Price of Honour

Also by Jan Goodwin

CAUGHT IN THE CROSSFIRE

Price of Honour

MUSLIM WOMEN
LIFT THE VEIL OF SILENCE
ON THE ISLAMIC WORLD

Jan Goodwin

LITTLE, BROWN AND COMPANY

For
Donald G. and Marilyn B.,
for the greatest gift of all . . .

A *Little, Brown* Book

First published in the United States by
Little, Brown and Company in 1994

Published in the United Kingdom by
Little, Brown in 1994

Copyright © 1994 Jan Goodwin

The moral right of the author has been asserted.

A CIP catalogue record for this book
is available from the British Library

Printed and bound in Great Britain by
BPC Hazell Books Ltd.
A member of
The British Printing Company Ltd.

ISBN 0 316 91074 0

Little, Brown and Company (UK) Limited
Brettenham House
Lancaster Place
London WC2E 7EN

Contents

Acknowledgments

PERHAPS BECAUSE OF THE GENDER segregation in the Islamic world, there is a bonding that occurs more rapidly among women in their culture than it does in the West. I am grateful to have been accepted into that consanguinity, and I admire the honesty, strength, courage, and continued faith of these women, plus their concern for my well-being in their world. It was they who took risks to talk to or assist me, particularly those who live under repressive regimes and whose names may not be openly listed here. I am proud to consider many of them new friends, and sincerely hope that there will not be reprisals — government, extremist, or societal — against those who permitted their names to be used.

I received enormous support and assistance from many others: journalists, both in the West and in the Islamic world, who opened their files to me and shared their sources and experiences, as well as academics, religious scholars, embassy officials, human rights activists, and interpreters, who gave unstintingly of their time in the countries through which I traveled.

During my odyssey, I also received sustenance for the body and soul at the homes of Lynn and Mustafa, John and Margaret Rodgers; the Rahmat family in Pakistan; David and Diane, Robert L., Bernice, L., and K. in the Gulf; T and Y in Jordan; and D. in Israel. Special mention should also go to Asma Jahangir's staff, who worked hard on my behalf, plus Nafisa Hoodbhoy and Tahir Malik; to Faribah, G., and J. in Iran; to Fatima, Faiza, and to S. and A. in countries best left unnamed.

Without the encouragement and nurturing of Rachel Rossow and D.K. during one of life's bleaker moments, *Price of Honor* would have been stillborn. Brigitte Georgevich's generosity in volunteering to transcribe dozens of tapes was noble indeed, and her sound editorial judgment invaluable. There was also vital hand-holding and/or advice supplied by Pam Hait, Janet Maughan, Irene Bell, Bill Jones,

ACKNOWLEDGMENTS

Sam McGarrity, and Beth Weinhouse, plus the diligence of research assistant Sharon Epperson.

Finally, there is Fredrica Friedman, an editor who believes a writer's reach must exceed her grasp and who manages to make the challenge exciting, and her fabulous team: Jordan Pavlin, Eve Yohalem, and Pamela Marshall. And, of course, there is Connie Clausen, an agent who palliates the pain with humor.

THE JOURNEY

The journey of my life
begins from home,
ends at the graveyard.
My life is spent
like a corpse,
carried on the shoulders
of my father and brother,
husband and son.
Bathed in religion,
attired in customs,
and buried in a grave
of ignorance.

HAND IN HAND

I want to walk beside you
through life
And you!
Want to put a ring in my nose
To pull me along.
Intoxicated by love,
I want to love you
And you!
Want to be god
Making and breaking me.
I want to dance forever in
the courtyard of your heart.
And you!
Singing songs of my helplessness
On the tambourine of my needs,
Want me to dance like a puppet.
I want to become a perfume
And permeate your body
But you!
Want to hide me in your pocket.
I want to cry:
And you!
Want to make me laugh as
you flick your fingers.

—ATIYA DAWOOD, SINDHI POET, PAKISTAN

THE MUSLIM WORLD

Percentage of population in each country that is Muslim

 0–10   10–25   25–50   50–90   90–100

Price of Honour

CHAPTER 1

Fundamentally Different?

*We have just enough religion to make us hate,
and not enough to love one another.*

JONATHAN SWIFT, 1667–1745

I T BEGAN WITH MARIA. She entered my life for a brief while when she was nine years old. I lost her two years later to a world that I then little understood. I was the mother that she did not have, and she was the daughter I had never given birth to. The last time I saw her, she was sobbing bitterly. Between gasps for breath, she said she wanted to kill herself. I shuddered as she said it, the shock no less than it had been the first time she spoke it six months before.

The final image I have of her is her face pale with grief, her brown eyes as dark as the deep shadows under them that no eleven-year-old should have. She moved stiffly, the bruises from her most recent beating still vivid. Maria was a bargaining chip in an auction that was closed to outsiders. I never saw her again, but there isn't a day that I don't think about her, wonder how she is, and ask myself, Could I have done more to stop the apparent inevitability of what happened to her?

In trying to locate her afterward, the cultural barriers came down to close me out as effectively as the four walls of *purdah* that went up and now confine her. A year later, I was told that Maria, still weeks short of her twelfth birthday, was pregnant with her first child. Forcibly married, she had been traded off at the age of eleven to a man described to me as "already having two wives, and so old he has lost all his teeth and shakes all the time," possibly from Parkinson's. In exchange for Maria, the ancient bridegroom had given one of his daughters to Maria's father, a widower who had wanted to remarry and could not afford the bride-price.

• • •

I first met Maria when she moved into my home after I went to live in Pakistan in 1988. Her father was a security guard for the house in which I lived in Peshawar. An ancient frontier town between Pakistan and Afghanistan and close to the fabled Khyber Pass, Peshawar is Islamically conservative. It was also violently volatile — bombings, kidnappings, and machine-gun assassinations were regular occurrences. A decade ago, the city numbered five hundred thousand; when I moved there the population had tripled with Afghan refugees who had fled the Soviet invasion of their country in 1979. Maria, her aged grandmother, and her father were part of that exodus, forced out of their homeland when Soviet MIGs and helicopter gunships obliterated their mountain village and killed the rest of their large extended family, including her mother, five siblings, and even her pet dog.

Their first home in Pakistan was a carport, closed on three sides only. Maria was put to work at the age of six, as a child-minder for the infant of her father's employer. When I met her three years later, she had never attended school. It simply had not occurred to anyone to enroll her. Within a few weeks of being in her company, I realized she had a keen and questioning mind, and a near-photographic memory. Her English vocabulary grew daily. With her father's permission, I entered her in the first grade of an Afghan-run girls' school.

Maria and I shopped for fabric for her school uniform, selected a serious-looking schoolbag, and filled it with exercise books, a pencil set, and a calculator. Together we worked on her homework and baked her favorite cookies. I told her bedtime stories; she told me stories about her life in Afghanistan and the country's folklore. I presented her with a puppy, a tiny stray I had found. She filled my house with flowers. I introduced her to birthdays and birthday cakes. (Few Afghans know when they were born or how old they are.) She explained Muslim holidays to me and asked me to fast with her during the month of Ramadan, which recalls the time the Koran was first revealed to the Prophet Mohammad.

By the following year, Maria had advanced to third grade, had learned to read and write, and was fluent in English and Urdu, as well as her own two languages, Dari and Pashto.

One day, when we were out walking the pup I had given her, she slipped her hand inside mine and said, "You are my mother, my second mother." And it felt that way.

Yet there were a number of occasions that indicated too clearly that I was not. To celebrate some minor success of Maria's that I no longer recall, I took her for an ice cream sundae, her first. At the time, the only place to find one was the town's sole four-star hotel. The comparative luxury of the lobby and the liveried employees clearly intimidated her and she clutched my hand tightly. But she relaxed and grinned widely when served with the enormous sundae. It was a simple outing, but for Maria it was a splendid adventure, and she talked about it animatedly with everyone she knew.

Friends of her father, however, were enraged and told him so, and a high-ranking and close Afghan friend of mine lectured me on the inappropriateness of what I had done. "But I asked her father's permission," I replied, pointing out that I had never made any decision, no matter how minor, concerning Maria without first obtaining her father's approval. In this archpatriarchal society, I had tried hard not to offend social mores.

"You are encouraging an Afghan girl, a Muslim, to be immodest," he continued. "What?" I asked confused. Maria and I were both wearing the local traditional dress, *shalwar kamez* — long, baggy pants worn under a long-sleeved, loose, knee-length tunic. Additionally, Maria's head and chest were covered by the large white sheetlike *chador* she had worn as long as I had known her, even though her religion didn't require it of her until she reached puberty. I also pointed out that there were other women present in the hotel coffee shop. "You are exposing her to a way of life that is alien to her, and should be alien to her. She does not belong in public places — you are encouraging her to be a prostitute."

I was too stunned to argue.

A few months later, I had to go out of town, and when I returned, I learned that Maria had been absent from school for the period I'd been gone. Eventually she told me that her father's friends had been advising him that education of girls was a bad thing. "It makes them argumentative and they become unmarriageable," they had said. That Maria was not yet eleven seemed irrelevant.

And then the beatings began. She suffered in silence at first. I found out about them accidentally when she had trouble rising from the floor cushions her family used in their quarters instead of furniture. Her grandmother told me what had happened and showed me both Maria's bruises and the thick ax handle that caused them.

Maria had trouble walking for several days. I wanted to confront her father, but neither she nor her grandmother would permit it. "You will only make it worse for her," Maria's grandmother told me.

"A man has the right to beat the women in his family. There is nothing you can do."

And certainly that had seemed the case nationwide when I had attended Pakistan's first conference on child abuse held the previous year. I had sat dumbfounded as doctors, lawyers, and legal experts had recounted how difficult it was to prevent, report, and prosecute cases of child abuse. "It is a man's right to discipline his family," local culture insisted. At that same conference a lawyer recounted a case of incest being thrown out of court despite the girl's having been made pregnant by her father. Incest doesn't happen in Islamic families, said the judge categorically as he quashed the case.

Maria's beatings continued, and increasingly her father confined her to her family's quarters. And then I learned why. "He wants to remarry, and he has found a new wife who won't want Maria. New wives in our country never want the other wife's children. He will give Maria to the man whose daughter he marries," explained her grandmother. "Maria must do as her father says. It is our way."

The child, who just months before had begun to have dreams that perhaps one day she could attend college, continued to resist. "He can kill me. It is better I should be dead. I want to die. I will kill myself."

Afghan friends warned me not to interfere. "Even if he does kill her, no authority here would challenge his right to do so," said one. "She is his daughter, she must obey him." An Afghan colleague suggested, "Buy her, offer her father money and just disappear with her." And while the thought of purchasing a human being was as abhorrent as the violence, I gave it serious consideration. A telephone call to the American embassy told me that adoption in Pakistan took at least two years. Additionally, I would have to prove she was an orphan or had been abandoned by her parents.

Shortly after that, Maria's family moved out, and despite many attempts to find her, I never saw her again. In another culture and because of our closeness, I could have expected her to find me. But the world outside her home was forbidden to her unless she was accompanied by a male relative. Her physical confinement I knew she would cope with as have other women in her culture; it was the imprisonment of her mind that would be as painful to her, being forced to marry a man she found repugnant.

• • •

It was because of Maria that I began this book. Was what happened to her merely a daily occurrence in underdeveloped nations throughout the world — children born into deprivation, raised in ignorance? Could her story be replayed just as easily in Africa or Latin America? Or was her experience intrinsic to her culture? I wanted to understand what it was like to grow up female in Maria's world. It was a pilgrimage that would take me through the Islamic heartland to ten countries: Pakistan, Afghanistan, Iran, United Arab Emirates, Kuwait, Iraq, Saudi Arabia, Jordan, West Bank and Gaza of Israel, and Egypt. During that journey, I interviewed hundreds of Muslim women, from royalty to rebels, from professionals to peasants. I also spoke to the men who demarcate the lives of their women: fathers, brothers, husbands, sons, Islamic scholars, and religious leaders, including the highest Islamic authority for 85 percent of the world's Muslims, the Grand Sheikh of Al Azhar. Al Azhar, the eleven hundred–year-old mosque and university in Cairo, Egypt, rules on all temporal, spiritual, and legal Islamic issues for Sunni Muslims.

Very early on in my travels, a subtext began to emerge, and by the time my journey ended, its underlying theme had become dominant, and too important to ignore. The leitmotiv in the countries through which I traveled was growing Islamic extremism.

Time after time, I found that the male militants I interviewed during my ten-country tour had been educated in the United States and frequently had been radicalized during their time in the West. Initially, I did not understand why. What was apparent, however, was that a neoconservative wave of self-styled religious literalists had begun attacking Islam from within, and by doing so, were changing the world in which they live, especially for women, and were frequently reaching outside it.

In the West, we regard the separation of church and state as an imperative progressive goal. In the Muslim world, however, Islam is a total way of life that affects all aspects of being: public, private, and spiritual. And because of the blurring of religion and governance, the increasingly militant Islamic revivalist movement is dictating how people should think, behave, dress, and live; it is also increasingly influencing how nations are governed.

Countries throughout the Islamic world consider the growing fundamentalist (or Islamist) movement the principal threat to existing regimes. The radical rage of religious extremists has so unnerved many Muslim rulers that in early 1993, Arab states began holding a series of meetings in the Middle East and Europe to discuss how Islamic fundamentalism could be crushed. Bombings, sabotage, assassinations, assaults, all in the name of Islam, have burgeoned in recent years. Incidents of violent and subversive activities have increased to such an extent that governments now recognize they must be countered.

Devout Muslims are always shocked to learn that the word Islam, which means "submission and obedience to the will of God," is becoming synonymous with acts of violence. And certainly, just as there are many shades of Christianity and Judaism, there are similar gradations in Islam. Moderate or more secular Muslims should not be labeled fundamentalists, and those who follow Islamic orthodoxy are not automatically fanatics and vice versa. The Western world also tends to overlook that not all members of organizations commonly perceived as Islamic are Muslim. One of the more violently inclined terrorists in the early PLO, and then of its extremist splinter group, the Popular Front for the Liberation of Palestine, is physician George Habash, a Christian. Other well-known figures in the Islamic world who are Christian include Tariq Aziz, Saddam Hussein's foreign minister, and Hanan Ashrawi, who was Palestinian spokeswoman in the Middle East peace talks. The latter's sole weapons have only ever been her keen mind and a silver tongue.

It is becoming increasingly clear that the new Islamic revivalists are considerably more radical than their predecessors. As they call for a return to an earlier, more spiritual (and certainly idealized) form of Islam, their rhetoric has more to do with demagoguery than purity of religion. The Islamists recognize what Machiavelli and Plato understood: religion can be used to legitimize power. And in recent years, the extremists have used Islam to sanction a desire for or a continuation of political control. In doing so, many fundamentalist factions have perverted for political ends the teachings of the Prophet Mohammad and the Koran that they claim to be reviving.

This is particularly true where Muslim women are concerned. The severe restrictions placed on women by the Islamist movement, such as confinement or complete veiling, have no basis in the Koran or the teachings of the Prophet, but are being stressed because of the role women play in the Muslim world. The honor of the Muslim family is believed to reside in women's chastity and modesty; hence the stress on her being a virgin until her marriage and the very real threat of death if she is not. It is for this reason that the Islamists insist women be completely covered and secluded from the outside world. As Hassan al-Turabi, the de facto leader of fundamentalist Sudan has said, "Women are the symbolic and substantive key to the new Islamic movements." New York political scientist Barnett Rubin, of Columbia University, agrees. "Women have become symbols of men's Islamic commitment," he says.

If Maria and her family returned to their homeland, as did many Afghan refugees when the resistance seized power in 1992, they would have found their country newly declared an archtheocratic state modeled after Iran and Saudi Arabia. And, like the two nations it emulates, Afghanistan's fundamentalist government introduced public executions. The first public hangings took place in September 1992 in the capital's main park; the crime: "Un-Islamic activities." At the same time, Afghanistan's female population found their rights immediately and almost totally eroded. After twenty-seven years of suffrage, they lost the right to vote, and they were no longer permitted to hold government positions or work in television or radio. A country where miniskirts had been a fashion statement in the capital during the sixties now required all women to be completely veiled. And yet fourteen hundred years ago, when Islam began, the Prophet Mohammad permitted women to be politically active, to work and mix with men, and they were not required to veil their faces.

As the Islamic extremism movement gains strength in countries throughout the Muslim world, those in power need to be viewed as complying with rigid religious leaders. Restricting women is visibly symbolic and an easy assuagement, at no cost to those who enforce it. Interpreters of religious texts, who are usually male, emphasize Koranic passages that reinforce Islam's patriarchal aspects while deemphasizing its clear injunctions giving women equality, justice, and education. For political ends, the Prophet's intent regarding women is both misinterpreted and misapplied, and his sympathy for women's rights is frequently no longer reflected in the law and practices of modern government. And because Muslim women are the first to be affected by such changes, their freedoms, or lack thereof, have become a key indicator of the political direction in which such states are moving.

• • •

In the West today, it is fashionable to designate all Muslims as the new pariahs: terrorists, fundamentalists, fanatics. They have filled the bogeyman niche under the bed where communists used to lurk. Not so long ago, *Time* magazine published a cover story entitled

"The Growth of Islam: Should We Be Afraid?" To many people, the answer was a resounding yes. The easy response to that, of course, is that ignorance breeds fear. Westerners find it convenient to draw a fence around the Islamic world, label it all Arab, and people it with bearded men with multiple wives swathed in multiple veils who walk two steps behind their husbands. There is a perceived oil well in every backyard, a stretch Mercedes and a camel in every garage, a Kalashnikov machine gun in every closet, and a harem in every home. It is a nonsensical view that comes from the same school of simplism that permits movies to define Americans to the rest of the world.

While Western-based Islamic antidefamation organizations work hard to reverse non-Muslim perceptions of Muslims, Islamic militants have begun exporting their violent radicalism. Several years after the last American held hostage by Muslim extremists returned home, and expatriate Muslims no longer felt it unsafe to openly admit their faith, a single act of terrorism in New York City did as much damage to Islam's image in the United States as did Khomeini's revolution. The bombing of the World Trade Center in downtown Manhattan in early 1993 killed six and injured over one thousand. It was the worst-ever terrorist attack on U.S. soil.

The young men arrested for the bombing were Palestinian refugees and Egyptians, all disciples of a rabid Muslim fundamentalist leader, Sheikh Omar Abdel Rahman. Four months later, another group of his followers, including several African-American Muslims, were arrested for allegedly plotting to bomb the New York United Nations building, the FBI offices, and the Lincoln and Holland commuter tunnels between New Jersey and Manhattan. Shortly after, Sheikh Omar himself was arrested, originally on U.S. immigration charges, and then with seditious conspiracy.

Rahman, who is Egyptian and who has been blind since childhood from diabetes, is the leader of a fundamentalist organization that is outlawed in Egypt. When the group, Al-Jihad (Holy War), was banned, Sheikh Omar simply renamed the organization Al Gamaat al Islamiyya (the Islamic Group) and continued business as usual. His fundamentalist organization and the sheikh himself were implicated in the assassination of Egypt's President Sadat. Sheikh Omar had authored the *fatwa*, a religious imperative, declaring Sadat an apostate — someone who has forsaken his or her faith — which can carry a death sentence under Islam. The *fatwa* was similar in style to the one Khomeini issued calling for author Salman Rushdie's death.

The Sheikh's organization was also linked to the slaying of Egypt's Speaker of the Parliament in 1990, and to the killing of author Farag Fouda in 1992. Fouda died because he mocked the extremes to which the fundamentalists had gone regarding women, one example of which was men being told not to sit on a bus seat vacated by a woman for at least ten minutes, until her body heat was no longer apparent. Additionally, the sheikh's group made death threats to a number of other prominent figures and writers in Egypt, including Nobel Prize–winner Naguib Mahfouz and Nawal El Saadawi, Egypt's leading feminist, causing the Egyptian authorities to place these individuals under around-the-clock armed guard.

In late 1992 and 1993, the sheikh's followers began targeting Egypt's tourist industry. Tour buses and Nile cruise boats were raked with machine-gun fire, and cafés and other sites frequented by Westerners were bombed, with at least three Westerners killed and many more Arabs injured. Within months of the campaign of terror, Egypt's tourism had plummeted 80 percent, costing the country most of the industry's $4 billion revenues, a sum the impoverished country can ill afford to lose.

After repeat arrests in the eighties, the sheikh fled across the border of Egypt to Sudan in 1990. Sudan, whose own fundamentalism has been financed and supported by Iran, has been training Egypt's religious extremists in special military training camps close to the Sudan/Egypt border. It was while Rahman was in Khartoum that he applied for and received a tourist visa to the United States despite his having been on the State Department's banned terrorists list since Sadat's death.

Shortly after Sheikh Omar arrived in the United States, another of his acolytes was charged with the assassination of right-wing rabbi Meir Kahane in New York. And a few months after that slaying, a colleague with whom the sheikh had had a falling-out over control of funding was found murdered in his Brooklyn, New York, apartment.

Sheikh Omar is a follower of Takfir wal Hijra, an ideology developed by Egyptian intellectual Sayyid Qutb, who was executed under Nasser's regime. Qutb became radicalized and fiercely anti-Western after spending 1949–1951 as a student in the United States. His abhorrence of the moral decay with which he claimed the West was riven caused him to join the Muslim Brotherhood. Today, the Brotherhood, founded in Egypt in 1928, is the largest Islamic fundamentalist organization in the world, and now claims a presence in most major countries, including the United States and countries throughout Europe.

More recently, the sheikh has threatened Egypt's President Mubarak, and has called for his overthrow on the grounds that he and his government are corrupt, anti-Islamic, and infidels. Labeling a Muslim an infidel or unbeliever is the same as declaring him an apostate, and under fundamentalist Islam that is considered to be a sentence of execution. It is this simple but flawed argument that the extremists use to justify Islamic assassinations.

Authentic Islam, however, is more merciful. Someone charged with apostasy is entitled to a trial, and if the accused recants, he or she is pardoned. If the accused refuses to disavow such a claim, then a sentence of death may be imposed. Islam also has very strict guidelines regarding the declaration of a Holy War. Getting rid of one's political opponents is rarely sufficient ground for declaring *Jihad.*

Sheikh Omar holds a degree in Islamic jurisprudence from the prestigious Al Azhar University, and has taught the subject in both Egypt and Saudi Arabia. This would indicate that he is an Islamic scholar of some learning and must know, therefore, the Islamic punishment for falsely declaring a Holy War or murdering another Muslim. Since his arrival in the United States, some major mosques have refused to let him preach because his sermons are too light on theology and too heavy on his fanatical politics.

In a crackdown against the fundamentalist violence that has shaken Mubarak's government, membership in extremist groups in Egypt is once again a crime punishable by death. It is harsh penalties such as this, plus the banning of many radical organizations in their country of origin, that has made Europe and particularly the United States places of refuge for Islamic extremists.

The major recruiting grounds for Islamic fundamentalism in the United States, I learned, are university campuses. The Muslim Brotherhood; the Indian subcontinent's equivalent, Jamaat-i-Islami; Sheikh Omar's organization, Takfir wal Hijra; and Lebanon's virulent Iranian-backed Hizbullah — which was responsible for the Beirut kidnappings of Americans and suicide bombings, including the one that killed 250 U.S. Marines at their barracks in 1983 — all have active student programs at colleges throughout America. From Berkeley in the west to Florida University in the east and many points in between such as Michigan State and Southern Illinois University, well-funded, professionally organized student organizations target

Muslim students. "Shielded from the watchful eyes of the police in their homelands, Muslim students in the U.S. have been recruited into a variety of Islamic organizations," says Professor Yvonne Haddad, an expert on American Islam. "Here they are able to forge links with students of other nations, providing the nucleus for an international network of leaders committed to the creation of an Islamic state, or an Islamic world order."

One of the largest and most active Islamist student organizations is the one based at Southern Illinois University in Carbondale, according to Dr. Scott Appleby, who is the codirector of the Fundamentalist Project, perhaps the most august authority in the United States on religious fundamentalism. Funded by the American Academy of Arts and Sciences and made up of leading scholars from some of the country's most prestigious universities, the six-year project is an "encyclopedic survey of religious fundamentalism worldwide." The results of the study will be made available to policy makers among others. According to Appleby, Carbondale's Islamic student body, which includes Muslims from the Middle East and Southeast Asia, "produces extensive literature and proselytizes widely outside its own campus."

Muslim students in the United States are attracted to Islamist organizations during their studies here also because they are frequently isolated from other students, fundamentalists told me during my ten-country odyssey. They talked of being mocked and patronized for their religious beliefs, and they complained of bigotry from students and faculty alike. "Muslims are the only ethnic group about whom it is still acceptable to be racist in America," an American-educated Arab engineer in the Gulf told me. "We have replaced blacks in this regard." He went on to explain that after any act of Islamic violence that makes the headlines, Muslim students in America are insulted and sometimes assaulted. "When Americans were held hostage by Iran, they called me a goddamn Iranian and told me to go back to Khomeini. When the Marine barracks were blown up, they called me a dirty Arab and told me to go back to Beirut. During the Gulf War, Arabs were labeled Saddam Hussein–loving sand-niggers and told to return to Baghdad. I knew many students who denied they were Muslims while they were in America to avoid such problems. I did so myself, after being physically threatened."

Today in the United States, ordinary Muslims are taking issue with such bigotry. After the World Trade Center bombing and its dramatic headlines, hundreds of Muslims demonstrated outside the New Jersey mosque associated with Sheikh Omar, carrying placards stating, "Islam Is Not Terrorism" and "We Will Not Tolerate Prejudice."

Religious fundamentalism of all kinds is on the march around the world says Dr. Appleby. "Whether it is Islam, Christianity, Judaism, Hinduism, Sikhism, or Buddhism, the failure and bankruptcy of secular alternatives in the late twentieth century have stimulated the rise of these movements. Many countries in the Middle East, S. Asia, and Africa experienced colonialism, and while they have been liberated from its presence, these societies continue to live in its cultural framework. The second- and third-generation–trained bureaucrats and administrators from this era, the Westernized elite, have not been able to bring economic prosperity or political freedom to their nations.

"There is discontent with this and a growing sense that people have somehow gone astray. Societies see a return to their religious roots, frameworks, and laws as a way of addressing such problems." In the oil-rich Muslim states, where poverty and deprivation are not factors, as they are in many Islamic countries, Appleby says Muslims are "deeply and morally offended, confused and troubled" with what comes with great prosperity. "Too often, it is seen as selling out the West."

The tremendous growth in Islamic fundamentalism in recent years is attributed in part to the success of the Iranian revolution. "In many countries, across the Islamic arc, and in nations as diverse as Nigeria, Malaysia, and Indonesia, Islamic leaders have been influenced by the success of the Iranian regime," says Appleby. "There is a new sense of nationhood; people feel empowered by the success of and the attention given to fundamentalist Iran." The modern fundamentalist slogan "Islam Is the Solution" is an appealing, and frequently the only, alternative in countries with corrupt, repressive, and ineffectual governments that have been unable or unwilling to supply jobs, housing, and other basic services.

The "Islamic Awakening" movement, a term the Western-educated and militant spiritual leader of Sudan uses to describe fundamentalism, represents modernity, he says, in Islamic societies. "Islam will come through evolution if allowed to come peacefully. Or it will come through revolution," insists Turabi. "It is up to Muslims to define what Islam is and whether it is militant." And increasingly, in countries around the globe, Muslims are engaged in that debate right now, oftentimes at the end of a gun.

Muslims who have accepted aid or military assistance from Islamist states or organizations invariably find that payment includes adopting the donor's radical ideology. And the rise of fundamentalism in Islamic countries marks dramatic and detrimental changes in the lives of women. The movement's rigidity of extremist thought and behavior has a profound effect on every aspect of women's existence. It is recognized, of course, that women do join the radical movements voluntarily, as happened in Iran at the beginning of Khomeini's revolution. Such women frequently become fundamentalists because they were among the disenfranchised who gained access to power for the first time, or because they are genuine believers in the ideology. Others feel that under fundamentalism, and if they are completely veiled, they will receive more respect and be less harassed by men. But in the vast majority of cases, women are forced to adhere to fundamentalism either because the men in their families require them to or because of threats of violence from Islamists in their communities.

．　．　．

The international Islamic extremist movement is not a nickle-and-dime operation. Arms and military training do not come cheaply. Nor does one of the more efficient propaganda machines in the world. And while Islamic fundamentalism is by no means monolithic, Sunni and Shi'a are increasingly working together. As I found during my travels for this book, the Islamist phraseology, philosophy, and didactics were invariably identical no matter which country one was in, or which group one was talking with. "The most powerful weapon the Islamic fundamentalists have is the uniformity of opinion and no deviation from the script," says Alon Ben-Meir, a New York–based political analyst specializing in Middle Eastern affairs.

A common misconception is that Iran is the main banker of the Islamic fundamentalist movement. While it is certainly involved in exporting incendiary fanaticism, it is a long way from being the main financial supporter of extremism. Iran's own economy is in a shambles because its regime of mullahs knows how to run a religious revolution but not a country.

The most generous countries in the fundamentalist funding arena are, not surprisingly, those that have the most to give — the oil-rich

Gulf states. Saudi Arabia, Kuwait, and tiny but fabulously wealthy United Arab Emirates, all close allies of the United States, have long played two ends against the middle politically. While openly supporting the Middle East peace talks, for example, Saudi Arabia has also funded Hamas, the Palestinian militant branch of the Muslim Brotherhood in Israel's West Bank and Gaza, which is adamantly opposed to the existence of Israel. In a single year, they have given Hamas, which maintains a permanent presence in Saudi Arabia, $72 million. The kingdom has also funded the PLO since the days it was also classified as a terrorist organization; one payment in 1989 totaled $85 million. And despite Riyadh's publicly denouncing the organization after Yasser Arafat supported Saddam Hussein in the Gulf War, the Saudis continue to fund it quietly through highly placed individuals.

Equally disturbing, Saudi Arabia has funded Sheikh Omar's deadly politics, as has Iran. And the Saudis have financed the Muslim Brotherhood, as well as its violent offshoots in Sudan, Jordan, Syria, and other Islamic states. Riyadh has, in fact, poured money into the Brotherhood since the fifties, when Nasser outlawed the organization after it attempted to assassinate him. Other extremist groups that have benefited from Saudi largesse include Pakistan's Jamaat-i-Islami and all four fundamentalist parties of the Afghan resistance, one of which has been implicated in training Sheikh Omar's followers in terrorism. The Afghan fundamentalists received $3.2 billion from Saudi Arabia during the Soviet occupation of Afghanistan, plus the bulk of the U.S. funding to the Afghan resistance, which also totaled $3.2 billion.

Islamists also employ charitable organizations and aid, which have cost billions of dollars, to make their ideology more palatable to the impoverished and disenfranchised. Much of the Saudi funding of fundamentalism globally, for example, is done through the semi-government organization, Rabitat al-Alam as-Islami, or the Muslim World League, the body that sponsored my visa so that I could enter Saudi Arabia. Rabitat also heavily supports many of the Islamist student organizations in the West, including a number in the United States, and is responsible for much of the Islamist proselytizing propaganda distributed worldwide. "It is easier to become established under a charity umbrella because it is culturally acceptable. Once formed, the institutions then inculcate a certain ideology," says Dr. Scott Appleby.

Over the years, vast amounts of funding from the Gulf states have enabled fundamentalist organizations to build infrastructures that can rival those of the governments in whose countries they operate, as has happened in Jordan. And because of the blurring of the lines, it is often not possible to separate the militant networks from many of the Islamic relief agencies. For example, in the Palestinian refugee camps in Jordan, such groups have obliged women to completely veil by paying men monthly supplements for every female in their family who is covered. In Kuwait and the Emirates, fundamentalist charities offer men substantial cash bonuses for taking wives polygamously.

"The Saudis have been indiscriminate in their support of extremist elements," says a State Department official. "The three Gulf states are paying ransom money to the extremists, and they do so out of fear," says political scientist Ben-Meir. "When the Saudis fund Hamas, even though the group has been undermining the Middle East peace talks, which Saudi Arabia openly supports, the inconsistency is overshadowed by a greater interest. The royal family does not want to be intimidated, threatened, or assassinated by these extremist groups. The Gulf states have been paying billions of dollars of such ransom money for years."

And of course, in a region where royalty and heads of repressive regimes rarely die of natural causes, such fear is real.

Kuwait, too, has long been similarly blackmailed. Between 1981 and 1987 particularly, militant groups were responsible for a series of bomb attacks in Kuwait. The Kuwaitis also now pay ransom to various extremist organizations, giving an admitted $60 million to Hamas in 1989 alone.

Equally nervous, the UAE has long financed similar groups and individuals, including giving millions of dollars to Abu Nidal, a terrorist known to Arabs as the "father of destruction."

Such buy-offs are a new twist to the "not-in-my-backyard" philosophy familiar to small-town politicians in the United States. Unfortunately, as became clear with the World Trade Center bombing, paranoia politics in the Middle East and Gulf can mean the problem is relocated to our neighborhood.

Today, also, some of the funding for radical Islam originates in the United States. According to Professor Ben-Meir, when the 415 Hamas members were expelled from Israel at the end of 1992, there were immediate fund-raising events in Detroit, California, and Houston, "at which one million dollars was raised on the spot." A senior member of the Muslim Brotherhood in Jordan told me that the MB has long owned businesses in the West and the States, which pour much of their profits into the movement.

• • •

A major factor in the growth of Islamic fundamentalism in recent years has been oil. When the Gulf states chose to use oil as a weapon against the United States, it turned out to be a two-edged sword that has been slashing at their stability ever since. The Arab oil embargo in 1973, triggered by the United States's rearming of Israel during the Yom Kippur War, hit America at its most vulnerable spot — its gas pumps. But while Americans suffered, so, shortly after, did the global economy. Petroleum prices increased fourfold, and a world-wide recession ensued. Among the hardest hit were the impoverished Muslim countries.

Israel has always wondered what quirk of fate determined the "Chosen Land" to be the only one in the region without oil. Pauperized Muslim countries such as Egypt, Yemen, Jordan, and Pakistan have always pondered what kismet blessed the three Gulf states with the smallest populations — Saudi Arabia, Kuwait, and the UAE — with the largest reserves of oil.

Saudi Arabia's oil revenues have been as high as $120 billion in one year, which, for a country whose population at the time was only nine million, was not a bad return. In Egypt, however, one in five of the workforce was unemployed, and the infrastructure of the country was collapsing, literally. In Cairo, apartment blocks regularly crumble into dust, killing residents trapped in the rubble. All that seems to soar in Egypt is the birthrate and government corruption.

In conditions such as these, the fundamentalist promise "Islam Is the Solution" seems increasingly more appealing. Cynical disenfranchised youths ask, "Even if it isn't, can it be much worse than now?" And certainly, during the 1992 earthquake that devastated parts of Cairo, it was the fundamentalist organizations that supplied emergency services to those in need. Egypt's bloated bureaucracy was, as always, indolent to the point of inertia, and couldn't even get drinking water to those who lost their homes.

And while it may seem axiomatic to talk of fundamentalism in archconservative Saudi Arabia, the kingdom's radical Islamic organizations are gaining strength, becoming increasingly militant and hostile to the royal family. Kuwait is flirting with what it terms "democracy," but the ruler has dissolved Parliament at a whim before in very recent history, and is expected to do so again if government by the people impinges on control by the Al-Sabah royal family. In Kuwait, as in Saudi Arabia, there is a growing Islamist opposition to the royal family's hold on the country and the nation's petro-dollars.

"The uneven location of oil in the Middle East has created a division between super-rich and dreadfully poor societies that has no equivalent in Central America or sub-Sahara Africa," says Paul Kennedy, director of the International Security Program at Yale University. The divide between the haves and have-nots, explains Kennedy, author of the book *Preparing for the Twenty-first Century,* is accentuated by the presence of millions of Egyptian, Yemeni, Jordanian, and Palestinian unskilled workers laboring in the oil-rich states, which increases mutual resentments. "Is it any wonder," he asks, "that the unemployed, badly housed urban masses, despairing of their own secular advancement, are attracted to religious leaders or 'strongmen' appealing to Islamic pride, a sense of identity, and resistance to foreign powers and their local lackeys?"

With the highest birthrates in the world, and with the majority of Middle East and Gulf states having 50 percent of their populations under the age of fifteen, the world's most unstable region will only become increasingly more incendiary.

Into this region, the West, the former Soviet bloc countries, and China have poured and continue to pour billions of dollars of highly sophisticated arms. Thus it is that in the part of the world most subject to war and conflict, "there are probably more aircraft, missiles, and other weapons than anywhere else in the world," contends Professor Kennedy. Since the Gulf War, the United States has sold $25 billion of military hardware to Saudi Arabia, the same amount that Iran has spent recently in its rearming program. In the mid-eighties, Iraq was the world's-largest arms purchaser, and while the Gulf War somewhat dented Saddam's weapons supply, he did not lose his highly experienced and capable legions of technocrats or their know-how. Like Israel, Iraq has long had an efficient weapons-production industry.

One can only wonder how much longer it will be before Saudi Arabia, with its second generation of technocrats who have enjoyed the best education petro-dollars can buy, and with the kingdom's enormous financial resources, emulates Israel and Iraq, and produces or clones weapons. (Pakistan recently became the first Muslim state to possess nuclear weapons, according to congressional sources.) After all, this is a nation that in three decades went from an impoverished kingdom with no asphalt roads in 1950, to one that produces astronauts and has become a major international wheat exporter after turning one of the most barren deserts on earth green.

For some time, Saudi radical groups have been calling for a joint Arab army of one million strong, as has the Palestinian Hamas. Iraq also has long sought for the four Gulf states with the world's-highest oil reserves — Saudi Arabia, Iraq, Kuwait, and UAE — to unite into a "material power that the U.S. and the rest of the West will be forced to reckon with." And even after the Gulf War, Iraq continues to propose such a unity.

A common refrain from government officials in Iraq to me when I was there in 1992 was, "Of the last two barrels of oil on earth, one of them will be from Iraq, and you can be certain, that oil will be used to punish America."

And Saddam Hussein is aware, according to statistics published in Iraqi newspapers, while most Americans do not seem to be, that the United States is increasingly Gulf-oil dependent, not less. The lessons of the 1973 and 1979 oil crises still have not been learned. At the time of the first oil embargo in 1973, the United States imported 36 percent of its oil. Twenty years ago, our automobiles — which account for half the oil consumption in the United States — guzzled a lot more petroleum than they do now. But despite the fact that our fuel efficiency has since improved by 50 percent, according to the American Petroleum Institute (API), we now import half our oil, and by the year 2000 we will import 60 percent. Our principal supplier of that imported oil is Saudi Arabia. "If for any reason, Saudi Arabia's production was stopped, we would be very, very up the creek," says Ed Ross, spokesman for the API. "If Saudi Arabia goes down, it will be a catastrophe for us." Even Wall Street is showing concern. Senior petroleum analyst Jim Clark, of First Boston Corporation's New York office, agrees that the United States is "vulnerable" because of our oil imports. "Islamic fundamentalism is exercising more of an influence over Saudi Arabia, Egypt, even Iraq," he says.

As Daniel Yergin, perhaps the foremost expert in the United States on oil, wrote in 1992 in his highly acclaimed book *The Prize*, about the history of oil, "Petroleum remains the motivating force of industrial society and the lifeblood of the civilization it helped to create. It is an essential element in national power, and a major factor in world economies." President Bush also warned that "American jobs, our way of life, our own freedom, would all suffer if the control of the world's great oil reserves fell into the wrong hands."

It was for this reason that he sent America to war against Iraq when it invaded oil-rich Kuwait.

The simple truth is that in the United States, which was once the largest oil exporter, petroleum production has fallen to the lowest level since 1960. At the same time, our consumption continues to increase. California alone now burns more oil daily than either Germany or Japan.

There is also a little-known U.S. agreement that was made with the Saudis and Kuwaitis twenty years ago and that is still in existence: unless the United States keeps their massive petro-dollar investments in America secret, both countries will stop pumping oil. The agreement was made in 1974 by William Simon, Nixon's Treasury secretary, one year after the oil embargo, when Riyadh literally had Washington over a barrel. The accord, which also includes the UAE and is referred to in congressional documents as "secret," has helped contribute to the current instability in the Islamic world. It also has very possibly compromised our security, and it has certainly wasted vast sums of American taxpayers' money.

Why did the Gulf states want such an agreement? "The Saudi Arabian Monetary Authority, SAMA [and the kingdom's national bank], makes investments in the United States," says congressional economist James Jackson. "In essence, however, the Saudi royal family is SAMA. And they are sensitive about having their private holdings made public. The Treasury agreed that the U.S. would withhold data that could be identified as the holdings of an individual person, whether that person is an individual by himself, or whether that person happens to be a government."

The situation is the same in Kuwait and the UAE. The national Treasuries and/or oil revenues of all three Gulf states have long been viewed by the ruling families as their private piggybanks. And because of the domestic political and economic vagaries in the Gulf, these revenues have been invested abroad. "Flight capital," as the practice is dubbed in the financial world, is also used by dictators such as Saddam Hussein and various other despots, who skim their countries' exchequers and hide the money in private investments outside their own countries.

"The ruler of Abu Dhabi [who is also head of the seven Trucial states known collectively as the United Arab Emirates], kept his country's entire oil revenues, approximately $10 billion a year, in flight capital because he was afraid of internal coups," said Jonathon Winer, legal counsel to Sen. John Kerry and head of the congressional investigation into the Bank of Credit and Commerce scandal. (BCCI has been dubbed the "financial supermarket for crooks and spies.") Collectively, all three oil states have had as much as $200 billion invested in the United States in a single year. Currently, it is estimated to be $90 billion. Said Winer, "This practice has been generally carried out throughout the Middle East and Gulf, and that is a very big secret. The rulers do not want their domestic populations to know they are keeping all their money, the nations' oil money, overseas."

"Simon's agreement changed the whole way the Treasury reports foreign investment figures," said Jackson. "Congress has never been able to circumvent it." This Treasury veil of secrecy has even blocked the CIA from giving Congress precise data on Arab investments.

Just where has Arab oil money been invested in the United States? Much of it has been in Treasury bills. American oil analysts estimate, however, that up to two-thirds of Gulf state investments in this country are not known even to the Treasury. Certainly, the Treasury has admitted to making between $37 and $75 billion "discrepancies" in calculating the total annual amount of Arab investment in the United States. Collecting the few details available on Arab holdings here is like playing some fabulous game of Monopoly. After a while, one stops noting any purchase that totals less than megamillions. Following the time-honored investment advice — buy what you know most about — Gulf Arabs have paid $1.5 billion for Saks Fifth Avenue, all forty-five stores, and for lesser sums they have acquired Tiffany's, the jewelers, Carvel Ice Cream, and a controlling interest in Gucci's. On a more mundane level, they paid half a billion dollars for Color Tile, a floor-and-wall–covering chain.

The Kuwaiti government spent $2.5 billion, paid in cash, when they purchased an oil drilling and production company, Sante Fe International, in California. And they own property parcels around the country, including the thirty-story Atlanta Hilton Hotel, the Baltimore Hilton, and South Carolina's resort, Kiawah Island. The Kuwaiti stock portfolio has included $100 million in AT&T, $52 million in Dow Chemicals, and $43 million in Atlantic Richfield.

A Saudi prince paid $590 million for 15 percent of stock in Citibank, America's largest bank. Saudis also purchased a half-interest in Texaco's refineries, plus their gas stations in thirty-three states. And they now own United Press International. At the time of buying the news service, a spokesman for the Saudis stated there was no "political motive in the purchase." Other Saudi investments include 6.8% in First Chicago Corp., 5.3% in Transamerica, 5% in Thermo Electron, and 1% in each of Chase Manhattan and J. P. Morgan & Co.

In 1975, Ghaith Pharoan, a Saudi tycoon then unknown in the United States, told a Chicago journalist, "Investment by Middle Easterners in the West should be welcome. Americans are always afraid outsiders will come and buy up everything. I don't know why anyone would be concerned."

Thirteen years later, Pharoan fled the United States as the four-year-long congressional investigation into BCCI began. Pharoan was head of the bank's operations in the United States as BCCI perpetuated the largest international banking fraud — $30 billion — in history. The bank, which was founded in 1972 by a Pakistani, was predominantly funded by the ruler of the UAE and by Saudis highly placed in their government and/or related to the king. Today, Abu Dhabi has refused to cooperate with the U.S. congressional BCCI investigation, and has withheld documents and key witnesses by placing eighteen bank officials under house arrest since 1991.

Saudi Arabia's approach has been more sophisticated: they intensively lobbied the State Department to have the charges dropped. But despite even the king's personal intervention, very prominent Saudis were indicted. Among them was Sheikh Kamal Adham, the brother-in-law of King Faisal, and one of his close advisers. Adham was also the first head of Saudi intelligence. In a most disturbing conflict of interest, while being a key player in a global crime organization, Adham was also the American CIA's chief liaison for the entire Middle East from the mid-1960s through 1979, and our chief negotiator with President Sadat during the Camp David talks.

Two members of the Saudi royal family who also owned sizable chunks of BCCI are Prince Turki, Adham's successor and the current head of Saudi intelligence, and Prince Naif, the kingdom's Minister of Interior. Khalid bin Mahfouz, a close friend of the current monarch, King Fahd, and his personal banker, was another Saudi implicated.

"Certainly, BCCI raises questions about U.S. and Saudi relations," says Jonathon Winer. "And had the William Simon 'secret' agreement not been in operation, Congress might have been alerted earlier to the U.S. holdings of the foreign princes involved in BCCI.

"BCCI was able to flourish because there is a lack of accountability in the Gulf countries, which were its principal funders," he added.

"The U.S. needs its foreign financial dealings to be absolutely transparent. With the Gulf states, those dealings aren't even translucent, they are opaque."

• • •

The beginning of the 1990s marked a radical shift in our nation's political interest. Cold War concerns have subsided and our security and energy needs are now inextricably linked to the nations of Islam, a culture that remains a mystery to us. Our ethnocentrism in this regard is both shortsighted and foolhardy.

Today, Islam is the world's fastest-growing religion, with one billion adherents. It is the faith of more than one-fifth of the world's population, and is second only in size globally to Christianity. The *World Christian Encyclopedia* calculates that since 1900, Christians have remained 34 percent of the world population. The number of Muslims has increased sixfold in that time, however, when, in the same number of years, the world's population has only quadrupled. And because Muslim countries have the highest birthrates in the world, demographers predict that the Islamic population will double to two billion in the next twenty years.

Similarly, when Islam began in the seventh century, "it spread across continents at an amazing speed," says Dr. Ismai'il al-Faruqi, a religion scholar at Temple University. "Its political power eventually eclipsed that of the Roman Empire — the greatest political and social organization the world had ever known. For a thousand years Islam was unparalled in its world power, affluence, high civilization, and culture. For a thousand years, it was the only challenger of Europe, and it came close to making a conquest of that continent."

In the United States, Islam is also the fastest-growing religion: for the first time, Muslims at 6.5 to 7 million now outnumber Jews at 5.7 million. Forty-four percent are African-American Muslim converts, many of whom point out that the Islamic faith was a part of their heritage. Nearly half of the slaves shipped to the Americas were Muslim; most were forcibly converted to Christianity. (Of the approximately eighty thousand recent white converts in the United States, 80 percent are women, the majority of whom have converted to Islam on marrying Muslims.)

Across the United States today, according to Fareed Nu'man, a spokesman for the American Muslim Council in Washington, D.C., there are 1,200 mosques and 165 Islamic schools serving Muslim populations, which are predominantly concentrated in California,

New York, Illinois, New Jersey, Indiana, Michigan, Virginia, Texas, Ohio, and Maryland. "There are two hundred thousand Muslim-owned and -operated businesses in the U.S., ranging from street stalls to substantial companies," says Nu'man. The nation's first Muslim mayor is Charles Bilal of Knoxe, Texas, and Detroit has a deputy mayor who is Muslim.

Jewish scholar Jonathan Sarna of Brandeis University notes that "Islam's emergence as a major American faith has failed to elicit much discussion in Jewish circles." Yet he points out that America can no longer be considered a Judeo-Christian society. "The U.S. has become a Judeo-Christian–Muslim society," says Sarna. "Jews in the next few decades will have to endure what mainstream Protestants went through earlier this century: the experience of status loss, of feeling almost dispossessed."

Sarna points out that Israel may well suffer the most from these changes. "The declining status of American Jews, coupled with the rise of American Islam and the growing political maturity of the American Muslim community will make it much more difficult in the years ahead for massive aid to Israel to win congressional approval. This change should occasion vigilance," he says, "but not necessarily alarm. On the brighter side, the rise of Islam and the widening parameters of American religion may in the long run promote closer Muslim-Jewish relations."

• • •

Despite the Islamic world's growing impact on our lives, Muslims understand us far better than we know them. Their upper echelons are frequently educated in the West, where they study our politics, economics, technology, and in the process become bilingual and bicultural. We cannot assume, however, that because of their familiarity with the West, they think and behave like our mirror-images. They do not.

Just as we learned with Japan, Islam is an ancient culture, one that is rigidly traditional, and one that was essentially closed to the Western world for centuries. It has its own way of doing things, its own philosophies, and, most important, its own religion.

"There is an incredible arrogance in the U.S. and in Europe regarding Islam," says Dr. Scott Appleby. "There is an assumption that Islam is widely irrational. And there is also the conviction of the superiority of the Western way of life, of Western religion, and our separation of state and church. So often, even with career diplomats who speak Arabic, their understanding of the culture is very rudimentary because while living in Islamic countries, they are essentially cut off from local people and spend much of their time with other foreigners.

"Westerners can't imagine what it is like to walk around every day with one's worldview not just informed by religious consciousness but largely determined by it. Muslim and Western nations may use the same words — negotiation, conflict resolution, democracy, consultation — but they are in such a different context in Islam. Consultation, for example, is not just experts sitting around the table with their own opinion trying to come to consensus. Instead, it always involves religious scholars and sources of Islam. In response to this, Britain's former deputy prime minister, Geoffrey Howe, for example, once told me, 'Well, we have biblical verses, but we would never bring this to bear at the conference table. We wouldn't impose religion on negotiations.' But Muslims do, and we need to understand that."

In the last two decades, Islam has had a dramatic impact on our lives; events like the Gulf War and the world's continued dependence on oil will ensure that it continues to do so for decades to come. As the Muslim world's power has grown, our miscomprehension of that culture has caused us to be held to economic ransom over the price of oil, and held hostage with increasing frequency at the end of a machine gun. And it has also caused us to confuse devout, peace-loving Muslims with violent fanatics and vice versa.

Our superficial understanding of the Islamic world has contributed to our intelligence agencies' being 180 degrees wrong in every major crisis in the Middle East in the last two decades:

- Twenty-four hours before Egypt invaded Israel in 1973 and started the war that led to the oil embargo, and even after the Soviets had evacuated their dependents from the country, the CIA told the White House that the military preparations then under way were not plans to initiate hostilities.
- Shortly before the Shah's regime fell in Iran in 1979, our intelligence stated that the Shah was expected to remain in power for at least the next ten years.
- And we were just as wrong when Saddam Hussein poised one hundred thousand troops to invade Kuwait, and possibly Saudi Arabia. The invasion took place at 2:00 A.M. on August 2. At the

end of July, the American ambassador in Baghdad presumed business as usual and left for home-leave.

In his first weeks as Clinton's secretary of state, Warren Christopher was surprised when a deal he cut with Israel regarding the Palestinians was not endorsed by Saudi Arabia, Syria, and other Arab countries. Christopher had accepted the Israeli analysis of how the Palestinians would respond. And both the Secretary of State and President Clinton were taken by surprise with the PLO and Israeli accord in 1993, which took place after secret negotiations in Norway to which the United States was not a party.

One week before the World Trade Center explosion, American authorities disagreed with Egyptian officials over cassettes made by Sheikh Omar in New Jersey that were being shipped to fundamentalist groups in Cairo. The recordings offer encouragement, said the Americans, not direction, for the violent challenges to the Egyptian government.

"The Islamic fundamentalist movement becomes unstoppable after passing a certain limit and that isn't yet fully comprehended in the West or by the media," says Palestinian-born scholar Hisham Sharabi, of Georgetown University, and author of *Neopatriarchy; The Theory of Distorted Change in Arab Society*. "If it is not contained, if an alternative solution does not become available, then it will be difficult to control. We have not seen anything like this before. Fundamentalism is the first political mass movement that the Islamic world has seen in the twentieth century. It is also a movement that can be hell for women."

Adds Islamic scholar Dr. Zaki Badawi, head of the Muslim College in London, "Very few Muslim countries have given women their full rights, and both Islamic law and the message of Islam have been violated. But today, petro-Islam with its vast amounts of money is letting loose on the Islamic world a wave of fundamentalism. The movement, largely funded by the Saudis and Kuwait, is pushing a doctrine that is antiwoman, anti-intellectual, antiprogress, and anti-science. I am extremely concerned with what is happening to women, and such doctrine is also very destructive for Islam." (Dr. Badawi, who was formerly on the faculty of Al Azhar University, still serves on the High Council of Islamic Affairs, the highest authority deciding on issues of Islam.)

Early on in my travels for this book, Dr. Badawi told me that the most important indicator of change in the Islamic world is the treatment of its women. "To understand the Islamic world, one needs to decode the way that society perceives women," he said. The manner in which Islamic culture relates to women reveals much about how that society is structured and how it relates to a host of other issues — sociological, political, and issues of basic human rights. Muslim countries currently face conflicting trends: on the one hand, growing religious extremism, and on the other, their vital need to communicate and compete in a modern technological world. How they balance the two in respect to the position and treatment of women will indicate how they are likely to succeed in integrating these two polarized facets of their society.

"Women are the recipients of family honor; the reasons for this are culture, orientation, inherent jealousy, concern, fear. It is the dominant role that has been enshrined throughout the generations," says political scientist Alon Ben-Meir. "And because of this, no matter whether Islamic fundamentalism is Sunni, Shi'a, or any other coloration, women are the first to be affected."

In essence then, Muslim women are the wind sock showing which way the wind is blowing in the Islamic world. And as the extremist movement grows, they are also, as one woman I interviewed put it, "the canaries in the mines."

CHAPTER 2

Muslims, the First Feminists

Treat your women well, and be kind to them.

PROPHET MOHAMMAD

D ESPITE ITS RAPID SPREAD, Islam is not a religion for those
who are casual about such things; adhering to its five pillars
takes effort and discipline. One must rise before dawn to
observe the first of five ritual prayers required daily, none
of which can take place without first ritually cleansing oneself. Sleep,
work, and recreational activities take second place to prayer. Fasting
for the month of Ramadan, undertaking the Hajj pilgrimage to
Mecca at least once in a lifetime, paying *Zakat* tax for relief of the
Muslim poor, in addition to accepting Islam's creed, which begins,
"There is no God but Allah, and Mohammad is his messenger,"
require a serious and energetic commitment. And the vast majority
of Muslims worldwide do observe those tenets.

Every condition and circumstance of life is believed contained
within the Koran, the *hadiths* (the reported traditions recording the
Prophet Mohammad's behavior and sayings), and the *Shariah*, the
Islamic code of law. The most minute details of everyday existence
are governed, such as the correct way to style one's hair, or by which
foot one should enter a toilet. The Koran's teachings, in their en-
tirety, are meant to be observed in their original purity. Unlike the
Bible, for example, the Koran may not be given contemporary inter-
pretation; it is considered incontrovertible, modern mores notwithstanding. It is for that reason that Muslims, no matter their mother
tongue, are expected to read their holy book in the original Arabic,
not in translation, which may change the meaning originally intended.

So it is ironic that the most outstanding contradiction regarding
the inequities suffered by Muslim women is that Mohammad, the
founder of Islam, was among the world's greatest reformers on be-

half of women. He abolished such sex-discriminating practices as female infanticide, slavery, and levirate (marriage between a man and his brother's widow), while introducing concepts guaranteeing women the right to inherit and bequeath property, and the right to exercise full possession and control over their own wealth. Islam, in fact, may be the only religion that formally specified women's rights and sought ways to protect them. Today's Islamic spokesmen frequently extol the Prophet's revolutionary innovations, but usually fail to note that they are rarely honored in reality.

They fail to observe, for example, that it is not the Koran that compels Islamic women to be enshrouded from head to toe or confined to their homes while men feel free to pester women who do venture out. Mohammad's directives on this issue were addressed to both sexes and could not be clearer:

> *Say to the believing men that they should*
> *lower their gaze and guard their modesty . . .*
> *And say to believing women that they should*
> *lower their gaze and guard their modesty . . .*

Said Islamic scholar Dr. Zaki Badawi, "This section of the Koran also states that women should not show 'their adornment except what normally appears.' This means it is left to custom. There has never been an Islamic obligation for women to cover at any time. In fact, veiling the face is an innovation that has no foundation whatsoever in Islam. Even in Saudi Arabia the covering of women from head to toe is recent; it was not required before the discovery of oil.

"The *hijab* veil (which covers all of a Muslim woman's hair) is also not obligatory. And in Europe, for example, it should be prohibited because it creates a lot of problems for women. If women are attacked because they are wearing the *hijab*, as happened in France not so long ago, then they should not wear it. I have spoken out on this issue on a number of occasions, and since I began doing so, a lot of Muslim women in Europe have started leaving off the head covering."

The veil originated as a Persian elitist fashion to distinguish aristocracy from the common masses, and has moved in and out of fashion ever since. Early Islamic scholars, for example, tried to enforce veiling by declaring "all of woman is pudendal." Islamic studies specialist Nancy Dupree, of Duke University, explained its more recent use. "At the time of national movements against colonial powers, it became a symbol of resistance against alien policies that were generally viewed as a move to encourage female overpermissiveness. After independence was won and governments embarked on their indigenous Western-oriented paths, the veil was discredited as an emblem of enforced orthodoxy and suffocating social control, an archaic social institution similar to slavery."

Like Pakistan's first female prime minister, Benazir Bhutto, many Muslim women who grew up in this less-restrictive era wore Western dress. Bhutto took to Islamizing her wardrobe only when she began her election campaign. Throughout her time in office she has had great difficulty keeping her head modestly covered simply because she is unused to wearing the *chador* intended for that purpose, and it keeps sliding off.

As Islamic radicalism rose at the beginning of the last decade, the pendulum for Muslim women swung the other way again. Once more they were to be hidden behind veils, a development that now seemed to legitimize and institutionalize inequality for women. In fact, calls by Islamist organizations in recent years for Muslim women to veil themselves have been followed shortly thereafter by demands that women stop working, stay home, limit their educations, and resign positions of authority. Insists Dr. Badawi, however, "This is not required by Islam. According to our religion, women have a perfect right to take part in society."

Despite the limitations placed on them, Muslim women have achieved amazing gains. In Islamic cultures, where education for women often began only three or four decades ago, women whose mothers are totally illiterate frequently earn advanced degrees. One need only look to the percentage of women teaching in universities in Muslim countries to see how fast change is occurring for women. "In 1981, in Egyptian universities, twenty-five percent of the faculty were women. In American universities at the same time, it was twenty-four percent and in Germany, twenty-five percent," says Fatima Mernissi, a leading Moroccan sociologist. "Even in conservative Saudi Arabia, women have invaded sexually segregated academic space. They are twenty-two percent of university faculty there." It was also in this era that Benazir Bhutto became the first woman to head a modern Muslim state, and many other women succeeded to public office. A number of Arab states, however, had female ministers as early as the fifties, long before most Western countries. These Muslim women are the ones who have been able to balance their culture's traditional customs and demands at home — arranged marriages, obedience to their husbands — with the progressiveness their careers demand.

Women who do work in Gulf and Middle Eastern countries often enjoy job benefits their female counterparts in the West would envy. Equal pay with men has existed in a number of the countries since the 1970s, while women in the United States and Britain still earn only slightly more than half a man's salary for the same job. In Iraq, where human rights are scant, a woman's employment benefits are extensive and include free child care while she is working and the right to retire with a full pension after fifteen years of employment. And in virtually all Arab countries, maternity leave on full pay is substantially longer than it is in the United States.

Dichotomously, as we near the twenty-first century, the majority of Muslim women still find their lives controlled by their closest male relative. They are the daughters whose future marriage partners continue to be determined by their fathers. They are the brides who must be virgins on their wedding nights in a culture where if they are not, honor killings are common and often carried out by the girl's own brothers. To guard against this, a simple surgical procedure — hymen restoration — is equally common in the Muslim world. Fratricide can occur when a young woman refuses to marry a man of her family's choice. Even though Islam states that a woman has the right to refuse a husband selected for her, in reality, familial pressures can be so strong, they may result in her death if she is not acquiescent.

Bride-price still exists in Muslim countries, a convention that only serves to confirm that a woman is a man's property. Once married, every aspect of a woman's life will be dictated by her husband: what she does, who her friends are, where she is permitted to go, how her children are raised, and even whether she may use birth control or be sterilized. She cannot obtain a passport or travel abroad without his written approval.

And if she is not obedient, her husband may take another wife. Polygyny is the specter that haunts every married Muslim woman: husbands are entitled to take four wives. According to Koranic dictates, should a man decide to marry again, he is supposed to obtain his first wife's permission. He is also required to treat each wife exactly the same, in affection, time spent together, material possessions, and status. In practice, if his first wife doesn't agree, he gets married anyway, and human nature being what it is, he invariably favors the newer and younger spouse.

I remember a discussion with a woman whose husband had taken a second wife when she was twenty-six and had borne six children. "He just moved her into our home. He didn't tell me. One day she wasn't there, the next day she was. After that time, I sit in the same room with them and he hardly speaks to me, he has never come into my bed again, and he ignores our children and favors hers. It is difficult to get him even to buy clothes for mine." Now ten years later, she is delighted that her husband is taking a third wife. "Good," she told me. "Now his second wife will know what it was like for me. She can watch, as I did, as he ignores her and spends all his time with the new wife."

Not so long ago, a young woman began a national outcry in Pakistan when she questioned in a letter to a newspaper why, if polygyny was really the Islamic right of men, Islamic law did not grant similar rights of polyandry to women. Outraged religious and political leaders publicly condemned the woman, terming her statement "illegal, immoral, and highly irresponsible." She was ordered to "repent, or she would be declared apostate."

The point the young woman was making that was completely overlooked in the furor is that polygyny was not intended to be an automatic right for Muslim men, a chance to trade in the old model for a sleeker, newer version. The Prophet Mohammad's original intention was to provide protection to widows and orphans. The Koranic verses on polygyny were recorded shortly after a major battle, when many Muslim males were killed, and women would have been left destitute unless the surviving males took additional wives.

Originally, in the pre-Islamic or Jahilliah period of Arabian society, often referred to as an era of ignorance, polygyny and polyandry were recognized institutions. Men *and* women were allowed to have multiple spouses. Islam, however, condemned these practices for both sexes. The Koran permitted polygyny only in exceptional cases, principally for war widows, whom the Prophet feared would become impoverished or "unprotected" once their husbands were dead. Later, when the early Islamic caliphate was replaced by monarchy, wealthy males with the assistance of the then half-educated ulema (religious and legal leaders) again revised the pre-Islamic form of polygyny. Polyandry for women, however, stayed banned. At the same time, men began to ignore the Koranic preconditions for polygyny, and instead of marrying unprotected widows, it became, and remains, the practice for them to take young, unwed women as their subsequent wives.

There is a continuing debate in the Islamic world over whether polygyny is outdated and should be expunged from Islam. Modernists insist it is inappropriate today, anti-women, and some go as far as to argue that when one man impregnates multiple wives, it only exacerbates the high birthrates in Muslim countries. Traditionalists insist polygyny is a Muslim male's right and that the word of God as recorded in the Koran may not be changed. But despite insistences that Koranic intent not be modified at all, concubinage and slavery — which still stand in the Koran — have been subsequently abrogated.

Tunisia prohibited polygamy in 1957. It cited the Koranic verse in which Mohammad acknowledges that men "have it not in your power to deal equally between wives, however much you may wish it. . . ." Tunisian religious authorities concluded that "unless and until adequate evidence was forthcoming that the wives would be treated impartially, which was virtually impossible, the essential conditions of polygamy could not be met."

In Turkey, Ataturk abolished the veil by decree when he came to power in the twenties, the first Muslim ruler to do so. But today, despite Turkey's now having a woman premier, in small towns and villages in the interior of the country women are rarely seen on the streets without being covered by a black *chador*, and polygamy is still practiced although it is legally forbidden. Feminists say that what Ataturk may have accomplished on paper still has to be accepted in practice by many Turks.

How is it then that Islam, the only religion to outline formally the protection of women's rights, is also the faith most perceived to oppress women? When Islam began fourteen hundred years ago, the women around the Prophet participated in public life, were vocal about social inequities, and often shared decision making with him. In fact, many women displayed traits that a modern-day feminist would recognize.

• • •

Theirs was a relationship as contemporary as today.

She was an international trader, forty years old and widowed twice, who headed her own thriving business. A mature, aristocratic beauty of substantial wealth, she moved in the elite circles of her world. And as an intelligent and determined woman, and an excellent judge of character, she was, not surprisingly, influential in her community.

He was a twenty-five-year-old freelance importer-exporter, a slim young man of average height, whose beard, like his hair, was thick, black, and given to curl. The aquiline nose was typical of his ancestors, but it was his eyes that caught one's attention: large and set wide, with long, dark lashes, they had a luminous quality that everyone who met him commented on.

Orphaned as a child, he began work at twelve. Thirteen years later he was still too impecunious to marry. His first marriage proposal was rejected; the girl's father considered him insufficiently established financially. By his twenties, his strongest asset was still only his professional reputation.

Considered honest, reliable, and trustworthy by the traders for whom he had worked, he was well known in his field. She needed someone with those qualities to oversee a large shipment of her merchandise that would be traded in Syria, and so she hired him.

He was a skilled businessman, and the commodities he brought home sold for double the amount of the original investment.

Shortly after, she asked him to marry her, and he accepted.

Fifteen years his senior and his employer, Khadija bint Khuwaylid became the first wife of Mohammad, the man destined to be the Prophet and founder of Islam.

It was a harmonious and monogamous marriage of twenty-five years that ended only when she died, and even after he remarried, he spoke of her constantly and with great affection. She bore him six children, four girls and two boys; both sons died in childhood.

Was Khadija unusual in sixth-century Mecca, in what is now Saudi Arabia? She was, after all, a publicly visible woman who was economically independent due to inherited wealth, and who had initiated her own marriage to a man many years younger than her. Pre-Islamic Arabia is believed to have been a male-dominated society, where women were scarcely more than sales commodities, and girl babies were so little valued they were frequently buried alive. Although many women were treated as slaves, in major cities and trading centers, affluent women like Khadija occasionally had opportunities to enter commerce. And in Khadija's case, according to Professor Leila Ahmed, chair of the women's studies department at the University of Massachusetts, "the wealth she earned from caravan trains freed Mohammad from working and enabled him to become contemplative, the prelude to his prophethood."

Certainly his first wife appears to have contributed to Mohammad's respect and concern for women. During her lifetime, she was his confidante and counselor, his strongest supporter. She shared his ideology, became his first convert to Islam and a leading proselytizer of the new faith. And throughout their marriage, he turned to her for reassurance when he was threatened by his enemies or bewildered by his religious revelations. It was she who held him close and reassured him that he was not insane or sick after he received his first vision.

Mohammad was forty years old in A.D. 610, when Angel Gabriel first appeared to him and commmanded him to read, a seemingly odd instruction to a man who, like most of his contemporaries, was illiterate. At that time he was meditating alone, as he did frequently, in a mountainside cave above Mecca, when he heard a voice tell him, "O Mohammad, thou art the apostle of God, I am Gabriel."

Over the next twenty-two years, Mohammad received many revelations, the contents of which became the Koran, the divine guide for all Muslims, who are required to accept every word as the literal word of God.

"Some eighty percent of Koranic rulings are devoted to regulating marital relations and the conduct of women," says Professor Ahmed, an authority on women and Islam. "The area in which Islam introduced the greatest reform was marriage and sexual relations." This is not surprising given the Prophet's statement that "marriage is half the religion."

Many of those rulings, most being of a practical nature and intended to improve and regulate the everyday life of Muslims, often occurred in circumstances when the Prophet had been undergoing some profound experience in his own life. The various domestic dramas that the Prophet experienced with his wives frequently were used as the sources of his own enlightenment.

When Khadija died in A.D. 620, Mohammad, then aged fifty, was bereft, and friends recommended that he marry again. They suggested two potential spouses, Sawdah bint Zam'ah, who was in her thirties and who had been recently widowed, or A'isha, the daughter of his closest friend, Abu Bakr. It depended, the Prophet was told, on whether he wanted to marry a virgin or non-virgin. The Prophet chose both, marrying Sawdah first. At his marriage to six-year-old A'isha a few months later, the child-bride was not present, and the union was contracted between Mohammad and the girl's father. Because of A'isha's youth, she continued to live at her parents' home, unaware of her new marital state.

Three months later, the Prophet married again, this time to Hafsa, whose husband had just died in a recent battle, and who was the daughter of another of Mohammad's most powerful supporters. It was after the Prophet's fourth marriage that the Koranic verses regarding polygyny were revealed to him: "Marry of the women who seem good to you, two or three or four. And if ye fear that ye cannot do justice to so many, then marry only one."

In the twelve years following Khadija's death until his own demise at age sixty-two, Mohammad married between nine and twelve women (the exact figure has been lost in history). He was apparently not subject to the four-wife restriction because of his position. He did, however, endeavor to treat all his wives fairly. After every marriage, a room of identical proportions was added to the Prophet's home to accommodate the new wife. Mohammad did not have quarters built for himself; instead, he shared those of each of his wives in turn.

Of all the world's religions, Islam is closest to Christianity, yet the Christian world has reviled it and its founder from the Crusades until today. A frequent point of attack was the Prophet's multiple marriages, which caused Christian critics to denounce him as "lustful"; Voltaire went so far as to accuse him of being sexually insatiable. Such arguments drew apparent support from the writings of the early Islamic chroniclers of the *hadiths*, who described Mohammad's sexual vigor as being "equal to that of forty men."

There were, however, sound political and social motivations for the Prophet's numerous marriages. At a time when Islam had gained many converts and Mohammad was well established as its Prophet, the new religion continued to meet with enormous resistance. By selecting the wives he chose to marry, the Prophet forged alliances with tribes that had been bitter enemies of Islam and in the forefront of battles against it. His marriage to Safiya bint Huyay, the daughter of an important Jewish chief, for example, diminished Jewish opposition to the Prophet's mission. Important clans suppressed longstanding feuds with Muslims and accepted the new faith.

Even the consummation of his marriage to A'isha when she was ten, an age later critics considered scandalously young, took place at the request of her father, who wanted to strengthen the bonds between the two families. It was A'isha's father, Abu Bakr, an important supporter of Islam, who succeeded Mohammad after his death.

With the exception of A'isha, all of Mohammad's wives were widows, many of whom lost their husbands during wars. By marrying widows in an age when few were permitted to remarry after their husbands died, the Prophet tried to ensure that women who would otherwise have been unprotected were cared for.

Mohammad is described as being tolerant, flexible, affectionate, and good-humored with his wives. But he was unable to live up to his own ideal of treating them equally. That he tried to, they recognized, as he drew lots among them to select a companion to accompany him when traveling, and systematically spent each night with a different wife. And it was he who stated in a *hadith*, "A man who marries more than one woman and then does not deal justly between them will be resurrected with half his faculties paralyzed."

The Prophet's downfall was Maryam, a Coptic Christian slave renowned for her beauty, who had been sent to him as a gift by the ruler of Egypt. Mohammad was so enamored of her he began to spend days and nights in her company, ignoring his wives, who became increasingly jealous. Eventually, the Prophet's wives became so resentful that Mohammad retreated from his household to meditate. While he was gone, rumors spread rapidly that he was about to divorce all of his wives. His followers were appalled, recognizing that divorce would destroy the earlier tribal alliances brought about by the Prophet's marriages.

During his long meditation, he received a vision in which he was shown how to bring harmony back to his home and restore peace among the women he loved. A month later, Mohammad returned to his family and told his wives God had given them a choice: either they could accept an ordinary life and be honorably divorced, or, if they "desired Allah and his Messenger and the abode hereafter, then Allah [would] prepare [them] a great reward. . . ." If they chose the latter, however, Allah required that they "stay at home and not display themselves as in the days of ignorance." Influenced by A'isha, his wives all chose to stay with the Prophet.

The Prophet's other wives were equally jealous of the time he spent with A'isha. It was clear he was fondest of her, and those who wanted to please Mohammad would donate their turn with him to her. But when they voiced any feelings of discontent, the Prophet chastised them. It was in A'isha's company, he told them, that he received the most revelations.

Zeinab bint Jahsh was another wife around whom many revelations occurred. She was the high-ranking and beautiful cousin of the Prophet, and Mohammad had given her in marriage some years before to his adopted son, Zaid, a former slave. The Prophet's intent had been to show that social class was irrelevant. Zeinab, an extremely proud woman, had not been happy in the marriage to a man she considered infinitely her inferior, and, because of her discontent, neither had Zaid.

Mohammad was visiting his adopted son's home one morning when he caught a glimpse of Zeinab as she was dressing, and, embarrassed by his feelings, he hurriedly left the house. When Zeinab later told her husband of the incident, she hinted that the Prophet was impassioned with her. In an apparently loveless marriage, and not wishing to stand in his father's way, Zaid offered to divorce Zeinab if the Prophet wanted to marry her. Mohammad refused. In Arabia at that time, an adopted son was viewed as a blood relative, and marriage with Zaid's ex-wife would have been considered incestuous. But the incident triggered a breakdown in Zaid's marriage, and the couple divorced anyway. Shortly after, in another revelation, God commanded Mohammad to marry Zeinab.

The potential scandal in the community was avoided by the fact that same revelation also told the Prophet that adoption was now no longer legally permitted, and so, did not confer the status of parenthood. Zaid, who had been known for thirty-five years by the name Ibn Mohammad, meaning "son of Mohammad," now reverted to the name of his biological father.

And since divorce was frowned upon by Islam, this divine revelation also decreed that all future marriages must be between consenting partners; the woman must also be consulted and must agree. A radical change in its day, this had not been the case when Zeinab's first marriage was arranged for her.

At the Prophet's marriage to Zeinab, another far-reaching divine decree was revealed. Mohammad became angry when wedding guests stayed too long in Zeinab's room talking to her, and that same day he observed male guests touching the hands of his wives, possibly as they offered food to their guests. Since his home was at the center of the burgeoning religion, and the Prophet did not have private quarters of his own, there was a constant flow of visitors to the house. A revelation shortly after led to the seclusion of the Prophet's wives. "Enter not the dwellings of the Prophet for a meal without waiting for the proper time, and unless permission be granted you. When your meal is ended, then disperse. Linger not for conversation. . . . And when ye ask the wives of the Prophet for anything, ask it of them from behind a curtain."

The same decree forbade Mohammad's wives to marry again after the Prophet died. By this and other divine verses it was made clear that the wives of the Prophet were to be treated, and comport themselves, differently from ordinary women. The rulings for them to stay home and be secluded behind a curtain, the literal meaning of *purdah*, were formalized into the religion. However, it was clear that such rulings were intended for Mohammad's wives and not for women in general.

But it was an incident with A'isha that not only led to the Koranic punishment for slander but also is believed to have instigated the initial rupture in Islam, which created the religion's Sunni and Shi'a sects.

In the eighth year of A'isha's marriage to the Prophet, she accompanied him on one of his frequent expeditions, and was traveling in an enclosed howdah on a camel. On one of their regular halts to pray, A'isha slipped away from the men to seek privacy to perform the ritual washing required beforehand. Adjusting her veil as she rejoined the party, she realized she had lost her necklace and turned back to find it. The beads had great sentimental value for her, having been a wedding gift from her mother. By the time she located the necklace, the expedition had left, assuming she was inside the howdah. A'isha had no choice but to wait for someone to realize the error and return for her.

As she waited, a young man she had known in the days before she married rode by and recognized her. He offered to help her catch up with Mohammad's party, and, seating her on his camel, he led A'isha back to the city. Gossip traveled faster than they did: people who saw the attractive couple together concluded that Mohammad's favorite wife, then only fourteen, preferred the company of· a younger man to that of the now aging Prophet. It was the beginning of a scandal that shook the community. The uproar came at a disturbing time for Mohammad; the Muslim community was showing signs of disunity, and his divine revelations had apparently ceased. He became cold toward A'isha, and began to question many people about her character and fidelity. All but one of the men with whom he discussed the issue spoke well of her. Only his cousin and son-in-law Ali, who was married to Mohammad's daughter Fatima, did not. "Women are plentiful, you can always change one for another," said

Ali, encouraging the Prophet to divorce A'isha. A'isha never forgave him for it. This antipathy between the two would later cause Islam to splinter into two main sects.

The drama was finally brought to a close with another revelation in which the Prophet was told that his wife was not guilty of the accusations against her. The Koranic verse still used today in adultery cases dates from this time: "And those who accuse honorable women but bring not four witnesses, flog them with eighty stripes, and never again accept their evidence. For such men are evil-doers."

Throughout his life, the Prophet's affection and concern for women, and for mothers in particular, was evident. On one occasion when asked by a follower to whom one should show the most respect and kindness, the Prophet responded, "Your mother." "And then who?" insisted the questioner. "Your Mother," Mohammad replied again. "And then who?" "Your Mother," responded the Prophet for the third time. The questioner persisted: "And after that who?" "Your father," Mohammad replied, positioning men in fourth place. Similarly, on another occasion, when the Prophet was asked whether there was a shortcut to Paradise, he responded, "Paradise lies under the feet of the mother."

And in what turned out to be his final public address to Muslims from Mount Arafat near Mecca, the Prophet exhorted them, "Treat your women well and be kind to them."

Shortly after, Mohammad, now in his sixty-second year, began to complain of debilitating headaches. The pain intensified, and he finally collapsed. He was carried to A'isha's room and was nursed by all his wives. A few days later, on June 11, in the year 632, the man known to Muslims as the final Prophet died in the arms of A'isha, his favorite wife, who was then only eighteen.

• • •

The unexpected death of a Prophet who left no male heirs created a major crisis in the Islamic world. Rebellions broke out all over Arabia, and for a while it looked as if the new Islam unity might revert to the former tribal factions. Immediately, those who wanted to appoint a successor to Mohammad split into rival camps. A'isha's father, Abu Bakr, eventually succeeded as first Caliph or representative of Mohammad, with only Ali initially refusing to acknowledge his authority.

The appointment of her father as Caliph helped to confirm A'isha's position in the Islamic world. Even as a teenager, because of her closeness to the Prophet, she was frequently asked to interpret verses of the Koran and religious traditions, or to rule on Islamic law. She became the most prominent of all of Mohammad's wives, and was considered a major authority on Islam and an adviser to Muslims. One description of her at the time was as follows: "There is no greater scholar than A'isha in the learning of the Koran, obligatory duties, lawful and unlawful matters, poetry and literature, Arab history and genealogy." Her juristic opinions were widely sought, and one-quarter of the Islamic *Shariah* law, which is based on the collection of *hadiths,* is believed to have been narrated by her.

Later, after her father's death and that of his successor, A'isha led the opposition against the appointment of Ali, her former antagonist, to third Caliph. Says Professor Leila Ahmad, when the two opposing factions rode out to the attack in what is now known as the Battle of the Camel — the first time Muslim slaughtered Muslim — A'isha was leading her troops. Ali, who recognized her as a rallying point for her men, ordered her camel cut down from under her, which caused confusion among the ranks and brought about a ceasefire.

The followers of A'isha eventually came to be known as Sunni Muslims, and those of Ali, the Shi'a. Today's Sunni Muslims, who make up approximately 85 percent of the Islamic world, believe the first four Caliphs were the rightful successors of Mohammad. While they respect the Prophet's family, they do not believe that the temporal and spiritual leader of Islam must be a member of it.

Shi'a Islam rejects the first three Caliphs and regards Ali, the Prophet's cousin and son-in-law, as the original Caliph. They insist that the Imam, Muslim leader, must be a descendant of Ali and his wife, the Prophet's daughter. They also reject the Sunni sect, and the *Sunna hadith* laws from which they take their name. Shi'as are found mostly in Iran, Iraq, Yemen, and Azerbaijan, and have sizable populations in Kuwait, the Emirates, Saudi Arabia, Afghanistan, and Pakistan. Since the murder of Ali in A.D. 661 to the present day, Shi'as have waged an on-again, off-again war to overthrow the Sunnis and make Shi'ism, which is older than Sunni'ism, the dominant faith.

After A'isha's defeat by Ali, he charged that by going into battle she had violated the seclusion imposed on Mohammad's wives by the Prophet. Her place, he told her, like that of the other wives, was at home.

It was then that A'isha retired from public life. "Women scholars and authorities were still to be met with in the following two generations, though in far fewer number," says Professor Leila Ahmed. "Gradually it became extremely rare for any teachers of the *hadiths* to have learned from a woman. This is the period typically blamed for the restriction on women's lives." Added an early biographer of A'isha, "Muslim women's position was now one of passivity and submissiveness. By the second and third centuries of Islam, the seclusion and degradation of women had progressed beyond anything known in the first decades of Islam."

• • •

It begins at birth. The delivery of a baby boy is greeted with felicitations, parties, and, in some Muslim countries, even celebratory bursts of gunfire. The birth of a girl, on the other hand, is invariably a time for mourning. Even in everyday speech in much of the Arab world, when a silence falls at a gathering, the phrase uttered is *Yat Bint*, "a girl is born." And when one is, midwives have been known to abandon a delivery the moment they realize the child they have just helped into the world is of the "wrong" sex. Even before the umbilical cord is cut, more than one mother has had her face slapped for daring to give birth to a girl.

Husbands frequently feel shame, women feel guilt, and their family and friends offer whispered condolences instead of the customary sweets. "It is God's will," they say sadly, using the same expression employed when someone dies. "Next time," the new mother is told, "next time, you'll give him a son."

Modern Muslim physicians recognize the problem. A woman obstetrician at a high-tech Arab hospital in the Gulf told me, "We never inform women of the sex of their baby-to-be after they've had a sonogram. We find they can cope much better and longer with labor pains if they don't know they are giving birth to a girl."

If a Muslim woman doesn't present her husband with a son, chances are high that he will eventually take a second wife. He may even divorce her, which, in much of the Islamic world, can render her a social pariah. In a culture where men, on being asked how many children they have, will reply, for example, "Four children," meaning four sons, and when pushed will reluctantly add, "and three daughters," women are blamed for the birth of girls. Few Muslim males, even educated ones, accept that it is he, not his wife, who determines the gender of their child. "My wife is worthless, she has only given me girls," is a common refrain. And indeed, a woman's place in many Muslim societies can be determined by her sons; without them she is frequently viewed as having lower status than other women. Similarly, the woman is held responsible if the couple is unable to have children.

The low value placed on the average female Muslim child may have its genesis in the title used to describe a girl before marriage: translated, it means "another's wealth." The epithet refers to the fact that any investment made in a girl in her early years will be enjoyed only by her husband's family when she moves in with them permanently upon marriage. Because she is seen as having only "temporary guest membership" in her own family, money, time, and effort spent on her childhood development may be minimal.

In 1985, the president of Pakistan established a commission to investigate the status of women. The report concluded, "The average woman is born into near slavery, leads a life of drudgery, and dies invariably in oblivion. This grim condition is the stark reality of half our population simply because they happen to be female." Not surprisingly, the government suppressed the report.

Few statistics are available in most Muslim countries for the simple reason that all information is tightly controlled by the governing regimes; concerning women, however, they scarcely exist, and when they do, they can be grim. In Pakistan women have a lower life expectancy than men. In fact, the country is listed in *The Guinness Book of World Records* for an unusual reason — the world's lowest female-male ratio: 936 women to every 1,000 men. The world average is the reverse: 1,110 women to 1,000 men. The main reason for this is poor health in women caused by the discrimination they face from the time of birth. A boy infant, for example, is breast-fed for two years as prescribed by the Koran. A female baby is frequently weaned much earlier. In the majority of families, girls and their mothers usually eat only after the male in the family; not surprisingly, therefore, girls have a much higher malnutrition rate than boys. And even in privileged homes, sons are more likely than daughters to be given milk, eggs, meat, and fruit.

Though she eats less than her brothers, a girl in an ordinary household does twice the work. Her fragile nutritional status leads to anemia and other nutritional deficiencies, and exposes her to infection. She is ill more often than her brother. But even when she is ill, studies show that she is more likely to be treated at home, whereas boys are taken to doctors or hospitals. Women and girls have died when the men in their families have refused permission for them to be examined by male physicians because of Islamic modesty dictates, and female physicians are still rare.

Studies show that in Pakistan, for example, female deaths between the ages of fifteen and forty are fully 75 percent more frequent than male deaths. A significant cause of this is the extremely high rate of maternal mortality — Pakistan has one of the highest in the world — which is caused by one of the highest nutritional anemia rates. A shocking 97.4 percent of all pregnant women in Pakistan are anemic.

Such cause and effect is not confined to Pakistan. Many Muslim countries share depressingly similar practices, except among the minority, the educated elite. And even then, while women's physical needs may be well attended to, frequently their emotional needs are ignored.

From the time a girl is five or six, preparation for the only acceptable role for her — wife and mother — begins. She is groomed to be a good wife: docile, obedient, and self-sacrificing. She will learn that her brothers come first in everything, and that even her younger ones hold sway in her life. I found it unnerving to watch a nine-year-old boy walk into a room and with barely a glance cause his seventeen-year-old sister to give up her chair to him and sit at his feet. I was told by a young woman graduate student whose class was about to go on a perfectly ordinary half-day field trip, "My father gave me permission to go. But my younger brother became very angry and said it was not appropriate for his sister to go out on such a trip. He was so angry, he said he would leave our house if my father permitted it. And so I couldn't go." A more depressing example of male dominance is a seven-year-old who told his mother he would not give her his permission to go out when she wanted to attend a course in mother-and-child health care, and she complied.

As a Muslim girl approaches adolescence, the injunctions to walk, talk, and dress unobtrusively — to be invisible — become more stringent. She is constantly imbued with such values as the following: "A girl should be like water, unresisting. It takes on the shape of the container into which it is poured but has no shape of its own." Even her movements and associations are strictly curtailed. Her place is at home, she is not allowed to play outside, and her friends are limited. If she is fortunate enough to have attended school, which is usually segregated by gender except for the very young, she is often withdrawn as a teenager.

And once she reaches puberty, her world will be severely circumscribed. How much her world is limited depends on where she lives, and to which class she belongs. Only after menopause does she attain any real authority. No longer able to bear children, she is often considered an honorary male. And if she has been totally veiled, it is at this age she may uncover her face, but by then she may no longer want to.

Feminism in the Islamic world, however, has a long history. The first Islamic feminist movement began in Egypt at the end of the last century and quickly spread to Turkey, Syria, and Iran. Women lobbied heavily for changes in polygyny, divorce, inheritance, and child custody laws, but won only minor successes. Then in the twenties in Egypt, women began to shed their veils. In Iran, the veil was formerly abolished in 1936 by Reza Shah, and the king did the same for Afghanistan in 1921. The law there was soon reversed in a conservative whiplash. But in 1959, Afghanistan's President Daoud reversed it again, and most women unveiled.

Between the 1950s and 1970s, women in a number of Muslim countries made great strides. Today, however, the situation is reversing, as Islamic conservative movements such as the Muslim Brotherhood, and Wahabi-backed groups and Rabitat-Islami, both originating in Saudi Arabia, grow and spread.

"For a period of time, Muslim women were able to obtain education, to work, and, in some cases, even join their country's armed forces. A middle class was born in some of these states, and women were an active part in it," says Iranian scholar and professor of Middle Eastern studies Shaul Bakhash. "Things began to reverse for these women at the end of the seventies. If you look at Muslim countries today, across the board the direction is toward Islamist movements. The current situation for women is not at all encouraging; the reverse, in fact: it is regressive.

"In countries like Iran where harsh restrictions have been placed on women, there is a tremendous amount of resistance against them from the new educated female elite. And because of this, Muslim movements back to traditionalism may have to yield on some issues. Conversely, in a number of Muslim countries, women are again being viewed as a potential source of corruption in the society (by their very existence), one that has to be watched most carefully so that such influence can be guarded against."

For Akbar S. Ahmed, an Islamic scholar of international repute, formerly of both Princeton and Harvard, the current change in the

Islamic world regarding the situation vis-à-vis women comes down to a simple equation: "The position of women in Muslim society mirrors the destiny of Islam: when Islam is secure and confident so are its women; when Islam is threatened and under pressure so, too, are they."

CHAPTER 3

Pakistan: One Step Forward, Two Steps Back

*Make not God's name an excuse for your oaths
against doing good or acting rightly.*

KORAN 2:224

LAHORE IS A CITY OF GARDENS, a rare Asian metropolis that
keeps the promise of the romantic East. Third World munici-
palities tend to be seedy and scabious, as mangy as the emaci-
ated dogs that roam their streets, but ancient Lahore's decay
is one of faded elegance. Its wide, tree-lined boulevards, canals, and
myriad landscaped parks, more plentiful than in many European
cities, provide vital retreat from the summer's searing heat. And its
proud Moghul history is evident at every turn. It was in Lahore 350
years ago that Shah Jahan, the creator of the Taj Mahal, built the
Shalimar Gardens, whose marble pavilions and fountains cool more
aesthetically and as effectively as modern-day air-conditioning. The
massive fort constructed by the greatest of all Moghul emperors,
Akbar, stands in Lahore, as does the vast and still beautiful Badshahi
Mosque, where four hundred thousand Muslims attend prayers on
Islamic high holidays. Throughout the city it is apparent that Lahore's architectural wealth dates from a period when Moghul architecture and art were at their zenith. But the region's history predates
the Moghul empire by millennia.

The Indus Valley civilization flourished here five thousand years
ago. Little known in the West, its culture developed at the same time
as ancient Egypt's and Mesopotamia's, and it is believed to have been
larger, more advanced, and better administrated than both of them.
It is perhaps not surprising then that Lahore, the thousand-year-old
capital of Punjab, Pakistan's most affluent and fertile province, is

also the country's cultural and intellectual center. Much of that refinement is imparted at Lahore's elite educational institutions, such as Aitcheson College, Pakistan's Eton, through whose doors many of the nation's leaders have passed. And it is evidenced at the pukka Gymkhana and Punjab clubs, where white-gloved waiters serve luncheon and dinner, and the membership is as restrictive as it was when the British were here. But behind the gentility of the city is a brutishness that stuns.

• • •

"It happened at such a happy time," says Ahmedi Begum. "I was so proud. I had just become a grandmother for the first time, a boy, praise be to God. My daughter was still in this bed recovering from the delivery," she says, patting the simple wooden bed covered with a quilt she embroidered herself that we are both sitting on. Ahmedi, now a sixty-year-old widow, was waiting for her nephew, Tufail, to return with a bag of cement for some repairs he planned to do in the courtyard. That she cares about her little home in Bukarmandi, a middle-class area of Lahore, is evident. Her tiny living room–cum–master bedroom is spotless, the turquoise paint on the walls bright, and there is lace trimming the shelves that house her collection of dishes and glassware.

Her nephew returned just as she was opening the gate to visitors. Two women in their twenties, both completely veiled, wanted to rent the upstairs section of the house that Ahmedi had been trying to lease because she needed the income. "I didn't know them, but they seemed honest and I was about to show them the rooms when there was a commotion outside and several policemen burst into the courtyard. In the shouting and confusion they arrested the two women and my nephew. He was just standing there holding the cement."

When her son-in-law came home from work later that afternoon, Ahmedi and he visited the police station to find out what had happened. The arrest didn't make sense since Tufail and the women were strangers to one another.

Even now, five years later, Ahmedi Begum finds it hard to talk about what happened next. "The police put me into a separate room and told me they were arresting me, too. I was shocked. 'I'm a respectable woman who has lived a respectable life. You have made a mistake,' I told them. 'You must let me go.' But they ignored what I said. They even took away my earrings and bracelets, my wedding gold. When the officer-in-charge came, I told him the same thing:

'I'm a grandmother, a widow, a respectable woman, why are you keeping me here?' He said they would free me in a little while." As Ahmedi talks, her work-worn hands turn over and over in her lap.

"As I was sitting there waiting, one of the police opened the door and said, 'If you want these other women, here they are,' and they pushed them into the room. They were naked, bleeding. . . . They raped them again in front of me. I covered my eyes," says Ahmedi, unconsciously doing the same thing again. "I couldn't watch."

Her anguished response angered the officers. Ahmedi was forced to her knees, her arms pulled to her sides. "Why are you covering your eyes? Watch it, watch it!" she was told. Then, while they still held her, a police officer thrust his penis into her mouth. "They were laughing and shouting 'suck, suck,' " says Ahmedi, as the tears slide down her face. "I, who have never known any man's body except my husband's. Such shame, such shame. I was a grandmother, a woman of honor. But they weren't finished with me." Just like the other two captives, the five-foot-tall widow was stripped and, like them, she was held down while one officer after another repeatedly raped her. "It went on for hours, and the same with the other girls. I cried, I prayed, I asked God why. I don't know how many policemen came through that room that night. It could have been fifty. I will never forget their laughter, their shouting."

Ahmedi thought it was over when they dragged her outside. "It was morning and I believed they would let me go," she recalls. "But they threw me on the ground, and holding me facedown, they began to beat my whole body with a wide leather strap. I thought they would kill me. Suddenly the beating stopped. . . . Then I screamed and screamed. I felt as though my insides were on fire. I have never known such pain." A police officer had forced a *lathi*, an oversize truncheon, covered in fiery chili paste, into Ahmedi's rectum. It was done with such violence that her rectum was ruptured, and the chili paste burned like acid on the lacerated tissue. Mercifully, Ahmedi passed out. When she regained consciousness several hours later she was in Kot Lokhpat Women's Prison.

"I couldn't walk, I couldn't speak, my mouth was too swollen. My clothes were covered in blood." Ahmedi lay almost motionless for days in her cell until a government minister made a VIP tour of the jail. During his visit, prisoners were required to sit on the ground with their criminal files in front of them. "He saw the blood on me and spoke to me, but because of my mouth I couldn't reply," says

Ahmedi. "He ordered a doctor to see me." He also ordered the police commissioner of Lahore to investigate the matter.

The medical report detailed the savage assault and documented that Ahmedi had been subject to "severe sexual torture." The other two women in the case had been charged with "roaming about," which can be viewed as prostitution in Pakistan. At the same time, Ahmedi learned that she was in prison charged with *zina*.

Zina, sex outside of wedlock, encompasses adultery, fornication, and rape, and its maximum punishment in Pakistan is stoning to death for those who are married. For unmarried transgressors, the punishment is up to one hundred lashes, and ten years' imprisonment.

Under the law as it stands in Pakistan, women who have been raped can be charged with adultery or fornication. The proof required for *zina* is that there be four Muslim adult males of "good repute" present who can attest to the act of sexual penetration. No male witnesses of good repute, of course, are likely to stand and watch a rape in progress without trying to stop it. And because of this requirement it becomes impossible to punish the rapists. Instead, the victim is prosecuted. Her legal complaint of rape is considered a confession of illicit sexual intercourse.

This is exactly what happened to sixteen-year-old Safia Bibi in 1983. Virtually blind, Safia was employed as a domestic in the home of a local landowner. She was raped first by her employer's son, and then by her employer. As a result, she became pregnant and subsequently gave birth to an illegitimate child. Safia's father registered a case of rape for his daughter. The judge, however, acquitted both the son and the father because there were not four male witnesses to attest to the assaults. Safia's pregnancy, though, was deemed in court evidence of fornication. In sentencing her to three years' rigorous imprisonment, a public flogging, and a fine of Rs. 1,000, the judge stated he was giving the handicapped teenager a "light sentence" because of her young age and near blindness.

In Ahmedi's case, she spent three months in Kot Lokhpat jail. She was released on bail after Asma Jahangir, a human rights activist and lawyer, took up her case. The Lahore grandmother was finally acquitted three years later. But in that time, her son-in-law abandoned and then divorced her daughter because he felt shamed by the gossip.

Ahmedi is still under treatment for a chronically ulcerated rectum.

She also suffers from constant back pain from the beating, as well as high blood pressure and frequent nightmares. She believes she was arrested because shortly before the incident she had refused to rent out rooms to a police officer from the station where she was assaulted.

Compounding her health problems were the visits she received from the police several times after she was acquitted. "They offered us thousands of rupees to drop the case against them, but they never gave back my dowry jewelry. I told them my honor is more important than their blood money. The last time they came, a police official said to me, 'These men cannot be punished. It is bad for the country, and will bring a bad name for the police, if they are.'"

The officers involved in the attack were charged but never tried. They were transferred outside the city to different parts of the province, as was the trial. The witnesses could not afford the frequent travel to the new location in Rawalpindi, seven hours' drive away. Such ploys are commonly used in Pakistan in cases against the police.

Tragically, Ahmedi's case is not an isolated one. Seventy-two percent of all women in Pakistan in police custody are physically and sexually abused, according to lawyer Asma Jahangir, who is also cofounder of Women's Action Forum, a national women's rights organization. Equally shocking is the fact that 75 percent of all women in jail in Pakistan are there under charges of *zina*. "Many can serve months, even years, waiting for their trials to be heard," adds Hina Jilani, Jahangir's sister, and a fellow human rights activist and lawyer.

But it isn't just law enforcers who see rape as a fringe benefit of their positions. In a country where a woman's chastity, purity, and honor must be preserved at all costs, even to death, women are subject to sexual assault almost daily, as Pakistan's newspapers attest. And it is an easy crime to commit because punishment for men is so rare.

Rape is a weapon commonly used for revenge. In August 1991, twenty-six men raped Allah Wasai, a woman who was eight months pregnant, to settle a score with her father-in-law. After the attack, she was paraded naked through her community. In November of that same year, two young women were subject to nearly identical barbaric assaults. In each case the young woman was gang-raped by eight men, and then had her nose amputated. "To cut off someone's nose" is a figure of speech in Pakistan that means to humiliate someone. The attacks in both cases were reprisals aimed at the women's brothers. In neither incident did the police conduct an investigation.

"These kinds of attacks against women are meant to humiliate and demean their menfolk," says a spokeswoman of War Against Rape, an organization based in Karachi, Pakistan's largest city, who was too nervous to give her name in case she became a victim of revenge herself. "It seems to be done with the same kind of motivation that makes kids who are angry with you go out and damage your property. No thought is ever given to the woman involved."

Rape is also employed as a weapon by political opponents. In April 1992, twenty female polling agents, including a former woman politician, were raped during a local election in Sindh Province in an organized effort to disrupt voting. One newspaper editorial commented at the time: "It appears that the Sindh government has once again reaffirmed its faith in using rape as an effective tool of political manipulation." Political use of assault on women made international news not so long ago when Veena Hayat, a longtime close friend of then opposition leader Benazir Bhutto, was gang-raped by five armed men who broke into her home. The attack on such a prominent woman, which led to demonstrations and a hunger strike by Pakistan's women activists, was allegedly carried out at the behest of the president's son-in-law. During the twelve-hour ordeal, the victim was repeatedly questioned about the activities and visitors of Benazir Bhutto. Once again, no one was arrested.

Other common reasons for rape are family feuds and revenge against a family that has defaulted on a debt. Majida Abdullah was eleven years old when she was abducted by her father's employers. A bonded laborer in a brick kiln — an occupation likened to slavery in Pakistan — her father owed money he was unable to pay. Majida was held for two months, repeatedly raped by her captors, one of whom was a government "anticorruption" official. She was also threatened with being sold into prostitution slavery. When her family tried to bring a case of rape against the landowners, Majida was charged with *zina* and jailed. Four years later, and now out on bail, her case is still pending. Yet again, her attackers went free. After the attack, Majida tried to commit suicide. "Pakistan is not a place for women. My life is over. Because these men were rich and I am poor, they considered me the same as the bricks in their factory — I was their property," she said.

In Pakistan, rape is also utilized as a show of raw power, and feudal lords in rural areas often use sexual assault publicly to enforce local dictates. And the crime is employed to penalize nurses, who are frequently accused of being immoral because they must work at night or care for male patients. Twenty-three-year-old Farhat Sadiq was a staff nurse working on the night shift at a Karachi hospital when she was raped at gunpoint by two male visitors to a private patient. "I reported the attack to the hospital matron and was told to keep my mouth shut. The patient was a prominent one," Sadiq told me. "I received the same response when I went to the hospital's medical superintendent. I was too afraid to go to the police in case they raped me again."

Ten days later, Sadiq was arrested, charged with *zina*, and she spent two months in Karachi's Central Jail. At her court hearing, where she was able to identify her attackers, she was found guilty, sentenced to five years' imprisonment, five lashes, and a 10,000-rupee fine. Her attackers were never charged. On appeal in a higher court, Sadiq was acquitted of all charges. But by then she had lost her job because her reputation was now "tarnished," and her fiancé had broken off their engagement because he didn't want to marry "a woman who was no longer pure." Says her mother, "I was so proud of my daughter when she became a nurse. It is good to work for suffering people. But men in Pakistan think because a nurse has to go out of the house at night to work, she must be a bad woman. These men who have ruined my daughter's life should be hanged. Instead, they went totally unpunished. Why is there one justice for men and another justice for women?"

In view of assaults like Sadiq's, it is not surprising that Pakistan has a severe shortage of nurses. According to Dr. Paula Herbert of the Aga Khan school of nursing, for every four doctors in the country there is only one nurse.

Such attacks on women substantially increased in Pakistan after the country was "Islamized" at the beginning of the eighties by its then martial-law president, General Zia-al-Haq. Zia, the grandson of a mullah, came into office when he overthrew Zulfikar Ali Bhutto, Benazir Bhutto's father, whom he subsequently executed.

• • •

Mohammad Ali Jinnah, who founded Pakistan in 1947, intended the country to be a Muslim homeland but a secular state. And like Turkey's Ataturk before him, Jinnah exhorted his fellow Muslims, "Take along your women with you as comrades in every sphere of life."

He noted that there was no Koranic injunction for women to be confined. "We are victims of evil customs," he said. "It is a crime against humanity that our women are shut up within the four walls of their homes like prisoners.

"I do not mean that we should imitate the evils of Western life. But let us try to raise the status of our women according to our own Islamic ideals and standards. There is no sanction anywhere for the deplorable conditions in which our women have to live." And for a while women in Pakistan appeared to be progressing.

President Zia chose to ignore his country's original secularism when, during his first speech to the nation after he seized power in 1977, he claimed legitimacy on the grounds that he was "fulfilling Pakistan's divine mission of becoming an Islamic state."

And it was under the U.S.-supported dictatorship of General Zia that the status of women in Pakistan dramatically eroded. This was achieved through the introduction of laws that were highly detrimental to women. Perpetrated in the name of Islam, these laws included the Hudood Ordinances, under which Pakistan's *zina* laws fall. Said lawyer Asma Jahangir, "The framing and implementation of the Hudood Ordinances were so slipshod that they lent no credibility to the object of Islamization. In fact, the bill showed a transparent political opportunism." Zia's new laws also decreed that in court hearings, the testimony of two women was equal to that of one man's, and that in compensation cases, the value of a woman's life was to be only half that of a man's.

Promising to return the country to "the purity of early Islam," Zia issued a series of directives aimed directly at women. Female government employees were ordered to wear Islamic dress. In Pakistan, this is a loose tunic that comes to below the knee and has long sleeves and a high neck, and is worn over ankle-length baggy pants. Over this, they were required to wear a *chador*, which covers the head and most of the body.

Overnight, female television announcers could appear on the air only with their heads covered and in full-sleeved dress. Then the ruling was extended to women's educational institutions for teachers and students alike. The code of conduct and dress for Pakistani women was to be modeled on Saudi Arabia and Iran, considered by many Islamic theologians to be the only truly Islamic societies.

Suddenly it seemed as if every aspect of women's lives was targeted. New laws were issued on obscenity and pornography, and women began to be generally regarded as synonymous with obscenity, immorality, and corruption. If women were harassed, killed, or raped in the streets or at home, it was because they had provoked these attacks by their speech, action, or just by their very presence.

The Koranic injunctions for men to cast down their eyes when in the presence of the opposite sex appeared forgotten. According to women's rights activists Khawar Mumtaz and Farida Shaeed, women were now being scrutinized in a manner that was previously unheard of. Theologian Dr. Israr Ahmad, who was also a member of the advisory Council of Islamic Ideology, and was handpicked by Zia for the Federal Council, actually stated on government-controlled television that no one could be punished for assaulting or raping a woman until an Islamic society had been created. By that he meant a total absence of female visibility. He and President Zia wanted women to return to the traditional *chador and chardiwari* — "the veil and four walls."

Under this custom, which is still practiced in conservative regions of Pakistan and particularly in the provinces of Baluchistan and the Northwest Frontier, it is said that a woman should go out only three times in her life: the first time, when she is born; the second, when she is married and taken to her husband's home; and the third time, when she dies and is taken to be buried. And on the occasions when she does go out, she is expected to wear a *burqa* veil, a tentlike garment that covers her from head to toe, shrouding her completely except for her feet. The only opening is a small embroidered grill at eye level, through which she is destined to view the world in blurred glimpses.

The *burqa* is stifling in Pakistan's extreme summer heat. Everyday errands, even going out for groceries, are undertaken by the males in the family. This confinement is frequently carried to such extremes that women suffer from a host of ailments caused by lack of physical exercise and exposure to sunlight. There is a high incidence of osteomalacia, a softening of the bones, in Muslim countries where women are completely veiled. The lack of sunlight reaching the skin also contributes to conditions such as eczema and to ulcers.

The segregation of women is taken so seriously that many houses in Pakistan are surrounded with eight- to ten-foot-high *purdah* walls. All rooms face inward, with windows on the ground floor either built close to the ceiling or with frosted glass to ensure that the women who live there are never seen by passing male guests or tradesmen. In the Northwest Frontier Province, it is illegal to build a house with windows that overlook the windows or garden of another house. In addition to these precautions, Muslim homes also have one room set aside for guests, which usually has direct outside access to further ensure that unrelated male visitors will not catch a glimpse of women living there.

When Benazir Bhutto first came to power after Zia died in a mid-flight airplane explosion, it was widely assumed she would improve the lot of Pakistani women. Part of her election campaign manifesto was "to repeal all discriminatory laws against women," particularly the Hudood Ordinances. "Women's rights will be strengthened to bring them to a par with men," she promised.

"Benazir did nothing for women apart from starting women's banks," says Hina Jilani. "Bhutto's first interest as prime minister was to mollify the mullahs, and to compromise with the establishment. Her popularity was rooted in the population's desire to better itself economically. Disadvantaged groups were drawn toward her because she talked about the oppressed. Unfortunately, she turned out to be part of the traditional system."

How did a young, attractive woman rise to hold her country's highest office in Pakistan, a domain of male supremacy? She was the first female head of a modern Muslim state, and, at thirty-five, Pakistan's youngest prime minister ever. Many of her country's mullahs were outraged and publicly declared her un-Islamic for presuming she could be premier. They urged believers to reject her for their own salvation. Pakistan's chief mullah, Maulwi Syed Mohammad Abdul Qadir Azad, of Lahore's Badshahi Mosque, issued a *fatwa* stating that any person voting for Bhutto would be rendered non-Muslim, and thereby sentenced to an afterlife in Hell.

Benazir's rise to power was preordained, or so she was informed when she consulted a medium in England to try to communicate with her dead father. "The medium told me I would lead my country," Benazir earnestly explained to me at her family's estate in Larkana, Sindh, when I interviewed her shortly before she was elected prime minister the first time. Preordained or not, her ascendancy once it began was rapid. And like most stars, at the beginning Benazir was luminescent. Soon she was being dubbed an Eastern Princess Diana, whom she promptly joined on the world's best-dressed and most-influential women's lists, and with whom she began to compete as an international media cover girl. Charismatic and charming, she was exotic enough to beguile Washington when she addressed Congress.

After a less glamorous early career that included house arrest and self-imposed exile endured under a media blackout, celebrity was a role Benazir enjoyed. And it was one she was willing to pay heavily for, literally. To maintain the limelight she suddenly found herself in, Benazir paid several hundred thousand dollars a year of her country's hard-found foreign currency to retain a Washington, D.C., political publicist, whose business it was to keep her in the public eye. That she was doing so, of course, was never publicized back home.

For a while, her publicist's job seemed easy as Benazir set out to prove herself a superwoman. She gave birth to her first child shortly after being elected, the world's first chief executive to do so while serving in office. She appeared in the National Assembly, Pakistan's parliament, the day before going into labor. And despite a severe postcesarean infection, she was soon back at work tending to affairs of state. And in between conferring with ministers, senators, presidents, and kings, she found time to breast-feed. To her countrymen, the fact that her first child was a boy confirmed her infallibility.

Her early background had suggested that Benazir was being groomed for nothing more demanding than a good marriage and managing a house full of servants. She was the oldest child of Zulfikar Ali Bhutto, who owned vast land holdings in Sindh Province, "as far as the eye could see," as Benazir described them. She enjoyed a pampered, Westernized childhood, complete with a fashionable wardrobe shipped to Pakistan each year by Saks Fifth Avenue. As in the case of many of the elite class in Pakistan even today, only English was spoken at home, and Benazir's early education was at a private, English-language convent school. Her poor knowledge of Urdu, Pakistan's national language, would prove to be an embarrassment when she was prime minister — her televised speeches to the nation contained frequent language errors and mispronunciations.

As her father before her, Benazir attended college in the United States, at Radcliffe, and then went to Oxford. Friends from her early student days told me that in those days she had a taste for brightly colored sports cars and parties. She became politicized when her father was executed in 1979. In conversations I had with her a few years after his death, it was obvious she regarded him as a deity. In fact, he was anything but.

Bhutto Sr. saw himself as an agent for modernization, and a voice of the people, but he also demanded to be treated like the feudal landlord he was. Although he did give women access to education and positions of power, he was stronger on rhetoric than he was on actual reform. He preached democratic socialism, but he practiced repression, including the creation of a brutal personal secret police force. As a sop to the ever-powerful mullahs, he banned all forms of gambling, forbidden by Islam, and changed Pakistan's weekend holiday from Sunday to Friday. But the hard-drinking Bhutto refused to give up alcohol, also forbidden under Islam, bragged about his liquor consumption in speeches, and told the mullahs that while he drank whiskey, they drank the blood of the people.

Finally, Bhutto Sr. so outraged the religious leaders with his high Western lifestyle, they helped to bring him down. Pakistan's impoverished majority, to whom he had guaranteed much but delivered little, were left with empty promises. They would not forget, however, that he was a leader who, unlike those who had gone before him, at least recognized their existence.

Benazir understood from the beginning that she owed her status to her father and manipulated his legacy brilliantly. She campaigned in her father's name so intensely, with his photographs and posters outnumbering hers, that during her oath-taking when she was sworn into office, the masses stood outside Parliament House chanting *Jeeay Jeeay Shaheed Bhutto* — "Long live the martyred Bhutto."

But having won the first race, Benazir faltered almost immediately after crossing the finishing line. It soon became apparent that Benazir was a prime minister of obvious style but little substance. While she had clearly inherited her father's feudal arrogance, she seemed to lack his political savvy. Like him, she was strong on rhetoric, but she did not have his abilities as a leader. As one editorial said at the time, "She inherited every single fault of her father, but none of his virtues."

Distrustful of outsiders, Benazir used nepotism and cronyism for support. Increasingly she turned to her husband, Asif, a polo-playing playboy until his arranged marriage to Benazir. While his wife played at governing, Asif allegedly acquired a new profession — using Benazir's name to circumvent government regulations, grab lucrative industrial licenses, and open doors for friends who would be grateful when their somewhat shady deals were pushed through without delay or question.

Colleagues and friends tried to warn her. But Bhutto, as always, was intolerant of criticism, confrontational, and autocratic. Despite this, when one aide tried to intervene, Bhutto declared in the fashion of a traditional, subservient Muslim wife, "Let my husband do what he will do."

Forced out of office after just twenty months, Benazir was accused of corruption and incompetence, and her husband was jailed. He was incarcerated for two years before being allowed bail. Several cases against him were dropped, but other charges were still outstanding that could have led to a stiff sentence. But then in the constantly shifting sands that are Asian politics, Benazir was again voted back into office, in October 1993, albeit with a very slim margin and in the lowest turnout in Pakistan's voting history.

Under her leadership the first time around, Pakistan's shaky economy worsened, its citizens remained among the poorest in the world, and the oppression and human rights violations against her country's women continued unabated.

Would conditions improve this time around? Early indications suggest not. Shortly before these latest elections, it was revealed that bank loans worth over $2 billion, or two-thirds of this impoverished nation's national debt, had been defaulted on by prominent Pakistanis. Among those named who allegedly used their political clout to have the debts written off, were Benazir, her husband, and her mother. Benazir's response at the time was simply to blast the publication of the list as "partisan politics."

During her political campaign, she vowed to repeal the recently imposed and much needed agricultural tax on wealthy feudal landowners like herself. And women's issues? In the political horse-trading that typifies Pakistani politics, Benazir's new coalition government includes all of the nation's religious parties. As she did during her first administration, Benazir is once again expected to appease the mullahs in order to stay in office rather than concern herself with the rights of women.

While Bhutto has yet to improve the situation for women in Pakistan, the man who followed her first term of office, wealthy industrialist Nawaz Sharif, made it much worse. His promises to the fundamentalist political parties that shored up his weak coalition government culminated in the passage of the *Shariah* Law Bill in May 1991. Described as being "the worst piece of legislative draftmanship" by Pakistan's former interior minister, Aitzaz Ahsan, a prominent jurist and a member of the National Assembly, the *Shariah* Bill was feared on the grounds that it would put Pakistan on a par with Saudi Arabia Islamically. Ahsan was concerned that it would give license to the fundamentalists to carry out the kind of actions witnessed under Zia when he first initiated Islamization.

Ahsan recalled that in 1980, a mob in Karachi, at the instigation of a mullah, stoned to death an abandoned infant on the presumption that it was illegitimate and therefore could not be tolerated or cared for by human hands. Similarly, a man's hand was cut off by a crowd led by a local clergyman who alleged, but had not proven, that the man was a thief.

Shariah means "pathway to God," and, based on the Koran and *hadiths*, it is to be the source of all law and policy making in Pakistan. It gives religious courts the power to overrule existing laws, and dissolve the Marriage Act and Family Protection Bill, both of which granted women a certain degree of protection in personal legal matters. "The *Shariah* Bill is a means to control women and marginalize them instead of bringing in a just order. It is a law that facilitates aggression against women but ignores the corruption in the country and it disregards violence against women," said one leading feminist.

International economists have long considered Pakistan to be one of the most corrupt countries in the world. President Ghulam Ishaq Khan, who forced both Benazir and her successor, Nawaz Sharif, out of office for "alleged corruption," was himself on the payroll of BCCI, as chairman of their international influence-purchasing foundation. According to U.S. congressional investigations, Pakistan's President Zia also received hundreds of thousands of dollars in 1985 alone from BCCI.

Less than a month after the *Shariah* Bill became law, the state-run Pakistan television began to censor its commercials. The first they whisked off the air was a tea bag ad that showed a man and a woman, both Islamically dressed, drinking tea together. That the couple are perhaps the best-known siblings in the country did not affect the decision. After much deliberation, the ad was allowed back on the air but only after a segment showing the couple smiling at each other and walking through a park together was cut. But a candy commercial was less fortunate. Its animated dancing jelly beans and sugar bears were permanently banished because dancing is un-Islamic.

Though dancing jelly beans may be considered too irreligious for TV viewing, the dancing girl industry in Pakistan is flourishing. It also receives official sanction even though it is generally known to be a cover for prostitution. The tradition of dancing girls in Pakistan dates back hundreds of years, and it is a profession that girls are either born into or sold into by their parents. Dancing girls are hired out to entertain at stag nights and prewedding bachelor parties, and also can be rented by the quarter hour in the country's red-light districts.

Pakistan has one of the highest child populations in the world — 45 percent of its 110 million people are under the age of fifteen. When money is short in impoverished families in Pakistan, a daughter may be sold into slavery, child prostitution, or simply for child labor. Studies show that Pakistan's carpet and brick-kiln industries would collapse if children, some as young as four, were removed from the workforce.

Young girls sold into prostitution serve as servants in brothels until they reach the age of nine or ten, when they are considered old enough to "entertain" customers. Prostitution in a Third World country is a short-lived career, as hepatitis and syphilis are rampant, AIDS arrived recently, and medical services are minimal. Many prostitutes are dead before the age of twenty-five. But now that a recent medical study in Karachi has found that 80 percent of dancing girls and other prostitutes suffer from AIDS, many may not live that long.

The most notorious of Pakistan's red-light districts is Hira Mundi in Lahore, in the shadow of the historical Badshahi Mosque. Just as houses of prostitution were historically established close to cathedrals in Christian countries, brothels and prostitutes operate near mosques and shrines "where the crowds are" in Muslim countries.

Finding a guide and translator to accompany me on a visit to Hira Mundi was difficult. Several men agreed and then backed out because it was "too dangerous," particularly since the government officially permits the district to operate only from 11:00 P.M. to 1:00 A.M. The pimps who control the area are notorious for their violence, and murders and beatings are not uncommon. Eventually, however, Tahir Malik, a journalist at one of Pakistan's national daily newspapers, who earned his Master's degree at Oklahoma State University, agreed to take me. Well over six feet tall and with the physique of an athlete, Tahir's presence was a comforting one in the dark and narrow lanes of Hira Mundi, where the ramshackle and ancient buildings lean perilously against one another, the whole conveying a Dickensian gloom. At first it appeared that despite the many men on the street, Hira Mundi was not yet open for business — windows stayed tightly shuttered and doors were heavily draped. But that is only for privacy, Tahir explained; customers here are meant to step inside and inspect the wares. Many of the men clustered in groups of three and four every fifty yards were, in fact, police officers, ostensibly present to keep the peace, but also well tipped for their presence.

At one venue, we stepped through a large wooden door that was bolted shut behind us by a male musician. Two sisters, Chandri, seventeen, and Tanya, who said she was twenty but looked younger, barely glanced at us as they mechanically strapped on heavy bell anklets. Their mother, seated in a corner below two gaudy pictures of Mecca, briskly started negotiations. "Five hundred rupees," she demanded. Five hundred rupees ($25) is the average worker's weekly salary in Pakistan. Tahir counter-offered Rs. 200. Tanya promptly snarled at her mother, "Take it, foolish woman, take it!"

The dancing was a blend of Western disco and Indian classical. Tanya and Chandri were dressed in vivid-colored satin *shalwar-kamezes*, richly embroidered in gold and silver, reflecting light as they twisted and turned, but the girls were sullen throughout the performance. Their faces were heavily made up and their toe- and fingernails lacquered bright red. Each wore expensive jewelry, the kind usually given to Pakistani brides for their dowry. Dancing girls normally receive such costly gifts from the customer who purchases their virginity or with whom they later find favor. The highlight of the girls' dancing was the fast-paced stamping of their feet, making the brass bells on their ankles ring, a movement considered extremely erotic by aficionados. The performance came to an abrupt end five minutes after it began, and we were expected to leave quickly. Interviews would have to wait until after hours. They feared losing paying customers: on a good night dancers can make Rs. 2,000, a month's salary for the average Pakistani male.

Later, a group of Hira Mundi's girls said that 90 percent of them were in the business because their parents were too poor to keep them. Most began dancing at ten, and resisted becoming prostitutes for about a year. "We have no other way to get money," said one, who, like the rest, was too scared to give her name. Pimps negotiated prices with clients, paid the heavy bribes to police, and provided security against violence. All of the prostitutes knew of instances when johns had turned nasty and had beaten or murdered a girl. Did they ever think of getting out of the industry? "What else would we do?" was their response.

Were they worried about their health? "We are very afraid of health problems. And we have heard of AIDS, but don't really know what it means, just that it has something to do with sex."

When I interviewed Pakistan's foremost religious leader, Mullah Azad, at his home on the grounds of Badshahi Mosque, I asked him why the government and the mullahs permitted Hira Mundi, which is directly below the walls of the mosque, to operate. After all, this was the man who had issued the *fatwa* stating that Benazir Bhutto could not be prime minister because he felt women were so weak they needed the constant protection of men. At that time, he had said that she, like most females, would be better off at home observing *purdah*.

Sitting on the floor of his living room, and playing with his prayer beads, Mullah Azad addressed his answers to my male driver, whom he had invited to join us. "It is true," he said, "that Hira Mundi is allowed to operate. I would like to adopt all these girls, and get them married." My driver and the mullah chuckled together. I pushed the issue. "Yes, yes," he responded, "I discussed the matter with President Zia, and he agreed to close it down, but nothing was done. I will take up the matter again with Nawaz Sharif."

The interview with Mullah Azad was lengthy, as he is given to sermonizing. It was also disturbing because he frequently contradicted himself, and because the opinions held by this highly influential man are regularly communicated to 110 million people. Fifty-five-year-old Azad has been chief mullah of Badshahi Mosque for eighteen years, and he likes to let visitors know he is an important man. "The Archbishop of Canterbury came to see me, we had Christian prayers in the mosque, which is good because all religions should come together." And almost in the next breath, "Christianity and Judaism are limited religions, they do not give rights. In Islam everybody has rights — husband, wife, father, mother, even animals have rights." To emphasize his point, he tossed a bone from a plate of chicken he had been eating to a cat in the hallway.

"I received the Order of Merit from the president of Egypt. I have always been a great supporter of America. I was the first man to condemn the American hostage–taking by Iran. Why should I not be nominated for the Nobel Peace Prize by the U.S.?" And minutes later, "America is Godless. Western influence here is not a good thing, our people can see CNN, MTV, kissing. . . . We are suffering from these things, they bring these new diseases like AIDS." And almost without pause, "I want to send my son to Harvard to study Islam."

He told me that his *fatwa* against Benazir Bhutto was necessary. "A woman is restricted; she cannot be the leader of an Islamic country. What happens if there is a war, and she is delivering a baby?" I asked him what would happen if a male prime minister had a heart attack at an equally inopportune time. "Medically, doctors say a man's heart is stronger than a woman's. Women's bodies and brains are weaker than men's, and they are particularly weak when they have their menses." He felt it was permissible for Pakistan's current ambassador to the United States to be female. "Abida Hussein is an old lady [she was then forty-five], so it is allowed. She is no longer fertile, so she cannot be corrupted by being in public."

His most worrisome comment came when I asked him why, in a strictly Islamic country, rape is on the increase, and why rapists are allowed to go free, when women victims are prosecuted. He responded, "Both the man and the woman should be convicted. And she should be forced to marry the man who has raped her. If she has been corrupted by this man, she must be married to him."

Mullah Azad, who has nine children, three of them girls, has two wives. Why did he marry twice? "My first wife is a grandmother, she is required to look after my fields. And since I am away from her, I needed another wife. I asked the first's permission, and she said yes, and she was present at the wedding. But I was not obligated under Islam to ask her. When a man is full of sexual power, he can marry again without seeking permission."

In 1991, Mullah Azad fell afoul of Islamic law when fifty cases of "gross misconduct under anticorruption laws" were filed against him in Lahore's District and Sessions Court. The charges arose after the official visit of Britain's Princess Diana to Pakistan in September 1991. The complainants were outraged that the mullah had received her at the mosque and "in full view of thousands, covered her head with a chador, presented her with a Koran, and showed her around the mosque." They charged that "the respondent was sacrilegious, and had defiled and desecrated the mosque and the Holy Koran." Their argument was based on the fact that Princess Diana was exposing her legs from mid-calf to ankle during the visit, and that the mullah did not know whether she had her period at the time he gave her the Koran, which would have rendered her "unclean" and unable to touch the holy book. After much deliberation, the court dropped the charges against him.

• • •

Karachi, the former capital in southern Pakistan, and still its commercial and industrial center, is a city that seems intent on committing suicide. The pollution of its air, drinking water, and coastline is so severe that the identity cards of its eleven million residents should be stamped "Living in Karachi is known to be dangerous to your health."

And yet what must rate as one of the most unlivable and unattractive metropolises in the world increases dramatically in population every year because of both its own soaring birthrate and the thousands of rural Pakistanis who move to Karachi in the hope of a better life. Not surprisingly, the city's services have long ceased to meet the ever-expanding demand. Power cuts and water shortages occur constantly.

In affluent sections of the city, such as Clifton, whose residents include, among other notables, Benazir Bhutto and her family, the luxurious homes have their own electrical generators and water systems to avoid some of Karachi's shortcomings. For the same reason, the large marble villas are secured behind high fortlike walls and guarded twenty-four hours a day by armed security men. Kidnappings for ransom have long been a problem in Sindh Province.

Overburdened, overpopulated, and underfinanced, Karachi is an administrative black hole. The closest thing to a social welfare program that the city offers is operated by a private charity, the Edhi Foundation, the founder of which, Abdul Sattar Edhi, has been dubbed the Father Teresa of Pakistan. During Karachi's many ethnic riots, Edhi's 250 ambulances are the only ones that will brave the explosive violence and thick gunfire. The Edhi Foundation runs nationwide emergency medical centers, homes for the retarded, troubled, abandoned, and orphaned, and many other services aimed at making life marginally more bearable for the marginalized.

Edhi and his wife, Bilquis, are peripatetic, and in trying to locate them, I found myself crisscrossing Karachi in one of their Suzuki van ambulances. Minus air-conditioning (the Edhis keep both frills and bureaucracy to a minimum) in the 120-degree heat, the vehicle was stifling, and the smells of the city assailed me. The open sewers and vast mounds of garbage reeked, and children waded in canals of viscous water that had a strange metallic sheen and an even stranger odor. Camels with bell bracelets on their calloused knees, and half-starved mules and donkeys towing overloaded carts all competed for limited road space with ancient Bedford trucks spewing fumes into the air, and completely covered with gaudily painted movie heroes and other escapist art.

I finally caught up with Bilquis Edhi at one of their centers in a network of streets so narrow that nothing wider than the Suzuki ambulance could have driven through them. Signs on the outside wall read "Enquire for Dead Bodies," and "Prayer Place for Dead Bodies." Inside, Bilquis, forty-four, was surrounded by women petitioners waiting patiently for assistance. One, a well-dressed young matron, told me tearfully that she was there to look at the abandoned babies. "I am barren. But I want to mother a child. This is the only place I can go."

Taking a break from fielding constant phone calls and questions, Bilquis took me into a back room equipped with two cots, where she and her husband live during city crises or curfews. I asked her what usually happens to children who are abandoned in a culture that does not recognize adoption. Placing a fat photographic album in my lap, she showed me photographs of dead newborn infants. "This is what happens to many of them," said Bilquis. The rest of that album and several more contained similar snapshots. The only other time I have seen such a grisly chronicle is in El Salvador during the early eighties when religious groups kept similar albums so that wives and mothers could check to see if their missing menfolk were among the previous night's body count, people slaughtered by the death squads in that country's civil war.

The Edhis keep the baby books for much the same reason: in case a relative or neighbor might be able to identity these infants. "More than five hundred of these babies are found every year in Karachi, in the gutters, the trash bins, on the sidewalks. The police bring them to us. Ninety-nine percent of them are girls — considered a burden in this society. A few babies are deformed. A few are boys. They are anywhere from a couple of hours old to several months. They are strangled, or suffocated with plastic, or just left to die. Dead boy babies are normally the children of unmarried mothers. If the mother is not married, she is usually killed by the men in her family."

In an effort to stop such murders, Bilquis started a program three years ago encouraging families to turn unwanted children over to their foundation. Outside every Edhi center hangs a metal crib with a sign that reads "Do not kill the innocent baby. Do not make the first sin worse." Rare is the morning when the cribs are empty. Since the program began, and despite there being no tradition in Pakistan for adoption, the foundation has been able to find homes for seven thousand unwanted infants. Those it cannot place it keeps in its own centers.

Six-year-old Kausar will probably be included in the latter category; her father is one of Pakistan's government-estimated two million heroin addicts. "Heroin addicts here sell everything — their wives, their daughters — to buy drugs," said Bilquis. In Kausar's case, her father had decided she would be more useful to him if she brought in regular income by working as a beggar. He also decided to optimize his earnings. Beating her with some kind of club, he badly broke her right arm and left leg. Then, using kerosene and matches, he systematically burned the rest of her body. Deformed and maimed children earn more as beggars. "He must have panicked that he had gone too far, that she was dying because he showed up with her here some months ago, told us to make her better, and left."

At first, it did look as though Kausar would die, but with first-rate nursing, her physical wounds began to heal, although her bone breaks were so bad, those limbs will never be normal again. "She wouldn't talk for a long time, she was so traumatized," says Dr. Salma Mazhar, one of Edhi's physicians. When Kausar finally spoke, her first words were, "Please bring my sister Shehnaz. My father is always beating her too." Unfortunately, the foundation has not been able to locate Kausar's father or sister.

• • •

Just as the affluent Clifton has insulated itself behind high walls from much of Karachi's wretchedness, so, too, does wealth help to cocoon Pakistani women from many of the strictures of their culture. For the junior Pakistani jet set, life and interests can be very similar to those of any yuppie community in the West: designer clothes, jewelry, cars, and hairstyles, and even designer drugs.

Muslim girls who have been educated in the West are, of course, exposed to different values from those instilled at home. A girl who has dated abroad may be loath on her return to give up a way of socializing that is abhorrent to her culture. And so the games begin.

She may leave home covered from head to toe, and in the company of a chaperon. Once she arrives at her destination and sheds her *chador*, she may be wearing a miniskirt, and she may exchange her chaperon for her boyfriend almost as quickly. In Pakistan, as in most Islamic countries, alcohol is illegal, but at private parties bootleg whiskey and gin are served, and she will be drinking. And in someone's home when parents and servants are away, her crowd will watch smuggled-in soft porn on the VCR. In Muslim countries where any physical contact between sexes or the display of a little flesh in movies is censored, the video industry has liberated many libidos. And just as in the West, her boyfriend may proposition her, and she may accept, having taken the precaution of stocking up on the contraceptive pill while she was abroad. And should she have the misfortune to become pregnant, she'll go abroad again, on the pretext of a shopping expedition, to have an abortion.

It is in this sophisticated society that marriages for love can be found, but even among the well-heeled, most parents still insist on selecting their children's mates. A privilege of the privileged class, however, is that veto power is easier to obtain. In such circles, chances are also good that the couple will be permitted a few discreet and well-chaperoned meetings before the match is finalized. Modern technology is also increasingly employed. "I met my fiancée a couple of times before we married," said Sohail. "But her family sent me videos of her so I could she what she was like."

In seeking potential brides for their sons, parents demand a good education, preferably a college degree, even if the majority of women will not be permitted to use it once married. And in turn, her parents prefer professionals, particularly those possessing an American green card or its European equivalent. Access to things Western, particularly residency visas, imparts status.

Once wed, a monied young woman's life is passed very differently from that of her impoverished counterpart. Instead of a day of domestic drudgery — all that is taken care of by the servants — she is likely to spend her time working out or playing tennis at the all-women's gym, shopping, or even doing a little illegal gambling with friends. However, there will still be the same pressure on her to have children as soon as possible, and to present her husband with sons. And later, when her marriage seems somewhat stale, both partners may indulge in a little adultery. His infidelities are considered pro forma among the sophisticated set; hers, on the other hand, are not. But, unlike her uneducated peer, if she is caught, she does not risk her life. Chances are very good, however, that she will be divorced, a fate that renders her an outcast in many Muslim circles.

A Pakistani male doctor friend of mine admitted after I had known him for some time that his sister, also a highly educated woman, was divorced. "We try to keep it a family secret," he said. "She never goes out. My mother is ashamed of her. It is considered shameful for our family." Why had the marriage broken down? "My sister refused to let her husband take a second wife," he said, "so her husband divorced her and married again anyway. Of course, my sister will never remarry even though she is permitted to, because men in our social circle would never consider marrying a divorced woman."

"The rules are very different for Pakistani's elite," says lawyer Asma Jahangir. "This factor helps to explain how in Pakistan a woman can become a politician or diplomat. It also is much less common for a wealthy woman to be charged with *zina*, for example. And there is no way I could do the work I do. I would have been silenced long ago if I did not come from a privileged family." Jahangir stands about five feet tall, and her build is as petite as her height. Soft spoken, and with a graceful manner, she could easily pass for just another well-bred, traditional Muslim woman. I first saw her at a lecture where she was the keynote speaker. Dynamic and articulate, she mesmerized the mostly male Muslim audience, who gave her a standing ovation. This is not the response, however, that Jahangir always receives for speaking out. Her brilliant legal maneuvering against legal inequities and human rights violations has won her innumerable discriminatory cases for women — and has also caused her life to be threatened on occasion.

Being a woman activist lawyer in Pakistan obviously comes with a price, as her chain-smoking in private attests. "I've only been in prison once — for three weeks under Zia's Martial Law," she told me, "and I know I'm lucky. If I didn't come from such an influential family, I would have been locked away a long time ago."

Jahangir's father was a leading liberal politician, and Asma learned her activism from him. After graduating from college, where she had been active in student politics, she made an appropriate marriage to a man who is now a highly successful businessman. "In keeping with tradition, I moved into his parents' home and tried to be the kind of wife I was expected to be — a person I am not — docile, domestic, obedient. I had to ask permission to do anything. And I was required to have my hair done weekly, dress in elegant outfits with matching shoes and handbags, attend coffee parties with my mother-in-law, and make polite conversation, never talking about anything unpleasant, including politics.

"And for several years, while having babies, I did this. But I hated the person I became. I became fat, dumb, I had no status, and I could see my husband losing respect for me. I was neither the chic coffee-party woman nor myself. I was an embarrassing disaster."

Jahangir persuaded her family to let her study law. The Dean of the Law School required her father-in-law to give his formal permission for her to do so. For family reasons, Asma studied at home and attended college only to take her exams. Once she had graduated, her husband forbade her to work in a "man's law office." So in

1980, Asma approached two friends and her younger sister, all new lawyers, to start the first women's legal practice in Pakistan. "We were so poor, we began with one secondhand typewriter, and cleaned the office, even the windows, ourselves."

Today, her office waiting room is always crowded, and, because of the nature of their business, 70 percent of their cases are pro bono. Some of her clients travel thousands of miles to see her, like Josianne Malik, a Swiss woman who journeyed from Geneva on an international custody case. Josianne's ex-husband, a Pakistani, had whisked the children out of Switzerland to Pakistan, evading an Interpol warrant for his arrest for allegedly abducting them. In the early hearings of the case, the judge made constant references to the Islamic law that grants the father, rather than the mother, custody rights. Josianne, who had not seen her two children for more than a year, was distraught. "It is impossible to fight religion," she said through her tears.

A constant in the lives of Pakistani women is a lack of knowledge about their rights, and a lack of recourse once these rights are abused. One of the more bizarre examples of this are women who are forcibly married by their families to the Koran, an event for which there is no foundation at all in Islam. Such weddings tend to take place when an extended family runs out of available male cousins for the family's females to marry. If she were to marry outside the family, when she inherited her portion of the family estate, the land would be divided. To avoid this, the young woman is forced to marry the Koran in a ceremony identical to a real wedding except that the bridegroom is nonexistent. The bride is dressed in a bridal outfit for the nuptials, guests are invited to the feast, and the ceremony is the same as if she were marrying a man. Once wedded to the Koran, the girl is not allowed to leave her home or see an adult male, even on television, for the rest of her life. Instead, she is sentenced to a life of isolation and emptiness.

Another crime against women that goes virtually ignored by the country's legal and religious authorities is what is known in Pakistan as dowry burnings. Newlywed young women whose dowries are considered insufficient despite prenuptial agreements are burned to death by their husbands or his relatives when the bride's family is unable to contribute more. In a ten-month period in 1991, two thousand women under twenty-five died in such cases; others may have gone unreported. Explained the relative of one such woman to hospital authorities, "We didn't report it to the police because we didn't want to create a scandal; and anyway, if she survives, she will have to go back to her husband. It will be bad enough for her as it is."

A typical case was related to me by Deputy Police Superintendent Farkander Iqbal. Iqbal, one of two female deputy superintendents in Punjab Province, is the chief of an all-female police station in Lahore, which was recently set up to handle only crimes against women. It is the first such unit in the country.

"A sixteen-year-old girl, Rahina Jasnin, had been married to an out-of-work laborer, and, as is traditional, after the wedding she moved into his parents' home. A few months later, her in-laws began to complain that the size of her dowry was too small, and started demanding a color TV and VCR. The girl's parents had barely enough money to survive; they couldn't afford such luxuries. In an effort to appease her in-laws, Rahina, now pregnant, sold her wedding jewelry, but their demands continued, and they began beating her.

"Neighbors heard the beatings and screams, but nobody intervened. She gave birth to a daughter and was criticized and beaten for that. One night shortly afterward, Rahina was awakened by her mother-in-law, who was holding her down while kerosene was poured over her by her husband and set alight. Neighbors ignored the screaming and later said they thought it was just a routine beating.

"When it was over, Rahina's in-laws, thinking she was dead, took her to the local hospital and reported she had killed herself. But the young woman, who was burned over ninety percent of her body, lived for two more days. Before she died, she spoke about what had happened to her.

"The local police dropped the case," Iqbal told me. "I reopened it because there was far too much evidence that she had been murdered." Iqbal complained that often the police were paid off to close investigations. "You find male police officers siding with the men under suspicion. They are not interested in the real story, only in taking money. These cases are increasing in recent years. We see ten to fifteen wife burnings a month at this location alone."

Pakistan is very different today from what it was fifteen or twenty years ago, according to Iqbal. "Before, crimes against women were relatively rare," said the thirty-five-year-old superintendent. "If a man misbehaved toward a woman, he was promptly dealt with legally and society ostracized him. Today, in Pakistan, respect for women no longer exists, and crimes against them have increased dramatically.

"They claim to have 'Islamized' us. How can you Islamize people who are already Muslim? Ever since Zia gave power to the mullahs, it seems as though every man feels he can get hold of any female and tear her apart."

• • •

While the picture seems bleak for women in Pakistan, organizations such as Women's Action Forum and War Against Rape are growing, and so are their successes. WAF was formed in 1981, when several women's organizations came together to fight the conviction of what proved to be a landmark case under the Hudood Ordinances. Fehmida and Allah Bux were sentenced to one hundred lashes each and death by stoning for fornication. The charge was brought by the woman's father, who claimed Fehmida, who had eloped with Bux, had been abducted by him, because her family refused to permit their marriage. By the time the police located the couple, Fehmida was pregnant with her first child. The Bux case was the first time the severe implications of the Ordinances were realized, and women turned out in force to express outrage at the sentence. The Supreme Court subsequently overturned the conviction.

And it was Pakistani women in 1983 who organized the first demonstration against Martial Law.

Professionally, too, some women are making gains and by doing so are setting precedents and creating opportunities for others. After a long fight to be granted commercial status, one female pilot was awarded a license on condition that she always fly wearing a *hijab* veil. On another occasion, a married couple both ran for office. She was elected, he lost. The ensuing outcry continued for weeks; naturally, the wife should give up her seat to her husband, the majority demanded. She declined to do so.

And not so long ago, female students demonstrated for one-and-one-half months, braving police beatings and arrests, to change the tiny quotas for women in medical schools. One of them, Iffat, the twenty-year-old sister-in-law of journalist Tahir Malik, told me, "I wanted to study medicine and my marks were thirty-five percent higher than boys who were being admitted. They were getting seats simply because of the quotas. It had been unjust for too long and we had to do something." Iffat took part in the daily demonstrations, and, like many of the participants, was arrested. She was released after a few hours. Finally, the students prevailed and quotas for medical schools were dropped. It was too late, however, for Iffat, who is now a psychology major.

There is at least one Islamic organization in Pakistan, "Daughters of Islam," in Karachi, which campaigns for women to liberate themselves through their Islamic rights. And while its founder and director Nilofar Ahmad might find Iffat's youthful feminism harsh, she is equally determined to change the lot of women in Pakistan. A Fulbright scholar in the States in the sixties, Ahmad led a mostly secular life until five years ago, when she found herself "becoming more intensely religious."

As Ahmad began to immerse herself in Islam, she realized that Muslim women had no idea of the rights given to them by their religion. "Most either could not or had never bothered to read the Koran in the original, and so they relied on the interpretations of it by men. Islam is a religion that liberated women, and that same religion is being used to oppress them. The backward position of Muslim women today is due to the misinterpretations — intentional or unintentional — of the primary sources of Islam."

Ahmad points out, for example, that for much of the last fourteen hundred years the majority of Muslims have believed that in Paradise men will be supplied with beautiful virgin companions. "When women ask what happens to them in Paradise, they never receive an answer," says Ahmad. "The Koran, in fact, originally said that both men and women would be granted good companions in Paradise.

"The gymnastics that have been performed with Arabic grammar in order to mistranslate some key words are incredible," she says. "For example, when the masculine gender is used in the Koran for an injunction that it is felt a woman must obey, it is interpreted to denote the common gender. But when the same pronoun is used for something that the male wants to preserve for himself, then it is interpreted to mean the masculine gender."

Ahmad cites numerous examples of what the Koran intended and how those teachings have been perverted today. In the areas of education, earnings, equality, divorce, inheritance, polygamy, veiling — just about every aspect that covers women in the Koran — her organization teaches women where translations and interpretations are made to favor men. She even takes issue with the famous verse 4:34, which states: "Men are the maintainers of women because Allah has made some of them to excel others . . . and therefore good women are obedient . . . ," and which has been cited by Muslim patriarchs for centuries to prove the superiority of men. "The Koran in the original frequently describes men and women as being the *awliya* of one another, which means 'friends,' or 'guides,'" explains

Ahmad. "In the key verse 4:34, a word of very similar meaning, *qawwamun*, is used, only in this case it has been interpreted as meaning the man is superior to the woman.

"Women have to remember that the Prophet said, 'Men and women are equal as two teeth on a comb.' Greed for power has led to the politicizing of Islam. If I have any message for Muslim women it is that they must study their religion for themselves, learn what it really says, not accept someone else's idea. Only then will they be able to fight for their rights with the very weapon currently used against them — the Koran."

CHAPTER 4

Afghanistan: "When You Can't Beat the Donkey, Beat the Saddle"

He who honors women is honorable,
He who insults them is lowly and mean.

PROPHET MOHAMMAD

SPENDING TIME WITH FATIMA GAILANI involves a certain amount of cognitive dissonance. Tall and slender, she has an elegance of manner, a gentle, subdued voice, and a grace to her every movement. In the Junior League–style outfit of a spring-green plaid kilt, toning cashmere sweater, single strand of good pearls, and fashionable short-haired bob, she projects an image of refined femininity.

Watching her preside over an afternoon tea tray in her tastefully decorated drawing room with its subdued silks and oriental carpets confirms the genteel picture. The trompe l'oeil aspect is indicated only in the discreet details of her surroundings: the sophisticated security system and complex locks, which are more expensive than the homes on the West London suburban street with its tranquil flowering gardens appear to warrant; and the solid and smiling cook, who does double duty as an omnipresent bodyguard.

There isn't a turban or Kalashnikov machine gun to be seen, but this amiable and courteous woman is as much an Afghan guerrilla as her bearded brothers and many of her countrymen. Fatima, aged thirty-nine but looking a good nine years younger, has been an official of the Afghan Resistance for the past twelve years, the sole female in the guerrilla army. She is the European representative of the National Islamic Front of Afghanistan. And while she has had weapons training, and has frequently met with European generals to request the arms needed by her military organization, the tools of her trade have been diplomacy, negotiation, and lobbying.

When Soviet troops invaded Afghanistan in 1979, Fatima was completing her Master's degree in Persian Literature and Islamic History at university in Tehran. She finished the course work but never received the diploma. All educational institutions in Tehran were closed down when the Iranian Revolution began ten months before her own country was attacked. Unable to return home because there was a price on her father's head, Fatima moved to England without being able to speak a word of English. But she immersed herself in the language for a year, and her first involvement with the war was to act as an interpreter for the severely wounded Afghan fighters and children who were brought to Britain for treatment by the British government.

Afghanistan, a country the size of Texas, which shares borders with China, Iran, Pakistan, and Russia, is one of the least developed nations in the world, in part because much of its topography long rendered it difficult to reach. Until the Soviets rolled their tanks into Kabul, the capital, on Christmas Day fourteen years ago, it was a land where time appeared to stand still. Only in Kabul and a few provincial capitals did Afghans seem to live in the twentieth century.

Turbaned Kuchi nomads, as flamboyantly dressed as their camel mounts are decorated, still traverse the country annually in search of pasture for their large herds of livestock. The simple mud-house villages that dot the countryside have changed little in three hundred years; their thick fortresslike walls were built to protect during frequent intertribal conflicts. Farming continues to be done mostly by hand or the occasional draft animals, and women still spend much of their day fetching water and wood or animal dung for fuel.

Afghanistan is a country of savage beauty: the vast mountain peaks, some of the highest in the world, of the Pamir and Hindu Hush ranges, where the rare five-foot-tall Marco Polo sheep, once hunted as big game, still roam like phantoms. The snowcapped, jagged summits counterpoint the barren plains and desolate salt desert, where only the wind is alive. And just when the eye feels assaulted by the harshness of the landscape, the occasional verdant valley appears, fragrant with wild thyme and lupine, shaded by mulberry and almond trees, where birdsong gives descant to tumbling mountain streams.

At the outset of the war, Fatima's father — Pir Sayed Ahmad Gailani, a former Member of Parliament and the spiritual leader of many Sunni Afghans — founded the National Islamic Front of Afghanistan (NIFA), which he still heads, one of the country's seven major Resistance parties. Gailani, whose family is revered as descending from the Prophet Mohammad, looks more ambassadorial than he does a religious warlord. An erudite man and a liberal specialist on Islamic law, he advocates secular democracy for a free Afghanistan. Not surprisingly, NIFA is one of three moderate parties.

By the time Moscow withdrew its troops in 1988, nearly two million people — one in eight Afghans — had died. Five million, one in three of the population, had been forced to become refugees in neighboring Pakistan and Iran, and the entire infrastructure of the country was in shambles. The absence of Soviet forces, however, did not bring peace to Afghanistan. Instead, the communist puppet government in Kabul, propped up with a constant and massive infusion of arms and money from Moscow, continued to fight on. Three years later, when that regime fell in April 1992, partly because, with the collapse of communism, the impoverished Russian government could no longer afford to fund it, the Afghan Resistance was expected to triumph. Sadly, the war of liberation became a battle for the different forces of Islam. Islamic extremist factions now fight one another for dominance, and as many as three thousand residents of the Afghan capital have died from rocket bombardments within a single twenty-four-hour period.

The fundamentalist leaders of the former Resistance have turned formerly moderate Muslim Afghanistan into a theocratic state as rigid as Iran and Saudi Arabia. And both of those countries have poured millions of dollars into the effort. The moment the Islamic State of Afghanistan was declared in May 1992 by the interim government's calling itself the Leadership Council, the *mujahideen,* holy warriors, took aim at Afghanistan's women. On the very first day of their existence, the avowedly Islamist government decreed that women must immediately adopt strict Islamic dress. Skirts, stockings, and high heels disappeared immediately from the streets of Kabul. Women television newscasters opted for safety and appeared for work with their hair covered with a *dupatta,* a chiffon scarf and modern replacement for the more enveloping *chador.* On arrival at the station they were told the new government had banned women from TV and radio altogether. Now the country's women were required to be completely covered except for hands, feet, and face.

The more fanatical groups demanded that even women's faces be covered, and the tentlike *burqas* suddenly appeared in every bazaar in the capital, and sold out rapidly.

In a country whose constitution in 1964 guaranteed that "both women and men, without discrimination and privilege, have equal rights and obligations before the law," and where women were granted suffrage in 1965, the new government immediately declared that only men could participate in future elections. The extremists among the leaders demanded that women should no longer hold government positions, or, indeed, work at all. And as the clarion call for women to return to their homes was sounded, the streets of Kabul emptied of women. Afghans recalled with fear how these same fundamentalist parties had violently forced Afghan women refugees in Pakistan into veils and *purdah*, and that abductions, stonings, and killings of women known to have liberal attitudes began in the early eighties and continue to take place.

"In Afghanistan currently, control of women is a symbol of the power of men, and of their honor," said Barnett Rubin, a political scientist at Columbia University, who is head of its Center for the Study of Central Asia, and a leading expert on Afghanistan. "Women are the one part of the society that can be controlled, so the Islamists manipulate them as symbols. Women have become the pawns of men in this Islamization process."

Recognizing this, Fatima Gailani is preparing to wage a different kind of *Jihad* from the one she has helped combat for the past decade. Concerned that the fundamentalists would take over because they have been better financed and better supplied with arms throughout the war, Fatima decided to do what Pakistan's Nilofar Ahmad also advocates: fight the extremist Islamists with the ideology they use — Islam.

"Women have become a very soft target for the so-called fundamentalists or hard-liners," she said. "Right now, the situation for Muslim women has become grave, even dangerous. It is time for Islamic women, the majority of whom are moderate, to take a stand. But to do that, we need to have a thorough knowledge of our religion."

Since religion and state are one in the Islamic world, leading theologians can wield as much, and sometimes more, power than political leaders. Fatima enrolled at the Muslim College in London in 1991 and is currently studying *fiqh*, Islamic jurisprudence, which covers all aspects of Muslim life. She is one of only five women at the college where men from all over the Islamic world train to become Imams. On completion of her jurisprudence degree, Fatima had planned to move to Al Azhar University in Cairo, but in late 1992, Afghanistan's interim and moderate foreign minister traveled to London to meet with her. "He informed me that Afghan women wanted me to take the leadership for them, to be their voice in the new Afghanistan," she said, adding, "and they so badly need to be heard." Canceling her plans for further study at Al Azhar, she decided instead to return to Kabul as soon as she graduated from the Muslim College.

"Muslim women have made a mistake in thinking that it is not their territory to be educated in Islamic law, or the Islamic way of thinking," says Fatima. "Told they cannot be judges, which is not true, or Imams or preachers, educated women turned their energies to medicine, research, et cetera, never to expertise in Islam. We left it to men and then we mourn and say, 'Oh, this is injustice, such injustice imposed upon us.'

"If something that has been given to us by God is taken away in the name of Islam, I will fight it. How else can we safeguard our part of the world, and ensure that no one abuses it? Women have been completely ignored for a very, very long time in our part of the world. And the most unfortunate enemy that women, and men, have in the Islamic world is ignorance: ignorant people facing selfish forces intent on using the religion for political reasons, reasons of power."

Fatima stresses she would feel exactly the same if children or men were being similarly oppressed. "I have taken up this struggle not just because I am a woman, but because this is an injustice in the name of my religion. And this misuse of Islam is a major factor in making my religion completely misunderstood by the West, something that need not happen."

She is particularly disturbed by the *fatwas* issued by fundamentalist Resistance leaders that banned or severely limited education for Afghan women in the refugee camps in Pakistan, which housed three million people, and in the city of Peshawar, where the Afghan Resistance has had its headquarters since 1979. With Afghan literacy rates among the lowest in the world, the ruling stunned and angered many. "To forbid education is a violation of Islamic order. The Koran insists we be educated," says Fatima. But it is not the first time education for women has been criticized. In a number of Muslim societies, an ancient adage was, "Teach a girl to read, so that she can read the Koran, but do not teach her to write, because she may write love letters to boys."

One *fatwa* that was issued to Afghan refugees in 1990 and circulated widely read in part: "It is the command of God that education is necessary for men and women. But the way of learning is different for both of them. . . . If girls or women want to learn, they must do so from their nearest relatives. . . . But this is not the right time for women and girls to become educated. Therefore, learning and writing is religiously prohibited for women. The united *ulema* [high-ranking Islamic scholars] of the Islamic leaders of the Resistance require that Afghans not permit women to attend schools and/or become educated, or else the Islamic movement will meet with failure." One-third of the *fatwa* document, which measured two feet by three feet, was covered by nearly two hundred signatures of mullahs, Resistance officials, and religious scholars. In the wake of the *fatwa*'s being issued, schools and training institutes for Afghan women were closed because they feared a wave of violence that normally follows the enforcing of such religious decrees.

One woman educator in Peshawar was forced into exile shortly after the *fatwa* was issued, after receiving repeated death threats, which culminated in an attempt on her life. Tajwar Kakar, a forty-two-year-old Afghan schoolteacher, does not run easily. Before arriving in Pakistan, she had already been imprisoned and tortured for more than a year in Kabul for her opposition to the Soviet invasion. With funds raised from Western donors, and with the support of the Afghan Resistance, she founded and became principal of Lycée Malalai, one of the few secondary schools for Afghan girls in Peshawar. The school, which numbered among its pupils young Maria, the child who lived in my home, was named after an Afghan Joan of Arc who led the country's men into battle against British colonialists in the nineteenth century.

In 1989, Kakar received a final death threat warning her to stop teaching refugee girls that Islam permits them to expose their faces and hands, which, according to the Koran, it does. "They are required to wear *burqas*," she was told, "and if you do not accept this we are going to kill you. This is the last warning you will receive."

At the time, Tajwar Kakar said, "We women have fought hard for the freedom of our people and our nation. We have been imprisoned and tortured and some of us have been killed. The women helped fight this *Jihad*, and now they forget about us."

There was no further warning. Months later, in the middle of the school day, gunmen attacked Lycée Malalai. A doorman who tried to protect Kakar was seriously wounded in a burst of machine-gun fire. Fortuitously, the students, though terrified, were unharmed. In the chaos that followed, Kakar was rushed into hiding. Days later, with the assistance of the United Nations Refugee Protection Program and a minimum of red tape, the Australian government accepted her and her family.

Incidents such as these underscore the deep ideological divisions among the Afghan Resistance. The fundamentalist power base in Afghanistan was created shortly after the Soviet invasion. In what became the last gasp of the Cold War against communism, the United States supplied the Afghan *mujahideen* with arms and aid worth nearly $3 billion in the largest covert military-support operation run by the CIA since Vietnam. But because the Afghan Resistance was based in Pakistan, President Zia demanded that the money be funneled to the Afghan parties through his military officers. And as part of his Islamization program, he heavily favored the fundamentalist parties over the moderates. Over a twelve-year period, 75 percent of American funding was channeled to rabidly anti-American Afghan Islamists by Pakistan, a move the U.S. State Department now acknowledges was an error.

Saudi Arabia matched American aid to Afghanistan dollar for dollar. Unlike the United States, it financed the Resistance directly, but only the parties that were as archconservatively Islamic as they are. Impoverished moderate Afghan *mujahideen* began changing their allegiance to the fundamentalist Resistance parties because they could keep them well supplied with arms. In the latter part of the war, there were times when the moderate parties had difficulty paying their phone bills, let alone buying bullets.

In addition to its financial-aid package to Afghanistan, Saudi Arabia also included in the deal Arab fighters whom they sponsored, and who were known among the Afghans as Wahabis. Wahabism is the most puritanical sect of Islam and has been followed in the region of Saudi Arabia since it was founded in the eighteenth century. Well armed and well financed, the Wahabi guerrillas also heavily proselytized among the Afghans in special training camps in Afghanistan and Pakistan. A number of the followers of Egypt's Sheikh Omar and at least one man implicated in the bombing of the World Trade Center fought with and received their military training from the Wahabi guerrillas in Afghanistan, as did at least a thousand Algerian extremists who are currently involved in fighting in Algeria. Wahabism was alien to Afghanistan. More than 80 percent of Afghans are adherents of Hanafi Islam, the least fundamentalist of all the Islamic sects.

According to Columbia University's Professor Rubin, the extremist Muslim Brotherhood, through its various Middle Eastern networks, also funneled vast amounts of money to the Afghan fundamentalist Resistance parties. "Today, there are large numbers of Arabs in Kabul, and in many provinces," he said, "and an Arab/Afghan alliance has been formed."

Another Arab country that was involved in attempting to establish a fundamentalist government in Kabul was Libya. Qaddafi acted as a personal go-between for Gulbuddin Hekmatayer, the most brutal and repressive Afghan Resistance leader, in his negotiations with the Kabul regime's president during an attempted coup d'état in the spring of 1990. Had the coup succeeded, Kabul's communist dictator would have been replaced by Hekmatayer, a man most Afghans abhor and fear. Afghan women in particular recall his followers using acid to attack women in Kabul who wore Western dress. Hekmatayer, who, at this time of writing, is Afghanistan's interim deputy premier, also offered sanctuary to Sheikh Omar when the United States arrested the fundamentalist cleric in the summer of 1993.

The 15 percent of the Afghan population who are Shi'a were not ignored, either; the Revolutionary Government of Iran has underwritten Afghanistan's Shi'a *mujahideen.* The assistance also came with extensive and constant proselytizing. And in the Shi'a regions of Afghanistan and in Kabul, posters of Khomeini and Rafsanjani are common.

The term "Great Game," coined for the political and military machinations played out in this region in the nineteenth century between Czarist Russia and the British Empire, suddenly took on ominous new meaning. Afghanistan has become a modern-day case study in how moderate Islam can be subsumed through the hegemony and petro-dollars of Islamic theocratic states.

Another concern of Fatima Gailani is the new Afghan leadership's reversing women's suffrage. "I was a child when women were granted the right to vote in Afghanistan," she said. "In those early days, women were elected to Parliament, we had a woman in the Senate, women diplomats, even women in the cabinet. These rights were given under a constitution that was approved by an Islamic *ulema,* in a country that is ninety-nine percent Muslim. At that time no one, including the current leaders, reacted against it. Nor did they oppose women attending university. Now Mohammad Nabi, a man who heads a moderate party, and who served in Parliament with women politicians beside him before the war, suddenly announces that women shouldn't vote, and that even elections are not Islamic.

"I would like to ask him whether, at the time he was elected to office and serving in Parliament alongside women, he was a *kafir* [non-believer] and has only recently become a Muslim."

Fatima tackled her own father on his lack of public support for the issue of women voting because even he, the most Westernized of Afghan leaders, had not spoken out in favor of continued suffrage for women. "His reply to me was 'For God's sake, let's have our country first, and then we can take up this problem,'" says Fatima. "But I know this will not happen because if you take a first step that is wrong, the rest of the way will be crooked."

Like Asma Jahangir in Pakistan, Fatima recognizes that her family connections make it safer for her to speak out. "Thank God I was born into my family," she said. "If I had been the daughter of someone who could be easily jailed, or whose house could be burned down, as has happened in Peshawar, or could be driven into exile like Tajwar Kakar, I couldn't do what I do. I have the protection of my family name, my father's position, and because I come from a privileged background, it is harder to wipe me out, kill me, than it is an ordinary Muslim woman."

Fatima feels that her advantaged background, however, requires more of her. "I have had a very, very privileged life, and it was given to me by the Afghan people. This places a responsibility on my shoulders to work on their behalf. And because of that position, I can afford to take more risks than others.

"But I cannot change things alone. Afghanistan has liberal religious and political leaders who know that I am right, and I need their support. This is not a fight for women, it is a fight for the preservation of authentic Islam."

Women's rights is not a cause Fatima Gailani has always espoused. In fact, she freely admits it was an issue she chose to avoid because it might damage her newly won credibility as a representative of the Resistance. Even now she shudders at the label "feminist."

Fatima denies she is a feminist because it is a Western term. "I am very Eastern," she says. "I am not looking for equality, simply for the rights granted to women under Islam." Feminism is also a label

that has become lethal in Afghanistan. The Revolutionary Association of Women of Afghanistan, whose aim was to emancipate
women, was forced underground in 1987 when its thirty-year-old
founder, Mina Kishwar Kamal, and two female aides, were assassinated. Because Kamal had been a Maoist during her days of student
activism in Kabul, Afghan feminism became equated with Chinese
communism, as hated by the Resistance as its Soviet equivalent.

Fatima's refusal to be branded a feminist is both prudent and
also accurate. Her women's rights philosophy would make Western
feminists blanch. On polygamy she says, "How I feel may not be
very popular with the Western women's liberation movements but
under certain circumstances, such as exist in my country right now,
where many women are war widows, I think polygamy should be a
temporary law, encouraged even, to give these women some kind of
protection. If a woman is a widow with young children and has no
means to support herself, why should she not become a second,
third, or fourth wife to a man?

"But on the other hand, Islam does not freely encourage polygamy. Therefore, it should not be considered an everyday right of
men. Under Islam, it is not," said Fatima, who recently divorced her
own husband of seventeen years shortly after he took a second wife.
She insists that any government has the right to ban polygamy when
it is no longer necessary.

Fatima asserts that if something is forbidden to women under
Islam, no matter how oppressive it may seem in the eyes of the West,
she will accept it. "I will accept it because I believe in God, believe
in the Prophet and believe in our Holy Book. The divine mind knows
what is best for us."

Almost as an adjunct to that declaration, she states that she does
not believe men and women are equal. "I think the duty of a man
and woman is different in Islam," she said. "For example, no matter
how rich a woman may be, whether from inheritance or her own
earnings, her husband is required by Islamic law to support her and
their children, and he is not entitled to any of her money, unless she
chooses to make it available. So Muslim women may complain, but
men can also do so."

While she willingly wears Islamic dress when in Islamic countries,
and covers her hair with a white scarf while attending courses at the
Muslim College in London, Fatima staunchly refuses to cover her
face and hands no matter how conservative or Islamically elevated

the company. She even refuses to do so in Saudi Arabia, where, in the capital, Riyadh, all Islamic women have their faces veiled. As the only woman in a position of authority in the Afghan Resistance, she is, of course, a major role model for the women in her country. How then have the *mujahideen* leadership responded to her?

"Their response to me initially was, 'You can do anything because you are not a woman,'" she said. What they meant by that was that because of her education and position, she had been designated an honorary male. "My reply to their denying my being a woman was that I had already proven I was. I have a daughter," said Fatima dryly. Her only child, Humeira, now aged fifteen, lives with her in London.

Fatima refuses to veil her face because, she insists, it is not required in Islam. As proof of this she cites the fact that when Muslim women go on the Hajj pilgrimage to Mecca, they must do so with their faces uncovered. "Even if they have worn a *burqa* all their lives, they must remove it during Hajj."

Due to factors like these, Fatima yearns for Muslim women to be familiar with their religion. She insists it is essential that they be able to distinguish whether the Koran is being quoted or interpreted accurately, or whether a statement is being taken out of context. "So often something is attributed to the Koran when it is not the case. Take Benazir Bhutto, for example. Educated in the West, she had little idea about Islam. When she returned to Pakistan to begin campaigning, she was told not to shake hands with men. Without doing the slightest research, she accepted it, and even began to hide her hands under her *chador*, as if a hand is something shameful. I remember thinking at the time, My God, is this going to happen to all of us?"

When Fatima returns to Kabul, a city where near anarchy rules, will she not feel concern for her safety, particularly in her new role as ambassador for Afghanistan's women? After all, outspoken liberal Afghans are being systematically assassinated, and Kabul is a capital described as having no security, no administration. "There's a different government on every street. And every day there are violent clashes between various groups. People do not feel their lives, property, and dignity are safe."

Matter-of-factly, Fatima replies, "I will return whether it is safe or not. I think Kabul will find me much more Islamically conservative than the people who lived under the communist regime. I do not agree with the way women are treated in villages, but I certainly do not agree with the Western excesses that were introduced under Soviet rule."

• • •

The first time I saw Kabul was the summer of 1985, and the Soviets had occupied the city for five years. In those days it was not a pleasant place to be. There were military checkpoints every few hundred yards throughout the city, and a nightly "shoot on sight" curfew. There were food and water shortages and regular power outages, and rocket attacks from *mujahideen* bases outside the city were a daily occurrence. I was the sole guest in the two hundred–room Intercontinental, which had been kept open to serve the occasional visiting communist dignitaries. Most of the staff had been laid off, and my footsteps echoed as I walked along the deserted corridors of the hotel.

Reeling drunks were common in the capital, as were billboards depicting gruesome automobile accidents, and exhorting motorists not to drink and drive, a strange ad campaign to run in a Muslim country, where alcohol consumption is forbidden. But in 1985, not only was alcohol readily available in Kabul, but the city had a new Soviet-built distillery that was producing vodka, cognac, and wine. A short stroll later through the five hundred–year-old gardens built by the Moghul emperor Babar found them peopled mostly with drunks, usually Soviet conscripts, and a few Afghans.

Heavy alcohol consumption may well have contributed to the dramatic increase in the number of rapes in Afghanistan's capital since the occupation. Western human rights organizations documented a number of instances of Afghan women and teenage girls being abducted and then sexually assaulted by Soviet soldiers.

In Afghanistan, rape victims commonly commit suicide; they recognize that society and even close family members will reject them afterward. In one particularly tragic incident during the war, Soviet soldiers attacked a village, and the women, fearing they would be molested, threw themselves into a fast-flowing river, where most drowned rather than be dishonored.

I was in Kabul to interview Dr. Anahita Ratebzad, the sole woman on the Afghan politburo. She wanted me to visit the various projects of her Women's Democratic Organization of Afghanistan (WDOA), the women's arm of the Afghan Communist party, in order to document their success. One of the stated aims of the Communist party was to bring needed reforms to the country, which Ratebzad said would be particularly beneficial for women. But carrying out such reforms in a country at war proved to be a logistical impossibility. Also, as I discovered during my visit to Kabul, many of the programs existed on paper only.

Ratebzad claimed that her organization was the first to be established in Afghanistan to emancipate women. She explained to me that the WDOA's goals were to stamp out illiteracy among women, to empower them through education and professional training, and to enable them to cast off the veil. Five years into the occupation, the organization was still only offering six-month literacy courses taught by high school students and needlework classes.

I also later learned that the WDOA was not new, but merely the renamed version of the Afghan Women's Welfare Association, founded by the government in 1946. This earlier organization had offered courses in foreign languages, business, and home economics, in addition to literacy and handicrafts.

A protégé of Ratebzad, twenty-four-year-old Sohaila Sherzai took me through some of the WDOA projects. Taking me to a literacy class in a mud-house village a few miles outside Kabul, Sohaila proudly introduced me to fifteen women, aged eighteen to sixty, who were chanting from poorly mimeographed primers. These women, I was told, were in the final month of the course. I noticed, however, that at least two of the students had made little progress — they were holding their books upside down. Later, a Western diplomat told me that despite claims made by the regime on their literacy program, party members privately admitted that fewer than two thousand women had been registered for classes outside Kabul. He also said that the WDOA's main agenda was to promote Marxist-Leninist ideology, and to recruit women for the state secret police. And, in fact, programs that benefited woman, such as free child care, had been curtailed since government spending had been redirected to the military effort.

Despite Communist party claims to the contrary, the veil was first banned in Afghanistan in 1921 when King Amanullah launched an emancipation program for women, and his wife, Queen Soraya, appeared in public with her face uncovered. The first school for girls was opened months later. And graduating students were sent to Turkey to obtain higher education. When King Amanullah was overthrown eight years later, the conservatives forced his successor to reinstate the veil.

Then in 1959, at the Independence Day celebration in Kabul, the wife and sisters of Prime Minister Daoud Khan appeared on the reviewing stand unveiled. It was the first step in Daoud's program for voluntary removal of the veil, and many women in the city quickly followed suit.

Influential clergymen organized protests, and in Kandarhar Province there was a near revolt. But Daoud, who saw the unveiling of women as part of his program of modernization, refused to back down. He promptly jailed the mullahs who led the demonstrations. Then, in an act designed to humiliate them further, he sent Musa Shafiq, the senior mullah of the royal family's palace mosque, to debate them on Koranic law. Shafiq, who would later become Afghanistan's prime minister, held a law degree from Columbia University, and was also a graduate of Al Azhar in Cairo. He was considered one of the country's highest authorities on Islam at the time. Daoud ordered him to challenge the imprisoned mullahs to find Koranic support for their insistence that women's faces should be covered. The clerics failed to do so, and Daoud's modernization program continued unhindered.

Nine years later, girls were admitted to Kabul University, although women's colleges had existed since 1946. The following year, in 1964, when the constitution granted equal status to men and women, coeducation in all primary schools began, and also in all the colleges of Kabul University, including the College of Theology. Rokia Habib, one of the first four women to be elected to Afghanistan's House of Representatives in the sixties, explained, "Two women were members of the Counseling Committee in charge of drafting the new Afghan constitution. Four others, myself included, became members of the Grand Assembly, which adopted the constitution that same year. The movement for women's emancipation in Afghanistan began long before the communist takeover."

In a number of ways, the occupation reversed progress for women. Family-planning clinics for women, for example, were opened in Afghanistan in 1968, funded in part by the Planned Parenthood Federation and USAID. Neither religious leaders nor traditionalists objected at the time. It was the Kabul Communist party who closed down the centers throughout the country in 1979. They claimed that "family planning was a concept created by imperialists to divert the attention of the masses from the true cause of poverty and underdevelopment to an unimportant factor, the number of children."

In my travels to ten of Afghanistan's twenty-eight provinces that year, and to other parts of the country in subsequent years, it was apparent that in rural villages, women's lives — like those of their uneducated menfolk — had changed little in centuries. Steeped in timeless traditions and given religious guidance by uneducated mullahs, whose Koranic knowledge was riddled with errors, women's rights had no meaning.

A young Afghan man I met, Azar Jhan, demonstrated how difficult some traditions are to change, particularly when cultures claim they have a religious basis. He was a subsistence farmer in Nangarhar Province, which borders Pakistan. Just a generation ago, his family had been nomads. At six feet six inches tall, and pure muscle, he could carry loads that would have crushed many other men. Aged twenty-two, he had married a fourteen-year-old girl the previous year. In the final stage of her pregnancy, she was suffering from high fevers. Would I take her to a women's hospital in Pakistan?, he asked me. At the hospital, doctors found that her child had died in utero. Azar Jhan's young wife told me that for more than a week before the fevers began she had spent every day "from light till dark" fetching water in heavy metal pots, and carrying wood in preparation for a wedding party.

Azar Jhan stoically accepted the death of his unborn child. "Allah will bless us with many more children; my wife is young," he said. But when I suggested that next time he should do the heavy carrying for his wife, he replied irately, "This is not men's work. Women must carry water. Islam says men and women's work is different. Ask our mullah." He stalked away. Another villager explained that Azar Jhan would lose face in the village if anyone saw him help his wife fetch water.

Completely illiterate rural women are, of course, unable to read the Koran themselves, and have no means of learning how the Prophet Mohammad intended them to live their lives. And for them perhaps it is easier than for those who are educated to accept the role their society has imposed on them, often because they are unaware of other existences. I met women among the Afghan refugees in Pakistan who illustrated this. Sarai, in her mid-thirties and unmarried because her fiancé had died, had only been permitted a couple of years of elementary school education. Now, her entire world was her home. Very occasionally, she would leave her family compound, heavily veiled in a *burqa* and always chaperoned, to attend a wedding or visit a relative. And while she became excited by her rare outings, she told me she was happy at home, and that it wasn't appropriate for women to go out more than she did. "Why do I need to leave the house?" she asked me. "All my needs are supplied here. Whatever I want, my father or brothers will bring it.

"I could never live as you do in America. I would be afraid. Coming home to an empty house every night. Don't you get lonely? Going out to work every day, competing with men, just so you have money to eat. What happens if you get sick, or when you get old? Who will look after you? Who will advise you? God chose to give neither you nor I children, but I am surrounded by family — brothers, sisters, uncles, and aunts, and all their little ones. You are alone. No, I don't want what you foreign women call 'freedom.' Our way is better, kinder, I think."

Hamida had been part of her family's first generation to go to college. She graduated with honors from Kabul University with a B.S. in mathematics, and briefly enjoyed a teaching career in a girls' school in Kabul.

When her world suddenly reverted to conservatism after her family became refugees, Hamida was required to stay home with the other women. Overnight, her wardrobe went from modified Western to traditionally veiled and her outings became rare. Hamida was bitter. "My brothers have total freedom, I have none, and yet I am as well educated, if not better, than they are. My education is going to waste. I am becoming crazy staying at home all the time." Her health was suffering due to her confinement. She now slept and ate poorly, was frequently depressed, and suffered from heart palpitations.

Feeling unable to fight against her restrictions, Hamida has exerted her independence in one area of her life — she has refused to marry. "My parents are probably more liberal with me, despite all my restrictions, than any Afghan husband will be," she insisted. I found that a little hard to believe. On one occasion, Hamida had been complaining how heavy and hot her thick, waist-length hair was under her *chador* in the summer. I suggested she cut it. "Oh, no, I cannot," she replied. "I asked my mother for permission to cut it. She refused, and said good Muslim women do not cut their hair." Hamida was then twenty-six.

Had Hamida been male, her refusal to marry would have been considered un-Islamic. The Koran requires a man who can afford to support a wife and children to marry. Marriage is only compulsory for a woman who has no other means of maintaining herself and who fears that her sexual desires will "push her into fornication." Muslim males may marry non-Muslims, but a Muslim woman is forbidden to marry outside her religion.

Marriage, meant to be a high point in a woman's life, is frequently viewed with fear in the Islamic world. A traditional Afghan bride does not meet her groom until the end of the wedding ceremony. Her first glimpse of her partner for life is in a mirror held under her veil as the couple are declared man and wife. Even if she is engaged to a close relative as a child, once the engagement is made formal, the couple will not meet again until the day of the wedding some years later.

During the ceremony, the bride is expected to look unhappy — it is considered more modest — and for most that isn't hard to do. For the majority of Afghan women, a woman's wedding denotes the day she becomes the property of her husband's family. Once she is married, an Afghan woman will see her own family again only with the permission of her husband, which he may or may not grant. After the wedding, the bride will move from her parents' home to that of her in-laws, where, unless they are wealthy, she can expect to be treated as a house servant for many years, until, with the birth of sons, she gradually moves up the hierarchy.

Afghanistan lays claim to some of the saddest health statistics in the world: the highest maternal death rate, the second-highest infant mortality rate, and the highest fertility rate. But doctors say that it isn't only poor hygiene, nutrition, and maternal health that are behind the high death tolls. "In so many instances, these girls start having babies long before their bodies are really mature enough," one woman obstetrician at the Afghan maternity hospital in Peshawar told me. "Their families seem to think that just because a girl is menstruating, she is old enough to get married and become a mother. A lot of these girls commonly start their menses at ten or eleven. They should not be having babies at that age. It can kill them. Also, in our part of the world, where women's and girls' health is generally poor, a fourteen- or fifteen-year-old body is a lot less mature, less strong, than her counterpart in the West."

An Afghan bride and groom consummate their union while the couple are still total strangers. As with all Muslim brides, she is required to be a virgin. She also is required to prove it publicly. Even today, a white sheet daubed with her blood from the breaking of her hymen is passed among relatives the day after the wedding. "She was a clean girl [meaning pure]; there was blood on the sheet," house servants told me after a wedding of an Afghan acquaintance last year. This tradition is a disaster for the young woman who does not bleed, unless the couple choose to fake it. If there is any doubt whatsoever of an Afghan bride's chastity, she will be immediately divorced and returned home to her family with the statement, "She was a woman, not a girl," no matter what her age. Should that happen, the chances are high she will fall victim to fratricide.

For Muslim women, marriage begins a life of sex on demand — his demand, that is. The Koran tells men: "Your women are a tillage for you; so come unto your tillage as you wish." Only during menstruation, when the Koran considers a woman polluted and therefore out of bounds, in late pregnancy, and for forty days after the birth of a baby, is she permitted to refuse her husband. A woman who rejects her husband sexually, said the Prophet Mohammad, is "condemned to have angels hurl anathema at her." And while the Prophet indicated that sexual satisfaction is a woman's right, for many Afghan women it is rare. In the large extended family of her in-laws' home, privacy is limited, as a number of people may sleep in the same room. Intercourse is usually furtive and very brief: foreplay is unusual and couples do not disrobe. A common belief among some Afghan tribes is that nudity makes the man impotent. (Male impotency is one of the few grounds for a Muslim woman to request a divorce under Islamic law. Other reasons include the husband's being insane or having leprosy.)

Many Muslim marriages, of course, are happy. Women frequently explained to me how love should follow the wedding, not the other way around, and how arranged marriages are so much more successful than Western ones. "Look at you," Shafiqa told me. "You are unmarried, and are responsible for finding your own husband. How can you do that? How will you know whether he is good or wise, or whether he comes from the right kind of family, or will be able to support you and your children? Our parents, who are experienced in marriage, know how to select two people who will be well matched in every way.

"When our family arranges a marriage for us, do you realize how much investigating they do? The man can hide nothing. In the West, you marry when you are in love. Both of you are trying very hard to impress each other. Only after you live together do you discover all those unpleasant surprises. I think our way is more practical. We know what to expect from the beginning."

When I first moved to Peshawar in 1988, for what became a four-year stay, I knew I would have to dress conservatively. From the moment of stepping off the plane, women are made to feel uncomfortable unless they are observing the Islamic dress code. In my case, I wore a *shalwar kamez*, baggy pants covered with a long and loose full-sleeved tunic. Only my head, hands, and feet were exposed, despite the fact that the temperature at the time was 120 degrees.

At the beginning, I was advised to wear the *chador*, to cover my head and drape it loosely around me to disguise feminine contours. This way, I was told, it was less likely that I would be sexually harassed on the street and in the bazaar, particularly since my bright red hair, I was warned, would attract a lot of attention. Muslim culture strives constantly to negate women's sexuality, yet I was never made as aware of mine as when I was in an Islamic country.

Because of the extreme heat, and the fact that my *chador* was always falling off my head or coming unwound, I soon abandoned it. Local Muslim women manage to hold their *chadors* in place with their teeth, a skill I never mastered and found exceedingly uncomfortable. Rather than veil, I began instead to practice what I later learned is called "eye *purdah*," averting one's eyes, a concept not unknown to women trying to steer clear of trouble when walking through the streets of New York City. In a Muslim culture, where little of a woman is visible except her eyes, eye contact is considered erotically enticing.

I quickly learned that it was unwise to go out for a walk alone because Muslim women would never do so. And bike riding, a form of exercise I enjoy, was out — to sit astride a bicycle was considered so immodest it could invite a stoning. A woman was, however, permitted to ride sidesaddle behind a male relative.

For an American woman who was very much part of the feminist movement's spearhead in the West two decades ago, moving to a conservative Muslim country was frequently jarring. I was, after all, a woman whose coming of age was marked by the advent of the Pill, who grew up with the voices of Gloria Steinem and Germaine Greer ringing in my ears, and for whom emancipation, equality, and the honorific "Ms." were so well entrenched they could have been engraved on my DNA. Yet in the Muslim society where I now lived, women were rarely addressed by their rightful names. Instead, throughout a woman's life she was usually referred to, even by close friends and relatives, by the name of her father, husband, or son, as in "mother of Abdul." Her own name is seldom used since, as a woman derives her status from the men in her family, it is considered insignificant.

It was not always easy to wend my way through cultural minefields without triggering explosions. I had to remember never to touch a Muslim male, never to tap his arm to get his attention, to pat him in encouragement, or touch his hand in sympathy. In this newly Islamized society, many Muslim males refused to shake hands with a woman, and after having several men pointedly step back to avoid mine, I soon learned not to embarrass them.

More disturbing was the fury I caused when I approached a young male acquaintance while he was with friends to inquire after his sister's health when she had been sick. He refused to acknowledge me, and the next time I saw him, he stormed at me that I had dared mention his sister, even used her name, in front of other men. He insisted my behavior had shamed him.

With the Afghan family, headed by a Resistance official, that adopted me during my stay in their world, I was initially treated like Fatima Gailani — as an honorary male. In the early days, I ate with the men, was included in male gatherings — the only woman in the house to be so — and even sat in on a number of meetings with guerrilla commanders. At these times, my opinions on events of the day, the war, and politics were sought out and listened to. Even during family television viewing time, when programs such as Western movies were deemed inappropriate for the womenfolk and they were ushered from the room, it was assumed I would be part of the audience.

But eventually, as I became more a part of the family, this changed. One day, as I sat chatting in the guest room with other members of the family, the call "Hide yourself," a traditional alert that male visitors are in the vicinity, rang out. The women scurried to remove themselves, their needlework, and other possessions that would be recognized as female from view. I continued to sit. Suddenly, the patriarch of the family was standing over me. "Hide yourself," he repeated curtly, impatiently snapping his fingers and pointing to the door. I was so surprised, and he was so authoritative, I found myself meekly getting up, and without saying a word, moving to another part of the house.

The other women chuckled when they realized what had happened. "Now you are one of us," I was told. And apparently I was. From that day on, I was no longer invited to join all-male outings, as I had been previously. "It isn't appropriate," I was told, and it was obvious that I was expected not to question that decision. Tradition had finally caught up with me. With it came a campaign by the family's grandmother for me to stop working and to stay at home with the other women. Every time she found me reading, whether it was a newspaper, research, or a paperback, she clucked sadly and said I didn't have to tire myself this way since God and her family would look after me.

One tradition I never became accustomed to was males in the family leaving the house without saying good-bye or telling their wives or other women, including myself, where they were going or when they intended to be back. To do so suggested that we were important enough to be informed.

· · ·

It was through my involvement with Afghanistan that I met Laili. She and her husband worked for a New York–based Afghan assistance organization for which I was one of the board members. Except for her maiden name, Zikria, I would not on first meeting have known she was Afghan. Her jeans and sweaters, knee-high boots and ponytail, and her unaccented English, made her seem thoroughly Western. She had arrived in the United States three years before the Soviet invasion of her country. Laili had not wanted to leave Afghanistan; like many Afghans she had a passionate love for her country, and even when I met her eleven years later, she dreamed of the day she would return.

Her family had been forced into exile because her grandfather, Faisal Zikria, the former foreign minister of Afghanistan, had been an outspoken critic of Prime Minister Daoud. Daoud had overthrown the monarchy in 1973, and Zikria had been close to Afghanistan's last king, Zahir Shah. Laili's teen years in Tenafly, New Jersey, were a mixture of Western and Muslim. At home alcohol was banned, even for American guests. The older women covered their heads, and the five daily prayers were observed, as was a month of fasting every Ramadan. Laili attended a coeducational high school, where she played volleyball and baseball, and where, like any American teenager, she learned to love the music and the dance of the seventies. But she was forbidden to date, and her family and she assumed that her marriage, when it came, would be an arranged one.

Laili was sixteen when the communists took over her country.

Almost immediately, her male relatives in Afghanistan were jailed, and many of them were tortured. "I became obsessed with what was happening in Afghanistan," recalled Laili. Her political involvement led to her meeting twenty-five-year-old Roger Helms, the blond, blue-eyed nephew of former CIA director Richard Helms. When he met Laili, he was already a political activist for Afghanistan. An M.B.A. student, he also had been studying Persian and Islam.

"My family was beginning to mention names of suitable Afghan husbands for me," said Laili, then a second-year psychology and communications student. "When Roger asked to start seeing me alone, I told him it was impossible. I was a good Muslim girl. I didn't drink and had never been out with a boy." But eventually the appeal of an American man who cared as much about Afghanistan as she did won out. "I hated lying to my parents, and had just made up my mind to stop seeing him, when he asked me to marry him."

Laili broke the news to her mother, who told her she was being ridiculous, that such a marriage was totally unacceptable to their family. Her father and other relatives were outraged. But despite family opposition, Laili and Roger, who had by then converted to Islam, were married at a mosque in Manhattan. Eventually her family forgave both of them.

Shortly after I moved to Peshawar, Laili and Roger followed. Within two days of arriving in Peshawar in 1988, they had been offered jobs with an American refugee relief agency. But returning to their hotel a day later, the couple found a death threat addressed to both of them. They learned the letter had been delivered by Afghans in a jeep, "who looked like *mujahideen*."

Shocked and scared, the couple went looking for advice. The American agency that had agreed to employ them had none to offer, and their jobs promptly evaporated now that they were considered a liability. The theories behind Laili and Roger's death threat were varied: the agency that had offered them work employed many fundamentalists who considered known royalists their archenemies; Afghans have been known to prolong feuds for decades, and Laili's grandfather had not been forgotten; Roger's family connection with the CIA was another suggested cause. The CIA was hated by Afghans despite the fact that they supplied them with arms. A final theory was that radical Islamists were enraged to see an Afghan woman cohabiting with an American.

"Because we were concerned about the last reason," said Laili, "I have worn an enormous *chador*, which covers everything except my eyes, since we have been in Pakistan. We knew that seeing an Afghan woman with a Western male would rub people the wrong way. And in the four years we have now lived in Peshawar, we have never gone to the bazaar together for the same reason."

Despite the death threat and other problems, Laili and Roger refused to give up and return to the United States. "Afghanistan is my country, and Roger is my husband," said Laili simply. Today, Laili works with the Afghan Women's Resource Center, and Roger, employed by USAID, monitors reconstruction programs in Afghanistan.

Laili has never gotten used to being completely veiled. "It is degrading to have to wear the *chador* to be perceived as pure," she said. "The Afghan women I work with feel the same. We resent it. It is damned uncomfortable, particularly in the heat of the summer. But to feel safe, Afghan women, especially those working with Western-funded agencies, have to wear it. Today, a woman is perceived by how she walks, sits, moves her eyes, if she giggles. I have to be careful. There have been too many incidents and threats."

Laili and Roger have lived in Peshawar during a time of violent anti-Western attacks and growing extremist activity against women by Afghans. In 1989 and 1990, during a particularly volatile spate, Western relief agencies had machine-gun guards and high walls topped with barbed wire. Shelter Now, an Australian agency, was attacked by an armed mob of five thousand Afghans after they were incited by an extremist mullah during Friday prayers in a refugee mosque. The mullah claimed that soap given to women refugees was made available to them because Westerners in the agency wanted to have sex with them. Soap, an expensive and valued commodity for refugees, was used as an incentive to get Afghan women to attend Mother and Child Care classes. The mob sacked the agency and burned its warehouses to the ground while Pakistani authorities refused to act. It made no difference that the warehouses contained tons of powdered milk destined for Afghan refugee children.

Two months later, the agency's director, Thor Armstrong, and his young son had their jeep sprayed with machine-gun fire by Afghan extremists. Injured only by flying glass, and severely shocked, Armstrong managed to drive the vehicle to the nearest hospital. The family left the country the next day. John Tarzwell, a Canadian office manager for the Christian relief agency SERVE, was not so lucky. He was kidnapped at gunpoint on his way to work by Afghan guerrillas one week before the birth of his third child. Believed dead, he has never been seen again.

Shortly afterward, the director of the American International Relief Committee had his life threatened, and was rushed into hiding until he and his family could leave the country. A little later, anonymously authored pamphlets were circulated stating that fifty Western Christian women employed by relief agencies were suffering from AIDS and had been sent to Peshawar to infect Muslims. This last piece of agitation propaganda was so ludicrous it might have been funny if it had not come during such an incendiary period.

At the same time as Western agencies were being threatened, so were the Afghan women who worked with them. Posters appeared all over the Afghan section of the city threatening the lives of any Afghan females who worked with or took part in any of the educational or income-generating programs offered by the agencies. Buses supplied to transport the women to their courses or to work were chased or fired at by machine gun–toting Afghan zealots traveling in jeeps. A nurse working at a refugee clinic who had previously received a bullet in an envelope was abducted from work. Her mutilated body was found some time after.

A *fatwa* was issued banning women from "wearing perfume or cosmetics, going out without their husband's permission, talking with men other than close relatives, walking with pride, or walking in the middle of the sidewalk." Mullahs announced that any Afghan woman caught with embroidery materials in her home (relief agencies offered such items for women who participated in income-generating projects) would be fined the equivalent of five months' family income. Later, they threatened to burn down the homes of any women who did not comply. Announcements were made that it was better for women to go to their graves than to leave their homes to work.

Laili and her female colleagues continued to work and continued to receive threats. USAID was forced to relocate the Helmses after Laili was threatened by Arab extremists. "The house next to ours was a fundamentalist Arab hostel," said Laili. "I had been spat at by these men when I left the house and they had thrown stones at me. Then one day I drove out in our car, and they followed in their vehicle brandishing their machine guns at me. They chased me for about ten minutes, trying to force me off the road. I was terrified, and convinced they were going to kill me." They abandoned the chase when Laili reached the heavily trafficked main road. Three of the Helmses' neighbors, all liberal Afghans like Laili, were assassinated that year.

"This is not the religion I grew up with," said Laili angrily. "The Islam I know is compassionate, tolerant, and understanding. What they are doing in the name of religion here is the complete opposite. They have corrupted Islam for political ends. The ritual and the overt signs of Islam, such as women wearing veils, has become the most important thing. But basic decency is not a part of that dynamic.

"Hypocrisy is now the mainstay of Islam here. Our mosques in Peshawar are built with drug and arms money; the Resistance newspapers are run by drug and arms money. Those who are the most overtly religious are the ones who are the most corrupt and violent." The opium poppy that has made Pakistan the major exporter of heroin to the United States has been grown in parts of Afghanistan as a major cash crop to help finance the war.

"It is hard to stay clean in a war, and in fourteen years of fighting, much of the Resistance has been tainted. People no longer feel represented by their leaders, and the children are growing up as fanatics without compassion."

Laili believes that what is happening in Afghanistan today is part of a broader picture. "The Islamic movements are on the march right now throughout the Muslim world; there is a major push going on. It started with what were terrorist movements in Iran and Lebanon, but the Muslim Brotherhood and similar groups have since become establishment organizations. Through publications, on the air, and through day-to-day pressures in the mosques, they are shaping the way Muslims everywhere think. In Afghanistan already two provinces, Kunar and Nangarhar, have fallen to Arab extremist money."

She sees a similar response in the agency where she works. The Afghan Women's Resource Center is a program designed to empower women. "But we are not empowering women so they can do things for themselves. We are empowering women to fit in to the neat little picture defined by the fundamentalists. Most of the women in positions of authority are those willing to toe the party line for the Muslim Brotherhood and the Wahabis. You can see it from our newspaper, which is full of reprints of Arab articles on the revolutionary Islamic movement taking over, and the Anita Hill–type plight of Western women. These women have no other choice: either they comply, or the extremists close down the program.

"The Afghan women here feel forced to dress from head to toe in black — faces, hands, everything covered. They look like beekeepers. This is not the way we ever dressed before. Women know they have to do it, although they are respected less for it than they were before. My colleagues often complain to me that Afghan men didn't use to stare at us this way. Now even though we are completely covered, they look at us as if we are whores. We feel oppressed because we are forced to veil ourselves, and despite that, these men view us as nothing more than sexual objects. They feel a woman should be unseen; if she shows herself, it is temptation. These men are being taught that a woman seen in any shape or form is a Western idea, and therefore un-Islamic."

Laili feels that since men are being oppressed themselves by the newly politicized religion, they in turn are oppressing women. "We have a proverb in Afghanistan," said Laili: " 'When you can't beat the donkey, beat the saddle.' Women are the saddle."

When the Kabul regime fell in the spring of 1992, Laili, like many Afghans, thought there would be peace in Afghanistan and wanted to go home. Persuading Roger to stay in Peshawar with their three-year-old son, she joined a group of refugees, friends of her family, on the sixteen-hour bus ride back to the city where she was born. The man who led her group insisted that the women wear *burqas* for the journey since they were traveling through Nangarhar, where the presence of Arab and Afghan fundamentalists was strong. "It was the first time I had worn a *burqa*," said Laili, who found it so heavy and hot in the 100 degree–plus heat, she began to feel faint. She arrived in Kabul the week that the Resistance government took over.

"I hardly recognized the city. All the buildings on the drive in to Kabul were burned out. There was still smoke coming from the windows of the museum and university. Wherever you looked, there was war damage. The city was full of Arabs, particularly the quarter where we had lived. There were also posters of Khomeini and other Iranian leaders all over the place. While I was there, girls' schools were raided and their books burned; movie theaters, viewed as irreligious, were attacked. The city was shelled daily by different Resistance factions. The *mujahideen* no longer know what they are fighting for, except absolute power for their particular party.

"For me, this time in Kabul finished any hope I had of moving back and having my kids grow up there. This is not the world I want to raise my children in," said Laili, who is pregnant with her second child. "I want them to know the Islam I was raised with, not this violent political movement that calls itself religion." Now, instead of settling down in Afghanistan, the family will return to the United States when Roger's contract expires. "Five years of living in this madness is enough," she said.

CHAPTER 5

Iran: "There Is No Fun in Islam"

*As to those women on whose part you fear disloyalty and
ill-conduct, first admonish them, then refuse to share
their bed, and last beat them, but then if they return
to obedience, do not seek a way against them.*

KORAN 4:34

OBTAINING A VISA TO IRAN is an endeavor that is not for
the impatient or easily discouraged. It also is an experience that is microcosmic of the rest of one's stay. My
first application in London received no response, and
follow-up phone inquiries were put on hold and disconnected so
frequently that it began to seem a quaint Persian method of refusal.

Trying again in Pakistan was a challenge of a different kind. At
the Iranian Consul in Peshawar, I was turned away at the entrance
because my head was uncovered. Suitably *chadored,* I made it the
next time as far as an interview with the vice-consul. He regretted,
however, that he could not accept my photographs for my visa application because they were "disrespectful." He explained, "Your head
is uncovered in them." I returned the following day with my own
head and my photographed version both swathed in fabric. Smiling
pleasantly, the vice-consul once again declined to accept my new
photographs. "The front of your hair is showing," he said, referring
to a small portion of my bang that was visible and apparently rendered my dress "un-Islamic." My third set of photographs was finally
accepted. But I was not, as I learned the following week when I
contacted the consulate. "Tehran has turned you down," said the
vice-consul. Why? "They probably don't want a single Western
woman wandering around Iran," he replied cheerfully.

Journalistic fortunes can change from one day to the next. Mine took an upswing when, just as I was being rejected by Tehran, a good friend of mine in the Afghan Resistance was appointed ambassador to Pakistan by the new Kabul government. I called to congratulate him, and asked if there was anything he could do to help. The following day I was summoned to the consulate. "Now, it is good," said the vice-consul. "You are a guest of the Afghan *mujahideen,* you will stay in their house in Tehran, you are not a woman alone. Please give me your passport." As I turned to leave, he warned me, "Please make sure you are wearing full Islamic dress when you arrive in Tehran. And wear it at all times in Iran."

My next stop was the Peshawar clothing bazaar, where the stall-holder assured me that the black full-length wraparound coat and large head scarf he offered me were correct Iranian *chador* and *hijab.* "You must wear black socks with this," he also told me, "and they don't permit makeup or nail polish."

On the flight to Tehran, I carried the Iranian version of Islamic dress in a plastic bag, and changed before we landed. It was not a flattering ensemble, but of course it was not intended to be. As we landed, I watched the women around me tug and pull at their Islamic costumes to make sure they would pass tough scrutiny at the airport. I had been warned that passing through immigration and customs at Mehrabad airport had become a lengthy process since the mullahs ran the country, and could take a grueling four to five hours. By the time I arrived, the process was more streamlined, although still not friendly. But the decor was the same: large photographs of Khomeini, his successor Ayatollah Ali Khamenei, and President Hashemi Rafsanjani.

Little more than an hour after arriving, I was sitting in a taxi and heading for my destination in northern Tehran. The vehicle, a decrepit Iranian-made Peykan, coughed and sputtered its way out of the airport, its leaded gas and ancient engine typical of most vehicles on the road in Tehran and a major cause of the city's lung-rasping pollution. Tehran currently has the third-highest level of sulfur dioxide of any city in the world, and on many days of the year, the government warns the elderly and those with respiratory problems not to leave their homes. The day I arrived, however, the air was gloriously clear and the snow on the Elburz mountain range at the northern edge of the city glistened in the sun. Iran's highest peak, Mount Demavend, at 18,300 feet, is just northeast of the city. The mountains, when they can be seen through the murky atmosphere, are the city's saving grace. Much of Tehran today is grimy, dilapidated, and dreary. It was little different under the Shah, but the mullahs have exhibited even less skill or interest in municipality management.

On the inside of the taxi's passenger door, where the "no smoking" sign can be found in American cabs, was a decal that I soon realized was ubiquitous throughout Iran. Showing the silhouette of a woman's covered head, it stated, "For the respect of Islam, *Hijab* is mandatory." The same four-inch-wide decal was on display in stores, restaurants, and every public building I visited. A storekeeper would later tell me, "It means we are forbidden to serve you unless you wear a proper *hijab*." As we traveled through the city, other *hijab* signs were common. "Bad *hijab* is prostitution," read one, an ironic statement since Iran's prostitutes tend to be more covered than ordinary women, even veiling their faces. Another that was intended to be more threatening than insulting stated, "Lack of *hijab* means lack of man's manhood."

We turned onto Freeway Shaheed Ayatollah Sayyed Mohammad Baqer-e-Sadr heading to Kamraniyeh, my final destination. Many of Tehran's roadways are named after the *shaheed*, or martyrs — those who fell in the revolution or the eight-year Iran-Iraq War, and were destined for Paradise after their Islamic sacrifice. In the neighborhood in which I was staying, so many streets were designated *shaheed*, it gave the area a somber air, a little like living in a cemetery.

Kamraniyeh edges up to the foothills of the Elburz Mountains. Its private villas with their high walls, ornately barred windows, and swimming pools rent for $2,000 a month. Its tree-lined streets are edged with small canals that were once the sole water source for the city, and are now a constant hazard for roadside parking. In Tehran's northern districts, where the air is clearer, the homes can cost as much as $2 million. The southern half of the city houses much of Tehran's industry as well as the workers employed in its run-down factories.

The home in which I stayed had white marble floors, stone fireplaces, a large American-style kitchen, multiple bathrooms, an outdoor swimming pool, a small indoor pool, and servants' quarters. Neighboring homes were similar. The luxury that such dwellings denote belong to a pre-Revolutionary Iran. Most of the privileged class fled to the West when Khomeini came into power, which is why the country has a dramatic shortage of doctors, dentists, and other professionals. In those early days, the Ayatollah had denounced professional expertise as being without value "because Islam alone will provide." For those who remained, the Islamic Revolution has been a great leveler.

The regime, of course, has spawned its own elite, which on occasion turns on its own. A few hundred yards from where I was staying was the enormous, machine-gun guarded villa of Sheikh Mehdi Karrubi, the former speaker of the Majlis, the Iranian Parliament. Karrubi, a leader of the radical wing of the clergy, is one of the most outspoken foes of closer relations with the United States. He and seven other like-minded leading radical clergy were publicly stripped of membership in the prestigious Assembly of Experts in late 1990 after failing examinations set for them on Islamic ideology and theology, on which their rarefied credentials were based. The exams were a move engineered by President Rafsanjani, who saw the extremists as a roadblock to mending relations with the West, a vital step for Iran if it is to repair the country's ravaged economy.

Khomeini's portrait is ever-present in Iran, but when I arrived in Tehran, there were even more portraits than usual. The city was observing a week of mourning for the third anniversary of the Ayatollah's death, and silk screens of the late cleric hung from nearly every lamppost and even many trees in the city's large Park-e-Millat. Large, black velvet-lined booths were set up as shrines on most streets and in the front of public buildings and schools. The posters of Khomeini were bedecked with red and white gladioli, and banners reading "Greetings Imam Khomeini," or "O Imam, you have left us, and we accursed must remain behind."

For the period of mourning, Iran's two-station television, which normally devotes a lot of time to religious affairs and readings from the Koran, daily aired hours of tape of Khomeini talking, teaching, or preaching, or of his funeral. They particularly focused on crowds of mourners beating themselves and wailing. Even children's hour did not escape: every single program showed youngsters, some just toddlers, beating their heads and chests and calling on the late Ayatollah. One female teacher told me, "This is so offensive, particularly for young children. Iran has been reduced to a country where any form of joy has been banned. But they put on such a show for sorrow, such ritualized sorrow."

Khomeini himself declared that joy was un-Islamic. Six months after the Iranian Revolution, he stated on national radio, "There is no fun in Islam. There can be no fun or enjoyment in whatever is serious." Certainly, that comment seemed to be taken seriously. The streets of Tehran look sorrowful the year round, with the predominant color being black, dominated by the women's *chadors*. I realized after a while that the only vivid color on the city streets came from the dresses of little girls. And because they brightened up the monochromatic cityscape, I found myself smiling at them, their bare arms and legs symbolizing a freedom soon lost. Legally, young Iranian girls must be entirely covered by the age of nine, although many are *chadored* long before then. Nine is the age that Khomeini declared girls mature enough to be married.

But even with strict Islamic dress, fashion has crept in. Many women now prefer to wear the *rapoosh,* an ankle-length coat that Tehran residents call by the French word for coat, *manteau.* The manteau is easier to wear than the *chador* since it buttons up the front, and is less likely to come unraveled and expose the wearer, a crime punishable by flogging or imprisonment. Now, along with black, one can see navy, dark green, brown, gray, and khaki, even the occasional dark purple and pea-green. Styles vary also, ranging from what resembles a maxi raincoat to more expensive embroidered versions. But all have enormous shoulder pads. *Hijabs,* too, are changing slightly. Although the predominant color is still black, whites, dark prints, and paisleys are beginning to appear. Manteaus cost from $40 to $200, and in a city where the average salary is $100 a month, this seems excessive. And since they are worn constantly — summer and winter — in restaurants, schools, in offices, on the street, they do not last long. Because the garments are imposed by the regime, many women feel that the government should make them available for free.

Women wearing styles that are considered un-Islamic are subject to arrest on the street. Such fashion offenses include buttons on their manteaus that are gold or silver or over-large, or splits in the back of the garment to facilitate walking that expose too much well-covered leg. Bare feet, or stockings that are not heavily opaque, are just as dangerous. In fact, the list of violations women can commit in Iran just by dressing is long: makeup, nail polish, and hair showing under the head scarf are just a few. According to Rafsanjani, a man frequently labeled in the West as moderate, "It is the obligation of the female to cover her head because women's hair exudes vibrations that arouse, mislead, and corrupt men." But Iranian women take most risk with their head scarves, pushing them back on their heads in a minirebellion, particularly in the summer, when the scarves and coats are stifling. Tehran, which means "hot locality" in

Farsi, is aptly named; the temperature is frequently over 100 degrees in the summer, and few buildings are air-conditioned. After the first day of walking around the city, I had salt stains from sweating across the back of my manteau.

"The trouble with all this," Zahra Qasim, a forty-three-year-old store clerk explained to me, "is that few of these restrictions are written down. They vary from time to time. No one has ever defined how big our buttons can be before they are considered un-Islamic, the authorities suddenly make a push through the city, and anyone with big buttons is arrested. Lipstick might be ignored one week, but not nail polish, and vice versa later on. Suddenly, without warning there is a clampdown. They particularly concentrate on crowded shopping sections of the city."

The *Pasdaran,* Revolutionary Guard, is more likely to crack down on Iranian women around holiday time or special events: they usually target the Iranian New Year, before *Ramadan* — the Islamic month of fasting — and the anniversary of Khomeini's death. But it can happen at any time. Kati Ghazi, the American-educated, Iranian-born correspondent for the *New York Times,* had been back in Tehran only briefly when she attended a Rafsanjani press conference that was being televised. That evening, when the conference was aired, Ghazi's image as she was posing a question to the president was purposely blurred. The following day she learned why, when she was summoned to the Ministry of Islamic Guidance and stripped of her press credentials because a little of her hair had slipped out from under her scarf.

Ghazi was informed that she would not get her credentials back until she "abandoned her Western ways." Apparently, the authorities had also observed her shaking hands with a male colleague when he had arrived to cover the Iranian earthquake in 1990. Ghazi was lucky: while she was unable to work for eight months, her press credentials were eventually restored to her.

Fifty-five-year-old Faribah was much less fortunate. She had just been shopping at a supermarket and had returned to her car with her arms full of groceries. "I was about to open the car trunk, when a guard stopped me. I didn't understand why. I was wearing what I always wore outside the house, my long manteau, sneakers, socks, and trousers. I couldn't have been more covered. And I wasn't wearing makeup, although sometimes I did. Everything I had on was very plain.

"Then I realized my head scarf had slipped back a little from my forehead, but with my arms full of groceries I didn't have a hand free to adjust it." Faribah was taken to a nearby fleet of buses with more than one hundred women ranging in age from fifteen to sixty-two. "The women arresting us all wore black *chadors* and were very quietly spoken. Usually they pick on the younger women to teach them a lesson. But there were a lot of women arrested who were my age or older. Many were with their husbands. I saw one young woman forced to give to her husband the baby she was carrying before they arrested her. It was a warm spring day and some of the women had on short skirts under their coats. Many were crying. Others were sitting on the bus frantically trying to chew off their nail polish.

"What angered me was seeing all the men standing just looking at us being taken to the buses. None of them said or did anything. Deep down, Persian men like to have their women covered, it makes them feel in control. When we wore bikinis before the Revolution, they didn't say anything but they didn't like it."

When the buses were full, the women were driven to Monkarat Jail. "There they wrote down our names and our crimes," said Faribah. "I was told my hair was showing and that the split at the back of my coat was too high. It only comes to knee length, but it must have seemed higher as I bent over to open the trunk. We were put four or five to a cell and told we would be held for a day or two until our trials were set.

"By now, people were very frightened and asking one another whether they were going to whip us." The penalty for bad *hijab* in Iran is one to twelve months in prison and/or flogging. More recently, some women have been given the option of paying a fine instead of being flogged. The price per lash varies, beginning at Iranian Rials 10,000 per stroke and up, so that 80 lashes could cost between six and twelve months' average income. "To calm myself more than others, I said, 'Of course they won't whip us. Some of the women are old enough to be grandmothers and there is even a pregnant woman with us.'"

Faribah was held seven hours and released after her husband turned over the deed of their home to authorities as required bail. Her court hearing was set for two weeks later.

As we talked, Faribah and I sat in her elegant apartment with a superb view of the mountains. I had first met her in a restaurant, when she had been dressed as drably as she was the day of her arrest. I had not recognized her when she opened her apartment door to me. She looked a good fifteen years younger with her face skillfully made up, and wearing a fashionable silk shirt, an above-the-knee–length skirt, sheer black hose, and very high-heeled black suede pumps. She could have just returned from a lunch on Madison Avenue. Styles worn at home in Tehran are little different from those in the States. Many of the women I visited in their homes were dressed in high fashion, and their daughters in tight stirrup pants or miniskirts. The underwear and lingerie on sale in some of the more expensive stores was a cross between Victoria's Secret and Frederick's of Hollywood. No doubt if one is forced to dress like a pre–Vatican II nun most of the time, scarlet satin underwear trimmed with black lace has a definite appeal.

From Faribah's sophisticated appearance, her impeccable English, many of her comments, and her surroundings, it was easy to imagine myself sitting with a Western woman somewhere in New York City. This was an impression I had often in Tehran. Because Iran under the Shah was very Westernized in the cities, urban women in Tehran were more culturally attuned to the West. I was amused to see while I was there that the best-selling book in the city was a bootlegged Persian translation of *Scarlet*, the sequel to *Gone with the Wind*.

Smuggled music and movie videos, including those of Madonna, are also available from private dealers. Western videos were banned in Iran when the clerics set out to rid the country of the decadence of Western culture. Anyone caught selling or renting them is now subject to a ten-year jail sentence. "Videos are an invitation to prostitutes from the East and West to come into your living room," states one widely distributed government poster. At one home I visited a young man who was sent out to rent a video came back carrying a cake box. "Here," he said to me, putting it in my lap, "Iranian heroin." Inside was a video of the movie *Pretty Woman*.

In Tehran, the box could just as easily have contained heroin. The drug is readily available in the city, although at chic villa parties Iranians prefer to consume it in its unprocessed state as opium. Both opium and heroin are shipped into Iran from Afghanistan and Pakistan. But drug dealers risk their lives in doing so. The sentence is death by hanging, one of 109 offenses in Iran under the regime that is punishable by execution. A drug dealer had been publically hanged in Tehran three months prior to my visit. "It happened in Qazvin district in one of the squares," Mohammad, a local journalist, told me. "They did what they always do, stop the traffic, drive in a crane and a car. They stand the prisoner on the car, attach the noose to the crane, and then drive the car out from under him. It's sickening for adults to see, but it is really disturbing when kids are in the area." The regime is more high-tech when it comes to Islamic amputations for crimes such as theft. Sophisticated electric guillotines, which were invented in Iran in the mid-eighties, can amputate a hand or a foot in the case of repeat offenders in a second.

Although Iranian women like Faribah were seemingly easier to understand and identify with than women in any other Islamic society I visited, the world she now lived in could not have been more different from mine. "When we went to court two weeks after my arrest, my husband and parents came with me," said Faribah as she served me tea and cookies. "We arrived at seven A.M. I was told I would have to go in alone and wait until I was called. There were a lot of women waiting, some were prostitutes, some drug addicts. These women had been beaten and their legs were covered in blood. Each of us was called in turn before a mullah. When my turn came five hours later, he read my charge sheet and began to give me a long lecture. Then I was told to wait outside."

A Revolutionary Guard informed the women arrested with Faribah that he thought they would be fined Rials 500,000, approximately three months' average salary. "One woman became very upset, and started shouting that her husband didn't have that kind of money. She said the Revolutionary Guards only arrest us so they can get rich," said Faribah. "Apparently, the mullah heard her shouting and called in the *Pasdaran*. I became scared then, worried what the reaction might be. When the guard came back he told us the mullah was furious and had ordered all of us to receive eighty lashes. The woman who was five months pregnant was terrified. I still didn't believe it. I thought they just wanted to scare us. I still thought we would be fined."

Faribah was herded into the basement of the building with the other women. "It was horrible looking, damp and dark. Some woman began to cry hysterically, and the guard told her, 'Don't scream, no one can hear, so don't waste your energy.'

"Two *Pasdaran* took me into a cell. One was holding a whip in his hand. They handcuffed me facedown on a wooden bed. All I could think was, This is not really happening, this is not Islamic, how can a religious government let men do this to women? Then they started whipping me."

Faribah pauses and exhales as if she has been holding her breath while talking for the last couple of minutes. "What they did to me hurt me more mentally I think than physically. Somehow I was numb to the pain, I was so shocked that this was happening. But it was the total helplessness and subjugation. The lack of power, being robbed of all dignity. It was a disgusting experience, so degrading, and as violating in its way as rape. And it has changed me in so many ways. These days I am frightened every time I go out. It also made me realize what this regime thinks of women. Is it normal to live in a country where as a woman you have to get up in the morning and make yourself ugly before you can leave the house? Where nobody dares to laugh in public anymore?"

And for a while, it seemed as though President Rafsanjani agreed with those sentiments. In a much publicized sermon in 1990 he stated, "Appreciating beauty and seeking embellishment are serious feelings. To fight them is not God's desire." But the crackdowns have since been increased and the government still sends patrols onto the streets and into schools, offices, stores, even medical clinics, where women doctors and patients alike are checked for appropriate dress.

Faribah insisted that the authorities had become so violent that the Revolutionary Guards drive around the city in motorbike gangs removing lipstick from women with razor blades. I was sure the tale must be apocryphal until I learned later that Iran's interior minister had given an interview on Tehran radio in which he stated, "The brothers who rallied on motorcycles all over Tehran against social vice had done so with the prior knowledge of the Interior Ministry." Rafsanjani's comment while he was preaching at Friday prayers was, "We see now that these people need violence to some extent."

Many of the gains Iranian women made in the half century before the Islamic Revolution were instantly reversed by Khomeini. The Family Protection Acts of 1965 and 1975, legislation that had substantially improved conditions for women regarding marriage, divorce, and child custody, were abolished, and abortion was declared illegal. At the same time, female followers of Khomeini voluntarily began to wear the veil. One of the strongest supporters of the veil was Zahra Rahnavard, wife of the former Prime Minister Mir Hussein Mousavi. In the sixties she wore miniskirts. Today she wears the most severe form of Islamic dress and is a fundamentalist ideologue. "Our *hijab* was a symbol of our resistance against the Shah," she said. Rahnavard, a playwright and university lecturer, insists women in the West have been enslaved by fashion, makeup, and turned into objects of sexual attention. "The veil frees women from the shackles of fashion, and enables them to become human beings in their own right," she claimed. "Once people cease to be distracted by women's physical appearance, they can begin to hear their views and recognize the inner person."

"The establishment of an Islamic regime in Iran in 1979 had a devastating effect on the status of women," said Eliz Sanasarian, an Iranian-born professor who now teaches at the University of Southern California. "Despite this, many Muslim women rallied behind these clerics, and became the spokespersons as well as the implementers of the fundamentalists' view on women." Many academics saw this as a reaction to the widespread corruption, decadence, and brutal oppression by SAVAK, Iran's secret police, that marked the last years of the Shah.

In the early days of the Revolution, women were removed from the workplace en masse. The Islamic Council of Guardians decreed that "a woman does not have the right to leave her home without her husband's permission, not even to attend her father's funeral procession. A woman is completely at the service of her husband, and her social activities are conditional upon her husband's permission."

All schools were immediately segregrated by gender and women were barred from vocational training schools and banned from studying engineering, mining, and agriculture. The latter was particularly ironic as two-thirds of Iran's women then lived in rural areas and performed much of the agricultural labor.

Child-care centers were closed, and at the same time the *ulema* banned birth control. The clerics insisted that procreation was essential, particularly to replace Iranians lost in the eight-year war. The birthrate soared, and the country's population leaped from thirty-seven million in 1978 to nearly sixty million today. When Iran's population growth rate hit nearly four percent, then the highest in the world, the clerics reversed the ban, but contraceptives are still difficult to obtain in much of the country.

Khomeini lowered the marriage age for females from eighteen to thirteen, but permitted girls as young as nine, even seven in some cases, to be married if a physician signs a certificate agreeing to their sexual maturity. "In his book *Tahrir Al'Vassilih*, Khomeini writes about the legal requirement for having sex with children," explained a woman lawyer who is concerned that child brides are dying since this ruling was instituted. "In villages where child marriage is most common, doctors often don't even see the girl," she told me. "They just take the family's word that she is physically mature enough to marry. Consequently, we have had very young girls badly injured when they have had what amounts to forced intercourse. Infection sets in and they have died."

"Only with girls under seven did the Ayatollah say that sex was forbidden." The lawyer was reluctant to give her name as women only recently have been allowed to practice law again. Women lawyers and judges were banned at the beginning of the Revolution, and Iran still has only male judges, most of whom are mullahs.

Other changes that were made by the regime concerning marriage included husbands being able to divorce their wives legally without their consent or without informing them beforehand, whereas divorce for women was made almost impossible to obtain. "Women were not given the right to instigate divorce because they are prone to emotional and irrational decision making," said the head of Iran's Supreme Court, Ayatollah Ali Moghtadai in 1992. The law requiring a husband to have his wife's consent before taking a second wife was reversed. Child custody was given to the husband after the child was over the age of two, and if the husband died, the child went to his or her paternal grandfather. To this day, the mother is not considered a suitable guardian in Iran. Similarly, in a divorce case, any property goes to the husband's father should the husband die.

Under Khomeini, adultery was strictly outlawed, and punishable by flogging or death by stoning. And men were legally permitted to kill their wives if they were unfaithful, which led to cases of women being killed when spouses were suspicious only.

Couples today are still stopped on the street or in a car and asked to produce documents proving that they are closely related, such as husband and wife, father and daughter, or brother and sister. Unrelated men and women are forbidden to be together. Women have been banned from attending soccer games because the players wear shorts. Even Tehran's ski slopes are segregated, despite the fact that women skiers are required to wear Islamic dress over their thick ski clothes.

Young unmarried women found at parties are given automatic virginity tests. If found not to be virgo-intacta, they are given a choice of one hundred lashes or forcibly marrying the man they are with at the party. In the fall of 1991, in a well-publicized incident, Revolutionary Guards burst into a private home in Zafaraniyeh district of Tehran and arrested seventy youngsters aged sixteen to twenty-three. "The girls were wearing short skirts, and there was a little alcohol," said Mehnaz, whose sister was involved. "They weren't even dancing to smuggled Western cassettes, as often happens, but they took all of them into custody and kept them for seven days. The girls were all photographed in their miniskirts, no doubt as evidence of their moral decay. Then they were tested for virginity, and five who were found not to be were forced to get married. The authorities seem to think as long as everything is legalized, things are fine."

The Islamic Republic had a different approach to virgins who were jailed and sentenced to death under anti-Islamic charges during the Revolution. Since virgins, like martyrs, are believed to go to Paradise automatically, the clerics wanted to make sure these young women did not. The regime ruled that any unmarried girl or woman who was condemned to die must first lose her virginity through rape or temporary *Mut'a* marriage to the guards. The practice was lambasted by Amnesty International in a report in 1986. The number of such cases is unknown, but in the first three years of the Revolution, twenty thousand girls and women were executed. Khomeini set the legal minimum age of execution at nine years for girls, and sixteen for boys.

Temporary *Mut'a* marriages are permitted only under Shi'a Islam; Sunni Islam banned them in the seventh century. They are contracts agreed on between two people that can last as long as the couple desire, from "one hour to ninety-nine years." At the end of the stipulated period, the union automatically ends without a divorce being necessary. A Shi'a male may have as many *Mut'a* wives as he chooses, in addition to the four wives he is legally permitted under Muslim law. A single Shi'a woman is permitted only one temporary marriage at a time.

Mut'a marriage was historically intended for men who were away at war or traveling with camel caravans for months, possibly years. Unable to take their families with them, it was an institution created to avoid prostitution. The practice was banned under the Shah, and brought back by Khomeini, who called it "a brilliant law of Islam," and considered it the appropriate Islamic solution to resolving men's "need" for multiple sexual partners. President Rafsanjani angered Iranian women in 1990 when he endorsed temporary marriages and stated they were not un-Islamic.

It is commonly accepted in Iranian society that *Mut'a* marriages are now predominantly employed by prostitutes. None of the clerics has addressed the possibility of AIDS' being spread through temporary marriage, though the health authorities of Iran acknowledge that there are at least eighteen known cases of AIDS in the country. Being out of touch with the real world is a charge often leveled at

Iran's mullah government. The workings of the state are defined by men who have barely traveled and whose education and energies throughout their life have been devoted predominantly to Shi'a Islam.

The world's oldest profession began to adopt *Mut'a* marriages as a way of doing business when Khomeini changed the penalty for prostitution to death by stoning without a trial. The first two women to be executed for this crime after the regime came to power were buried up to their necks and then had small stones thrown at them so they would die slowly. Despite this gruesome punishment, prostitution has increased recently in Iran because the economic situation is so severe people are struggling to survive.

• • •

Despite the many restrictions on them, Iranian women refuse to be cowed. Among the most educated of all Muslim woman, they can often be outspoken and determined. I was introduced to Nazila Noebashari two days before her wedding. A dynamic and intelligent twenty-six-year-old, she manages her father's company. She had just spent the afternoon at her lawyer's office having a marriage contract drawn up that permitted her the right to divorce. "It may seem a very strange thing to do just before your wedding day," she told me. "But unless I have the right to divorce written into my marriage contract, I would have to prove my husband is insane or has not lived with me for many years before a court would grant me a divorce.

"A close friend of mine has been trying to get a divorce for three years and so far the court has not approved it. Her husband went to America, and when she flew to join him, he didn't even bother to pick her up at the airport. He was out every night with different girlfriends, and finally moved in with a woman with whom he has a baby. He doesn't want his wife, but he doesn't want to divorce her. It was an arranged marriage and he doesn't want to anger his family by formally divorcing her. There is nothing his wife can do. She is stuck. And I am determined this will not happen to me. Divorce was a right granted me and other Muslim women fourteen hundred years ago.

"If I have the right to sign large checks and contracts in business as I do, I have the right to obtain a divorce if my marriage isn't working. I know this will be difficult for my fiancé to digest. He will be angry, but I hope eventually he will understand. I don't want a divorce tomorrow. I may never want one. But I am not a woman of the Middle Ages, and I hope he will respect what I have done."

Nazila sat back and then giggled. "Don't let people tell you life for Iranian women is all pessimistic. We still do a lot of things, we still travel. We dress how we like underneath these manteaus; my mother dresses like a duchess at home." Nazila looked more as though she shopped at The Gap, her sweater-and-pants combination giving her a certain yuppie air, as did her aviator glasses, and her electronic notebook in which she keeps all her appointments. She smiled again, "My mother is absolute ruler in our house."

And then she made a comment I heard from many Iranian women: "I think Persian husbands are very different from Arab husbands. Men and women are more equal with each other in personal relations. It is not uncommon here to see a man out carrying his baby. Couples do things together — that is rare in the Arab world. Even wife abuse is not so common here."

Women like Mina, aged fifty-two, also see Iranian women as strong. A former academic, she explained that she and her husband, also a professor, were "purged" at the beginning of the Revolution. "I went to work one day in early 1980 and found my name on a list of people said to be unfit to work at the university. I just left the building and never went back. I didn't even ask them why. My husband lost his job in a similar fashion. But he dealt with it very well. I remember him telling me, 'It is correct that they throw us out. We don't belong to them, their movement. Now they have to have their own place, their own position.'

"We couldn't work for the next three years, and we had no income. Thank God we had built our house years before. My in-laws supported us, but nevertheless it was a very difficult time, with considerable hardships. I call it our Persepolis [the ancient capital of Persia razed by Alexander the Great]. My husband never complained or grumbled.

"But I watched the men my friends were married to who had undergone similar experiences, those who had been executives or had held good government positions. Once these men lost their jobs, they completely lost their bearings. Stripped of all their advantages, they became frozen. You could see men walking the streets of the city in a daze. The blow came so quickly, they couldn't absorb it, and in many cases it paralyzed them.

"It was these men's wives who suddenly became the breadwinners, even women who had never worked before. They started businesses from their homes, cooking, sewing, making things, anything, so the family could eat. The women became the core of the family, and held it together. I was amazed how strong and resourceful they turned out to be. I am not sure that the men in that class in this country have recovered yet. Women on the other hand have become more self-confident. Because of the suppression, they've accumulated such strength to survive."

Mina and her husband also started their own business, which she asked me not to describe for fear it might identify them. "You know, the Islamic Revolution cost heavily, but it also had some definite pluses. Certainly, life was more affluent before the Revolution. Children were better educated, better fed, the health care was better; these systems have broken down in Iran under the mullahs. Under the Shah, however, life was a big fake, every aspect of it. Morally, mentally, this nation was bankrupt. The Revolution has been like a gold assay, to find out what is real and what is not. Friendship particularly has been tested during this time.

"Yes, the price of this revolution has been very, very high. But Iranians have also discovered values, dignity, and principles they had forgotten or buried."

Mina, most of whose friends are academics like her, or writers and artists, attributes the Revolution with bringing about a cultural revival in Iran. "Artistically, culturally, this country was pauperized under the Shah," she said. "Life revolved around materialism — spend, spend, spend. Iranians were decadent and very superficial. People went from parties to nightclubs to discos to bars, and if they had any free time, they watched trash on TV. They can't do any of those things anymore, and so they began to read. They were looking for clues about what had gone wrong. Today, they are so much better informed.

"We become so biased when criticizing our enemy, we tend to forget they may have some positive points. We focus on the pain, the despair, the bleeding, and certainly, this Islamic Revolution has had all of that. There are times when it has been nightmarish. Perhaps, however, one has to be sick sometimes to become healthier."

One of Iran's better-known women writers, Moniroo Ravanipoor, who would seem to have reason only to criticize the regime, sees its positive points as well. Ravanipoor, aged thirty-eight, was jailed at the beginning of the Revolution, and recently her books were banned. Yet despite this, she can still say, "The Shah gave us illusion, nothing but illusion. Iran was like a decaying building, it was collapsing and crumbling, but under the Shah the government kept covering the damage with paint. The Revolution stripped away the paint so that we were looking at the actual construction, and we could see it wasn't stable. Thirteen years ago, we touched our history, and our rot. We are stronger now."

• • •

Call for change in Iran for women has come from some unlikely quarters recently. In October 1992, Khomeini's oldest daughter, Zahra Moustafavi, a professor of philosophy at Tehran University, and president of the Iranian Women's Association, who in the past has always supported her father's doctrines, spoke out briefly. "Islam gives men and women equal rights. If a woman wants to work outside the home, Islamic law allows her to, but the obstacle is the man. . . . There should be a revolution of women in the home. They must rebel against some men."

Moustafavi, who is still "very involved in politics," works from early in the morning until midnight most days, often not stopping for lunch until 6:00 P.M. "I have always worked," she said. "Even when my children were growing up. It didn't occur to me to stay home. There is nothing in Islam that prevents women from working. Even during the Iran-Iraq War, women's work was a real support to men."

Moustafavi describes her father as having been "humorous, kind, and affectionate" to his family. During Khomeini's exile under the Shah, Moustafavi was charged with recording his speeches and distributing the tapes throughout Iran. Today, she sees her major role as helping families develop "moral understanding." She believes there is no discrimination between men and women in Islam. "If a woman is doing the same work as a man, she should enjoy the same salary and the same advantages. And for working mothers, they should have nurseries, and the right to work three days a week for half salary."

On political issues, Moustafavi said, "The Iranian woman has the right to vote and be elected to any level. If she has not reached a ministerial level, it is because she has not had the right qualifications."

President Rafsanjani has said publicly that women, half the country's human resources, should be utilized to full potential to assist Iran in becoming more productive. But a secret report in 1992 by a special commission for Iran's Supreme Council on Security listed women, along with ethnic minorities and corruption, as potential threats to national security.

Despite being reelected in 1993, President Rafsanjani has been seen as losing ground in the power arena. Never the liberal progressive his foreign supporters made him out to be, Rafsanjani had appeared more forward thinking, less insular, than his colleagues because he recognized that Iran needed to regain international respectability in order to attract foreign investment and technology to jump-start its economy. Recently, however, there have been signals of a clerical backlash against his rapprochement program with the West. The coalition he put together fell apart almost immediately, with fellow clerics, including Ayatollah Khomeini, abandoning him. Indications were strong that his authority was being limited to defining economic policy. Ayatollah Khomeini was seen as taking over the controls of foreign policy, internal security, and cultural affairs — all areas that his predecessor, Khomeini, had dominated.

Around the same time, the hard-liners refused to abrogate the death sentence against writer Salman Rushdie, and instead doubled the reward for killing him to more than $2 million. The move was seen by Western diplomats in Tehran to reflect the power struggle in the Iranian government between the West xenophobes among the arch-Islamists, and those who want to open dialogue with the West. Because Rushdie was born a Muslim, Khomeini had charged him with apostasy.

Rushdie's book *The Satanic Verses* was perceived as insulting the Prophet's wives. For a Muslim, also, the title of Rushdie's book was perhaps a poor choice. "Satanic Verses" is the name given to a revelation to Prophet Mohammad, which he later recognized as being imparted to him by the devil. References to these verses have been expunged from most commonly available Korans. Under Islam, it is considered an unforgivable sin to refer to the story contained in the verses. A Muslim who repeats the verses commits apostasy.

The reason given by many analysts for the government's apparent reversal to Khomeini-era rigidity is Iran's moribund economy, which has caused soaring inflation and rioting in a number of cities in the last couple of years. In 1992, Rafsanjani admitted that since the clerical regime had been in power they had failed to alleviate any fundamental economic problems. He acknowledged that government institutions were riddled with passivity and doubts. The clerics may be unresponsive to the country's everyday needs, but Iranians are increasingly demonstrating their anger.

While I was in Iran, there were major riots in Mashad, one of the country's most famous pilgrimage cities. A reported 112 rioters were executed after city authorities demolished makeshift homes on the outskirts of the city. In the weeks preceding my trip, other Iranian cities — Tabriz, Arak, Shiraz, Ardebil, and Natanz — all experienced similar violence resulting in the execution of scores of demonstrators and the arrest of thousands. Tehran has also seen repeated rioting in the last two years on its southern border, because, as in Mashad, the government has demolished shanties. Iran's cities have a dramatic shortage of affordable housing. Even middle-class couples live in dread of a lease coming to an end because a rental deposit for the average apartment is now running the equivalent of five or six years' salary. For unskilled workers, many of whom have moved to Tehran in the last decade from rural areas, the only housing available are shanties they build themselves. Most shanties do not have water or electricity.

The move from the countryside to the cities started at the beginning of the Revolution because of the lack of good seed, farming implements or spare parts, and water, as irrigation systems fell into disrepair. Many of Iran's industries have also seen production markedly diminish, partly because Western embargoes on exports to Iran have caused major shortages of spare parts. The regime's own statistics show that heavy industry is functioning at 25 percent of its pre-Revolutionary capacity.

A country that was once sufficient in food production now has major shortages. While I was in Iran, milk was impossible to find, and sugar and cooking oil were rationed. Meat was available, but at $5 a kilogram, a schoolteacher earning a government salary of $70 a month could not afford to buy it. At the bazaar near the house where I was staying, bread was often in short supply. Ironically, in the same shopping district, however, I saw Lancôme cosmetics, Vidal Sassoon shampoo, and Retin-A on sale. A severe hardship for the last two winters in Iran has been an acute shortage of kerosene, used to heat many Iranian homes; winter temperatures often drop below freezing. Alcohol, however, was available at a substantial price. Iran's Christian Armenian population is permitted to produce it for their own consumption, and much of it finds its way to Muslim customers. The raisin-based moonshine sells for $1.50 a bottle. Imported wine or whiskey, which is smuggled into the country, was running at $70 a bottle.

Government employees receive a variety of benefits ranging from subsidized food, medical care, and housing to sports facilities, but they, too, are frequently forced to take two or three jobs to make ends meet. Car owners use their vehicles as gypsy cabs, and every street corner is peopled with men and veiled women selling cigarettes singly or in packs. Homelessness in Tehran has increased, and I was frequently accosted by beggars of both sexes.

"This is a country of tremendous resources and well-educated technocrats and professionals," one woman physician told me, "and yet right now before we can do surgery we have to ask the patient's family to supply equipment, even surgical gowns. There is also a dramatic shortage of syringes and insulin. The uneducated mullahs in the government seem to have no idea how to run the country; instead they are running it into the ground. The great Islamic Utopian bubble has burst." By 1993, government officials admitted that serious and often fatal diseases, such as tuberculosis, anthrax, and rabies, had grown to alarming proportions in Iran.

The U.S. dollar, which has an official exchange rate of 70 rials, trades at twenty times that level. Black market money changers were offering upward of Rials 1,400 for the dollar when I was there.

One body that feels it can do a better job of running the country, and that received American congressional support in 1992, is the National Council of Resistance, made up mostly of the People's Mujahideen of Iran. The organization, which has its own National Liberation Army of forty thousand troops, was founded in 1965 to oppose the Shah, but was little known outside Iran for many years. As an Islamic movement committed to secular democracy, it then dedicated itself to overthrowing the clerics' regime, which it claims has betrayed the Iranian people. "The mullahs are facing a tremendous crisis," said Mohammad Mohadessin, head of the movement's foreign affairs department. "The regime's economy is on the brink of bankruptcy with enormous foreign and domestic debt, 50 percent inflation, and unemployment created entirely by the mullahs."

The *mujahideen* organization is jointly run by husband and wife Massoud and Maryam Rajavi. Maryam Rajavi is a thirty-nine-year-old former metallurgical engineer, and she has been instrumental in mobilizing Iranian women against two suppressive regimes. One of her sisters, Nargass, was executed in 1975 by the Shah's SAVAK secret police. Another sister, Massoumeh, was executed while pregnant by Khomeini's regime in 1982, as was her husband. If caught, Maryam's fate would be the same.

The organization, which has attracted many highly educated Iranians, boasts that 40 percent of its 837-member Central Executive Council are women, as are one-third of its troops and half of its military leadership. And the general of the forty thousand–strong National Liberation Army is a woman. As deputy commander-in-chief, Maryam Rajavi is credited with mechanizing the six-year-old NLA, which by standards of resistance movements the world over has an impressive display of might. Based just across the border from Iran in Eastern Iraq, Maryam's forces boast 140 British-, Soviet-, and Chinese-made tanks, and entire tank units comprised only of women. They have scores of heavy artillery pieces, dozens of armored personnel carriers, and batteries of rocket launchers, much of which was captured from Iranian government forces.

The NLA has made a number of successful military strikes against the regime, but its largest offensive was a 150-kilometer thrust into Iran in 1988. Military observers say it is the only army in the world that deploys its female combatants in the front lines of battle. During four days of intense fighting, the *mujahideen* lost eleven hundred soldiers, a number of them women, and claims to have inflicted thousands of casualties, wounded or dead, on Iranian forces.

The NLA's female *mujahideen* make Rafsanjani's comments on women seem farcical. In a 1986 interview with an Iranian newspaper he said: "The regime's officials believe that men are stronger and more capable than women in every regard. The differences in height, sturdiness, voice, growth, muscular structure, and physical strength, endurance of hardships and illnesses in women and men show that men are stronger and more capable in all of these regards. Men heed reasoning and logic, whereas women tend to be emotional. The urge to protect, as well as courage and daring are stronger in men. These differences affect the delegation of responsibilities, duties, and rights."

The Iranian regime has consistently stressed that the best job for a women is to take care of her home and children. "This is basically why there are no women in any of the decision-making organs of the regime's judicial and executive branches," says Maryam Rajavi, "and why there are only a few women in the Parliament — all of whom share the mullahs' views."

She also feels that it is not enough to provide legal safeguards for equality. "Equality must be realized in all aspects of political, social, and family life in a realistic and nonformalistic manner. The rights of women should not be observed out of compassion, or in a purely theoretical sense, but on the basis of the reality of their equality with men."

More recently, the People's Mujahideen of Iran launched a campaign to "expose the huge arms purchases by the regime, including nuclear and chemical projects." Rafsanjani admitted allocating more of the budget to arms purchases now than during the eight-year Iran-Iraq War. In 1992, Iran took delivery of three stealth-type Russian submarines and is negotiating for more. Iran observers are concerned that these super-quiet submarines could create havoc in the Persian Gulf, and in the nearby sea lanes through which tankers transport oil to the industrial world. Iran has also purchased scores of MIG fighters and Sukhoi bombers, and hundreds of North Korean SCUD missiles, more than four hundred top-of-the-line tanks, and armored personnel carriers. Following the *mujahideen*'s revelations on Iran's program to produce nuclear weapons, mostly with China's help, Germany formally suspended its nuclear cooperation with the regime.

Money for Iran's new arms buildup comes from its oil industry, which currently produces only 58 percent of its pre-Revolutionary capacity. Said one European diplomat, "Iran's oil industry, however, is struggling and is nowhere near as efficient as it used to be. Their production has dropped from 6 million barrels a day to a current 3.5 million. Oil prices are substantially lower on the world market, extraction is proving more expensive, and the country has also increased its population by 62 percent in the same period." The major customer for Iranian oil is Japan, and in 1993, Iran also began supplying Cuba.

U.S. officials confirmed that Iran is known to be seeking two large nuclear reactors from the former Soviet Union. According to a Washington, D.C.–based *mujahideen* spokesman, Alireza Jafarzadeh, "a number of nuclear experts from the republics of the former Soviet Union are in Iran to advance its nuclear project."

Shortly after the *mujahideen* disclosures, the U.S. House of Representatives and the Senate called for support of the National Council of Resistance of Iran. A 1992 congressional statement said: "The NCR, and the NLC, backed by the populace, and in step with strikes and demonstrations in Iran, is capable of establishing freedom and democracy in Iran. Due to Iran's economic bankruptcy and internal crises, the Rafsanjani regime is obliged as never before to oppose regional peace, and to export terrorism and fundamentalism abroad. . . . The dramatic increase in Iran's official public executions, a new wave of suppression of women, and terrorism abroad, has thus ended the myth of Rafsanjani's moderation."

By mid-1993, the Clinton administration was taking a "wait and see" position regarding the Iranian Resistance. The U.S. State Department has refused to meet with delegations from the NCR since the days the Shah labeled his opposition socialist. Shortly before he became Vice-President, however, Al Gore did meet with the *mujahideen* leadership. And based on the reports of the massive rearming of Iran by the hard-liner government, the United States concluded that Iran must be isolated politically and economically, in the same way as Iraq is treated, until it curtails its military buildup, including its quest for nuclear weapons, and halts its support of fundamentalist terrorism in the Islamic world.

In recent years, Iranian-trained militants have launched terrorist attacks in Egypt, and through Hamas and Lebanon's Party of God, have attempted to disrupt violently the Middle East peace talks. In the newly independent Central Asian states, Iran also has been establishing a political presence. Another target for Tehran is Islamic Africa, where it would like to see the establishment of a chain of Islamic theocratic states from Sudan to Algeria.

• • •

On June 4, 1992, Iran observed the third anniversary of Khomeini's death. I decided to join the throngs of mourners at the cemetery where he is buried. Sima and Qasim, the young couple who offered to take me, recommended we leave early. Sima cautioned, "Please wear only black, no jewelry and no makeup, not even mascara. Your scarf should be tied tightly over your forehead. This is not the place to get caught with any hair showing," she said.

As we drove through the city, Tehran was just waking up. Behesht-e-Zahra, the vast martyrs' cemetery where Khomeini is buried, is just south of Tehran. The government has plans to turn the area around the Ayatollah's tomb into a park and build a religious university, hotels, and a large shopping center. The residents in Tehran's shanty towns not so far away feel the money would be better spent piping water and electricity to their homes.

Behesht-e-Zahra is the final resting place of thousands of the one million troop casualties of the Iran-Iraq War, some of them as young as twelve. Normally, a forty-five-minute ride from the part of Tehran where I was staying, the trip that day took two-and-a-half hours. As we reached the industrial part of the city, we found ourselves in heavy traffic jams with hundreds of buses, trucks, cars, and taxis crammed with black-garbed passengers and all heading to the same location.

Thousands of families had been camping out for days at the cemetery, their blankets, food, water containers, and ubiquitous red plastic shopping baskets spread on footpaths or between graves. We passed the infamous fountain of blood, which had flowed with gruesomely realistic crimson water throughout the Iran-Iraq War to symbolize the blood of the fallen.

Sima, Qasim, and I joined the masses of somber-faced, black-garbed mourners. Soon a long phalanx of *Pasdaran* with bullhorns began to divide the crowds, men on the right, women on the left. In Iran, even grieving is segregated. As soon as we were herded into the large courtyard reserved for women, the mood of the crowd changed. Thousands of women separated into family units, staked out with blankets or plastic rugs and overrun by hordes of grubby children. The youngsters, even the toddlers, were wearing *chadors* and most carried placards of Khomeini. Overlooking us were sixty-foot-high banners of a sometimes avuncular, sometimes fierce Khomeini hanging from every mosque wall. Despite these and the taciturn Revolutionary Guards attempting crowd control, the place began to resemble a picnic, one that might perhaps have been staged by Fellini, and the day took on a holiday air.

An elderly woman with only two teeth remaining, one of them gold, unwrapped a grubby white cloth, and offered me some of the coarse flat bread and homemade yogurt she had brought from home. Both were far superior in taste than what we had been eating in Tehran. She told me she had been at the cemetery for three days and had traveled from her village by bus. "It takes seventeen hours," she said, "a long way, but it is worth it. This is the third year I have come." Her leathery hand clutched mine as she said, "The Imam in heaven can see that Iran has not forgotten him. This country was Godless before. Imam Khomeini saved us from damnation. He could have saved the world, but he died too soon. He is the holiest man this country has seen in my lifetime. And I miss him. Iran misses him."

As I sat, women around me touched their heads to the ground in prayer and I realized that Iran is a Muslim country where outside the mosques and people's homes you rarely see anyone pray. In other Muslim countries, at prayer time it is common to see workers stop by the side of the street, or cars and buses disgorge their passengers, who unfurl small prayer mats or scarves before bowing to Mecca. Similarly, in Tehran, *azan,* the muezzin's call to prayer, is heard much less often. In most Muslim countries, the echoes of *azan* reverberating from one mosque to its neighbor fills the air at prayer time. In Tehran, however, in the late sixties, more secular citizens complained that the prayer calls were waking babies and invalids. The mosques were ordered to turn the volume down. It was one ruling the Ayatollah didn't reverse.

In the courtyard of Khomeini's shrine I spotted a team of ten men with what looked like fumigating tanks on their backs spraying the crowd. I wondered whether the Ayatollah, like Rafsanjani, had objected to the odor of the unwashed if loyal masses. In the pulpit at Friday prayers of the Tehran University mosque the previous year, Rafsanjani had told the faithful to stop using piety as an excuse for unkemptness. "When you go to some mosques the smell of bare feet is repugnant," he said. The fumigating tanks, however, held rosewater, which is commonly used at Iranian funerals to spray mourners.

A young woman nearby who had only her eyes uncovered, and who had apparently overheard me talking English to Sima, leaned over shyly to ask me in stumbling English where I was from and why I had come today. "I am here only because our school bused us here. It was required," she told me. "The government pays for buses to bring people from the schools, colleges, factories. They even go to the villages. The factory workers get double salary to make sure they come." Dropping her voice, she added, "Otherwise no one would be here . . . well, many fewer than today."

Not sure if she had convinced me, she added, still whispering, "Do you think I dress like this at home? No, of course, I don't." And to prove it she flashed open her *chador* to show me her jeans and lavender T-shirt underneath. "I hate it, hate all this. I am sixteen, this is my time, my youth, I should be having fun. Instead, I am here, dressed like a peasant grandmother, to mourn a dead old man who hated beauty, hated happiness. If God meant us to dress in black, if he meant us to have no color in our lives, why did he give us flowers? That's what I would like to have asked that dead Imam," she said, jerking her head in the direction of the shrine.

Suddenly she realized that Sima was beginning to look uncomfortable with the conversation. Flustered, the teenager tightened her *chador* over her nose, said a rushed, "I apologize, forgive me," and turned tail into the crowd.

• • •

Just as New York is not America, Tehran is not Iran. Iran is a large country stretching 2,250 kilometers across from Afghanistan and Pakistan in the east to Turkey and Iraq in the west. When a new friend, Mehri, offered a trip to Isfahan and Qom, the holy city where Khomeini was educated and taught, I agreed.

Between Tehran and Qom there is a new freeway built by Khomeini to facilitate travel to the holy city. Shortly before Qom, the highway passes the large Daryache-Ye-Namak (Salt Lake), which marks the edge of the Salt Desert. Its surface shone like snow. Mehri refused to tour the city with me. "No, no, you go, I am not properly dressed. They are very strict here," she said apologetically. In Qom, all women wore the severe black *chador* and *hijab*, most also covered their faces. Mehri's concern was that her khaki Burberry-type manteau would be unacceptable. "There are probably more hard-line mullahs in Qom than in any other place on earth," she said.

The city has been a major center for Shi'a scholarship for centuries. The domes and minarets of its many mosques dominate the skyline. Qom's main industry is producing mullahs. Khomeini was arrested here and exiled from Iran in the sixties after helping to incite heavy rioting against the Shah's reforms, particularly those concerning women.

Qom was heavily bombed repeatedly by the Iraqis during the war, striking at what they considered the country's spiritual heart. Four years after the ceasefire it was hard to spot war damage, just as it was in Tehran, which had also been shelled regularly. Apart from the mosques and the many mullahs on the streets, the most prominent feature was all the storefronts and house walls painted the same Islamic green and white by order of the city fathers.

Qom is a city that strictly adheres to Khomeini's maxim "There is no fun in Islam." The religious center and its citizens are serious, solemn. Even the city's famous souvenir is as somber as the late Ayatollah used to be. Burial shrouds are the main tourist purchase in Qom, as they are considered more holy from this city of Islamic learning, and many Iranians purchase them on visits to the city to keep for their deaths.

Since non-Muslims are forbidden to enter the shrine of Qom, we didn't stay long in the city, and Mehri was relieved to go. We left the freeway behind and began meandering through the countryside, most of it arid and dun-colored. By accident we found ourselves in the village of Abayaneh, an ancient red adobe community that predates Islam to the Zoroastrian fire-worshipers, the religion of the Magi, the biblical three wise men from the East who traveled to Bethlehem for the birth of Christ. The village had been on tour bus routes before the Revolution. Today, it was a sleepy backwater of pomegranate gardens and cherry orchards. Like many Iranian villages it was semiabandoned, and a number of the mud houses were beginning to crumble, their shutters swinging at odd angles in the breeze.

The only difference the Islamic Revolution made here is that the tour buses no longer come. The women, who didn't know who Rafsanjani was, still stitched replicas of their brightly colored clothes that they used to sell to tourists as souvenirs. In Abayaneh, the *chadors* were scarlet and covered in flowers, and they were worn because of tradition, not because of Tehran-made law. Zahra, a woman who invited us for lunch of corn bread, cucumbers, and yogurt, pointed to the stack of full skirts and embroidered tunics she had been making in the long winter evenings "because one day the foreigners will come back." With the simple wisdom of countryfolk everywhere, she said, "Nothing lasts, all things change, even revolutions end."

CHAPTER 6

United Arab Emirates: The Playground of the Gulf

*A man loves first his son, then his camel,
and then his wife.*

ARAB PROVERB

ARRIVING AT DUBAI AIRPORT after a two-hour flight from Tehran is a little like landing on Mars; it feels many light-years away from Khomeini-style controls. The ultra-modern airport whisks travelers through immigration in minutes, and baggage is already waiting. Why waste time when passengers could be shopping at the boutiques in the baggage hall? With arguably the best duty-free shopping in the world, the Dubai government sees no reason that incoming passengers should not be offered the same bargains as outgoing travelers: Baume & Mercier, Piaget, Christian Dior — names reminiscent of Rodeo Drive — are all available, and a precursor to the conspicuous consumption that epitomizes this superwealthy but minuscule Gulf state.

In Dubai I found myself overdressed for the first time since beginning my travels in the Islamic world. Everywhere I looked there seemed to be suntanned female flesh displayed under backless T-shirts, spaghetti-strapped mini-sundresses, even shorts. In Miami, no one would have looked twice. After Iran, it was like wandering into a photo shoot for *Playboy* magazine.

Admittedly, all of these women were foreigners, but they set the tone for the rest of the principality, where Islamic pragmatism has been raised to a fine art. Eighty-five percent of the Emirates population is expatriate. Pakistanis, Indians, Sri Lankans, and Filipinos are the house servants, drivers, and construction laborers. Americans and Europeans supply the know-how and the managerial skills. It is for the latter group that superb five-star restaurants offer extensive alcohol lists, and supermarket chains have entire sections given over to pork items. Standing in front of the sign reading "For non-Muslims only," I marveled at the honor system operating here.

There is much to marvel at in Dubai, the second-largest of seven tiny sheikhdoms that makes up the United Arab Emirates, which nestle between Oman and Qatar, and are across the Strait of Hormuz from Iran. Twenty years ago Dubai was little more than sand. Today, it is a cross between Beverly Hills and Miami Beach. Tinted-glass office buildings and futuristic apartment houses give way to whole neighborhoods of deluxe villas, which rent for upwards of $4,000 a month, and are interspersed with occasional palaces. Beachfront complexes, right down to their bathroom fixtures, seem to have been imported in their entirety from Palm Beach, Florida.

Traffic appears to consist wholly of BMWs, Ferraris, and Mercedes, along with Jeeps and Landcruisers, plus a fleet of Toyota Cressida taxis. Four-wheel-drive vehicles are used here for a weekend activity known as "Wadi-bashing," going off the beaten track to the desert, where sand dunes can drop as steeply as cliffs.

Telecommunication is first-rate, and business cards are crammed with the numbers of telephones, mobile phones, faxes, and beepers. At the Dubai Men's College of Technology, students are now required to check mobile phones and beepers on entering because lectures were being constantly interrrupted.

In this shop-till-you-drop Neiman-Marcus environment, there are more multistory air-conditioned malls than the population warrants, with new ones under construction. The number of banks and jewelry stores per capita is the highest in the world, but so is the discretionary income. A Dubai Citibank official told me of a sheikh who had recently spent $30 million on jewelry for his new wife. But this is small potatoes compared to the ruler's annual gardening budget; Sheikh Maktoum Bin Rashid Al-Maktoum loves trees and flowers, and has been spending a fortune turning his 3,900-square-kilometer desert sheikhdom lushly green. And, as part of the sheikh's greening-of-the-desert program, Dubai now exports strawberries to Europe.

The UAE's seven-channel television, which shows a medley of British and American soap operas and series, is uncensored. And the ubiquitous video rental stores cater to a Western audience. The American veneer of the Emirates is one reason that Khomeini referred to its ruling sheikhs as "Puppets of the Great Satan, America." In fact, the UAE has so many Western comforts overlaid with all the opulence petro-dollars can purchase, it comes as a surprise to open a copy of *Time* magazine and find a photograph of a Rubens nude blacked out by the censor. Despite the Emirates' liberal television viewing practices, local newspapers are strictly censored. The *Khaleej Times,* one of the two English-language dailies, resembles in content a British guts-and-gossip tabloid minus the topless models. On closer examination, all the Hollywood gossip is there, but any news that reflects badly on or offends the government — corruption, mismanagement, rape, or AIDS — is not. The *Khaleej Times*'s competitor, the *Gulf News,* ran afoul of the government several years ago when it published an article on the increase of AIDS in the Emirates. Journalists claim they were told they could write about AIDS in general but they were forbidden to be specific about the situation locally, and if they were, the paper was threatened with closure.

Medical personnel describe the Emirates as the AIDS capital of the Gulf. And while statistics are not published and are believed still to be low compared to many countries, they talk of delivering HIV babies, of HIV-positive foreign prostitutes being deported, and of the incidence of AIDS caused by contaminated blood that was imported from the United States before the days of screening. Doctors and nurses agree that the major cause of AIDS among the Arab population in this Gulf Peninsula is packaged sex tours to Bangkok's brothels and nightclubs, where more than 90 percent of the prostitutes are known to be infected with AIDS.

Major hospitals in Dubai now have AIDS-awareness programs and patients are routinely checked for HIV on admission. One doctor told me, "Young men here have so much money, they are being spoiled. They can either afford to visit foreign prostitutes locally, or they regularly go to Thailand on sex tours." A nurse in a women's hospital added, "We have seen whole families who have tested positive. The women here are so ignorant on these matters, and the men have such totally separate lives, that wives have no idea what their husbands are doing.

"I'm particularly concerned about my sister-in-law. Her husband is always going to Bangkok with his friends and everyone in the family knows why. I've tried to explain to her that it is only a matter of time before he and then she is infected. I said, 'You're an absolute fool if you do nothing about it.' Her response to me was, 'Yes, I know what he is doing, but what can I do? He is a man. It is in God's hands.'"

Soaring drug abuse is a subject the government does discuss

openly from time to time, claiming the nation's youth is "led astray by the effects of affluence." Fouzya Ghobash, an undersecretary of Youth Rehabilitation feels that oil revenues — which have brought about better social and economic conditions — have also led to a dramatic increase in the last six years in drug abuse. "In Western countries, the poorer segment of society tends to resort to narcotics. In the UAE, it is our wealthy youths who are involved. And they are not only drug addicts, they are also pushing drugs, and trading in narcotics." Dubai now has a hospital dealing only with drug-addicted patients. In a comment that sounds remarkably Western, Ghobash blames a lack of parental guidance for leaving the country's children "in social turmoil." He continues, "Parents, particularly fathers, are too busy to monitor their offspring."

Dr. Naima Al-Ali, a clinical psychologist at Tawan Hospital who has authored an award-winning paper on the problem, says that before the oil boom in the Emirates, children were raised in large extended families and received a lot of mothering. "Today many mothers are watching VCRs all day, and the children are raised by foreign maids. Everyone has at least one housemaid, and very few of them can communicate in Arabic to the children. They also tend to move on after a year or two, so there is no continuity for the child." Dr. Ali has labeled the syndrome "wealthy neglect."

Prostitution is another industry whose growth is attributed to the oil boom. Local journalists describe three categories of prostitutes. The first are expensive European and American women flown in on month-long contracts that can pay as much as $30,000 plus substantial fringe benefits. First-class airfare each way is standard, as is accommodation at a five-star hotel, where single rooms run nearly $400 a night, and gifts of jewelry when they leave. Such top professionals claim they need only work three months a year.

The second category is expatriate women, mainly Western, who are attracted by the get-rich-quick opportunities in the Gulf and who moonlight as prostitutes. Less protected than contract women, they are more prone to being caught. And more than one expatriate husband has had his work permit suddenly revoked because his wife was arrested for "immorality."

The last category, made up mostly of Africans but some Asian and Arabs from impoverished nations as well, caters to the Asian serving class. Unskilled workers in the Emirates are brought in on "bachelor visas" and may not be able to visit their wives at home for two or three years. Most are housed in dormitories, and the government naively seems to expect them to live as monks. Pakistani taxi drivers in Dubai, for example, earn between Dirham 5,000 and 6,000 per month, the equivalent of eighteen months' salary back home. And while most of it is sent back to Pakistan to support their families, a substantial amount stays in the Emirates as well.

• • •

The United Arab Emirates, formed in 1971, is a loose federation of sheikhdoms. Each of the hereditary rulers of the seven Emirates is a member of the Supreme Council of Rulers, the highest federal authority. Those same seven sheikhs, however, are absolute monarchs in their domain.

The largest and the most populous of the Emirates is Abu Dhabi, and its leader, Sheikh Zayed Bin Sultan An-Nahyan is also president of the UAE. The Emirate's vice-president is the ruler of Dubai. Abu Dhabi, like Dubai, was little more than sand until 1962, when commercial exploitation of petroleum began. Until that time there were no paved roads, only one hospital, and three schools. A sixty-four-year-old woman told me, "Before oil we lived in small groups of about fifteen families. The landscape was empty. The wealthiest of us had slaves from Africa, mostly Ethiopians. Otherwise, men married more than one wife to help with the work. Life was simple, we lived for the day, and tomorrow was God's decision. Our diet was dates, fish, honey, and bread. In the hottest four months of the year, we moved to Ras Al-Khaimah [the northernmost Emirate] because it was cooler, and as there were no roads then, we traveled there by boat. Suddenly, when they found oil we went from living in palm-frond houses in the summer because they were cooler to having air-conditioning. It seemed to happen overnight."

A 1961 tourist guide described the area, then known as the Trucial States, this way: "Barren coastlands [are] largely populated by nomadic tribes. No commercial oil has yet been found. Fishing and pearling are the main industries." Aerial photographs from the early sixties show Abu Dhabi as a cluster of small buildings around what is now the Center for Documentation and Research. Ten years later, a city was in place. Today, the Corniche Highway, which gives a sweeping view of the Arabian Gulf on one side, is as developed as Cannes is on the other. The region once famous for piracy and pearl-diving is now more modern than much of America. With a population of approximately two million people — most of them foreigners — the UAE owns 10 percent of the world's oil reserves, and also has large reserves of natural gas. Both are concentrated in Abu Dhabi, with Dubai being the second-largest producer.

The Emirates are extremely competitive with one another and seem in a constant contest to construct the largest shopping mall or the highest building. Currently the tallest building in the union, a thirty-two-story Trade Center, is in Dubai. And in an area smaller than Maine, five of the Emirates have built international airports. Dubai also maintains its own army independent of the Emirates Union Defense Force, but both forces are more decorative than deadly. The other five Emirates struggle to keep up. Sharjah, the third-largest, lost a major source of income in the eighties when Saudi Arabia bailed it out financially and forced it to go dry in return for its help. It is the only one of the seven Emirates where alcohol is forbidden. Tiny Ras Al-Khaimah, Ajman, Fujairah, and Umm-Al Qaiwain are much less developed than the other three, and survive largely on handouts from Abu Dhabi and Dubai, which keep them compliant.

Today, Dubai's Jebel Ali Free Zone is built around the world's largest man-made harbor. Its thirty-seven-berth port handles billions of dollars of imports and exports annually. The state has become a banking, finance, and insurance center in recent years, and would like to replace Hong Kong as a hub for international trading after 1997.

Despite UAE's commercial progressiveness, they are still very much oligarchies. The local telephone directory may list twenty-two pages of the ruling sheikhs' phone numbers, their palaces, residences, even their mothers' numbers, in a seemingly egalitarian move, but those same Arab princes head up all the government ministries. And while the government's tolerance for things un-Islamic appears extensive, Western expatriates in the Emirates say they never meet Arab women socially, or are invited to the homes of their Arab business associates. Diplomats attribute this to a near siege mentality, brought about because Emiratees are so heavily outnumbered. No doubt it would have been as difficult for me to meet Emiratee women if I had not become friendly with one of the sheikhas when I was invited to Dubai several years ago to lecture.

Sheikha Lubna bint Khalid bint Sultan Al Qasimi of Sharjah is a people collector, and her friends are both Western and Eastern, reflecting the two discrete parts of herself. Like many Arabs educated in the West, she has a foot in each culture, but unlike many of her peers, she is truly at home in both. Educated in California, her command of colloquial English and her machine-gun rapid-fire speech give her accent definite New York overtones. But then Lubna does everything fast, and time spent in her company is usually time spent on the go, as she dashes from appointment to engagement, sweeping companions along with her. At five feet two inches and a little more than a hundred pounds, the woman is a petite dynamo with the energy of a hummingbird and the intellectual focus of a laser. Despite her quick, creative mind and easy ability to bring ideas to fruition, she can display the fabled Bedouin patience when it comes to dealing with the restraints that culture, gender, and her royal lineage impose upon her.

Lubna's father should have been ruler of Sharjah. The Al Qasimis also rule a second Emirate: Ras Al-Khaimah. But when Lubna's paternal grandfather died, her maternal grandfather grabbed the reins of power, and passed the title to his son, one of Lubna's uncles. Lubna's father and other male relatives who could have threatened the new succession were exiled with their families to Saudi Arabia. She spent her early years there, returning to the UAE when still a child.

The sheikha refuses to talk about this part of her family's history: she is too politically savvy and too loyal to her uncle, Sheikh Sultan bin Mohammada, the current ruler of Sharjah. For such details, one has to turn to reference books. Lubna will only say vaguely, "It all happened a long time ago." And indeed, for her, such familial maneuverings appear to be ancient history. Her older brother seems not to have forgotten; his Rolls-Royce bears the license plate "Sharjah 1."

Aged thirty-six, Lubna, a computer specialist, holds an executive position in the government's General Information Authority, helping to develop government human resources. Her spacious elegant office, with its butter-soft leather couches and gray flannel chairs, attests to her success, but it has not been easy getting there. She is part of the first generation of women for whom higher education was a possibility. Her own mother is barely literate and, like most women of her generation, she still wears the face mask, called a *burqa* here. Emiratee *burqas* appear to be made of leather and at one time they were. Today, the two broad bands covering the forehead and mouth, plus a wide vertical strip covering the nose, are made of stiffened fabric and dyed indigo, which leaves a faint blue stain on the wearer's face when the *burqa* is removed. In addition to the *burqa*, traditional Emirate women wear a black *shaylah* head covering, which wraps around the head and neck several times, and a black *abaya*, a full-length silk or synthetic coat.

This stricter form of dress is making a comeback with the neoconservatives among the younger generation. Islamic fundamentalism arrived in the UAE in the beginning of the eighties and has received support from similar movements in Kuwait and Saudi Arabia.

Lubna, like many of her female contemporaries, is concerned about the Emirates' recent religious extremism. "There is a resurgence of religious fundamentalism all over the world, in my religion and in yours," she said. "The movement came here from Khomeini. We are very close to Iran, and what happened there had a lot of influence on us, and we have a large Shi'a community. We now see very young women who are covering themselves completely, even their faces, which is not Islamic. They are using fundamentalism as a shield, a blanket, or a wall. It becomes something to hide behind. They cannot say: I do, or I will, I can't face this, or I will work through this. It is always what the Koran said, or what Islam said. They never speak on their own behalf, only through Islam.

"Islam is an individual faith: it's between oneself and God. No one stands in between, as does a priest in Christianity. It is not influenced by a mosque or a religious movement. But the fundamentalists are changing all that, and they are making a big issue out of small things, particularly regarding women. They insist women have to be home, but forget that in early Islam women were active. They even fought in wars. The extremists are twisting Islam around. For example, they say 'Let's protect women, so let's have each man marrying four'!"

In the Emirates after the Gulf War, the Islamist Muslim movements emulated Kuwait and launched a campaign for men to marry polygamously, insisting it was their Islamic duty to do so. In Kuwait, the move came about ostensibly because there were women widowed during the war. The UAE did not have war widows, but the well-financed fundamentalist groups, in a move approved by the government, began offering to pay financial bonuses of Dirhams 35,000 (approximately $10,000) to men to take co-wives, and also to pay for many of the wedding costs. One reason for the financial marriage perks is believed to be the government's concern that many Emiratee women are now considered unmarriageable because the bride-price there can be $75,000 or more. The wedding costs, plus gifts to the bride, can easily boost that sum by another $250,000. Consequently, many Emiratee men are turning to Muslim brides from Lebanon,

Egypt, India, or Pakistan, whose families are content with dowries of only $1,000. The government worries that the region's Emirate Arab identity will be diluted.

Says Lubna, "The West wonders whether it should be afraid of the current growth of Islam. If it is the militant extremists using Islam as a political movement, then I think the world should be concerned. Khomeini in his war with Iraq gave an example of what extremist religion can do to people. How *could* a twelve-year-old child, wearing a white robe and carrying a plastic key he'd been told would open the door to Paradise, walk in front of soldiers to explode mines for them? Those boys knew they were going to die, and they all believed they were going directly to Heaven. The psychological conditioning was tremendous. The fanatics have tremendous influence."

While Lubna wears a *shaylah* over her head, and throws a black shawl around her torso, she refuses to veil herself in the style of her mother, or as the fundamentalists require. "I move too fast," she says. "I'm very active, very physical. I'm running around constantly. You can't do that when you are completely covered. I pray regularly, I fast, I've been to Hajj, but to cover in that way I cannot, and I will not."

In other areas of her life Lubna accepts the strictures placed upon her by her society out of a profound respect for her culture and religion. Or she will gently suggest change and will wait for seeds sown to finally sprout, maybe years later. And like many women in her world, she submits to tradition the way a Muslim is meant to submit to Islam. This is why she is still unmarried at an age in the Islamic world when many women are becoming grandmothers.

"I wanted very much to marry. I love children and I wanted my own," she says quietly. "But in my family we are only permitted to marry cousins. Since I delayed marrying to get an education, now there are no unmarried cousins left. And so I will remain single.

"Education was very important to me. It gave me a sense of freedom and power and achievement. Women here live such sheltered lives. For Muslim women, an education is the only chance at a personal identity they get, to find something of their own. I told myself, go to college and work for a few years and then get married. I believe women should work before marrying; it matures you to mix with other people. Your exposure is different from the limited one our women have at home. It makes a woman a better wife and mother.

But life doesn't let you set up neat little formulas about how you will structure your future."

Could Lubna not marry outside the royal family? After all, one of her brothers has had three foreign wives. "He is a man," she replies. "For the women, we cannot. The family simply wouldn't permit it. The ruler would not give his permission and he has to approve my marriage, and neither would my mother." (Lubna's father is dead.) The only other option open to the princess is to marry a cousin who is already married and become a co-wife, which she says she has no interest in doing.

"If I chose to marry against my family's wishes, I would have to be prepared to separate myself from them. They would disown me. I am financially independent, I have lived abroad for many years, have traveled extensively. I could live in any country, I'm very adaptable. I am, however, emotionally very tied to my family, they are very important to me. And I would not risk my closeness to them because of a marriage of which they did not approve."

Accepting that she would remain single was not easy for Lubna, however. "In my twenties I went through a depression because of it; it was a very emotional period. It made me feel very lonely, longing for something to happen that I knew would not. Now I am aware that I am not the only person in the universe in my situation."

The next obvious question was how does she handle the emotional and physical needs that a spouse, or, in a less restricted world than hers, a lover, would meet? Ever blunt, Lubna responds, "You mean a full life, a sexual life with a man? When I was at college in California, I had a friend who was forever lecturing me on this. She told me I was immature, a child who had never grown up to ask for a woman's needs. 'What do you mean, you are never going to have a boyfriend?' she would demand.

"I cannot say I wasn't curious about sex. I was. I have a very curious mind. So I began to read, just about everything I could find on sexual education from *The Joy of Sex* to textbooks. I read extensively on the subject," she chuckles. "Now I am in the position where when friends here have problems in their marriages to do with sex, I want to respond. I want to be able to say, 'Well, maybe it is because of such and such. . . .' But as a single woman in this culture, I am not supposed to know these things.

"Now I feel, Okay, so I'm a virgin, and it looks as though I will remain one. That's not such a terrible thing. I just accept it, I don't protest. Let's put it this way: I've watched my friends come full circle in the States. There are real problems there now with AIDS, and we also know that sexual freedom comes with a lot of emotional baggage. In the U.S. today it is considered more sophisticated to be less liberal about sex."

Lubna attended college in California in the late seventies when drug use, alcohol, and sex were extracurricular activities. "I didn't step over the line and try these things when everyone around me did for one simple reason: fear. Before I went abroad to study, my family gave me the responsibility of staying faithful to our mores, which is a lot more scary than having someone watching and waiting all the time to punish you if you go wrong." Her family did refuse, however, to allow her to take an apartment with a female cousin. Both girls were boarded instead with Mormon families.

The sheikha ran into similar family resistance when she graduated, returned home, and wanted to start working. "It was in 1980, and in those days here, any place I wanted to work was all men. My family was not comfortable with that, and they said no." With little other alternative, Lubna returned to the United States to study for a Master's degree. "By the time I came home again, more women were employed. Little by little, my family grew to accept that I could also go out to work."

But like other women in Sharjah, she then found that the local government refused to permit women to work in their ministries. Her job today is with the UAE's federal government. But even in federal ministries, women complain that a lot of their hiring is tokenism, that the glass ceiling may start barely above entry level. For Lubna, this has not been the case; today she manages a department of twenty-nine people.

The sheikha's family also resisted when she asked to attend a professional conference, which meant traveling away from home. "My mother simply rejected the idea. Once my family understood the nature of my work, slowly, gradually they began to accept it. It took years. I had to be very patient."

Lubna says that her experiences at home are mirrored by other Arab women in the UAE, a society that has traveled about one hundred years in two decades. "With education has come a certain degree of independence. For the first time, women are questioning their world. In the UAE, for example, we are seeing more divorces. Earlier, a woman was totally conditioned to accept an arranged marriage and her role within it. She never argued with her husband. Now if there are differences between a couple, the woman is more likely to speak out, debate the issue. When women had limited life-style choices, they were stuck with marriages that made them unhappy."

Certain aspects of Lubna's life have not changed, however, and she seems content with the status quo. She lives at home with her mother, another sister, and various servants, and has never contemplated moving to a place of her own. But being at home means asking permission to go out on social engagements and also occasionally having the request denied. Last year, Lubna was introduced to sailing by an American friend and loved it. "The second time I wanted to go my mother said no. She didn't think it was appropriate and I had to accept that. I think she was concerned that there may be men in such a group occasionally.

"There are similar limitations professionally. I meet men all the time in my business but I am not permitted to attend dinners or receptions because it would be frowned upon. All Muslim professional women are restricted in the same way.

Lubna says she tries hard to keep a balance in her life between her new-won freedoms, familial and societal approval, and what is expected of her as a Muslim. "I long ago learned that culture can dictate many things; it can even overrule religion in this part of the world. But my faith is important to me. I like being Muslim, I enjoy the spiritual side of my life. Islam has given me a core of strength. If I hadn't had my faith I don't think I would have survived in the West. It helped me say no to drugs when everybody around me was using them, or putting me down because I refused to date. Today, it gives me peace, brings structure to my life. Islam is consistent and very structured, and because of this I believe it is an easier religion to follow than any other. Here everybody is fasting or praying at the same time. In the U.S., there are so many different religions, it must be very confusing."

Lubna believes that the way to combat the growing Islamic extremism movement is through education, that people are less easy to manipulate when they have been taught to question, rather than blindly accept. A particular concern of hers is the lack of science education in the Gulf. "Right now the UAE is a consumer market. We buy technology and we buy the technocrats to run it, and when we train our own people, we don't train them enough. We seem to feel we will always have the money to buy the labor of others. We tend to forget that the transfer of technology is not necessarily the transfer of know-how.

"One day our oil resources will diminish. While we have the wealth we should be creating a society for scientists here. So many countries can no longer afford expensive scientific research, even in the West. We can. Historically, the biggest scholars of sciences came from Islam; they took their knowledge to the West, not the other way around. We should have a Foundation of Sciences in the Islamic world. I was shocked when I started to investigate how much Gulf countries invested in research; the UAE invested zero. The Gulf War should have taught us one thing. You cannot simply sit and let things happen to you. Things must change. It is not enough just to be a consumer, to buy whatever you want, and have it shipped over. With the wealth countries like ours have, there is no reason we cannot become the future Japan or Korea technologically."

Inadequate training of Emiratees is a problem that the UAE government is beginning to recognize. More recently there have been discussions about reducing the number of expatriates in the country. They cannot do this, however, until Emiratees can run the country without the assistance of foreign managers and technocrats. One of the steps taken to achieve this end was the opening of the Men's and Women's Colleges of Higher Technology. The country's only university at Al Ain, on the border of Oman, has often come under fire for not equipping its students for the real world. Al Ain has nine thousand students, two-thirds of them female, and some members of the faculty believe that factor is a major reason that less attention is paid to the university by the government. Many male students are sent abroad to study, but parents are still reluctant to let young women leave home to go to college.

Dubai Women's College of Technology (DWCT) had its first graduating class in 1992, and international corporations were scrambling to hire its graduates. In the past, foreign-run corporations in the UAE have been reluctant to hire Emiratees, preferring instead to import more highly skilled foreigners. This reluctance meant that most graduating students had two options, either to join a government ministry or to start their own business. Today, the ministries are bloated, which is another reason given for the soaring drug abuse among young men. "The ministries themselves are young and so are the people working in them," said a Western diplomat. "It may be years before positions open up for new graduates. Consequently, many young men are going out of their minds with boredom. Idle youths with a lot of money — that's a deadly combination. I get telephone calls all the time at the consulate from stoned kids who are randomly calling to talk. They have so much energy and nothing to do."

At the women's college, the three-year-diploma course includes banking, computer sciences, information systems, business management, marketing, and communications. Most students arrive in chauffeur-driven cars, in their best dress-for-success Arab-style outfits, chic long skirts and over-blouses, or full-length dresses. Beepers and mobile phones do not disturb these classes, but the clanking of jewelry often raises the decibel level. Many students attend class wearing thousands of dollars worth of gold jewelry. Every semester, however, more students are attending school Islamically garbed from head to toe in black, with a number covering their face and wearing gloves. One student in a class I sat in on took her gloves off to write, but kept her face covered throughout, even though everyone present was female.

Says Ellie LeBaron, the U.S. consul-general's wife in Dubai, and a lecturer at DWCT, "Initially, it was tough motivating some of the girls. U.S. students know they have to work when they graduate. These students know they can afford not to. This is an English medium school, and we ran into problems in the beginning with students having their Filipina maids, who speak good English, doing their homework for them. But once the students become excited about the opportunities this place gives them, then we find they work hard and do very well. They know that if they are not here, their alternatives are very limited: stay home, visit relatives, or go shopping."

An estimated 50 percent of the graduating students, however, will not be able to accept the plum jobs being offered them. Many parents, brothers, and fiancés are happy to see the young women educated but refuse to let them work because it will mean exposure to men who are not related to them. Even those whose families permit them to work after graduation expect their careers to be short-lived. Twenty-year-old Amal had already been hired by the Dubai Petroleum Company. Her family, however, is also making marriage plans for her. And Amal herself feels it will be inappropriate for her to continue working once she has a husband. "It will give my children a bad idea if they see their mother out in the world, working in an office. It is better I stay home and use my education to teach them."

The question in the UAE at the moment is to what extent working women will be permitted to use their brains and educations. I spoke to many women with very solid credentials who were frustrated because of the lack of promotions and raises, and the far fewer benefits they received than men. Listening to their concerns was like listening to my own peers more than two decades ago, when the feminist movement in the West was beginning. Emiratee women, of course, were a long way from *burqa-* or *abaya* burning, nor had they organized themselves to campaign for professional rights. The women's rights movement in the West also did not coincide with a fundamentalist crusade determined to remove every small gain women had made and plunge them back into the Dark Ages.

In the field of medicine, women physicians also complain of blatant discrimination. The Al Wasl Women's Hospital is as luxurious as a five-star hotel. The marble edifice with its fountains and tasteful murals is a cool oasis from the searing heat outside. The 305-bed hospital plus VIP wards was built in 1986, boasts state-of-the-art equipment, and the standard of medicine is high. Thanks to oil revenues, medical care in the UAE is free to nationals, as is education, and the government also gives housing allowances.

When women marry, however, they lose many of these benefits. Said Dr. Nadia Al Sawalhi, a senior obstetrics and gynecology specialist at the hospital, "If my husband were the doctor instead of me, we'd be rich. As it is, I earn six thousand dirhams a month [$1,700], the same as a taxi driver. Medical record clerks in the hospital make more than that. I don't get the housing allowance or the school fee allowance, and as my husband is employed in a private company, he doesn't get them either." Male doctors receive grants to buy land and build homes, some of which can be as high as $200,000 to $300,000. The allowances are withheld from women because the government is invoking the Koranic law that states the man must support the woman.

Dr. Al Sawalhi, her husband, and two young children live in a tiny second-floor apartment and drive an aging Chevrolet, one of the few nonluxury cars I saw in the UAE. Doctors at Al Wasl work hours that only interns suffer in other countries' hospitals: thirty-six hours on duty, twenty-four hours off. "I am so tired I tried to resign a year ago, but the hospital wouldn't permit it. I've had to send my son to nursery school early because I didn't have time to take him to a park or out to play with other children, and the apartment is too small for my children to play in."

Dr. Al Sawalhi recalled with frustration a meeting male and female physicians had with the hospital's Director General to discuss the issue of financial discrimination. "Male doctors said they were ready to contribute a percentage of their income to the women physicians so that both sexes would receive equal sums. The Director General refused, saying he had to follow government rules.

"I am on the teaching staff of the medical school here, and the government used to give us a thousand extra dirhams per month for teaching, then they reduced it to eight hundred, and they haven't paid that for six months." (Dubai's medical school recently introduced a compulsory course for all students: Islamic medicine. The program seeks to link all modern medicine, including genetics, to the Koran. Such courses have their genesis in orthodox Saudi Arabia. The Saudis have spent considerable sums on medical conferences at which leading Western scientists are asked to confirm that Koranic verses, which seem vague to the layperson, are in fact specific predictors of modern science. Videos and pamphlets from the conferences have been circulated throughout the Muslim world by the Saudis.)

The Emirates, of course, cannot plead poverty when it comes to women's salaries or their allowances. "They certainly have money to spend when it comes to sports," said Dr. Al Sawalhi. "A football player, if he wins a game, gets a Rolls-Royce or a house from the government, or they give him five hundred thousand dirhams. Whoever wins a camel race receives a five hundred thousand–dirham Mercedes, or a boat, and cash. If they can offer so much in these cases, surely they can give us an extra two to four thousand per month."

To avoid such flagrant sexism in the workplace, many women, even members of the royal family, have become their own bosses. Sheikha Jamila has been running a very successful school for the hearing impaired and mentally handicapped since 1983. A psychologist by training, she saw the need and rolled up her sleeves to make it happen. Today in the Arab world, it is considered one of the more progressive such institutions, and has recently added an early-intervention program. The waiting list is long and includes disabled children from other Middle East and Gulf countries. At the end of her full working day, thirty-two-year-old Jamila begins a second shift: fund-raising. UNICEF and the UAE government fund 20 percent of the school, but the remaining 80 percent has to be raised by Jamila. "In the beginning I didn't have time to sleep," she says. "Now it is a little better. Fortunately I'm single, and therefore my time is my own." She also appeals to other Arab women to get involved as volunteers in their community. "So many of our women sit at home all day and do nothing, because that's traditional. There is so much a woman can do, either as a volunteer or a worker. Too many say we are not able, we don't know how. But women can do anything, if we only try."

Sheikha Eman, a thirty-four-year-old mother of six, saw a need of a different kind, and started a business to fill it. Her "for women only" Le Café opened two years ago, not far from the "for women only" park in Sharjah. The café is the only one of its kind in that Emirate, and she started it so that women could meet women friends for coffee free of sexual harassment by Emiratee teenage boys. "Boys aged sixteen to twenty here are very irresponsible," said Eman, choosing her words carefully. "They annoy women, trying to force them to take their phone numbers, following them, or inviting themselves to sit at a table with women in a restaurant. Ignoring them doesn't work, and it is impossible to stop them. As a married woman, I would hate for my husband to have to witness such a thing. So I decided to open this café for women only."

In the Emirates, women are also plagued when shopping. At the multistory Al Ghurair Mall in Dubai, groups of youths drop their telephone numbers at the feet of veiled women, or insert them into videocassette cases, in the hope that a woman will contact them. They also speed alongside vehicles driven by young women, flashing their telephone numbers at them on large pieces of board. Telephone relationships between the sexes are common in the Islamic world, where family control makes it difficult for young women to meet young men privately. Frequently, youths simply call numbers at random in the hope that a woman will answer.

Suggesting in print, however, that all is not perfect in paradise can be a risky business, as Dhabia Khamees, a local woman journalist, author, and poet discovered. From the time her career began, her choice of subject matter as a journalist put her on a collision course with the government. She frequently focused on democracy, women's rights, and human rights. "And of course the UAE doesn't have all three," she said. Khamees is the author of ten books, two novels, and eight collections of poems, but all of her works have been published only abroad. Her books and publications carrying articles with her byline have been banned in the UAE for the last decade. And much of that time she has lived abroad in Egypt and England in self-imposed exile because of fears for her safety. At the time we met, she was in the UAE to be with her mother, who had terminal breast cancer. "My family didn't want me to come back. They were afraid I would be arrested again."

Khamees became the Emirate's first female political prisoner when she was arrested in 1987. The writer herself refers to her arrest as a kidnapping. "I was snatched from my home with no formal charges made against me. I was mistreated, my life was threatened, and my family did not know where I was for three months. I think that description is of a kidnapping, not of an official detention," she says angrily.

Khamees dates the beginning of her real problems with the government to 1983, when the six country members of the Gulf Cooperation Council instituted new censorship laws. "Saudi Arabia wanted all policy to come from Riyadh, and they were and still are very keen on censorship. Things became much tougher here then, particularly regarding what could and could not be published. The Saudis began the Association of Reform and poured money into it to encourage Islamic Fronts, with particular emphasis on women."

Shortly after, Khamees's writing was banned, and she started to receive threatening phone calls. On advice from friends and family, she left the country and lived in London until 1985, when, believing the Emirates were becoming more liberal, she returned home. Almost immediately, the threatening phone calls began, her mail started being opened, and Khamees became aware that she was being followed. Finally, in May 1987, she was awakened from an afternoon nap by a pounding at her door. "I opened the door and found seven guns pointing at me. The seven men and one woman were in civilian dress, but it was obvious they were from the government." She was blindfolded and driven to the Ministry of the Interior in Abu Dhabi two hours away.

"I had no idea where I was, or why I was arrested. I could hear voices, but I didn't know who the people were." Khamees was kept blindfolded, with her hands handcuffed behind her for weeks. "I couldn't tell night from day. They interrogated me for hours. I would no sooner go back to my cell than they would order me to return. They knew every tiny detail about my life for the past several years. They read me letters I had written, they played tapes of my phone calls, they had drafts of my articles and photographs of friends I had met in restaurants. They had a complete log of everything I had done every day.

"I was told I was degrading women by my writing. That I had

been an ambassador for this country but I had turned against the government." As the interrogations continued, and she became disoriented from constant blindfolding, Khamees fell ill. "I began to have trouble breathing, I started to pass out. I asked for a doctor, but they wouldn't bring one." During her incarceration in what she later learned was the central intelligence building, her family tried frantically to learn what had happened to her. When they contacted the police and other officials, everyone denied knowledge of her whereabouts. "Finally, after three months, my brother found out where I was and was allowed to visit me for five minutes. It was the only visit I had. I was not allowed to exercise, and when they finally took the blindfold off, the only reading material permitted was the Koran."

The following month, without warning, she was released. "The day before they had been threatening to kill me. Then at two A.M. that night, they suddenly opened my cell door and said I was being released. [Later Khamees learned that her release coincided with her mother's being hospitalized with a heart attack.] They forbade me to talk about my experience in jail. Then they warned me that if I ever went back to writing, even poetry, they would put a bullet in my head. They said, 'No matter where on earth you are, we will find you, and assassinate you.'"

• • •

Challenging the authorities is hard to do in an oligarchy like the UAE. It can be even more problematic when one's complaint is about a member of the ruling royal family. When the laws are made by the same people one is fighting, and when they can change them at will, protesting their decisions can be a Sisyphean endeavor.

The first ten years of Sonja Ohly's marriage sound like an excerpt from a glitzy romance novel. By the time the marriage ended in 1991, her enviable lifestyle had turned to ashes. She was divorced without being informed, lost her home, her possessions, her rights, and worst of all, her four children.

Sonja was twenty when she came to the UAE from Frankfurt, Germany, to represent her family's travel business. Multilingual, with auburn hair and the style and figure of a model, she has always been a head-turner. She was equally impressed with Sheikh Sultan of Sharjah when she first met him. Educated in England, Sultan is intelligent, urbane, and charming. Three months after they met, the sheikh, then twenty-six and newly divorced, proposed to Sonja and she accepted. She married him shortly after in a ceremony that she didn't attend; male representatives stood in for her. The couple honeymooned in Paris and then the Far East.

Recalls Sonja, "I was so in love with him. He was very correct, so polite, and he can talk knowledgeably on any subject — immunology, biology, religion, politics. I have never met a man whose conversational range is as broad as his. He was also very relaxed about his culture. I never wore long skirts or covered my head." When I first met Sonja and her husband at a party in the Emirates in 1988, I had been surprised to learn that they were husband and wife. Sultan was wearing a white *dishdasha,* the full-length traditional Arab dress, and Sonja looked as though she had just stepped off a Milan fashion runway. From her sculpted hairstyle to her high-style emerald-green silk jacket, a micro-mini black silk skirt, and her sheer black hose that emphasized her long legs, she epitomized Western jet set glamour.

And Sonja's life was glamorous and cosmopolitan. The couple traveled a great deal, entertained extensively, and Sultan's gifts to her included a green Rolls-Royce and seven horses. She gave birth to four children, all sons: Majid, now ten, Khalid, eight, Fahim, six, and Rashid, four.

In 1990, with her youngest son attending kindergarten, Sonja received her husband's permission to work. "If he had said no, I would have accepted it. Having married into an Arab royal family there were certain freedoms I didn't have. I always asked his permission before I visited women friends, for example." Sonja began an advertising agency. About the same time, although she does not see the two as connected, her marriage began to disintegrate. She insists that it wasn't cultural differences that caused it to break down. "What happened to us could have happened to any couple of the same nationality." Sonja refuses to be specific but does say that friends opined that she was too strong, and she may have caused her husband to feel insecure. "Arab male pride is very strong, and also very fragile," she said.

Sonja was divorced in May 1991, but was not informed. "I had no idea," she said. "I had not signed anything, nor been told. In September I learned that my husband had remarried again, a Palestinian woman we both knew well. At first I thought she was a co-wife, then a few days later I received a divorce certificate in the mail that showed our marriage had ended five months before. The letter also said I would have to leave the country, and leave alone, that my children would stay behind. I had no choice, I had to leave. I was not permitted to take any of my possessions from the house, not the presents my parents and friends had given me, not even photograph albums."

A few months later, Sonja returned to the UAE because she missed her children so much and wanted to be close to them. She moved into an apartment in Dubai, an Emirate where she could still obtain a visa. The apartment continues to be very sparsely furnished and has obviously been decorated on a budget. Next to the sofa is a large basket of knitting. "It's what I do with most of my free time these days," said Sonja. "It's therapeutic."

Under Islamic law in the UAE, Sonja, thirty-three, is entitled to the custody of her two younger sons until they reach the age of seven, when custody then changes to the children's father. As she chain-smoked, Sonja said quietly, "I haven't been permitted the visitation rights that I am legally entitled to. The only time I have seen my children is during term time, when I go to their school and have five minutes with them before they are picked up. They are not even permitted to phone me.

"At Christmas, Majid was in the hospital so dehydrated he was on an I.V. drip." Sonja's voice quavered. "Nobody telephoned me. I'm his mother." She stopped speaking. Excusing herself through her tears, she rushed from the room. More composed a little later, she returned. "My husband is not a cruel man. I do not understand what has happened or why. I knew about Islamic laws of divorce and how they affected women, but never in a million years did I think this would happen to me. If I had, I would have been more clever like some of my Arab women friends. I would have had a marriage agreement that specified my rights in the case of a divorce.

"I loved this man, we were so close. I've given him such support. Now, after twelve years of marriage, my husband sits in our house with our four children, and I cannot reach them or talk to him. I have nothing."

Friends and even some of Sultan's family have advised Sonja to appeal to the ruler. In Arab societies, ruling sheikhs are often asked to settle such disputes. "I don't know him very well, and I don't believe he would intervene." Other friends have suggested that she snatch the children. "I would never do such a thing. No matter where I went, I would never feel safe. And I wouldn't do it to the children. Children need both parents, even if those parents are divorced. I also could not rob my sons of their birthright. They are royals in this country — sheikhs. I wouldn't take that away from them."

Sonja plans to appeal to the Emirates' courts for custody of her children. It is a lengthy process that could be dragged out until her sons reach the age that her husband receives automatic custody, and there is also no guarantee they will rule in her favor. Her husband's position is certain to influence the outcome. "Islam gives women many rights in theory. In practice it is something else again," she said.

. . .

Secret divorces in the Islamic world are common, as are secret marriages. Often the wife is the last to know. This was the case with A'isha. When her husband took a second wife, family and friends chose not to tell her, to spare her the pain as long as possible.

A'isha is tall, made taller by four-inch heels. Her full-length *thoab*, the Emirates' female version of the *dishdasha*, emphasized her height also. She is not conventionally attractive, but her vivacity and infectious throaty laugh are very appealing. She is upfront, outspoken, and at ease with being so. It is hard to imagine her in the passive role her marriage forced upon her.

"I was married at twenty-four to a cousin who was twenty-two. I didn't know him because he had been educated in the U.S. And because of that he seemed very Westernized. He even drank alcohol at the beginning. But we were no sooner married than he became very Islamist. I'm a good Muslim, but it is as if he went back in history. He refused to have any furniture in the house, just carpets and cushions.

"We didn't have servants. He didn't want to see the face of female servants, and he wouldn't permit me to see male servants. He would not permit a television or radio in the house. He said they were sinful. And my friends were not allowed to visit. I was very lonely but all the time I told myself, he is my husband, my cousin, I must obey him. Whenever he wanted to have sex, we had sex. In Islam, it is not permitted for the wife to refuse her husband. And I wanted to be a good wife.

"When we went out, he insisted I be completely covered, a black veil over my face, and that I wear gloves. I had never dressed like this before. I was not allowed outside the house without him, even to go shopping with my mother. The veil was so hot, I couldn't breathe. My family told me, 'This is ridiculous. This is not the life you are used to.' But I did it because he wanted it. It was my duty to be compliant."

After three years, A'isha's husband returned to the United States to complete his studies and she went with him. Even there, he insisted she be veiled completely. Around the same time, both families of the couple began to question why A'isha and her husband had not yet had children. In traditional Muslim marriages, it is assumed that the bride will become pregnant in the first year. "Children are extremely important in our culture," she said. "I suggested to my husband that before we left the U.S. we consult a fertility specialist."

Tests at a hospital in Los Angeles proved that while A'isha was fertile, her husband was sterile. "It was a very difficult time for us. I love children very much. Now I had to accept that I would not have any." Under Islamic law, if she had been unable to conceive, that would have been grounds for her husband to take another wife. In the reverse situation, A'isha was not given that choice.

"In our culture it is considered very unmanly for a man not to be able to have children. To permit my husband to save face, I told our families there was something wrong with me. My mother-in-law wept when she heard."

At the end of that year, A'isha's husband took her on a two-week vacation. "It was unusual. We didn't take vacations together. Toward the end of the trip, he gave me money and said when we returned home I should go shopping with my mother, to buy anything I liked. This was even stranger. He had never permitted me to go shopping with her before. As we were packing to return home, I found out why his behavior was so different. He told me that the day before we had left for the trip, he had married again.

"I was stunned. 'I have always been a good wife to you. I have obeyed you completely. Why have you done this?' I asked. He said it was because he wanted children. 'But you can't father children. We still have the medical file,' I told him. His response to me was, 'Those were American doctors, not Muslim ones. They don't know anything.'

"Back in the Emirates I told him, 'You are newly married, you should be with your new wife.' I returned to my parents' house, I didn't want my husband to see me cry. There I discovered my whole family knew that he had planned to take a second wife. Only I hadn't known. One of my sisters had insisted I be told. But my mother said, 'No, let her be ignorant, remain happy, until the moment she must know.'"

A'isha was devastated, refusing to leave her home for a year, and spent most of that time weeping. She felt betrayed, and she also felt a failure. Eventually, however, her family began to pressure her to return to her husband. "My mother told me, 'It is your duty to return. He is your husband; he is permitted more than one wife. You must go back.' I remember replying that this man was a cousin; if a family member could treat me so badly, I wouldn't live with him."

Slowly, A'isha began to return to her former life, and to her former way of dressing. Her husband divorced her two years later, and, like Sonja, she was not informed. "I found out because a relative saw the papers in court."

Now thirty-five, A'isha would like to marry again. As with women her age in the West, she recognizes that if she wants to have children, time is running out. Like many Muslim women, she is required to marry within her extended family. It is a tradition she perceives as unjust, as men are permitted free choice.

"Maybe it is time to break this tradition," said A'isha. "Someone has to be the hero and marry outside the family for the first time. Maybe that hero should be me."

CHAPTER 7

Kuwait: A War of Independence

They differed with me over what time we are living in,
It is not democracy when a man can talk about politics
without anyone threatening him,
Democracy is when a woman can talk of her lover without
anyone killing her.

POEM BY SHEIKHA DR. SOUAD M. AL-SABAH

"THE WAR CHANGED ME. I'm not the woman he married, but I'm not sure if he realizes that yet. I'm much stronger than before, and he seems so weak, so passive. I know we will divorce, but I don't know how to tell him. It will not be easy. "He also doesn't know I've been having an affair for the last year. It began just after the war ended. I pray he never finds out, because if he does I will lose my son."

Leila is thirty years old, outgoing, smart, and sassy. It's hard to picture her as the shy, submissive, traditional wife she insists she was. In her form-fitting white linen slacks, casual but chic striped T-shirt, and short swinging cap of hair, plus a gold Rolex watch and designer diamond bracelets, rings, earrings, and gold chains, she looks like an up-to-the-minute Scarsdale yuppie. Her silver Mercedes convertible with its car phone that always seems to be ringing, and her Filofax that is bursting at the seams only confirm the image.

At initial meeting, if one had to choose an adjective to describe Leila, over-indulged might first come to mind. American expatriates dub women like her "MAPs," Muslim Arab Princesses, the Middle Eastern equivalent of JAP, or Jewish American Princess. It is an easy choice; international media described the Kuwaitis collectively at the time of the Gulf War as spoiled, hedonistic, dissipated, even decadent. Media coverage of the invasion often focused on the seventy-plus wives of the ruler of Kuwait, or how the scores of sheikhs and their families fled the country in the first hours of the invasion and passed the war in pampered luxury at five-star hotels in the West, in Saudi Arabia, or the UAE, as did three out of four of all Kuwaitis. Photographs of various members of the Al-Sabah royal family at the gambling tables and discos in London, dressed in drag at a wild party in Paris, and at play at various other sybaritic pastimes didn't help, as Americans, Europeans, and other nations' Muslims risked their lives in the war to defend the Kuwait these noble citizens had abandoned.

Kuwaitis are the Arabs other Arabs love to despise. In Egypt, where they descend on Cairo in July and August with large entourages of servants and take over whole floors of five-star hotels, service staff refer to them openly but out of tipping earshot as "whoremongers and drunks who come here to buy women and drink alcohol." In the UAE, where Kuwaiti women wear bikinis and shorts on the beach that they wouldn't dare wear in public at home, they are labeled "Muslim hookers." In New York, it is claimed they need supermarket carts when shopping at Van Cleef and Arpels, and Tiffany's. Such comments have their genesis in the fabled wealth of the average Kuwaiti. Non-Gulf Arabs will tell you that there are only two classes in Kuwait: "billionaires and millionaires; there are no poor people." This isn't true, of course. While there are many wealthy, there is also a sizable population in Kuwait wondering where its next meal is coming from. But public perception can be damning. There also is an element of truth in many of the criticisms. However, just as Leila is more than the sum of her expensive accessories, so is Kuwait more than the stereotype. And just as with Leila, it takes a little time to get to know Kuwait, to get beyond the excessive externals.

Like Dubai and the other Emirates, Kuwait is a city-state, but it lacks the energy and efficiency of the Emirates, and is certainly not as pleasing to the eye. Even before the war, this was a country that was being strangled by its own red tape and a passive and apathetic bureaucracy. Ninety percent of the Kuwaiti workforce is employed by the government, a substantial number of whom do not show up for work but still collect their salaries. Those who do attend mostly ignore the government working hours of 7:30 A.M. to 1:30 P.M., and instead put in an appearance between 10:00 and 11:30 A.M. Despite what has been estimated to be the shortest working week in the world, male government employees can retire on full pensions after twenty years' employment, female after fifteen years.

"Who is running the country?" asked a European diplomat. "'By and large, no one,' is the cynical answer," he said. "The country was run by three hundred Palestinians, but since they were expelled after Arafat supported Saddam Hussein in the Gulf War, very little works. At least the Palestinians knew their way through the amazing maze of red tape required to be navigated to get the smallest task done. While they were here, the economy and public sector cruised along. Once the system was stalled with the war, however, there has been no attempt to jump-start it."

This is also true of Kuwait's postwar appearance. Many buildings have not been repaired; hotels, office blocks, palaces, and homes were still burned out. Windows that served as gunports continued to be bricked in, and even sandbags were still in place. A number of the beaches were still mined, as was the small park opposite the Sheraton Hotel in the middle of the city. According to government figures, at least four thousand civilians have been killed or wounded by mines and by handling unexploded ordnance since Kuwait was liberated. The automobiles Kuwaitis drive — they have the world's highest car per capita ratio — are expensive and frequently new, replacing those pillaged by the Iraqis, but offices, public buildings, hospitals, and the university remained stripped of much of their equipment.

Telephone communications were difficult; directory assistance had not functioned since the invasion; many numbers had changed after the war; and telephone directories were impossible to find. The Ministry of Information did not know the current numbers of the Bayan Palace, the seat of the Kuwaiti government, where officials tune their office televisions to Western soap operas instead of working.

Kuwait's landscape is flat sand desert and the city, too, is mono-chromatically sand-colored, a shade favored by architects for their structures. Empty sandlots are common, as are buildings without pavements, seemingly set adrift in sand. There is little that is green in Kuwait, a country slightly smaller than Connecticut. The government claims at one time to have planted a million trees to protect buildings from frequent summer sand- and dust storms, but there was scant evidence of them in the summer of 1992, and many may not have survived due to lack of care. Instead of trees, Kuwait has high-tension pylons, veritable forests of them, particularly lining the highway to Ahmadi, the oil town just south of the airport. The pylons are so dense in number that the electromagnetic radiation rates in the houses built beneath them must be among the highest in the world.

Kuwait's petro-billions, unlike Dubai's, have not been spent on a country beautification program. Instead, much of the oil revenue has been invested abroad by the government's Kuwait Investment Office, which has "lost" at least $5 to 7 billion in recent years. The government and two members of the royal family have since been accused of massive corruption and mismanagement of the nation's finances. Historically, the fifteen hundred–strong Al-Sabah royal family has had tight and secret control of Kuwait's enormous oil revenues. And when the opposition won the October 1992 elections, the first to be held since the National Assembly was dissolved in 1986 by the ruler, it demanded investigations into a series of government fiscal scandals. "Without public scrutiny, there has been a massive abuse of public trust," said one opposition member.

The Emir of Kuwait, who can veto legislation, has ignored earlier parliamentary demands to investigate previous financial scandals. These include a big bailout of speculators, many of whom were tied to the royal family, after the Souk al-Manakh, Kuwait's unofficial stock exchange, crashed in 1982. It was this crash and the ensuing financial crisis that led to the suspensions of parliament and the constitution four years later and the tightening of newspaper censorship. Opposition officials claimed that the Emir dissolved parliament because it was in the process of examining the financial dealings of some of the royal family. This time, however, parliament has passed a law giving itself the right to monitor all state investments and to stiffen the penalties for embezzlement. How meaningful that may be is still unknown, and the Emir continues to retain the right to dissolve parliament if it becomes too assertive.

The 1992 elections came about because Kuwait had been under substantial pressure from its Persian Gulf War allies to become more democratic. But while opposition members won thirty-one of the fifty seats, the Emir, in a public slap in the face to the electorate, reappointed his heir, the Crown Prince, as prime minister. The major ministries were also retained by members of the royal family. Only six of the sixteen cabinet posts went to newly elected members of parliament.

Nineteen of the thirty-one opposition seats were won by Muslim fundamentalists, more than double the number of seats they received in the previous election. Today, three of the fundamentalists are government ministers. It is this growing Islamist movement in Kuwait that wants to amend the constitution so that *Shariah* law becomes the sole source of legislation. As in other Muslim countries, Kuwait's religious conservatives see Islam as the solution, and certainly an alternative to a government that for years has been marked by royal nepotism and cronyism, resulting in slothful, inept, and dishonest administrators. The Islamists do have at least one thing in common with the ruling royal family, however: neither group wants women to be able to vote or run for political office. It is Kuwait's liberals and Shi'as who support women's suffrage.

Ironically, Kuwait's constitution declares that all Kuwaitis are equal before the law in prestige, rights, and duties, with individual freedom guaranteed. But that is not true for women and a category of nationals officially designated "second-class citizens," Kuwaitis who cannot trace their roots in the country to before 1920, no simple task in a country that then was mostly illiterate and has very uncertain records. Only "first-class" Kuwaiti male citizens over twenty-one may vote. In the 1992 elections this meant that only 81,400 Kuwaitis out of a population of 606,000 were permitted to cast ballots, which resulted in "democracy for the few." The total prewar population of Kuwait was 2.1 million, three-quarters of whom were foreign labor.

During the 1992 elections, Kuwaiti women marched to various polling stations in a demonstration for women's suffrage. Carrying banners stating "The Voice of the Women Is in the Nation's Interest" or "With You in 1996," they braved the anger of men from the four conservative Islamic groups who shouted at them to return to their homes. They also continued despite scuffles with police, who tried to turn them back at one polling station. "If it was okay for women to take part in this country's Resistance during the war, and to die and be tortured for Kuwait, it certainly should be okay for them to have the vote," said one.

Three months into the Iraqi occupation, in October 1990, the Emir and the Crown Prince Sheikh Saad Al-Abdullah Al-Sabah told Diaspora Kuwaitis at a conference in Saudi Arabia that once Kuwait was liberated women deserved a better deal in society. It was later perceived to be nothing more than a morale-booster for women who were risking their lives; after the liberation of Kuwait, the Crown Prince modified his statement and said that democracy has its limits. Fatima Hussein, the only woman editor of a Kuwaiti daily newspaper, the *Al Watan,* has little patience with such comments. She is one of the organizers of the Constitution League, which was established so that women could obtain the rights given to them in Kuwait's 1962 constitution, and which they have never received.

"The first anti-Iraq demonstration three days after the invasion was made up of only women and children," said Hussein, who helped organize the march. "We thought the Iraqis would never attack women and children, but they did. In the second demonstration a number of women were killed. After that we stopped the demonstrations and organized underground newspapers. Kuwaiti women played a major role in the Resistance. They completely veiled themselves, which gave them a certain invisibility and enabled them to move around the country more easily than men." Kuwaiti women frequently smuggled arms and Resistance documents past Iraqi checkpoints by hiding them under their full-length *abayas,* which they adopted for the purpose.

The morning we spoke, Hussein had just published a scathing editorial attacking the minister of education, a cousin of her's, who once again had decided not to permit top female students to study abroad on government grants as male students have done for decades. "At a press conference yesterday when he was asked about the subject, he said there is nothing against it, that we have to study the matter. They have been saying that for thirty-eight years! So I skinned him in print. I said we are sick of these non-decisions on women's issues."

In the West, Kuwait has a reputation for being more liberal toward women than many Islamic states. And in some superficial ways it is. Women work with men, often in Western dress, and it is not uncommon to observe female office workers engaging in rambunctious behavior or flirting, giggling and gossiping with male colleagues. Six young women whom I saw hanging out the windows of a BMW, screaming like adolescents as they chased two men from the Ministry of Information around the car park pretending to run them down, hardly seemed to resemble the shy and modest women of other Islamic cultures. In the evenings, after the temperature goes down a little, groups of women wearing *hijab,* sweats, and sneakers speed-walk through the streets of Kuwait City "for exercise, to stay in shape." Yet despite the seemingly Western ways of the younger generation, the restrictions continue to outweigh the freedoms.

Twenty-two-year-old Afrah Khami meets Olympic sprinting standards, for example, but has never been allowed to participate in international women's competitions. The Kuwait Girls Club, of which she is a member, applied to the Kuwaiti Olympics Committee for her to participate in the 1988 games. "Both the Committee and the Ministry of Social Affairs say, 'Yes, yes, of course,'" said Najat Al Sulta, the club's president. "But when budget time comes around, they tell us there isn't any funding allocation for women."

As newspaper editor Fatima Hussein told me, "We have a saying in Kuwait: 'It's the low wall that everybody jumps over.' Women are that wall, and as long as we cannot vote, nobody will protect our rights."

Kuwait's feisty feminists can and do speak out, but unable to effect change legally, they are watching the Islamists gradually gain more power over their lives. The royal family's attitude to the religious movement, like that of many Middle Eastern and Gulf regimes, is one of appeasement, believing that placation is better than subversion of their own rule. "Fundamentalists have gained much more power over things big and small in the last few years," a Kuwaiti woman told me in 1993, shortly after they persuaded the government to ban male hairstylists in women's beauty salons. "As if the government shouldn't be engaged in more important things than who cuts a woman's hair." But Kuwaiti fundamentalists are not ignoring the larger issues, either. They are lobbying to weaken the country's close military and political ties with the West, especially the United States. Many would prefer instead to see Kuwait have good relations with the Islamic government of Iran.

Recently some extremists have started turning to violence whenever their views are challenged. Kuwait University's dean of medicine was targeted after he banned female students from wearing the *niqab*, the black face-covering, in 1992. Dr. Helal Al Sayer instituted the ban after seeing a student's veil dragging on a cadaver being dissected. "It is unacceptable and unsanitary," he said at the time. There was also concern that less talented or lazy students could have exams taken for them by brighter students by using the veil to hide their identity. The prohibition led to a strike by angry students, who described it as "an interference with their personal freedom, which Islam guarantees."

For the past decade, the students' union at Kuwait University has been controlled by the Islamists, and all university elections have been won by them. And on this occasion, the students' union issued a statement that read: "Preventing veiled students from continuing their studies for a reason that does not conflict with the quest for knowledge is prejudiced and wrong. . . . All this commotion is not for a crime they have committed or for falling behind in their studies, but because of adherence to Islamic modesty." Shortly after, the dean's car was blown up. Dr. Al Sayer refused to back down.

Then a month and a half later, while I was in Kuwait, the dean was targeted again. A twenty-pound bomb was planted outside the living room of his home in the Yarmouk area of Kuwait City on a Friday afternoon, the Arab weekend and a time when his family would be expected to be at home. The explosion killed the forty-five-year-old Iranian gardener of his neighbor, Sheikh Mubarak Sabah Al Nasser, and destroyed another neighbor's Mercedes. Dr. Al Sayer's family members, who were in a different room at the time, were unhurt, but the dean of Medicine, who rushed outside after the large explosion, had the gruesome experience of finding pieces of the gardener's body, including his severed head, scattered throughout his yard.

At the same time as the Medical School banned face veils for women, Kuwait's traffic department prohibited women from wearing *niqabs* while driving because they diminish visibility. *Niqabs*, which may be up to four layers of fabric, dramatically diminish peripheral vision, and turn a bright sunny day to night. A female ophthalmologist, who herself is veiled, discounted the problem. "There is no proof that it affects the vision at all," she said. "And if women see less well at night, well, no good Muslim women should be out at night unaccompanied." The physician made a case for the face veil protecting vision. "There is an eye condition you find in countries with a great deal of bright sunlight called pterygium. But it is very rare in women whose faces are veiled, so they obviously benefit."

Kuwait's traffic department remains unconvinced. "Women apprehended breaking this law will be subject to penalties," said Lt.-Col. Ismael al-Khalidi. Despite the threat, however, and Kuwait's tough traffic rules — speeders can go to jail for thirty days — many veiled women continue to drive, and traffic police, not wanting to be targeted by extremists, are reluctant to stop them.

The head of one Islamic women's group, Islah Social Society, asked why many women were allowed to use makeup and Western dress under the pretext of personal freedom, while there are objections to their wearing veils. "Veils also should be treated as personal freedom," said Suad Al Jarrallah.

When the Islamist Charity Association called for Kuwaiti married men to take more than one wife to combat female celibacy, the response was almost as controversial as that over veiling. Only this time, the country's feminists became enraged. In addition to the $10,000 wedding gift, the organization offered long-term loans to help support more than one wife, plus free furniture, the use of a wedding hall, kitchenware at cost, and a gift at the birth of the couple's first child.

The organization's head, Dr. Ahmad Al Muzaini, who has two wives himself, said in media interviews that no woman should have any problem with polygamy. "If they do, they are listening to the devil and their pride is getting in the way. We are trying to implement Islamic *Shariah,* which allows polygamy. Enemies of Islam, particularly secular and pro-Western elements, prohibit more than one wife but permit lovers and girlfriends, which is totally banned in Islam. Restricting marriage to one woman while allowing illicit affairs has led to the spread of corruption in the world. A visit to some hospitals in Kuwait will provide evidence about the spread of AIDS, drug addiction, and alcoholism."

In letters to the press, angry women responded. "This is not a charity organization; it's a committee whose aim is to destroy homes," wrote Mouda al-Motairi, a thirty-five-year-old mother of two. Khadija Sellers, an American Muslim convert who is married to a Kuwaiti and is the mother of four, said in a letter to the English-language *Arab Times:* "Dr. Al Muzaini has been talking about Kuwait having too many spinsters, and about Kuwaiti men flying to Bangkok on sex tours because their sexual urges are bigger than the average man. Now he wants to match up these spinsters with such men! Why should unmarried women be so unfortunate as to be matched up with men who may expose them to AIDS?" A third woman, thirty-four-year-old Sara Mataqi said, "I'd cut my husband into pieces if he even thought of marrying another woman."

Some of the increase in fundamentalism has been attributed to the many Kuwaitis who spent up to a year in strictly conservative Saudi Arabia because of the Gulf War. "They were infected by the conservativism around them and brought it back to Kuwait when they came," said one Kuwaiti.

The Gulf War, like most such conflicts, was also a catalyst for change for women. In the West, World War II's "Rosie, the Riveter" made it acceptable for both American and European women to work outside the home. In Kuwait, women who participated in the Resistance, or those like Leila for whom the war was a belated coming of age, are reluctant to give up the independence that they assumed during the Gulf War. And they watch the growing Islamist movement with concern, afraid their wings might be clipped before they have really had a chance to fly.

Prior to the conflict, Leila would never have participated in a women's rights march, as she did at the time of the elections. "I married at twenty-one, moved into the home of my husband's parents, and was totally passive," she said. "It never occurred to me to be anything else." The large, sprawling house, with its Persian carpets and expensive furniture, was obviously built to be an extended-family home, and Leila, her lawyer husband, and child have a suite of rooms upstairs.

The family Leila married into is more conservative than her own. Her father-in-law had three wives, although he has since divorced one. Leila's mother-in-law is the first. The second wife is maintained in a house nearby, and Leila's father-in-law splits his time between the two homes. "My mother-in-law appears to have absolutely no interest in her husband's other wife or his life with her," said Leila.

"Once I married, I spent nearly all of my time at home. If I went to visit girlfriends or relatives, my mother-in-law insisted I be home no later than nine P.M. It didn't occur to me to argue. Just as I didn't argue when she insisted I cover and wear the *hijab*. I obeyed everything she said, and so did my husband. Even when I wanted to leave the house, I asked her permission before I asked my husband. I was under the total control of my husband and his mother. Her behavior with me wasn't unusual; she is a typical Arab mother-in-law. I never argued. I had no personality, and this was considered appropriate."

For Leila the most difficult part of her early years of marriage was not the restrictions, but the fact that she did not become pregnant. "I longed to have a baby. I also knew it would please my in-laws and my husband. And motherhood would have filled my day. Watching television most of the time was driving me crazy. Finally, after five years of marriage, I became pregnant. It was very exciting. And once I was pregnant, it was as if I had been accepted into a club. Other women discussed their intimate lives with me. It was then that I learned that I didn't have a normal sex life. My husband was making love to me only once every two months or so. I had been such an innocent, I thought that was normal. When you are sexually ignorant in this part of the world, it can be difficult to acquire knowledge."

Looking back, Leila now attributes her husband's lack of interest in her sexually to his heavy drinking. What triggers his alcohol problem she doesn't know, and no longer cares to find out.

Leila had been married nine years when the invasion of Kuwait occurred. "When we heard the helicopters flying very low over our house, we rushed outside. They were Iraqi troop carriers, and soldiers were standing in the open doors ready to jump. I began to scream. I became totally hysterical. I couldn't control myself. I was convinced we would all die. I cried and sobbed for three days, I had diarrhea from terror, I was totally useless.

"There were tanks on the street, and Iraqi soldiers everywhere. We knew we had to get supplies, bottled water and food. And it was decided that the men shouldn't go outside in case they were arrested. So I went with the women to stock up on food. We veiled ourselves completely; we hoped it might protect us. I felt better the moment I had something to do. I didn't join the Resistance as other women did. But for me I became much more courageous, began to help other people find food. Before I had been such a spoiled child. I wanted to do more, maybe help in a hospital, but my mother-in-law wouldn't let me."

It was at her mother-in-law's insistence that Leila's family left Kuwait six weeks after the invasion began. Leila and her husband's family went to London, where she immediately became involved with the organization Citizens for a Free Kuwait. "There was so much my husband could have done to help. Instead, he spent every day in front of the television watching the war and drinking. I, the woman, was suddenly the one who was handling everything for the family. By the time we returned to Kuwait, I realized I was the stronger of the two of us. He is weak, too weak for me. I see that now. We will divorce; it is only a matter of time."

The divorce rate in Kuwait increased dramatically after the war. One-third of all marriages now do not survive, an extremely high percentage in an Islamic country. Dr. Fahad Nasser, a sociologist at Kuwait University, attributes some of the divorces to the breaking down of the extended family. "The extended family played a controlling factor. Marriage was not between two people but between two families, so divorce was a very major step. If a marriage was not going well, both families became involved. That control is diminishing. It began with the advent of oil wealth. Couples wanted to live separately from their parents and could suddenly afford to do so.

Other factors include the education of women, and women being exposed to the outside world as they were during the Gulf War."

When Leila and her family returned to Kuwait, she retained the Western wardrobe she had worn in London. With her newfound authority, no one challenged her right to do so, nor did they challenge her when she declared she would begin working, and took a job at one of the Ministries. Her affair with Hamid, a married man with whom she works, began a few months later.

"He paid a lot of attention to me, and that in itself was seductive. My husband has hardly touched me since I became pregnant with my son. Hamid awakened me sexually. I was a mother, but I knew so little about sex. He taught me so much, how to caress and be caressed. It was the first time a man has ever slept in my arms. Once my husband has had sex with me, he doesn't want to touch me. Hamid is not like that."

Leila and Hamid spend a few hours together midweek at friends' beach chalets, the weekend houses most affluent Kuwaiti families own, or, when they can arrange it, in the apartments of discreet friends. "I just have to take such care that my husband doesn't find out. He would divorce me, which is okay, but he would take away my son to punish me, and that I could not survive."

It was Leila who drew my attention to the poem on democracy in the weekend paper by a member of Kuwait's royal family that begins at the top of this chapter. "That's what democracy means to me, too," said Leila. "Freedom to be treated the same as a man."

• • •

I caught up with the author of Leila's poem a few days later. Sheikha Dr. Souad M. Al-Sabah, an economist, is also a human rights and women's rights activist, writer, and one of the better-known poets in the Arab world. This is an unexpected combination in a woman who is a member of a family described by the former head of America's National Organization of Women as "a despotic, clan-run monarchy, guilty of gender apartheid."

Dr. Souad is the widow of His Highness, Sheikh Abdullah Al-Mubarak Al-Sabah, the son of the founder of modern-day Kuwait. Despite her lofty connections, her writings have twice been banned in Kuwait, once in 1985–86, and again in 1988–89. On both occasions all media in Kuwait were prohibited from publishing or broadcasting any literary work or economic study by Dr. Souad, and from mentioning her name in connection with any social or cultural event. Not content with that, on the second occasion, the Kuwaiti authorities tried to make the ban universal throughout the Arab world by requesting that other governments also not publish her. "This was possible because, as you know, most of the mass media in the Arab world are, in one way or another, controlled," she said. Although the Kuwaiti government gave no reason for such measures, her work as a human rights and women's rights defender was assumed to be the cause.

"To understand what it means to be banned as a writer, one has to consider it within the context of the Middle East," she told me. "Expressions of views have always been subject to censorship, either directly or indirectly, explicitly or implicitly. Therefore, to be banned from writing in the Middle East has always been a common occurrence. What was so different in my case was being banned while a member of the ruling family, and by definition I am, therefore, expected to be a supporter of the prevailing regime. In effect, I am. However, a supporter or believer of the validity of the system does not necessarily mean that I become a blind rubber stamp. The real service is to be an intelligent assessor and objective contributor."

Dr. Souad is a founding member of the Arab Organization for Human Rights. "This work covers many issues, whether relating to political matters, those concerning women, or any other sector where injustices have been perpetrated on a weak segment of society. Human rights, and, in fact, the value of humans, have for a long time in the Middle East been given very low priority to say the least." With statements like these it is easy to see how the princess might run afoul of the royal family to which she belongs.

Like Afghanistan's Fatima Gailani, Dr. Souad is part feminist but also very much a product of her environment. Her approach is low-key and quietly determined. She is soft-spoken to the point where one almost has to strain to hear her comments. Above the sofa where she was sitting was a large portrait of her late husband, who died in 1990. His fifty-year-old widow talked about him with reverence and great love, and frequently as though he were still alive. "We had thirty-two years together," said Souad. "He was my husband, my father. Emotionally, physically, he was everything to me." The sheikh also was the man responsible for Souad's strong beliefs and opinions.

Souad was fifteen when she was betrothed to the sheikh, who was then forty-two. The arranged marriage made her the sheikh's sixteenth wife. The princess was perfectly matter-of-fact about this.

"No," she said, "I didn't mind. They were tribal marriages, intended to build tribal alliances. The Prophet did the same thing. My husband married these women when he was building his political life." Unlike the Prophet, however, Sheikh Abdullah divorced his wives after a month to a year of marriage.

I asked her how the brides felt about these marriages. Had they any idea the relationship might be measured only in days or weeks? "Oh, yes. They know," she said. "They are happy to be chosen; it is a great honor. To marry a royal sheikh is considered a great honor both by the woman and her tribe. Even after she is divorced, she is respected for having been his wife. Many men then want to marry her because through his wife he will have access to the sheikh."

Souad went on to explain that the many marriages of the ruler of Kuwait were also to cement tribal alliances. The Emir, Sheikh Jaber, reputedly has had seventy-two wives, but even the royal family has lost count. Three have been permanent wives, but the remainder have been brief tribal marriages for political reasons. Sometimes the unions lasted only a week or two. Now that the ruler is seventy-one, he is said to be slowing down in the matrimony stakes. At last count, the Emir had thirty-eight sons; no one to whom I spoke seemed sure of the number of his daughters.

Souad's husband, however, had only one living child from his various marriages and alliances before her. The surviving child, a daughter, was raised by the sheikh and Souad. Didn't her husband's former wife, the child's mother, object to this arrangement? I asked. "Oh, she was not the daughter of one of my husband's wives, she was the daughter of one of his slaves." For the second time in a matter of minutes I was silently nonplussed. Souad continued calmly as if we were discussing the price of groceries. "The mother was black, from Zanzibar. During the time of Mubarak the Great, my husband's father, our slaves mostly came from Africa. Later, white Russians were preferred."

Such comments indicate that both Kuwait, like other Gulf oil states, and Souad herself have changed dramatically in the last few decades. Despite her husband's sixteen wives and concubine slaves, Souad considers him to have been very progressive. And certainly, where she was concerned, that seems to have been the case.

Souad was still in high school when her father informed her that Sheikh Abdullah had asked for her hand. "I was very excited. I knew of his reputation and had been dreaming of marrying this man. He was strong, generous, and brave; for me he was like one of your

Western knights. The first time I met him, I was so in awe of the great Abdullah Al-Mubarak, I was terrified. My father and I were invited to have tea with him at the White Palace [now her home]. I took such care with my appearance, kept changing my outfits, my hair. I was a typical fifteen-year-old. I couldn't make up my mind even though I was going to be covered by an *abaya*. I was shown into his salon alone, and was so scared I was shivering. He realized how nervous I was and talked to me gently, asking me about school and my exams. And as I relaxed a little, he asked me whether my father had pressured me into agreeing to the marriage. I told him no, but I couldn't find the words to tell him how pleased I was. I kept looking at the floor. This was one of the country's great men, and I was overwhelmed."

Once married, Souad stopped attending school, but her husband encouraged her to attend his daily *diwaniyas,* the Arab salon or council at which politics and other important issues of the day are discussed with leaders. It is also the forum to which citizens bring problems to be adjudicated by the sheikh. *Diwaniyas* are male-only events in the Islamic world. Souad attended her first one in 1958 when she was still only sixteen. "I was the first woman to attend a *diwaniya.* I also went with my face uncovered. If the men present were surprised, they did not say anything out of respect for my husband. Two hundred men at a time attended — ministers, politicians, intellectuals, journalists, even King Saud of Saudi Arabia. These gatherings were my school, my real education. I was like a sponge. At first I was too shy to participate, but gradually I did, and my husband encouraged this. I traveled abroad with him and met kings and presidents. And I learned so much. Today, I have more male friends than female because of my involvement in my husband's work."

Later, when her husband was posted to Cairo and London, he encouraged her to attend universities there. She obtained her M.A. and Ph.D. at the London School of Economics. Along the way, the couple had five children, one of whom later died.

"My husband also encouraged me to write from the time we married, and to be published. He never censored me. Even when my writing was banned, he encouraged me to continue. He supported me with my work in human rights. At the time of the first ban in 1985, newspapers began to attack me because I was planning to attend a foreign conference. They said a woman shouldn't travel or attend such an event. I was extremely upset. But my husband told me to ignore the criticism and continue as before."

I mentioned to her that I was surprised that newspapers would attack someone whose husband was so prominent. And while she didn't say it, I was left with the impression that the sheikh, then in his seventies, had seen the mantle of power taken up by younger men. Said Souad of the move to attack her, "I know who was behind the move; they want to pull the carpet from under all Arab women, all over the Arab world. The conservative Islamic movements do not want a woman to be well known. I am more fearful of them now than I was when my husband was alive.

"Islam gave women all sorts of rights. Khadija, the Prophet's first wife, was also his employer, and she participated in all activities. The Prophet sought advice from his wives and his sisters-in-law. Kuwaiti women should take their full rights, and they should have the right to vote. Women are fifty-two percent of the population here. The authorities are aware women will change the balance of elections if they are permitted to vote."

• • •

There is more than one female maverick in the Al-Sabah family. Sheikha Dr. Rasha-al-Hamood al-Jaber al-Mubarak Al-Sabah, the first cousin of the Emir, could not be more different from the stylish and coiffured females in the royal family. Instead of Chanel or Dior, Sheikha Rasha's style is more thrift shop — the men's section. On the two occasions that we met, once for dinner in a restaurant and again several days later at her home, she was dressed identically, in baggy sweat pants and a peach-colored polo shirt. When relaxing at home she often prefers the comfort of a man's *dishdasha*.

Sheikha Souad may have been the first female to attend a *diwaniya*, but Sheikha Rasha decided to go one step further and host her own, the only woman in the country and the rest of the Gulf and the Middle East to do so. Another unusual aspect of Rasha's *diwaniyas* is that she invites men and women together. Souad and Rasha are very dissimilar people, but both are iconoclastic in their own ways, each having challenged the establishment to which they belong.

In Islamic countries, where substantial portions of the population are still illiterate, change, particularly for women, is invariably instigated from the top, the educated elite, instead of from grassroots organizations as it usually is in the West.

Rasha, like Souad, prefers to be known by her academic title rather than her royal one. Dr. Rasha's Ph.D. from Yale University is in Italian Renaissance Literature. Her confrontation with the ruling family came a year after the occupation, when as a vice-rector of Kuwait University, she publicly accused the school's administration, the secretary-general, and the minister of education of corruption. All the individuals she named were government, or Al-Sabah, appointees. But just as accusations in the past against the ruling circle have traditionally been ignored, so were these. "My complaints fell on deaf ears," said Dr. Rasha, despite the fact that she was charging that vast amounts of university funds had been siphoned off, and despite her closeness to the ruler.

She claimed the funding began to disappear shortly after the occupation, when the government allocated the equivalent of $120 million to the university as a six-month recovery fund in addition to the $90 million operational budget. "The University was devastated during the war," said Dr. Rasha, who had worked at the school for fifteen years and was a tenured professor there. One of the top priorities after the war was to reopen the university by September 1991 because Kuwait's students had missed an entire academic year. In order to meet this target, the large emergency budget was appropriated. "A month after the money was made available, the university authorities were tearing out their hair about what to do with all these millions in the set period of time. Shortly after, I noticed that books were being fiddled with: computers, library equipment, and all sorts of things would be ordered but never appear in the university. The entire carpeting was changed twice. It was brand-new; there was no reason whatsoever to change it. One thousand air-conditioning units for the school were ordered. They cost $1,380 each [a total of $1,300,000]. The university doesn't use air-conditioning units; it's all central air!

"I was very concerned about this. This was not a matter of difference in educational philosophy, or how to treat students. This was a point of personal integrity, ethics. I went to my family elders in the government and told them what was happening. I recognized I was putting them in an awkward position. I was telling them the rector and the minister were rotten. Many people in this country feel the entire government has long been rotten. But they couldn't afford to get rid of the minister. I think they felt vulnerable because this would be admitting that the government was not at the level expected by the average Kuwaiti.

"It is a question of courage. The people I went to had chosen the people I was complaining about. It was a case of, 'If you criticize them, you are indirectly criticizing us.' When I recognized that the misconduct on several levels — financial, administrative, and legislative — was being ignored, I resigned."

Rasha now feels she is being penalized for refusing to stay silent. "By comparison with other countries in the region, one can say a lot here and get away with it. In Kuwait, we don't have midnight visitors, we're not clamped down on, or thrown into jail for differing with the system. Here, they deal with us in a very subtle way. If you show any sign of dissent, you are ostracized. And sometimes, because it is more subtle, it is more painful than being thrown into jail; if you are jailed you become an instant popular hero. This kind of ostracism is very demoralizing unless you are very strong. I am going through it right now. Because I dared say in front of the press that the minister and these officials are rotten, and that most of the government officials are a bunch of twerps. Now these same people are dealing with me in a very sophisticated way.

"For example, I resigned seven months ago, and I still have not been given another official position. That in itself is not so important, but I feel that in the present situation in Kuwait, with the country trying to rebuild, people like me, in all modesty, are of some value to the academic community, to the government. If I weren't being ostracized, I would have been offered another position long before now. Instead I have been relegated to a wasteland.

"The university is part of me, it's in my blood. Fifteen years is a long time. I'd love to go back, but I cannot, not while the system is so bad. The war changed me. You lose your country, your identity, and then get it back. I think I became more intense, stronger, in trying to achieve certain goals, or breaking down certain taboos and barriers."

Dr. Rasha also has spoken out on women's rights. During the occupation she had her own consciousness raised and has since been trying to do the same for her fellow countrymen. "Before the invasion when one heard people say, 'Political rights for women? Oh, no, they haven't reached political maturity,' one was nauseated, but one had heard it before. But during the war, when women were being killed, or raped, then such statements became intolerable. I began talking out vociferously to the leaders of the country because I have access to them, they are family.

"I told them our constitution states all citizens are equal, and it is unconstitutional to deny women their rights. I also reminded them of all the pledges they had made." At the October 1990 Kuwait conference in Saudi Arabia to discuss Kuwait's future, at which the

Crown Prince promised a better deal for women, Rasha was also invited. "But then the Saudis disinvited me when they realized I was a woman. I got a phone call saying, 'Would you mind not coming?'

"On another occasion, I was invited by the Legal Sub-Committee of Parliament to talk about women's rights. They also invited the Islamic Reform Society to attend, and their representative got up and cited *fatwas* from years ago from Al Azhar in Cairo stating that women should not vote. I responded by saying that since then Al Azhar had issued other *fatwas* confirming the right of women to vote. I pointed out that in Egypt women not only have had the right to vote for many years, but they also have sat in parliament and been appointed ambassadors and ministers." Despite such arguments, Kuwait's political conservatives prefer the status quo, where power is not shared with the opposite sex.

"In Kuwait, the traditionalists are playing on either tradition or religion to block women from getting their rights," said Dr. Rasha.

After some months of being professionally exiled, the princess appealed to her cousin, the Emir, and told him that unless her situation was changed, she would leave Kuwait and work abroad. " 'I feel I have to go,' I told him, 'because I cannot sit at home doing nothing.' "

Since resigning, the princess has done what a lot of retirees do — go fishing. "I hang out with retired pearl divers. They are octogenarian fishermen, men from simple, modest backgrounds. I like to spend time with them, sit and hear their stories of how this country used to be not so long ago, before oil." Rasha's boat reflects her very unregal lifestyle. "It's not a yacht, it's a simple fisherman's boat, twenty-five-feet long, with two eighty-five horsepower engines, and a large open area for the net."

Coming from the very privileged branch of the Al-Sabah family, the arm that she admits is enormously wealthy, the princess could afford to buy pretty much anything she desires. Since the war, however, her lifestyle, materially, has more in common with a monk than it does with megarich oil sheikhs. During the occupation, her palace home was plundered and rendered unlivable, and virtually everything she possessed was stolen. But it isn't her looted Maserati, Jaguar, or other luxury items she mourns. "It's no big deal for me not to have my Piaget watches, and my Chanel and Valentino. It's no big deal for me not to live in a house full of servants." Rasha used to have fourteen. "It's my collection of five hundred T-shirts from all over the world, and I had worn every one of them. These I mourn. I'm not the kind of person you give gold or diamonds to; those are things I never wear. I throw them in a drawer and forget them. I tell people close to me who want to give me a present to get me a carton of engine oil for my boat — it costs about seventeen dollars — or sports socks; mine are getting threadbare."

In her new spartan life, Dr. Rasha shares an apartment with American academic and author Margot Badran, who hosted her in Cairo during her wartime exile. Rasha escaped from Kuwait just ahead of Iraqi troops trying to round up any member of the Al-Sabah family; she dressed as a Bedouin and posed as the second wife of a shepherd. "The pickup I escaped in came complete with sheep." Her new home is so modest that I was convinced I had the wrong address when I went to visit her. The apartment block, which is university housing, is scruffy, down-at-the-heels, with peeling plaster, chipped, dingy brown paint, and a view of a large parking lot. And while the paint is fresh in Dr. Rasha's home, there are no books and no pictures on the walls. The apartment is totally devoid of character, as impersonal as a low-budget hotel room, and yet the princess has lived here for a year. Chain-smoking the Dunhill cigarettes she is never without, she told me, "I don't like a lot of clutter. It's more restful for me to see white walls; it's bare, but I like it. I've simplified my life."

The three items she salvaged from her previous homes are stacked against a wall, not displayed. There is a large but damaged photograph of her as a child, a silver-framed photo of Margaret Thatcher inscribed to Rasha, and a large picture of one of her brothers, who disappeared at sea a few years ago on a solo fishing trip of the kind that Rasha likes to take. Reports at the time suggested he may have been captured by Iranians, but it is not a subject Rasha talks about easily.

The forty-two-year-old princess is unmarried and doesn't see her status changing. For years she has avoided society weddings, where arranged marriages are frequently made in the Islamic world. Mothers of eligible males inspect the single females present. "It's like a cattle market," derides Rasha. "The mothers who go on and on about 'my son,' the women who think they are fabulous, throwing themselves around to attract attention. Lavish functions with people dripping in diamonds. For me, it's such a circus, I try to avoid it. My attitude was very painful for my mother when she was alive. But these functions were hell for me. Just the other week, there was a very grand wedding, a sheikha's daughter, and it didn't take me a second to say no, I wouldn't attend. I think that is a privilege that comes with age."

Rasha's own mother and sisters were married at thirteen. The sheikha avoided that by attending British boarding schools from the age of eight. Instead of being married as she entered her teens, she was "kept busy cleaning the tennis shoes of senior girls." Some of her eccentricities, particularly her sartorial tastes, which would seem perfectly normal among the British upper crust, may well date from that era.

In Kuwait, where everyone knows everyone or believes they do, people talking about Rasha assume she is gay. Her being single in a culture where marriage is usually a forgone conclusion, her interests in traditionally masculine activities (Rasha is also the only female member of the Kuwait squash club), and her laissez-faire appearance, make it easy to draw that conclusion. The princess denies it without being asked. "I don't have boyfriends, I don't have girl-friends," she responds to a question about her private life coming under public scrutiny. "I don't have sex. I don't have liaisons. I'm not on drugs. I'm quite boring."

She looked at my face and laughingly asked, "Are you skeptical? Maybe I'm suppressed or married to my books . . . or maybe I've never married because I've never met a man who fits the ideal of my older brother, Salim. He's the person I'm closest to, whom I respect, love, and lean on emotionally. He's gentle, extremely intelligent, and extremely wise. With an elder brother in this part of the world, you are supposed to be obsequious, pay your dues. Salim isn't like that at all. He supports me even in the things that I do that are considered very untraditional here."

As unlikely an Al-Sabah as Dr. Rasha is, she stills sees her family as being the bond that holds Kuwait together. "There may be people here who are frustrated by the Al-Sabah regime, certain trends that are at odds with them. The Emir is a grossly misunderstood man. He's portrayed as being a despotic recluse, who doesn't like his own people. The depiction is utterly distorted. He's very sweet and gentle, a modest and pious man. The interests of the country are extremely important to him. And the majority of the Kuwaiti people will not accept any other leaders except those they elected back in 1752.

"I dread the day when our family, the leaders, become so weak, or so ostracized, they are reduced to symbolic rulers only. At that time I think the Islamists, the fundamentalists, will go for the kill.

The Islamic forces here are very powerful, and tightly organized. I fear that what has happened in Algeria and is happening in Egypt will happen here. And it could. When Islam is taken as a vehicle to create antagonism between compatriots, then I feel it is very dangerous."

According to Dr. Rasha, the Islamists in Kuwait are funded by the Islamic Reform Society, a movement founded in Saudi Arabia. "They receive funds from the Kuwaiti government, from the Muslim Brotherhood, and other such international organizations, and they control the Students' Union on campus, where they've had a lot of influence. Interestingly, it is the women students who always elect them. Six years ago the university Islamists managed to get the cafeteria and classes segregated and sixty percent of the girls now wear *hijab*. That was not the case before; only a handful did. And we've had the bombing of the medical school.

"This extremism is an instant knock-out with the youth. They are looking for guidance. And the Islamists are offering a solution to how to shape your life, how to lead your life. Their platform is 'Islam Is the Solution.' You can go around wearing your Cartier glasses, using your Cartier pen, and driving your Maserati, and still be looking for some kind of guidance. Islam has become a bandwagon for them to climb on. This fundamentalism sends shivers up my spine."

• • •

Mixing with the Al-Sabahs and the people close to them could easily lead one to believe that all Kuwaitis live on Easy Street. But for three hundred thousand people who were recently declared non-Kuwaitis despite the fact that their grandparents or even great-grandparents were born in Kuwait, life is very different. Many of them have been reduced to begging to survive. And the people who are most in need are now excluded from Kuwait's "cradle to grave" lavish welfare system, which includes heavily subsidized housing, food, medical care, gasoline, utilities, and free education.

The *bedoun*, the stateless, are Kuwait's settled Bedouin or nomads, and before they were declared non-Kuwaitis they comprised one-third of the country's citizenship. Poorly educated, they held the lesser-paying jobs that the more affluent nationals had no interest in: the police and fire-fighting forces, the army, porters, and bodyguards for the royal family. They were appointed the latter because Bedouin traditionally are considered extremely loyal, a poignant irony in view of Kuwait's recent treatment of them.

Their problems began in the fifties when the government required all Bedouin who wanted to have official citizenship to be registered. The system, like all of Kuwait's bureaucracy, was complicated and cumbersome, and it required a number of visits to the registration offices. Because the population then was mostly illiterate, many Bedouin did not understand the importance of registering, or they went once and thought that was sufficient. Many women were not registered because their menfolk did not think it was necessary. As far as the Bedouin were concerned, if they were born in Kuwait, and their fathers and fathers' fathers were born there, too, they were Kuwaiti, and a piece of paper didn't change that.

But the Kuwaiti government changed the rules, and at the time of the Gulf War, when the three hundred thousand–strong Palestinian middle-management population was declared traitorous and expelled because of Yasser Arafat's alignment with Saddam, so too were the Bedouin arbitrarily declared non-Kuwaitis and deprived of their legal right to live in the country they consider their homeland. The argument in their case was that nomads could include Iraqis and other nationals, and the easiest way to detect a few was to get rid of them all. Kuwait is now importing large numbers of Egyptians to do the jobs the Palestinians and Bedouin formerly held.

When Kuwait's Bedouin stopped living in tents in the desert, the government relegated them to special settlements outside the main cities, not unlike America's Native American reservations, but with fewer facilities. The Bedouin ghettos are in Sulaibiya and Jahra. When I visited the former, it reminded me of the poorer parts of Soweto Township in South Africa. Row after row of shoddily constructed cinder block houses with bare cement floors, separated by narrow lanes, are a far cry from the opulence of the average Kuwaiti home forty-five minutes' drive away. In fact, the Bedouin houses are not as big as most Kuwaitis' garages.

The temperature on the day that I went was a brutal 125 degrees, and inside the tiny three-room home I visited, it was even hotter; sweat ran in rivulets off guests and hosts alike. Forty-three-year-old Umm Hamid, mother of Hamid, offered us tepid water to drink. This family of fifteen could not afford to give a guest the iced sodas or juices normally offered. Before the Gulf War, Umm Hamid's husband had been a school guard earning Kuwaiti Dinars 355 ($1,225) per month. When the Bedouin were declared stateless, they were all fired from their jobs and forbidden to work, and their children were banned from attending school.

"The government did these things because they want us to leave Kuwait. But where can we go? We are Kuwaitis, our family has always lived here. I was born here and so were my parents and grandparents," said Umm Hamid, whose face is adorned with the indigo tattoos of a tribal Bedouin, and who has never attended school. "My brother registered when it was required, but they didn't register me. They didn't think it was necessary for girls. Now it is too late." Umm Hamid's thirteen children are able to eat now only because of her brother's charity. Her twenty-five-year-old son, Ahmad, was selling fruit and soft drinks on the street in Kuwait City to help support the family, but was warned he would go to jail the next time he was caught working. Checkpoints on roads entering the city turn back the stateless. The younger children in the family, who are closed out of their former school, have nowhere to play. The settlements have never had parks or recreational facilities, and the desert area around Sulaibiya was heavily mined by the Iraqis and is not on the priority list for mine clearing. A number of youngsters in the settlement have been killed or injured by mines.

"When they stopped our children from going to school, I was very sad," said Umm Hamid. "They were good students, and I thought education would give them a better life than the one we had. Now that possibility is finished. Our lives are in the hands of God. No one else cares."

The day I visited the settlement was the day the government announced that the Emir had donated $2.5 million to the London Zoo to save it from closure. Many of the Bedoun in Sulaibiya were angry. "The Al-Sabahs can feed another country's animals, and they let their own people starve," said one man outside the grocery store. He gestured to a veiled woman sitting on the sidewalk with her baby in the scorching heat in front of a pile of secondhand clothes she was trying to sell. "I have to make seven dinars [$24] every day," she told me, "or else my children will go hungry." Many days she didn't succeed. Children playing in the dust near her were barefoot; their parents could not afford to buy them shoes.

Hala Diham Homood Al-Thafery also lives in Sulaibiya, but I didn't meet her there. I was introduced to her at the Kuwait Association to Defend War Victims, a nongovernmental human rights organization in eastern Kuwait City. Hala had gone there braving checkpoints because she was desperate to obtain the small food ration packages the association occasionally gives out to particularly needy cases. As I passed her and her eleven-year-old son, Khalid, in the hallway, she clutched my arm. *"Min fadlak.* Please, I will kiss your feet if you can help me," she begged. The Bedouin tribes are extremely proud and dignified people. I knew how difficult it was for her to accost a stranger this way. But Hala was near despair. Khouloud Alfeeli, a twenty-seven-year-old journalist at the state-run Kuwait News Agency who volunteers at the center, showed her into an office where we could talk. Hala asked if her son could leave the room while she recounted her story to me. "He doesn't know what happened to his father, and he shouldn't know," she said.

When the invasion occurred, Hala had urged her husband, Jasser, to take her and their seven sons to Saudi Arabia with other fleeing Kuwaitis. "He said I had nothing to be afraid of. He wasn't a military man, the soldiers wouldn't bother poor people like us. And at first they didn't. Then, two months after the occupation began, the Iraqis came to our area. It was late, the children were sleeping. The soldiers began to search our house and found an envelope of papers from the Ministry of Health, where my husband worked as a porter. They started to beat him and kick him, pulling him by his hair and his beard. They threw him on the floor, tied his hands behind him, and then kicked him repeatedly in the head. He told them if they were going to kill him to please take him outside and not do it in front of the children. Then they took him away."

The young Bedouin woman stopped talking. Her work-roughened hands began compulsively to make small pleats in her *abaya.* Hala, who was pregnant with her eighth child at the time of her husband's arrest, did not know whether to take her sons and leave, or whether to wait so Jasser could find her if they released him. She chose to wait. "Two days later, the Iraqis came back and said my husband wanted to see me. I wasn't allowed to take my children, or any clean clothes for Jasser. 'Just see your husband and then you'll come back,' they said.

"I told my eldest son, 'If I don't return, take the other children to your uncle's wife.' The soldiers took me to the local courthouse and began to question me. They said, 'As the wife of a Resistance member, who does your husband see?' I told them he wasn't in the Resistance, he wasn't even in the army. Then they asked why my head was covered, and they pulled off my *hijab.* I became very upset, and said, 'You are our Muslim brothers. Would you treat your sister so in front of strange men?'

"The officer became angry. He called me the daughter of a whore, and said he would teach me to respect Iraqis. Then he began hitting me. . . . " Hala broke off from her story again. Suddenly, she began to rock back and forth in her chair, emitting a low keening sound that chilled me. Silent tears rolled down her face. Khouloud, who had been interpreting, got up to comfort her. "I don't think she's going to be able to go on with the interview," said Khouloud. "I think she's too upset." Hala continued to rock agitatedly, the wailing sound coming from her describing the pain of her memories more vividly than words.

After some minutes, Hala dried her tears on the worn sleeve of her *abaya*. Did she want to stop? She shook her head. "No, you should know what happened to us. . . . The soldiers ripped my clothes. I told them I was pregnant. They laughed. Then they raped me, four of them. They left me bleeding on the floor, and kicked me in the stomach, cursing me because I was making them dirty." Hala did not know it at the time, but she was miscarrying.

"Kuwait and all its money can never bring back my honor. If water is poured onto the ground, you cannot put it back in the jug. I am not a modern girl, my honor was the most important thing I owned. It is lies what they say about Arab brotherhood, if Muslim can do this to Muslim."

Hala did not see her husband, and did not know if he was alive or dead. When she was released after three days in custody, she and the children hid in basements of empty homes, terrified of going outside until hunger drove them to look for food. After liberation, she was informed that Jasser, like many Kuwaitis, had been in prison in Basra, Iraq. The first she knew of his release was when she was contacted by Kuwaiti hospital authorities and told her husband was there for treatment. "When I went to visit him, I saw him and screamed. They had put out burning cigarettes on his face. He didn't ask how I was or how the children were, he just kept staring at the wall. Then the doctors said they needed to speak to me. They told me they were transferring him to another hospital, that he was bleeding from his penis, that he was damaged inside, and needed an operation."

Jasser had been repeatedly sodomized by his Iraqi torturers, and a broken bottle had been jammed into his rectum, causing multiple internal injuries. He also had been hung from ceiling fan hooks for hours at a time, a common Iraqi torture. After recovering from surgery, Jasser, who was still emotionally very traumatized, was transferred to a psychiatric hospital where he remained for three months.

Hala clenched her teeth. "I never told Jasser about my rape. I was afraid if he knew it would kill him. It is such a shameful thing to happen to a man's wife. Once, after he came home, our youngest son asked him why he kept crying. The boy said, 'The soldiers took Mother, too, but she doesn't cry all the time.' Jasser asked me if I had been raped. I told him no, and swore on the Koran to convince him. I asked a religious sheikh' if what I had done was a sin and he said no, because the truth would have affected my husband's mental health. Even now my husband is taking pills to make him sleep, and all he can say over and over is that everything, his life, has been taken away from him. It breaks my heart to look at my husband. He won't leave the house because people know what happened to him and he is too ashamed.

"Now I am the one who has to look after the family. I am illiterate and because we are now called stateless, we are not permitted to work. I went to my husband's office to try to get his last month's salary that the Ministry of Health owed him. It was only one hundred and sixty dinars [$552]. They said they would give it to me if I brought papers proving we were leaving Kuwait. I told the man our families were born here, so where would we go? He didn't care. So now I beg for rice so my family can eat. I go from mosque to mosque asking for food. I come here. And then I begin again. I don't know how much longer I can keep putting out my hand to strangers.

"If the government deports us, they will send us to Iraq. We are not Iraqi, and how can we go to Iraq after what they did to us? They would kill us."

The one in three Kuwaitis who, like Hala and her family, were arbitrarily deprived of their nationality and who have been reduced to begging, are a side of Kuwait the regime would rather the world did not know about. And because they do not meet the criteria for refugees, the United Nations cannot help them. Just as Kuwait's corruption and mismanagement is causing Kuwaitis to join the religious extremism movement, the stateless, like many disenfranchised Muslims, may eventually have no choice but to turn to the Islamists as the only solution to their problems.

CHAPTER 8

Muslim Missionaries, American Converts

*And who believe in what has been revealed to you
and what has been revealed to those before you,
they are certain of the Hereafter.*

KORAN 2:4

T HE WOMEN ARRIVED DRESSED from head to toe in black: dark, shapeless, and silent shadows of indeterminate age and social standing whose personalities and characters were effectively erased as the garments intend. Floor-length *abayas* disguised their figures, *hijabs* covered their hair, and their faces, except for their eyes, were hidden behind *niqabs*. Despite the summer heat, a number wore black gloves and socks or stockings. Leaving their shoes at the door as they entered, and shedding their Islamic coats and face coverings, the greetings began.

"Hi, Debbie, how ya doing? . . . Have you seen Tracy? . . . Where shall I put these goodies, in the kitchen? . . . Ah, there's Angie." Fresh-faced young women, as American as their names and with accents from Chicago, New York, and North Carolina, were gathering at Mia Ponzo's house. Apart from their head scarves, which they kept on and wore low over their foreheads, their full-length skirts, and several pairs of hands decorated with henna swirls, it could have been a kaffeeklatsch anywhere in the United States. As the mothers caught up on local gossip, their toddlers, several of them blue-eyed towheads, played at their feet in the center of the room. The twenty Americans and two very shy Filipina women who did not unveil were waiting for a twice-weekly Koran class run by a conservative Islamic organization in Kuwait — The Society of Islamic Heritage Revival — to begin.

Their religious teacher, Hind al-Anati, who was dressed the same way as her students, had been selected by the organization to teach the class for Islamic converts because of her fluent English. Thirty-three-year-old Hind, who holds an M.A. from the University of Southern California, is an impassioned and serious woman. A charismatic speaker familiar with American culture and Christianity, she is extremely knowledgeable about her own religion. I had been introduced to Hind earlier in the week and she had brought me along to her foreigners' class so I could meet former American Christians who had "embraced Islam."

"The Prophet, Peace Be Upon His Name, said it is the duty of Muslims to convert people to Islam. 'If you convert one man, it is better for you than a red camel,' he told us. Red camels were very rare and expensive," explained Hind. Hind numbered among her conversion successes her Filipina servant, a former Seventh Day Adventist. "I used to talk to her about Islam, and one day she said to me, 'There is no difference between your religion and mine.' I asked her, 'What more do you need? Supplicate to Allah, become a Muslim,' and she did."

Hind assumed that my knowledge of Islam went deeper than a journalist's interest. "You've read a lot about Islam, you're familiar with the Koran. If you know the Prophet is the Prophet, why not become a Muslim?" It was a question posed repeatedly by Muslims in my four years in the Islamic world. Muslims in this part of the world invariably assume Westerners are Christian, or, less commonly, Jewish. Faith is such an integral part of people's lives in the Islamic world, it doesn't occur to them that others may be agnostics or atheists. And to avoid lengthy repetitive debates, Westerners, whatever their beliefs, tend to concur that they are indeed Christian. At one of my several meetings with Hind, she gave me a greeting card in which she had written, "Dear Jan, I can find no better present than these words: Supplicate to Allah. If Islam is the only right and accepted religion, He guides and opens your heart to it. If Christianity in its present condition is accepted by Allah, then He keeps you on it."

Hind's organization is one of many such Muslim associations in both the Islamic world and in the West involved in proselytizing. Newspapers in the Gulf and Middle East regularly carry articles about expatriate conversions, like the one entitled "600 Embrace Islam," which was published in the *Arab Times* while I was in Kuwait.

These particular converts, foreign workers in Kuwait, were attributed to the Islam Presentation Committee, which is funded by the government and private charities. IPC was planning to further expand its activities of introducing Islam to non-Muslims in the United States and Asia. I remembered the head of Pakistan's prison system telling me that he had been invited to teach Islam in New York's Rikers Island Prison, and had done so for a year. His prison program claimed that converts to Islam did not become recidivists. Black Muslim movements in the United States have been credited with turning inner-city youths away from drugs and crime.

Hind opened her class that night with an evangelical theme. "We are messengers of Islam all around the world," she told her students as they sat on the floor with her, or on chairs arrayed around the edges of the room. "You have a great mission before you. When you go to the United States, people will ask why you became Muslims. They will know Islam through you. We are facing rising suspicions globally against Islam. Muslims are being tortured just because they are Muslims. Look at Yugoslavia. When you visit America, don't be afraid when people 'stand in your face' and cause problems for you and your family. Stand firm, let them know what you believe, and they will be affected by you."

Tracy, wearing a cream *hijab* and black *abaya*, interjected, "Americans, even my father, always talk about amputating the hand of a thief when they talk about Islam. It is all they know. People in the States are afraid of what they don't understand. They think Islam is a cult like the Moonies."

"When you are in the U.S. you are like the pioneers in the Prophet's days," said Hind. "If you are firm in your heart, as the early Muslims were, then Islam will come to Americans. In the U.S. of course, there is a problem because the media often equate Islam with terrorism. . . ."

"That is because the American media are controlled by Jews," interrupted our host, thirty-one-year-old Mia Ponzo, from Syracuse, New York, who, like the rest of the women in the room, was married to a Kuwaiti, her third husband. Mia had had two short-lived arranged marriages to two other Kuwaitis. "Prostitutes in the U.S. are Jews, men who run the striptease industry are Jews."

"Weren't Jews, like Christians and Muslims, considered believers, people of the book, by the Prophet?" I asked Mia.

"Yes, they were people of the book, but the Torah and the Bible have been changed so much, they are no longer the actual word of God," she replied. "The Jews have thrown out most of their basic creeds. They've even thrown out the hereafter. Now because they no longer have a hereafter, they have to get the most out of this life. The Jews had a million chances to respect God, and to obey him, but instead, they kept killing his prophets." Mia was referring to the hundred thousand–plus prophets mentioned by Mohammad, twenty-five of whom were Jewish or Christian and are discussed in the Koran. "Now the Jews are a wandering people, without respect, without a homeland, and with a lot of diseases," she said. "But we are not fighting other religions; they are fighting and torturing us. Islam *should* be the religion that rules the world!"

At this point, Hind decided to get the evening back on track and changed the subject. She began to talk about worldly temptations. "In Kuwait, the major temptation is money. The more you have, the easier it is to do whatever you like. Here, it is fashionable to care about materialistic things, to want to be close to wealthy people, to be tempted by higher rank." Hind, a rapid speaker, slowed down and began to enunciate slowly. "To overcome temptation, read your Holy Koran." As if it were a mantra, she repeated the same two phrases six times, as the women listening to her nodded their heads. "Once you have refused the first temptation, it is easier to refuse others.

"The Holy Koran is not just a story book. It is a book on science, finance, sociology, meditation, everything. Any question that you have, it can answer. If you have a problem, go to the highest Lord of the Universe. When you buy a television or a VCR, the first thing you do is go directly to the instruction book. The one who created the machine is the most knowledgeable about it. So it is with our world. Allah created us. If you have questions, in Islam there is always an answer. In Christianity, that is not the case. There are not answers to many of your questions; you are told to have faith. Take your problems to Allah. Supplicate to Allah, bow your head to the floor one, two, three, a hundred times.

"But remember, Satan is always with you. Stay close to strong believers, people who constantly mention the name of Allah. Try to improve yourselves. If you do not go up, you will go down. Paradise is a land of flowing water, of milk, honey, wine, and fruits. Those who do not go to Paradise will be destined to drink boiling water that will cut their bowels to pieces."

Hind paused as Mia's Filipina maid went around the room, serving glasses of Coke and other sodas. As the kids tumbled and wrestled on the floor, Hind handed out tracts in two languages, English and Filipino, on that evening's main topic: embryology and the Koran. Her lecture closely mirrored a scientific video produced in Saudi Arabia, which I had been loaned by the Rabitat-Islami organization. "Little was known by science about the stages and classification of the human embryo until the twentieth century," began Hind. "Certainly, knowledge of embryology was unknown in the seventh century, when the Koran was written. And yet the Koran clearly defines the stages of embryonic development: when the ovum is fertilized it looks like a blood clot. The Koran describes it as looking like a drop of blood. And of course, the ovum was not discovered until the eighteenth century. Prior to that it was believed that the male sperm alone was responsible for procreation.

"In the second very early stage of development, according to the Koran, the embryo looks like a leech, which we now know it does. Forty days after fertilization, the embryo resembles a piece of chewed meat. You can see what look like teeth marks on it. The Koran describes this stage of the embryo as looking like something chewed." Hind passed around drawings illustrating what she was saying. "In the fourth stage, the Koran says, the bones develop and then the bones are clothed with flesh. Dr. Keith Moore, a leading embryologist, president of the Canadian and American Associations of Clinical Anatomists, and author of reference books used in medical schools, says medical science has only in recent years discovered these various stages."

In the Saudi video, Dr. Moore states: "The Koran emphasizes the internal stages of embryo development. There is no way Mohammad could have known such detail; he was an illiterate man, with no scientific training. And such knowledge would have required sophisticated technology, which of course was unavailable then. For example, when the Koran describes the embryo as looking like a leech, this is around twenty-three or twenty-four days after fertilization. At that stage, one would have needed a microscope to see it, which was not developed until very much later. The only reasonable explanation is that these details were revealed to the Prophet by God. Now modern technology is able to prove what Mohammad wrote fourteen hundred years ago. Divine intervention was obviously involved in what Mohammad was able to write."

For Hind, embryology being described in the seventh century is not surprising. "The Prophet also said metal would walk and talk and today we have cars, radio, and television."

Islamic medicine, tying modern scientific developments to Koranic verses, was a topic I ran across a number of times as I traveled through different Muslim countries. Just as the subject had been newly added to the medical school curriculum in the UAE, it appeared to be a recent addition to an international Muslim studies curriculum. When I spoke to Dr. Moore, who, until he retired recently, was Professor of Anatomy and Cell Biology at the University of Toronto, the eminent embryologist and son of a Presbyterian minister said, "We don't know what information was available during the Prophet's day. A lot of scientific research and studies were done in Alexandria, which were later destroyed or lost. [Alexandria, under the Ptolemies — 323–69 B.C. — was a center of scholarship that attracted outstanding scientists and mathematicians, such as Archimedes and Euclid. The Great Library of Alexandria was destroyed during the Roman civil wars.] Skeptics might say that they knew about such things at the time of the Prophet, and such information was later lost during the Dark Ages. But I don't think it is unreasonable to believe that this kind of knowledge could have been passed on to Mohammad, in the same way a lot of things were passed on to other prophets and to Jesus."

Hind ended the hour-long class with the *al-maghreb* prayers, the most important of the five daily observances. The women rose, put on their *abayas* and *hijabs*, and arranged themselves in lines across Mia's guest room facing Mecca. I was asked to sit behind them, as no one is permitted to come between those praying and Mecca. As Hind led the prayers, "*Bismallah al-Rahman a-Rahim . . .* " (In the name of Allah, the merciful, the compassionate . . .), they bowed their heads to the ground in a ritual as unchanging as the faith to which they now subscribe.

Hind insists that the reason she chose to go to graduate school in the United States was to spread the word of Islam. "I was the only veiled woman at the University of Southern California, and I knew it would make people ask me why, and then I could get into discussions on Islam. Most of the discussions I had with my professors were about Islam. I grew up in a religious family, thanks be to God. My parents were praying all the time. I was completely covered from the time I was very young, and I had been a pioneer in Islamic dress at Kuwait University. At the time I was there, only two or three of us were veiled, now more than half the women are. I didn't care what others thought. If you see what you do is right, you do it." Hind would prefer to be more covered than she is. "The companions to the Prophet said a woman should cover all but one eye, so that she can see her way. I drive a car, so this is not practical."

Hind does, however, insist on wearing the *niqab* when she drives, despite its being illegal in Kuwait. "I am much less of a traffic hazard than women wearing Western dress and makeup. Just the other day, a car nearly hit me at a traffic circle because the man driving it was so busy looking at a woman driver whose hair was uncovered and who was wearing cosmetics.

"Islamic dress is designed to make women look unattractive. That is why it is black. It is why I cover my hands; they are part of my body. Allah likes beauty in its correct place. You do not take flowers into a bathroom. Therefore, a woman's beauty should be seen only at home by her husband. Look at the Western world nowadays. There is such confusion. Human beasts are eating women, just because they are uncovered. A Western woman has to go out by herself, do everything by herself. This is not freedom. Freedom is to be safe. I do not want eyes following me as I walk.

"Scientifically, we know men are more sexual than women. Studies in America show men are thinking of sex every fifteen minutes. Men are different this way from women. When a woman laughs with a man, she may just be laughing. But to a man, her laugh is much more than that. Something else is happening inside him. This is why it is not enough for a woman to cover in front of a man. Her entire manner and behavior has to fit her appearance. She mustn't laugh with a man, or walk in a way that he might find appealing. When women go shopping, we mustn't talk loudly or laugh with a merchant. This is why I do not bargain very much. My voice should not be heard by a man who is not my relative."

For this reason, Hind, a mother of four, stopped working as an English teacher. "Mohammad the Prophet gave women all the benefits they need in Islam. A woman doesn't need to work; her husband should take care of her, provide for her. I stopped teaching for the sake of the family, and for Allah. My children need me to take care of them. And I need to be rested so that I am in a good mood to receive my husband. My husband has a right. He didn't marry so that he could come home before me. A wife is the one to receive the husband, to soothe him. Allah created men physically stronger. As a woman, I have to be sensitive, nice, and nurturing."

Hind's Koran classes are not considered work but a religious duty. And as she pointed out, they take only two hours a week, she is only with women, and she is not paid to teach.

"It is the Western way to run after everything materialistic, as you see in the U.S. Earning is in the hands of Allah." I reminded Hind of the Arabic maxim "Trust in Allah, but tie up your camel." She responded, "You have seen my home. It is a simple place. Why put all your efforts in making your life in this world comfortable? It is a waste of time. This life is temporary. We should be working hard for our permanent life in the hereafter.

"If a woman is unmarried, she still should not work. Her father, brother, uncle, grandfather, her male relatives should support her. A woman should not have a career where she can mix with men."

How should a single woman spend her time? "She should pray, fast, or talk to Allah. She can learn to sew and save the family money. But it is better for all women to get married. Her role is to have children."

Not unlike many Christian fundamentalists, Hind feels that the revival of her religion may portend the end of the world. "The Islamic revival started ten to fifteen years ago. The movement is growing more and more. It is now the time for Islam to spread. There is a *hadith* that says Islam will rule the world just before the world ends. At that time, there will be a war between Muslims and Jews, a lot of killing. Jesus Christ will guide the Muslim troops as a Muslim. We believe he will come again and break the cross. He will show he was a prophet, not the son of God. The world will benefit when it is Muslim. Everyone will feel at ease."

Debbie Harris, whose home was in Charlotte, North Carolina, before she married Jamal Madouh, an engineering instructor, agrees with Hind. "Islam has given me such peace of mind. When I accepted Islam it was as if somebody opened my heart and put back new life."

Blond, blue-eyed, and as bubbly as a cheerleader, Debbie met her husband when he was in the United States as a student. "We dated for six years because Jamal was on a scholarship and the Kuwaiti government does not permit students to marry foreigners; otherwise they lose the scholarship." Debbie was then a Presbyterian. "When we married in 1985, I told Jamal I didn't want to convert to Islam, and he said that was okay. But he insisted our children be raised Muslim. When I was pregnant with our first child, I kept asking myself how I could allow a youngster to be raised in a faith I didn't believe in. And so I started to take Islamic classes. As I began to read, I found Islam made a lot of sense. It was not contradictory like my own religion. I didn't convert until 1988, however, because I wanted to wait until all my questions were answered. I had been so confused with Christianity. Whenever I asked questions at my church, I got the runaround. My husband would ask me, 'Why do you believe Jesus is the son of God? Why did God need to send his son? Why did he need a mediator?' And I could only say that is what we believe."

The Western converts to Islam with whom I met and spoke in various countries all described their feelings of confusion with Christianity, with what they saw as too much reliance on blind faith, or what they felt were contradictions in the Bible. When I asked for examples of the latter, I was told that in one place in the Bible King Solomon was described as having a thousand horses, yet in another, ten thousand horses. Someone else mentioned that in the Old Testament the eating of pork was banned, but it was permitted in the New Testament. A number of the Islamist organizations publish pamphlets listing such biblical contradictions. I pointed out that there were similar inconsistencies in the Koran, and cited chapter 31, where it is stated that infants should be breast-fed for two years, and then chapter 46, where it says thirty months. Were such minor details so relevant? Yes, I was told. There are far more of them in the Bible. Explained Brenda, "The difference of nine thousand horses for King Solomon may not be so critical. But the point is the Bible has been changed so many times by human hands, and translated into so many languages, modernized so many times, it is no longer possible to know what is the authentic word of God and what isn't." For Brenda and other converts, the Bible had clearly lost much of its credibility.

The converts I met with also told me they felt reassured that the Koran gave specific answers to their specific questions, which they said the Bible did not do. Another benefit that Islam gave them, they said, was the much tighter structure of their everyday lives. In the West, where societal rules are constantly evolving, many individuals do, of course, feel adrift. The occidental converts living in the Islamic world also preferred having definite gender roles to follow: "Life is much less confusing this way for both women and men."

For Debbie, the Koran is as comforting and practical a guidebook for life as Dr. Spock is for new mothers. "For example," she told me, "if I want to know how late a woman can stay out, the Koran tells me. It says whose permission I need when I want to go out. And it tells me at what age I should discipline my child, or when youngsters should learn how to pray. The Koran even tells me how many miles a woman can travel from home without a *mahram,* a male relative chaperon. It is forty-five miles. Whatever I need about everyday life, it is there, as straightforward as a cookbook."

Debbie insists that it was not hard for her as a Westerner to adopt the Koran's guidelines regarding women. "I have very definite rights under Islam as a woman. And if I had to make any sacrifice of what might back home be considered a woman's freedom, I did it for Allah. I am glad not to go out to work. It pleases me to stay home with my children. I think it is where I should be. The beauty of Islam is that everything is for society. Nothing is for yourself."

As I sat talking to Debbie and the other students in Hind's class, I became aware of a certain irony. Women in the Islamic countries through which I had been traveling were striving toward a level of independence, freedom of choice and movement more commonly equated with women in the West. For them it was a major break-through when families permitted them to go out to work or to travel freely. Tahir Malik's sister in Pakistan refused to wear *hijab* or a *chador,* insisting that her character and modesty were unaffected by her mode of dress. Women in Iran had no choice legally in what they wore in public, but insisted that at home they were equal to the men in their lives, if not stronger.

The Americans at the Koran class had willingly turned their backs on the emancipated world in which they had been raised. This partic-ular group had chosen to adopt one of the strictest forms of conser-vative Islam. For them, the unrestricted lifestyle in the United States did not represent freedom. Instead, in many ways, when they looked back, they found Western latitudes threatening. To them, security was to be found in the Islamic world, where men protected and women complied.

A number of the women with whom I spoke had become Muslims independently of planning to marry a man from an Islamic culture. Iman Barber, one of Hind's students, was one; she said she wanted to talk to me, but not that evening. "I make a point of never being home later than eight P.M.," explained Iman, adopting for herself the same kind of restriction that had been placed on Leila by her mother-in-law. It implied that devout Muslim women were never out alone at night. Instead, Iman invited me to her home for coffee and cake at a later date.

Iman's apartment block was in Jabriya in the eastern part of Kuwait City. It was not an attractive neighborhood. Sand and garbage whirled around the buildings and through their open lobbies in the hot, dry wind. Iman's first-floor one-bedroom apartment was decorated in pastel pinks and blues with artificial flower arrangements in the same colors sitting on lace tablecloths. The only indications of a second person in the small apartment were the two toothbrushes in the bathroom and the man's *dishdasha* on the back of the bedroom door.

Iman, once a Sunday school teacher, became a Muslim sixteen years ago in Portland, Oregon, her hometown. Now forty-two, she has been married four times, three times to Muslims. She is currently the polygamous second wife of a Kuwaiti. This is the second time she has been a co-wife, and on both occasions her husband kept his marriage to her a secret from his first wife and family.

"There are a lot of secret second wives here," she said. "The men are afraid to tell their first wives and her family. But they do it anyway and just keep it quiet." A tall, slim, attractive woman, Iman appears supremely confident. Her personality commands a presence, which is why it is hard to see her in the role of a victim, but it is one she has found herself in a number of times. Like the other women at the Koran class, Iman is completely veiled whenever she goes out in public.

Religion has always been an important part of her life. Her father, a civil engineer, was Catholic, her mother Baptist, and she attended a Lutheran Sunday school. "Some of my family were Holy Rollers. You know, 'Hallelujah this, Praise the Lord that.' I eventually became a Baptist. When I was thirteen, my parents separated and I was cared for by a woman who was very active in the church. She had enormous faith, and influenced me tremendously. I was active in the church's youth group. I taught Sunday school." At sixteen, Iman dropped out of high school to marry her childhood sweetheart. By the time she was twenty-one, Iman had two sons and was divorced.

Iman's first introduction to Muslims was through her church's coffeehouse. The church had invited some local Saudis to use it because they did not have anywhere to socialize. "I found myself drawn to them because of the way they cared about one another, and the closeness of their family units. I guess I envied it."

Iman was also on a religious quest. "I was searching. I went on a lot of spiritual retreats. I began to study the Bible intensively, and started discovering a lot of inconsistencies. I had also found a book on the life of the Prophet and saw that Islam and Christianity had some similarities. I mentioned this to an elder of my church. He told me I was reading the book of the devil, and that I should give it to him and he would burn it. This really bothered me. I found I wanted to learn more about Islam. When I mentioned to my family what I was doing, they became very worried and thought I was joining a cult."

During one Sunday school class, Iman mentioned to the children that she had read a book on the Prophet Mohammad. She was promptly dismissed by the church authorities. "I was shocked. I couldn't understand why they couldn't be more open-minded about other religions. I was just reading about the subject."

Two years later she converted to Islam, and shortly after, her ex-husband sued for custody of their sons. "At that time, people had no idea what Islam was. It seems strange now, but that was the case then. My ex-husband claimed I was an unsuitable mother because I associated with Arabs. The legal brief described them as black people, and also suggested that Islam was a cult." Despite character witnesses who testified that Iman was in a stable community that didn't drink alcohol or use drugs, "both of which were very common in Oregon in those days," she says, she lost custody of her children. "I was stunned. I realized I was being penalized for following a religion people didn't know.

"I remember my ex-husband's new wife saying to me during the hearings, 'Why can't you be an American?' and she tried to take off my *hijab*. Even my father thought I was going through a phase. He looked at my *hijab* and long coat and said, 'You won't get married again looking like that. If a man can't see your hair, or know what you look like, he won't marry you.'"

Having lost her children, Iman immersed herself in her new religion and applied to the UAE to study Arabic and *Shariah* law at the university in Al Ain. "It was amazing: twenty-one days after sending my letter, I was in Al Ain. The tuition and board was free, everything was sponsored by the ruler."

When Iman graduated, she made the Hajj pilgrimage to Mecca, and then began teaching English at a school in Dubai. "It was then I realized I wanted to get married again. I met the father of one of the boys in my class. He had just divorced his wife, and had kept the house and their three children, who were all under five. He proposed to me three weeks after his divorce. I was lonely. I liked the idea of a ready-made family, and I accepted. I loved those kids.

I read to them at night, they called me mom. I felt as close to them as I had to my own children."

But the relationship with her husband did not work out. "We had little in common, he was never home at night. A year later, he divorced me. When I lost those kids, it felt the same as when I lost my own two. These three had been yanked away from their natural mother, had had a bunch of different housemaids looking after them, and a father who was never home. I put everything I had into those children. I was devastated when I lost them. See, I still have some of their books," said Iman, pointing to a small bookshelf containing a series of *Winnie the Pooh* books that she translated for them.

Iman decided that if she were to have another relationship, it would have to be with the most religious man she could find. "I wanted to find a man who practiced Islam the way the Prophet taught it." Friends introduced her to a Kuwaiti who was visiting Dubai and who was a senior official in the Ministry of Islamic Affairs in Kuwait. "I met him once, and when he returned home, we talked on the telephone daily for three months. I knew he was married, but when he proposed, I said yes. I thought a religious man, one who held the position he held in the government, would treat both his wives equally as the Koran states. I had read a lot about polygamy. Arab women accept it, and I felt I could. I wasn't a child, and I didn't think I would be jealous. I'd been a first wife, and that wasn't successful. Seeing a man every other day didn't seem so bad. It could be exciting waiting for him."

Iman's fiancé, who had five children with his first wife, flew back to Dubai to marry her and then returned home alone. A month later, he sent her a plane ticket, and she gave up her job and apartment and moved to Kuwait. "He had found me a two-bedroom apartment and furnished it for me. He told me he would see me every day. His job at the Ministry was spreading Islam, and we were supposed to work together doing that.

"But when I arrived, he hadn't informed his wife or their families about his second marriage. He said that because of his powerful position in the government, his marriage to me could cause him political problems, so he would have to keep it secret. I was disappointed, but I could see his point.

"He visited me three times in the first two weeks. Then he just disappeared . . . abandoned me. I knew his telephone numbers but I thought I should be patient and wait. Obviously, he wasn't able to make the commitment of treating both wives the same. Then he wrote a letter that said he could no longer be my husband, that he was divorcing me, but he could be my Islamic brother. I was so hurt, depressed. I had given up my life in Dubai, a circle of friends I considered family to come here and be with him. I remember thinking, How can he be a leading Islamic official and pull this stuff? I didn't have any friends here at the time. I don't think I have ever felt lonelier."

Perhaps because of her abandonment and isolation in Kuwait, Iman turned to the only person she knew, her divorce lawyer. "I poured my soul out to him. I had no one else to talk to in Kuwait then, and I desperately needed to talk. I remember saying to him that there are second-wife situations that work, and asking, Why didn't mine? We discussed the fact that it can work if the husband follows Islamic guidelines on polygamy."

Shortly after, her thirty-five-year-old lawyer, who is also married and has five children, proposed to Iman, and she accepted, agreeing yet again to be a second wife. Iman had married him a month before we met, and as with her first polygamous marriage, her latest husband had not told his first wife. "He's had a second wife before; she was killed in the Gulf War. And there were such bad repercussions from his family when he married her. His father kicked him out of the house for a while. I can understand why he hasn't told anyone.

"Now I see him for about two hours on Fridays, and three hours midweek. He knows it is not correct Islamically, and that he should be spending equal time with both wives. I just have to trust to Allah that he will change."

My own reaction was less generous than Iman's. As we sat in her living room, sipping mugs of coffee and eating the spice cake she had baked, my immediate response when she told me was very Western. "Iman! Are you nuts?" I blurted out. "You are an attractive, intelligent female. Why place yourself in the same untenable position you've just been in?" Yet even before she responded, I understood it in the cultural context in which Iman lived. She had felt vulnerable, and he had responded in a way that was Islamically acceptable.

"He says he loves me. And I care about him a great deal. In the U.S., a married man will have a girlfriend. Here they have second wives. They are legal mistresses. The man is religious enough to fear God and not play around, but not religious enough to treat both wives as the Koran decrees. In Kuwait, it seems a second wife is looked upon as something sinful. It is more accepted in the Emirates.

"I know part of my husband's attraction to me was that I am an

American, and that made me more exotic. For me, I guess I can't be single. There are a lot of temptations for a single woman in the Middle East. And Islamically, I don't think a woman should be tested that way. When a woman is alone, unmarried, it is open ground for the devil's work. I'm praying for him and hope he will change."

Iman's husband supports her financially; she is not currently working. Her husband does not ask her how she passes the time when he is not with her. "He trusts me completely. I don't give him any reason not to. There are times when I have felt very low and alone, when I've broken down in tears and been a basket case. But praise be to God, I've bounced back again. I do feel, however, that Arab men do not know what empathy is. They can't put themselves in somebody else's shoes. Their entire lives are handed to them on a plate. Arab men are raised as princes. He lives in a society where women never question his movements. It's quite acceptable for him to go home only to sleep. There are very few interactions with a wife. He doesn't play with the kids. There are times when I feel I am better off having only a part-time husband. Arab husbands can be very demanding, they want twenty-four-hour service. The man's needs must always be met."

So far, Iman's husband has stayed with her only one night, when his wife was away on Hajj. "I wish he would do it more, but I don't like to push him. Otherwise he'll go away. No matter how I feel when he visits, I try to be as soft, as gentle as possible. I pray his religion, his belief in Islam will become strong enough for him to treat both his wives equally. I also wish I had an Arab brother who could intervene with my husband on my behalf. Family backing can help. The husband knows the wife is not alone, and they may not treat her as badly. Foreign women here are isolated; they have to deal with everything alone. And in a culture where family is so important, it is easy to take advantage of them.

"If this marriage doesn't work, I will not try again. But no matter how bad things might have been, it has never occurred to me to return to the States. I belong here. None of this has shaken my faith. In fact, Islam has kept me together when things have been tough."

• • •

When I returned to my hotel that evening, the apparent emptiness of Iman's life depressed me. I couldn't imagine myself being prepared to make such personal sacrifices, but then, of course, I also didn't share Iman's staunch faith in her religion. And I found myself wondering about single friends and colleagues in the United States in their thirties and forties who, like Iman, were bright, attractive, personable women. Many of them complained they went years between relationships, even between dates. If offered a chance to be a second wife in a society that accepted polygamy, a chance to have a part-time husband, rather than coming home to an empty apartment night after night, I wasn't sure they would all refuse.

Once common in the Islamic world, polygamy began to die out in many Muslim countries in the 1960s and 1970s. As life became more expensive, fewer men could afford to support more than one wife, and as more Muslim women became educated, they began to resist becoming co-wives. For Muslims emulating a Western lifestyle, polygamy simply stopped being fashionable.

The Islamist movements are working hard to reverse that trend. Friday sermons in many mosques encourage it, hefty financial inducements are offered, and women themselves are encouraged personally to select another wife for their husbands, as an ultimate expression of their respect and esteem both for their spouse and the religious orthodoxy they follow. Over and over it was stated that not only was polygamy a man's Islamic right, it was also his biological necessity. Fidelity to one partner was a requirement for women, for men it was not deemed desirable.

Hind, Iman's Islamic teacher, had raised the subject at one of the meetings at her home. She had said that if her husband announced that he wanted to marry again, she would not deny him permission. "I don't say I wouldn't feel sad or jealous. I'm a human being, I have feelings. But I much prefer that one man take care of two wives, two sets of children, instead of my husband having one wife, and then going to a prostitute and bringing home AIDS or some other disease to me. I also believe that if I give up something in life, such as being an only wife, Allah will give something else instead.

"Certainly, the first time my husband goes to his new wife, spends the night with her instead of me, I may not be able to sleep. For the first few times, yes. But I can overcome these feelings of jealousy. When he is with his other wife, I can be using that same time to read the Koran, to pray, to revise my religious classes.

"A man is not everything in my life. Allah gave him to me, and I respect my husband. But I have always thought of a man as if he is an arm to me. If my husband dies, should I die also? No, of course not; life will go on. I respect my husband, but I also have my own life, my mission, my children."

As a conservative Islamist in a movement that views polygamy, like veiling, as a major focus of the religious revival crusade, Hind's comments were predictable, if theoretic. And it is also possible that in practice she may well have accepted it. But in the case of both the converts and Muslim-born women with whom I spoke, polygamy threatened their self-esteem and emotional security like no other issue in their lives. That was confirmed again when I visited a colleague of Hind's. Noura and her husband were both relatively recent Islamists, and, like Hind, Noura was also a religious teacher. I had made an appointment to visit her because I was interested in discussing her involvement with the conservative movement. I had been told that formerly Noura had been much more secular, had even worn miniskirts, although now she is completely veiled. I was interested in learning what had influenced the changes in her, and what advantages she felt her new life gave her.

Noura's home was in Bayan, not far from the Bayan Palace, in an area of new and expensive villas. Her large and luxuriously furnished living room, with its white raw-silk sofas, white marble floor, and silk pastel-colored Persian carpets, made Noura's lifestyle seem enviable. Forty years old, she looked like an Arab Natalie Wood. Her first comment as we sat down was, "My husband is in Syria this week." I thought we were making small talk, and asked if he was there on business. "No," she told me. "He's getting married again."

It was a little like hearing Sheikha Souad say she was a sixteenth wife, or her husband had concubine slaves. Letitia Baldrige's etiquette guide falls short on polite responses to these kinds of statements. I asked her how she felt about it.

"He does it all the time," replied Noura. "He marries them and then he divorces them. This is the third time."

Noura had been married to her husband, Ahmed, a successful businessman, for twenty-two years. They had three sons and two daughters. "I thought we were happily married, and then ten years ago, he came back from a business trip to Syria and told me he had just taken a second wife. He said he had done it ten days before, and he had left his new wife in Syria.

"I was shocked. Our youngest daughter was just two months old. I was angry, and then I became so upset I wanted to kill myself. I lost ten pounds in a week. I was breast-feeding, and my milk dried up. I was sad, depressed. I pleaded with him, 'If there is something wrong with me, tell me, and I will try to make it right.' His response was, 'No, you are good, but I still have to have another wife. I can't live with just one woman.' He said it was a sexual need: he wanted to know how it was with other women. He also said a man is entitled to four wives; it is a religious requirement. I argued with him. I told him Islam required him to ask my permission, and he hadn't.

"I said I wouldn't permit him to move another wife into the house. He would have to give her another house, and his mother who lives with us agreed. He told me I was the first to know. Did that make it better? Finally, he said to me, 'Don't get angry, I will sacrifice, I will divorce her.' And he did."

Families can and do exert tremendous pressure in such cases, and as a result many such marriages are not made public. And when extended families live together under one roof, it can be hard for a dissenter to hold out. "They can wear away opposition more effectively than the ocean wears away a rock," one man told me.

On a visit to Mecca last year, Noura's husband married again, also without telling her beforehand. "Then after twenty days, he divorced her. I have no idea why; he won't discuss it with me. But I knew he wasn't planning to stay with her because I found condoms hidden with the divorce papers. In our culture, a man who plans to keep a wife wants her to get pregnant. He wouldn't use condoms when he was newly married.

"The woman he is marrying now is a seventeen-year-old student. I asked him how he can divorce these women after a few days. If you are not going to finish the glass, you shouldn't sip from it. What about the woman's feelings? My husband is taking these women as possessions and then returning them like used furniture. I begged him not to keep doing this. It's very bad, people talk. I told him next time to keep her, have children with her. A stable second wife would be easier for me to accept.

"It's possible he's been married to other women and I don't know about them. I do know he has had other engagements in the last couple of years because he told me each time.

"It is his right in Islam to take other wives, but it is hard for the children and for me. I don't love him anymore. I don't even like him. It's not a pleasant way to live. Through the years, because of this, he has trained me to hate him. But in front of him I try to pretend I am happy, and I try to laugh and sit with him. We still live together as man and woman, we still share a bed."

Despite her own unhappy experience, Noura believes that polygamy serves a useful purpose. "It is a point of salvation for a woman who cannot have children or is sick. Instead of divorcing her, sending her back to her family, he can take another wife. For this reason, I don't think this part of Islam should be changed. But the man should do it according to Islam. There is a *hadith* that says men should treat their wives like glass, as if they are very fragile. This means gently.

"My husband is a very religious man. And I have tried to fight him with religion, to tell him that what he is doing with all these wives is not Islamic. But I have given up. It's worthless, it brings me pain. He doesn't listen."

According to Noura, neither she nor Ahmed was particularly religious when they married. For her husband, his involvement in the Islamist movement began when he was a graduate student at the University of Florida in Gainesville. He joined an Islamic student organization on campus, and gradually became more orthodox. In those days, Noura wore fashionably short skirts and cutaway dresses, and, like many Kuwaitis, they both lived a Western lifestyle. "At that time, we wanted to have a modern life, be Western. But then as my husband became more religious, gradually so did I. I began to cover, and then when we went to Saudi Arabia for Hajj, I veiled my face, and now even my daughter does. He asked me to stop working, and I did, although I didn't want to. I was a teacher of home economics, I loved my work, and I was very good at it. My husband felt my place was at home, and so I had to obey him. But I enjoyed meeting and talking to people. I have so much energy it's hard for me to stay at home most of the time. Since I haven't been working I do have much more time to study my religion, and that is good.

"Today, like my husband, I am an Islamist, and I think the Islamic revival is better for the country. *Inshallah,* God willing, Kuwait will become much stricter Islamically. We should take the good things of the West, the technology and the science, and mix them with an Islamic way of life, Islamic values. My husband would not agree with me. He would prefer to go back to a completely traditional life, except of course, he wouldn't want to give up air-conditioning and cars and other modern comforts.

"I think my problems with my husband have made me closer to my religion, not more distant. Reading the Koran calms me, brings me comfort. It's what I do whenever I am upset."

As Noura saw me out, we passed a row of hooks with black *abayas* hanging from them. "My mother has just returned from Hajj. She is having a women's party in her wing of the house. It is our tradition to welcome someone back from pilgrimage with a party. You know, not so long ago, we used to say about a good Muslim woman, 'She doesn't have an *abaya*.' This meant she was such a good Muslim that she didn't need one because she never left the house."

• • •

Bernard Lewis of Princeton University, one of America's leading authorities on Islam, put it well when he wrote, "Islam is one of the world's great religions. . . . It has brought comfort and peace of mind to countless millions of men and women. It has given dignity and meaning to drab and impoverished lives. It has taught people of different races to live in brotherhood and people of different creeds to live side by side in reasonable tolerance. It inspired a great civilization in which others besides Muslims lived creative and useful lives and which, by its achievement, enriched the whole world. But Islam, like other religions, has also known periods when it inspired in some of its followers a mood of hatred and violence. It is our misfortune that part, though by no means all or even most, of the Muslim world is now going through such a period, and that much, though again not all, of that hatred is directed against Americans."

And while Lewis cautioned that the dimensions of the problem should not be exaggerated, since the Iranian hostage situation in 1979 there has been fear and loathing of America on the part of many Muslims in the Islamic world, and similar feelings on the part of many Americans for much of the Muslim world. Of the ten Islamic countries I traveled through to research this book, only one, Kuwait, fifteen months after the Gulf War, was free of frequent "Death to the USA" graffiti, or impassioned anti-American sentiments that came up often in conversations.

For Americans marrying Middle Eastern Muslims, the first major hurdle is often overcoming bigotry, racism, or simple hostility in their own country and in that of their husband's. Women in the United States who have dated or married Arabs or other Muslims have found themselves called "sand-niggers" by people they know or by strangers on the street. Others have to cope with ignorance on the part of both sets of parents. I remember Bernice Amiri in the Emirates saying that when her father learned she wanted to marry an Arab, he told her, "Arabs stink, they are ignorant, they marry lots of women, keep them in a tent, beat their wives, and treat them like slaves." Her father was so angry that he refused initially to allow her fiancé, Aessa, inside the house, and he stopped talking to Bernice.

A Texan Hispanic Catholic, Bernice was then a nineteen-year-old student nurse. She had never heard of Aessa's country, the United Arab Emirates, and had no idea whether her father's comments were accurate or not. "But I did know Aessa was the most gentle, supportive, and undemanding man I had met. He treated me as though I was special. I was very insecure about my appearance in those days; I had a lot of zits. He accepted me for who I was. It was a wonderful feeling.

"He also was a man who didn't smoke, drink, do drugs, éven sleep around. The American boys I knew in those days were into all those things. It was a refreshing change to meet a man who was kind and considerate."

When Bernice's fiancé informed his family by telephone that he planned to marry an American, their response was similar to that of Bernice's father's. "It was horrible. The family called him from the UAE, and for a minute or two everything was normal. Then suddenly I could hear all this shouting from the phone. . . . They wouldn't consent to Aessa's marrying a foreigner. They told him all American women are prostitutes, no good. The only one who gave her permission was his grandmother, bless her heart."

A year after their American marriage, Aessa and Bernice moved to the Emirates. "I was terrified. I knew very little about Islam and even less about Muslim countries. In those days I was so immature and naive. But I wasn't thinking of religion. All I was thinking of was, I don't know what I've gotten into, but I loved my husband so much, I would go anywhere with him. I think I would have died for him. I just wanted to please him."

Bernice traveled to the UAE with a suitcase full of long dresses and scarves. Meeting Aessa's large extended family for the first time, none of whom spoke English, was unnerving for her. One of Bernice's more vivid early memories of her mother-in-law was her throwing an *abaya* at her. "She just threw it at me, and told me to put it on. I was terrified of his family. I think I was in a state of shock. It took years on both sides for us to warm up. Fortunately, my husband realized we couldn't live with his parents and moved us into a small villa. The only one who came to visit was his grandmother. We couldn't talk to each other, but her presence meant so much to me.

"Because of this experience, for three or four years I refused to learn Arabic and I didn't want to get to know other Arabs. It was only when I was pregnant with our first child that I decided this was my home, I loved my husband, I wasn't going anywhere. I told myself I had to learn the language, the mentality, and the culture. It was a turning point in my life. My first child was a son, and then Aessa's family warmed up to me, and I to them. Eventually, my father came around also.

"Throughout all these problems, my husband was so supportive, understanding, and reassuring. I guess if he hadn't been, we would have divorced long ago. Now we've been married eleven years, we have two children, I'm expecting a third, and I couldn't be happier."

For Brenda Ghalib, a Californian transplanted to the UAE, the initial bigotry she faced was her own. She met her husband, Mohammad, an electrical engineering student at the University of California at Berkeley, in 1979. "I asked him what religion he was, and when he told me Muslim, I thought, How can he admit that publicly? He should hide it. At that time there was tremendous hostility in the States because of the Iranian hostage thing. Later my husband told me he was threatened a couple of times at college because people believed he was an Iranian."

When Brenda, now thirty, started dating Mohammad, they kept the relationship secret because they were concerned about people's reactions, and when she began studying Islam in order to convert, she did so in private for the same reason. "I used to lock my door when I was praying, in case anybody walked in and thought I was weird." Fortunately for Brenda and Mohammad, when they married in 1981, both sets of parents welcomed the union.

Once Brenda moved to the Emirates with her husband, at Mohammad's request she began wearing full Islamic dress. "I feel so blessed with my life, with my children. I thank God, I'm so happy. Since I have been a Muslim, I'm very sure of myself. Islam has given me peace, an inner peace. I think in the West, especially in California, people are very unsure of themselves. They are always searching, searching.

"An Islamic society is a wonderful place to be a mother and raise children. It is incredibly supporting. There is such a sense of community. When I go back and meet my friends from university, they ask, Aren't you bored being just a mother? blah, blah, blah. My generation was raised to believe if you are staying at home, you are nothing. I think a lot of American women are isolated, confused, and lonely. The family has broken down in the States. My friends feel that when a baby turns six weeks they must put it into day care and go out and fulfill themselves in their career, even if their career is just being a secretary or working in McDonald's. To them it is more fulfilling than raising children. Life revolves around material things in America today. I have friends who say they have to work. If you ask them why they have to work, they respond, To live in a three hundred thousand–dollar house, have three cars, put their children in the best private schools. People even get involved in a church because it offers the best activities, not because of religion.

"For me, I can only say I have gained since I became a Muslim. My sister has run the whole gamut of religions from Baptist to Catholicism, which she quit. She's always looking, looking. And whenever I go back to California, she tells me she wishes she could have found the peace that I have found. But in the States, there is such a stigma now attached to Islam, just the name of it even, because of the unfortunate things that have happened in its name, that becoming a Muslim is not really an option for her at this point."

Chatting with Brenda in her comfortable home as her two children, Yasmin and Majid, played in the background, she acknowledged that there is a "big move here toward fundamentalism. I think it is a reaction, a whiplash, because everything became so Westernized here for a while."

Despite that, a year ago Brenda stopped wearing the *abaya* and *hijab* she adopted when she first married. Today she dresses conservatively in long skirts and tunics, but doesn't cover her hair. "I decided to stop completely covering because I felt like a hypocrite. I was doing it to please my husband and his family, but every time I went back to the States, I wore Western clothes. And I kept thinking, This is silly, this is hypocrisy. So I stopped covering.

"My husband is not happy about it. He says he is known as a religious person in town, so how can he have his wife running around in Western clothes? Other Islamists ask him, 'If your wife's not veiling, how can you be so religious? Why don't you make her cover?'

"We've had a lot of discussions on this issue. But I've told him it is between me and God. I do not feel I am doing anything wrong. I dress modestly, I just don't cover."

"Doesn't the Koran require you to obey your husband?" I asked Brenda. How did she justify her decision?

"The Koran places considerable emphasis on how hypocrisy is forbidden, doing things for show, praying for show, or acting in a certain way to impress people. The Koran considers this a much bigger sin and devotes much more space to this issue, whereas it mentions women covering only once and very briefly. It is a tiny portion of the religion. The Koran mostly talks about kindness to your fellow man, being a good human being, doing good deeds, taking care of the poor. The *hijab* is scarcely given a mention.

"I tell my husband I am trying as hard as I can to be a good Muslim, to pray, to help people. I just don't believe that it is crucial for me to be covered. My husband knows that my religion is from my heart, that I didn't convert for him. I am a Muslim because I want to be. And I think I am mature enough to make my own decisions about what to wear. I found here that when I covered a little bit, I was told I needed to cover more, and then to cover my face. And when you do that, they tell you that you shouldn't drive, or go out, or take your kids out anywhere, or work. It gets out of hand, becomes never ending. At some point you have to draw the line and say, 'I worship my God, I'm not here to impress anybody, certainly not the newly radical. I'm just here to be me.'

"One of Mohammad's sisters has become involved with the fundamentalist movement in the last year. She now covers completely, and her goal is to make me do so. It has caused a bit of a rift between us. The Islamist movement is beginning to quite frighten me because it has grown so quickly. The other night, I saw the video *Not Without My Daughter,* about the American woman who moved to Iran with her husband, who then became a fanatic and refused to let her and her daughter leave. The movie scared me. I found myself thinking, We really don't know how close we are to something like that. Iran turned overnight, and they were more progressive than we are here. It's frightening to me. My husband has always been religious. I can't really picture him going totally fanatic, but then again, you can't say what's going to happen tomorrow.

"I showed the video to lots of my Western women friends who are married to local men. And we all had the same reaction: 'Oh, my God, we are quite close to something like that also.' If the American woman the movie is based on was married to her Iranian husband for so many years and still didn't know him well enough to see how he would turn out, who can say what will happen here, when you've got this wave of fanaticism taking over everything?"

Brenda's husband, Mohammad, was out of town when I visited her home, but she set up a lunch date for me with him at a restaurant near his office when he returned. A tall, princely looking man, Mohammad became an Islamist while he was at college in the States. "I joined Rabitat-Islami's Arab Student Organization at Berkeley," Mohammad told me. Like his coreligionists, Mohammad wears a beard and *dishdasha* and Arab headdress. Despite a full-time career, he devotes at least two hours a day to working at a fundamentalist charity organization that has donated funding to Muslims in Bosnia and Afghanistan, and is active in Islamic missionary work. He views himself as an activist in the current Islamic revival movement. "People like me who have studied abroad and seen the problems of other countries — family disintegration, drugs, AIDS — realize very quickly that Islam is the only solution. So many people have become lost in the West. Here, if something happens, we can depend on God.

"Unfortunately, the West looks down on us. We can even see it in their eyes when they check our passports when we arrive. Of course, it makes us feel bad. American media always degrade Islam. I'm optimistic that now that Saudi Arabia has purchased the American United Press International, you will see better coverage of Islam in the States.

"The Muslim world is currently controlled by the West, which wants our resources cheaply. It wants to keep Islamic countries down. Look at Pakistan: the U.S. clamps down on its nuclear program because it's afraid it will make a bomb. Yet it ignores the same programs in neighboring India and also in Israel.

"People in the West fear us because they know Muslims will die for a cause. *Jihad,* Holy War, is part of our religion. And Islam encourages us to be courageous. I wanted to fight in the *Jihad* in Afghanistan; unfortunately, I did not have the chance. In the West, people have to be ordered to join the army. This is not the case in Muslim countries if the cause is Islamic. If the Islamic states united, we could be a superpower."

CHAPTER 9

Saudi Arabia: The Custodians of the Two Holiest Places

If a man and a woman are alone in one place, the third person present is the devil.

PROPHET MOHAMMAD

"I N SAUDI ARABIA, women are raised to be mindless, like babies. Even the most intelligent woman is told she cannot take care of herself, she isn't able. They just want to control people through religion. And if a woman disobeys, they treat her like a bug — they don't think twice before placing a foot on her to kill her."

The speaker was a twenty-four-year-old Saudi woman who made international news in February 1993, when she was granted political asylum in Canada on the basis of gender discrimination in her home country — a first in human rights globally. The young woman had fled Saudi Arabia because she feared persecution for refusing to veil, for walking in Riyadh alone, and because she wanted to pursue a university education in the field of her choice. In a telephone interview that was set up by her activist lawyer on condition that the young woman's real name not be used, "Nada" said that she feared government reprisals on her family if she was identified. "I hated veiling my face and when I didn't, men on the street threw stones at me, people called me a prostitute, and the religious police tried to arrest me. And things became a lot worse with the Islamists. The government cracked down on the women first. I wanted to study physical education but it was forbidden. In Saudi Arabia, even in school, if they see a girl jumping or running, they punish her. I couldn't live that way anymore."

Her first application for asylum in Canada was denied. Sounding a little like the Saudi authorities himself, the refugee and immigration commissioner stated in a written rejection that Nada would do well "to comply with the laws of the country that she criticizes, and to show consideration for the feelings of her father, who, like all the members of her large family, is opposed to the liberalism of his daughter." Until human rights activist lawyer Marie Louise Côté took up her case and subsequently won it, Nada lived in hiding in Canada and under the threat of constant arrest and deportation. "If asylum hadn't been granted and I had had to go back home, I would have been jailed, possibly even executed," she said.

In Saudi Arabia, defiance of religious authority can be as serious as appearing irreligious. A seventeen-year-old youth, Sadeq Abdul-Karim al-Allah, was arrested and subsequently beheaded in 1992 after he was accused of making slanderous comments against "God, the Prophet, and the Holy Koran."

Saudi Arabia is a country that takes itself very seriously, its gravity stemming from the fact that the kingdom is the birthplace of Islam. King Fahd Ibn Abd al-Aziz as-Su'ad refuses to be called "Your Majesty" and insists instead on being referred to as "The Custodian of the Two Holiest Places." The title refers to Mecca and Medina — the two most sacred Islamic sites in the world.

Mecca, the focus of the Hajj pilgrimage and the site to which Muslims all over the world bow in prayer five times a day, is the birthplace of the Prophet Mohammad. It also is the location of the Ka'bah — Islam's central shrine, which substantially predates Islam and is said to have been built by Abraham, from whom the Arab race traces its descent. Medina, 277 miles north of Mecca, is the burial place of the Prophet, and the second-holiest city in Islam. It is these revered sites that give Saudi Arabia religious preeminence in the Muslim world. The kingdom is also the most orthodox of all the Muslim countries.

Yet despite this, there is a growing Islamist opposition to the ruling royal family, which, as in Kuwait, has made charges of government corruption and economic inequities. In late 1992, 107 ultraconservative religious leaders, *ulema*, presented the king with a petition in which they criticized most of the kingdom's policies. In a country that is already the most conservative of all Islamic states, they were demanding a more rigorous application of Islamic law by placing special religious committees in government office to review all laws and regulations.

And rattling the "Swords of Islam," they also said it was time to "stop building palaces" and create instead a Muslim army of one million strong "to fight Islam's enemies all over the world."

Saudi women have less freedom than women in any other Islamic country, yet the *ulema* demanded further restrictions on them, including a total ban on their employment. Other changes listed in the petition included the substantial increase in religious TV and radio programming, which already takes up nearly 70 percent of all air time. And the clerics wanted a supreme religious council to review all of the media's material before it is presented to the public. Tightening censorship further in the kingdom would be hard to do. In the Saudi press, any article critical of the royal family, Islam, or Saudi Arabia is forbidden, as are those on sex, Judaism and/or Israel, and any other subject deemed unsuitable. In foreign publications advertisements for pork products or alcohol or those that show "too much" female flesh, which can mean even an elbow, are torn out or obscured with black ink before they go on sale. Four pages of *Time* magazine, for example, were removed because of a medical article on AIDS. The advent of the fax machine, however, has enabled many Saudis to circumvent the censors. "We just ask friends abroad to fax us the missing pages if it seems as if it could be interesting," one writer told me. "With modern technology, more attention is now paid to the censored material than would be if the magazines and newspapers were left intact."

In mid-1993, in an unexpected move, the Islamists opened the kingdom's first human rights organization: the Committee for the Defense of Legitimate Rights. Ten days later, Saudi authorities fired all the employees, arrested its spokesman, and closed down the organization, charging that it was, in fact, an incipient political party, which is illegal in Saudi Arabia. It was feared, apparently, that the organization would be used to further institutionalize the power of the Islamic clergy. The government's official comment, however, was that the committee was unnecessary because the state was already ruled by Islamic *Shariah*, and the religious laws were sufficient to deal with any human rights injustice.

The fledgling human rights committee was made up of prominent Islamist religious leaders, academics, and tribal heads who, according to political scientist Mamoun Fandy, could pose a very "serious threat to the Saud royal family." The committee, he said, was simply requesting that Saudis be protected from "arbitrary arrest and torture." If the Saudi government does not heed that request, says

Fandy, Islamists may be radicalized into using armed force against the regime.

The growing Islamist movement is seen as the most serious threat to the Saudi monarchy since Muslim extremists took over Mecca in 1979.

•   •   •

Entering Saudi Arabia is not easy. The kingdom does not issue tourist visas, and is also reluctant to issue press visas (with the exception of during the Gulf War). Sponsorship, male of course, is key. Well-connected friends arranged an unimpeachable sponsor for me: Dr. Abdullah Naseef, head of Rabitat-Islami, or the Muslim World League. Rabitat, a semi-official body established by the Saudi government in 1974, is a major player in the conservative Muslim revival movement throughout the world. The sophisticated and super-rich League is involved in the spreading of Islam globally, and to this end has recently built multimillion-dollar mosques in Moscow, Milan, Caracas, Düsseldorf, and even Gibraltar. As well as being very active in international relief to Muslim countries, Rabitat also rules on religious ethics; it approved, for example, organ transplants for Muslims. Another major role the organization plays is sociopolitical: it frequently bankrolls Islamist organizations in various countries.

Notwithstanding my Rabitat sponsorship, arriving at Jeddah airport, I was stopped by an immigration official who asked me, "Where is your husband?"

"I'm not married," I responded.

"But where is your *mahram*?" he asked, meaning "male chaperon," without whom a woman, Saudi or foreign, may not travel in the kingdom. Had I been Saudi, my *mahram* would have been a male relative whom I would not be permitted by Islamic law to marry. As a foreigner, it meant a male who was responsible for me. I explained that I was being met by Dr. Naseef's driver. "Unacceptable!" I was told. "You cannot enter the kingdom until your male sponsor either shows up or sends written notification that he is responsible for you." In Saudi Arabia it is unthinkable for a woman, no matter her age, to be responsible for herself.

It was 3:00 P.M. on a Thursday afternoon, the beginning of the Muslim weekend, and Dr. Naseef could have been on his way to his family's summer house up in the hills of Taif, two hours' drive from Jeddah, for all I knew. "But . . ." I began. The official responded with the Arabic version of no buts. "Wait! This is not the West, where women can do as they please. Here women, especially unmarried women, must be properly regulated," he said curtly. I waited.

Two-and-a-half hours later, the driver returned with the appropriate documents, and I was released into his custody. As we left the airport, we drove past the vast Hajj terminal, which, the Saudi government states, is 25 percent bigger than the world's-largest office building, the U.S. Pentagon. The award-winning roof design, based on Bedouin tents in the desert, is meant to remind the two million pilgrims who pass through it each year of the pilgrimage's historic past. An eight-lane highway leads from Jeddah on the Red Sea coast to "Mekkah," forty-five miles due east. Non-Muslims are forbidden to visit the holy cities, even to glimpse them from the highway. Instead, they are routed away from religious sites, and Saudi authorities are scrupulous in making sure that no nonbelievers slip through.

Another major highway sign pointed out the route to Rabitat's headquarters. I, however, was heading for the Al Attas Hotel in downtown Jeddah, an unlovely hostelry despite its four stars, with a view of the busy Al Amir Fahd Street overpass. The Al Attas was where Rabitat's guests were placed but the hotel could not remember any previous ones being female. They were surprised and discomfited by an unaccompanied female trying to register. In Saudi Arabia it is illegal for an unchaperoned woman to stay in a hotel unless the management receives documentation certifying that she is not a prostitute. Hotel employees have gone to jail for ignoring this ruling.

Once again, I was in official limbo while the driver went in search of the correct document. Minutes slipped into hours as I waited in the poorly air-conditioned lobby, the tedium marked only by drops of sweat falling onto my *abaya* from under my stifling *hijab*. Three hours later, feeling tired and overheated, I kicked off my shoes, and irritably removed my *hijab*. I should have done it much earlier. The night manager, obviously concerned that I might further disrobe in public, scurried over to say that perhaps it would be okay if I waited in a guest room after all.

The following day, when Rabitat's car came to pick me up, I learned that, because of my gender, I was assigned for the duration of my visit to Dr. Naseef's sister, Fateema, who is head of the women's division of Rabitat. Fateema holds a Ph.D. in Islamic Studies from Mecca University, and was dean of the women's section at the King Abdul Aziz University in Jeddah until she resigned from the post five years ago because her religious responsibilities were too demanding.

Today she teaches a few courses at the university in Islamic studies, religious law, and *Da'wa,* the propagation of Islam. Her classes are so popular that four times the average number of students attend them.

Throughout Saudi Arabia, Dr. Fateema Naseef is a well-known figure. She also is the only woman in the kingdom, and probably the entire Muslim world, sanctioned to issue *fatwas.* The authorization came from Sheikh Abdulaziz bin Abdullah bin Abdulrahman bin Mohammad bin Abdullah Aal bin Baz, the highest religious figure in the kingdom and head of the Committee for the Propagation of Virtue and Prevention of Vice, the arbiter of all that is Islamically proper, correct, and permissible in Saudi Arabia. The *matawain,* Saudi's religious or morality police force, comes under this committee.

Sheikh Bin Baz is an anachronism even in reactionary Saudi Arabia. Aged eighty and blind since he was eighteen, he is fond of telling the king that women appearing on Saudi television are too enticing, even though he can't see them. On such statements, the king has disagreed with him. But on most occasions, Bin Baz, who memorized the Koran before losing his sight, goes unchallenged, and his retrogressive opinions are given great prominence in Saudi Arabia. In 1969, the sheikh declared that the earth was flat. Three years previously, when he was president of the Islamic University in Medina, he had stated that the sun revolved around the earth. So convinced was he that he wrote a paper accusing Riyadh University of heresy because of its teachings on the solar system. In it, he claimed that God had made the earth immovable, and had "fixed it down firmly with mountains in case the earth shakes." He was obliged to revise both claims after a Saudi astronaut flew in a space shuttle and broadcast back to the kingdom television images providing evidence to the contrary. Such antediluvian opinions did not disqualify Bin Baz from becoming the President of Scientific Research, *Da'wa,* and Guidance Directorates, a position he has held since 1976 and one that gives him the rank of minister.

Archaic pronouncements from Bin Baz are frequent and they are why one Islamic country, Algeria, has an organization called "The Committee for Protection Against Saudi Ignorance." In Saudi Arabia, however, the sheikh is revered by many and was appointed to his high office to rule on Islam by the monarch in the late seventies.

In November 1990, Bin Baz declared it was illegal for women to drive, making Saudi Arabia the sole Islamic country to do so. The prohibition, which has no Koranic basis, came after forty-seven women in Riyadh gathered in a Safeway supermarket lot, dismissed their chauffeurs, and then drove a fifteen-car convoy through the city's downtown. The women, many of them academics at the King Saud University in the capital, were promptly arrested by the police and the *matawain*, some of whom called for their beheading. The women, along with their male relatives, were accused of renouncing Islam, an offense punishable by death in Saudi Arabia.

At King Fahd's request, the governor of Riyadh, Prince Salman Bin Abdel-Aziz hastily assembled a commission to investigate the matter. The Saudi government looked foolish when it was discovered that the women had not broken any religious law, only tradition, and that during the Prophet's time women had routinely led camels, vehicles of their day, through the desert, and that Bedouin women had driven their tribes' pickups for more than thirty years. Sheikh Bin Baz was not deterred, however. Calling the women drivers "portents of evil," he promptly issued a *fatwa* stating that henceforth "women should not be allowed to drive motor vehicles as the *Shariah* instructs that things that degrade or harm the dignity of women must be prevented." In a Catch-22 ruling, the forty-seven women who had not broken any law because at the time no such law existed were punished for it anyway, and more than two years later they are still being penalized.

In December 1992, Dr. Nourah aba AlKill told me, "Twenty-five months after the demonstration, we are still banned from working." The thirty-eight-year-old former assistant professor of public administration at King Saud University, like the other academics involved, lost her teaching position two days after the demonstration. "The university called and told me not to come back. I was very sad. After all my education and training. . . ." Dr. Alkill has a Ph.D. from Britain and a Master's degree from the United States. For both degrees, she won full government scholarships to study abroad in the days before Saudi Arabia banned women from doing so. Like the other demonstrators, she spent nine hours in police custody after her arrest. "The police were very kind to us, but the *matawain* were very bad." Dr. AlKill was too nervous to elucidate but, at the time, the women were called "corrupters of society, fallen women, whores, and communists" by the fundamentalists, who thereby ignored the Koranic ruling against slandering innocent women. Before being released from jail, each woman and a male relative had to sign pledges agreeing the women would never participate in such a demonstration again.

Within days, the *matawain* had circulated lists of the women's names and their home phone numbers, and many of the demonstrators began to receive menacing telephone calls and death threats. "We were afraid we were going to end up like Salman Rushdie," said one woman at the time. In mosque sermons throughout the country, mullahs reviled the women, demanded that they be executed and that "their heads roll in the gutters." The women's telephones were tapped, they were stripped of their passports, as were their husbands, and women who were studying abroad could not continue their studies.

A Saudi male journalist who took photographs of the driving demonstration was arrested and jailed for five months. At least one Western human rights organization claimed he was tortured while he was incarcerated.

The driving incident made headlines around the world. Unasked was the question, Why did the Saudi authorities respond so vituperatively and punitively to the women's action? "To be frank, these women were a useful tool," a Saudi government official told me off the record. "They played right into the government's hand. By punishing these women, the king was able to stop the religious sheikhs from focusing on half a million American troops arriving on our soil, which outraged them."

Eleanor Abdella Doumato, a Middle Eastern specialist and visiting scholar at Brown University, believes that action taken against the women may also have been related to the king's request for women volunteers to assist in the war effort. Made two months prior to the driving demonstration, it too had outraged the country's fundamentalists. An illegal radio campaign at the time screamed, "Does the king believe our honor is so trivial that we will allow our daughters to stand next to Zionists and U.S. soldiers — pork-eaters, sinners, and those infected with AIDS?" "The timing of the women's demonstration couldn't have been more fortuitous for the monarch," said Doumato. "Here was a ready-made platform with which to deflect attention from serious questions being asked in the kingdom."

Once again, women were being used as sacrificial lambs. The Saudi government had taken similar action in 1979 when a former seminarian student and former protégé of Sheikh Bin Baz, Juhaiman ibn Saif al Utaiba, and his extremist followers stormed the Grand Mosque of Mecca with 250 armed followers and declared himself the *Mahdi*. (According to the Koran, Al-Mahdi is the "Chosen One," who will appear on earth before the end of the world. Many Shi'a

Muslims believed Khomeini was the *Mahdi*.) The Mecca insurrection took two weeks to put down and it cost the lives of 130 Saudi soldiers and 102 insurgents. The extremist and sixty-two of his followers were subsequently beheaded. But the Mecca attack — which jolted Muslims around the world and called into question the right and ability of Saudi Arabia to defend the two Holy Mosques — sent shock waves throughout Saudi society.

According to Professor Doumato, the Saudis' immediate response was to mollify citizens and to divert attention away from the main issue by clamping down on women. Scholarships for Saudi women to study abroad were abruptly canceled (and are still banned), as were commercial licenses for women to run their own businesses. A woman could now only travel if accompanied by a male guardian. And morality police began rigorously disciplining unmarried couples who rode in cars or ate together in restaurants, and "improperly dressed" women. Until then, most women had been wearing short jacket-length *abayas,* and few covered their faces. After the Mecca attack, they were harassed into covering completely. Judith Caesar, an American professor who taught at Riyadh University for five years in the eighties, also feels that "repression of women in Saudi Arabia is part of a larger scheme to keep the king in power." Any time the government comes under fire, the public's attention is deflected by action against women.

The politics behind the punishment of the forty-seven women drivers were less important than the fact that being banned from working in a country with few other outlets for women is almost tantamount to being under house arrest. Cinemas, theaters, and public libraries are prohibited in Saudi Arabia. Women cannot swim in public or hotel pools. They may not mix with men in any public- or workplace. They are not permitted to attend mosques, except during Ramadan, when they must sit at the back. They may not even be present at their sons' school or university graduation ceremonies. It is illegal for single women to live alone. Many Saudi women who do not work are so bored they sleep most of the day, and telephone calls to their homes are answered by maids who tell callers, "Madam never gets up before four P.M."

"Now that I'm forbidden to work, I read a lot," said Dr. AlKill, who is single and lives with her family. "All my life I have been busy either studying or working. Life is a little boring right now. But I don't regret taking part in the demonstration. It was necessary. And despite what happened, I still think it was worth it. At the time we did it, we expected some problems, which is why we all covered our faces except our eyes with *niqabs*, in addition to wearing our *abayas*. But none of us expected the government to respond the way it did. We never thought we would lose our jobs and be stopped from working for more than two years. Our demonstration wasn't such a big deal." Ironically, Dr. AlKill holds two driving licenses, one from the United States, and one from an Islamic country, Egypt, where she drove when she was an undergraduate student at Cairo University.

When I applied for an interview with Sheikh Bin Baz, I was told, "Sheikh Bin Baz feels it would be un-Islamic to meet with you, a woman." My response, if a little acid, was, "Oh, really? Why? The Prophet himself sat and talked to women who were not related to him. Why would the sheikh consider it irreligious?" The question was rhetorical, of course, because Bin Baz would not have been able to cite an Islamic source for his refusal. And certainly the head of Al Azhar in Egypt, to whom the king of Saudi Arabia turns when he wants to overrule Bin Baz, agreed to be interviewed by me when I later arrived in Cairo.

In Kuwait I had met a niece of Sheikh Bin Baz, a charming and striking twenty-four-year-old computer science student, Nadia Al Baz, who told me, "I am glad my family lives in Kuwait and not in Saudi Arabia. I could not live there. My uncle is a good man, but he is very strict. When I visit Saudi Arabia, the women are jealous of my freedom, jealous that I am able to drive in Kuwait, and wear the clothes I want to wear. There is so little they can do, even professionally. Women are not allowed to have any ambitions. I ask my cousins, 'How can you stand it?' It is like being in prison to be in Riyadh. For most of them, all they do is shop or stay home. It is as if they are dead women."

In Kuwait, Nadia does not wear *hijab*, although she has been debating whether she should. "I haven't reached that level yet. Maybe in five years I will wear it, but not now. I had to be completely covered in Saudi Arabia, even my face. I hated it. The Koran doesn't say we should cover our faces, but it also doesn't ban women from driving, as my uncle has. I guess if he saw me with my head uncovered, he would kill me," she said with a small giggle, blushing.

• • •

With the myriad restrictions on women in Saudi Arabia, I was amazed that Rabitat's Dr. Fateema Naseef, who is also referred to with the honorific "Sheikha" because of her religious authority, was permitted to issue *fatwas*. Perhaps I should not have been surprised to learn, however, that she had never done so. "I haven't issued any yet," she said with a small smile, "because if I write one and they disagree with me, I will be fighting with them." "Them," of course, refers to Sheikh Bin Baz and other religious leaders. I was reminded of the comment made to me by a professor at the women's section of King Abdul Aziz University, where men are prohibited. Because there are not enough female professors, 30 percent of all classes are taught by men over television monitors. She said, "Yes, we have women professors and women deans here. But all decisions, big or small, are made by the authorities at the men's university."

Having come through the same university system, Dr. Naseef obviously recognized that *fatwas*, once issued, are like missiles — hard to recall. Instead, she gets her message across through frequent religious lectures around the country — to women only, of course. As her audiences number as many as five thousand, her word carries weight. On one occasion, the women in the audience donated Riyals 6,000,000 ($1.6 million) after she spoke of the urgent need to assist Muslims in Bosnia. Dr. Naseef, aged forty-eight, also functions as an informal marriage counselor. "Women come to me with their marital problems, and after I speak to them, I speak to their husbands to see if I can mediate. Many times it is possible."

Dr. Naseef is tall and angular, and her scrubbed face and glasses perched on top of her aquiline nose give her a severe mien. Her appearance, combined with her take-charge manner, bestow on her the demeanor of a school principal. Time spent with her at her large Western-decorated home near the King Fahd Hospital in Jeddah reminded me of being with Pakistan's Benazir Bhutto. Telephones rang constantly, and she was continuously called away by various Sudanese maids to speak to someone. Callers arrived every few minutes, and, like Bhutto's feudal supplicants, they bent to kiss the sheikha's hands and face as a sign of their respect. Some brought large parcels of Riyal banknotes wrapped in scarves; Dr. Naseef, like Sheikh Bin Baz, is authorized to collect *Zakat*, the tax the Koran states the rich must pay the poor each year. The Koran forbids the establishment of a bureaucracy to collect *Zakat*, and there is no system of accounting. It is an honor tax, which many Muslims pay on pain of punishment in their afterlife. Dr. Naseef oversees the distribution of the poor tax to Jeddah's needy, such as widows.

Helping her as an assistant and acolyte is Suhair Al-Querishi, an articulate thirty-two-year-old, who holds an M.B.A. The daughter of a diplomat, Suhair spends considerable time each day working with the sheikha, despite holding down a full-time job as head of quality assurance at King Fahd Military Hospital and caring for her six-month-old son. Apart from having abundant energy and drive, she has the ideal attitude for her role as Naseef's chief of staff. "If you have a strong leader, you follow," she said of the sheikha.

Two years ago Suhair married Dr. Naseef's older brother, and she is extremely close to Dr. Naseef. She probably spends as much time in the sheikha's home as in her own, but she has never met Fateema's husband. Arabic *mashrabiyya* lattice screens separate public and private areas of the sheikha's home, so that her husband and Suhair can come and go without seeing each other. "Fateema and I are as close as sisters," said Suhair, "but it is not correct that I meet her husband. If her husband divorced Fateema and if I were unmarried, I could marry her husband. He is not *mahram* for me, that is, not a relative forbidden for me to marry. And no, I am not curious about him; it is not my place to be."

Suhair refused to remove her *abaya* and *hijab* in my company at the sheikha's home for several days, despite complaining of being very hot. "Why on earth don't you make yourself comfortable?" I asked as she was mopping her face. She replied, "It is not correct that I uncover in front of you. You are Western. Maybe you will explain how I look, how my hair looks, to others." I assured her I would not, and she finally removed the garments. But throughout the time we were together, she had openly breast-fed her son in my presence. A Saudi woman physician remarked to me later, "Women here frequently find it much easier to uncover a part of their body for a doctor to examine than to bare their head or face."

In the past, Suhair, who was educated in London and in Washington, D.C., did not veil. "But then one of our maids from Eritrea gave me an Islamic cassette. And when I played it — *click* — I realized what was missing from my life. Being a good Muslim is like studying for an exam: it depends where you want to be placed. If you want an A-plus, you work hard. If you want to be judged a good Muslim by God, you do everything you can, and as a woman, that means proper Islamic dress. I also think women are more respected when they cover.

"And I believe that men should be responsible for women, particularly when they travel. The driving demonstration in Riyadh was stupid. We don't want a corrupt society. Already we have too much exposure to things in the West through going abroad to study, through dish satellites, and through foreign media. You can't control the society once you get all these things. We need to educate the society, instill proper Islamic values before letting women drive. Young men want cars to have fun and to speed. If women drive, these young people would bother them." Perhaps then, I suggested, the boys should be restricted instead. Suhair raised her eyebrows disapprovingly. "You interpret freedom differently from me.

"Fortunately, there is a move back to the real Islam both here in Saudi Arabia and in the rest of the Muslim world. People are lost and are searching for the truth. They need a power to lean on. Look at all the famous people in the West who acquire success and material possessions. They want these things, they get them, then they commit suicide. They have tasted everything and they still have nothing. Certainly not peace of mind. Humans are made up of flesh and spirit, and in the modern world we give nothing to the spirit. And yet we know that religious people are cured much more quickly physically and mentally than those without faith. When you embrace Islam, it is like pouring something sweet into your heart. Nothing bothers you again."

After yet another interruption, this time for praying, Dr. Naseef rejoined us and began a long dissertation on Koranic law and rulings. "When foreigners talk about Islam, they mention only amputating hands. Yes, we have it. It is necessary. But it is not done very often. Have you ever seen a man with one hand in this country?" she asked, slightly belligerently. I admitted that I hadn't, and that I hadn't seen one in any other Islamic country either.

Under Saudi law, judicial amputations are imposed only after the third offense of theft. Writer Robert Lacey, who lived in Saudi Arabia for eighteen months, reported that during that time, only ten such sentences, which are a matter of public record, were carried out. "It is the same with stoning for adultery," said Dr. Naseef. "It is necessary, but it rarely happens." A Saudi lawyer I spoke with concurred. "This country has a lot of faults," he told me. "We have oppression but usually without physical force. On the whole, it is a civilized form of police state. Few Saudis fear going to jail, and even fewer suffer the more severe forms of *Shariah* punishments. The executions that are carried out, for example, are mostly of foreign workers, Pakistani drug dealers, and the like. When they want to penalize Saudis, they tend to be more subtle. With me, they hit me financially." The lawyer had run afoul of the government after writing an opinion piece for a Western newspaper during the Gulf War. "The year after, I lost $150,000 worth of government business. They let me know clearly, and where it hurt, that they were not happy."

In 1992, Saudi Arabia publicly beheaded sixty-six miscreants. Perhaps the most publicized execution in recent years was that of Princess Misha'il bint Fahd bin Mohammad, who was the subject of the Western television docudrama *Death of a Princess*. Saudis close to the royal family with whom I discussed her 1977 execution claimed she would not have died if her elderly grandfather, Prince Mohammad ibn Abdul Aziz, had not insisted on it when he learned she had committed adultery. Other senior family members tried to talk him out of it. But the rigid conservative and brother of the king refused, and did not even invoke *Shariah* law.

For him, the princess's adultery had shamed the family's tribe, and for that he demanded her execution to uphold tribal honor. "Prince Mohammad was an old man, and easily shocked," one woman told me. "Everyone in the family tried to change his mind, but he felt Misha'il had committed the worst sin. Even the Prophet tried hard to avoid having a woman stoned when she came to him and admitted committing adultery. Twice he turned his head to one side, so he couldn't hear her confession. It was only when she told him the third time, when she insisted on her punishment, that he ordered her to be stoned."

The princess had been married to a much older relative, who reportedly showed little interest in her. She turned for affection to a man much closer to her age, but the relationship did not go undetected. And when Misha'il tried to flee the country in the company of her lover, they were arrested at the airport. Because of the princess's royal birth, she was shot to death; her companion was beheaded. As in other conservative Muslim countries, judicial stonings occur rarely. Tribal honor killings for adultery, such as that of Princess Misha'il, take place more frequently.

The Saudis tried to keep the execution a secret because Misha'il was royalty, but it was captured on videotape by a foreign visitor. The subsequent British television movie based on the incident was aired widely in Europe and the United States. Saudi Arabia's royal family was so enraged that they appealed to Downing Street in an effort to prevent the docudrama from being shown. When that failed, they threatened to expel all Britons working in the kingdom, and finally settled for expelling the British ambassador.

Dr. Naseef changed the subject from Saudi jurisprudence to the Islamic Law of Necessity. "Islam is a practical religion, and this is something else foreigners don't recognize. For example, a woman is forbidden to travel without a *mahram* for more distance than a camel can travel in three days. Since few of us now travel by camel, this today is considered to be forty-five miles. For distances beyond that, a *mahram* is necessary for a woman's security, to be her bodyguard, to help her on her way." I chuckled when she said the latter. On the few occasions I had an official *mahram* in Saudi Arabia, when flying from one city to another, I struggled with my baggage in front of them, while it never occurred to them to offer to assist. "If a *mahram* is not available, and the woman's journey is absolutely essential, a matter of life or death, the Koran says she can take a group of trusted companions instead, and this can be a group of responsible women. The Law of Necessity also applies regarding pork and wine, both of which are forbidden to Muslims. But if it is a case of starvation or death by thirst, the Koran permits us to consume both."

Dr. Naseef also felt that Westerners did not understand the concept of arranged marriages. "It works very well. The man tells his family what he wants in a woman, and they find him such a girl. In Saudi Arabia, he is permitted to see her once before they marry for only ten minutes in front of her parents. But more than once isn't necessary. Look at my brother with Suhair. She was all covered except for her eyes when he saw her. He wanted a wife; it wasn't necessary to see her. And look at your novels. It is written in your books that one glance is enough for a man to fall in love. If they don't know each other . . . well, who does until they have lived together for a long time?" Fateema excused herself again to pray.

In Saudi Arabia, all businesses, schools, government offices, and stores are required by law to close for prayers. Even television viewing is interrupted. The screen becomes blank except for a still shot of Mecca and a legend reading, "We would like to inform viewers that it is now time for prayers."

Evening shopping in the Western-style malls can be a frustrating event. The *al-maghreb* prayer lasts from approximately 6:30 to 7:00 P.M. Emptying out department stores takes time, and the religious police even insist that metal security grills be closed. Thirty minutes later, the stores reopen, only to shut again an hour later for *Isha* prayers, the last observance of the day. Stores then reopen once again until they finally close for the night at 10:00 P.M. Since evening prayers are keyed to sundown, their timing changes constantly. I invariably arrived at the wrong time and found myself obliged to wait with hundreds of other shoppers until the mosques were empty.

I quickly realized that it was during prayer time that young men and women took the opportunity to mingle. As soon as the *"Salaat"* prayer warning went out, shoppers not going to the mosques rushed to secure places on the mall benches. In what was almost a party atmosphere, groups of young men hovered around benches of young women, who felt free to talk to them from behind their veils. I saw what appeared to be the exchange of telephone numbers several times during such meetings. And despite my wearing an *abaya* and *hijab* myself, not to mention my being old enough to be the mother of some of the youths, I was frequently propositioned myself.

Once again, it seemed that it would be easier and certainly fairer to veil and restrict young men, at least until their roiling testosterone went off the boil or they had a culturally legitimate outlet for it in marriage.

To counteract attempts by young men and women to mingle, one store, the Music Master, in the Al Madinah Shopping Center, bears a sign stating "No Women Allowed." The Baskin-Robbins ice cream parlor has a separate section with a separate entrance for women, although women complain that they never get any service in their section. And many stores and boutiques had their fitting rooms closed after the religious police claimed an unmarried couple had been seen going into one together.

When Dr. Naseef returned again after praying, she picked up where she had left off in her religious commentary, pointing out, "Christianity, Jesus, is not our enemy. We believe in Jesus, as a prophet, of course, not as the son of God. Mohammad's name is mentioned in the Koran only four times, Jesus is mentioned forty-three times. There are a number of things in the Christian faith that Muslims also believe.

"Islam, however, has been asleep for three centuries. The Muslim civilization, which once led the world, declined as Muslims became wealthy. Then the source of knowledge moved to the West. Thanks be to God, at this time, Islam is waking up again, and the religion is spreading. Those who do not believe in Islam have become the enemy of Islam. God said Islam will spread until every person in the world becomes Muslim. Now we are heading toward that goal, but not because we are forcing it. Islam is forcing its own way. It is the power of God. We don't say, Please come to us. People come to us and say, please teach us. And this we are doing."

• • •

Jeddah, a city of two million people, is the largest seaport on the Red Sea. According to Saudi lore, it is also the place from which Eve is said to have traveled to meet Adam. Legend claims that Jeddah is the site of her tomb; Jeddah in Arabic means "grandmother," in this case, Eve, the grandmother of us all. Unlike Christianity, Islam does not attribute the expulsion from the Garden of Eden to Eve. Instead, the Koran blames Adam for the downfall. It also does not state that Eve was made from Adam's rib; according to the Koran, both were created "of like nature from a single being."

Until the early 1930s, Jeddah was a city that boasted only one tree, which is not surprising since the city had virtually no fresh water, either. Until relatively recently, potable water had to be transported into the city. Today, the four tall stacks of the massive desalination plant dominate the skyline, and more than eight million trees, many of them henna, have been planted. Perhaps as a symbol of this dramatic change, Jeddah now possesses the world's highest water fountain.

The city also has a twenty-mile Corniche beach road, which is the center for Jeddah recreation — for those few pastimes that have not been banned. The beach road is deserted during the broiling heat of the day, but comes alive between 10:00 P.M. and 3:00 A.M. when, in the cooler temperatures, it is bumper-to-bumper traffic. A number of the luxury vehicles are crammed with young men in white *dishdashas* and *ghutrah* headdresses cruising for action Saudi style — exchanging phone numbers with girls of their choice, the precursor to intense telephone conversations but usually little more.

Along the Corniche is a large amusement park, but even here innocent pleasures are segregated by gender. The kingdom of Saudi Arabia never forgets for a moment the Prophet's statement "If a man and a woman are alone in one place, the third person present is the devil." Lining the Corniche are the new five-star hotels. At the Sheraton's outdoor swimming pool café, and in the 100 degree–plus evening heat and humidity, women shrouded completely in black lift their *niqab* flaps to sip cappuccino while men, the chosen gender, swim back and forth past them. In any other country, watching swimmers is an innocent pastime. Here it feels almost risqué.

In Saudi Arabia, it frequently seems as though the city fathers and the doyens of the government have imbued every aspect of life, even the more mundane, with sexual connotations. Outside the women's banks guards are stationed next to large signs stating "No Men Allowed." Though banking is hardly an erotic event, in the women's branch of the Saudi American Bank, I spotted a young woman, completely veiled in black like the rest of the customers, wearing flame-red, four-inch satin heels that peeked out from under her *abaya*. In the repressive Saudi environment, they were about as sensuous a statement as a woman could make. Shoe stores in the Gulf would delight any foot fetishist. Shoes tend to be in Day-Glo colors, often covered in beads or brilliants, and with towering stiletto heels. Perhaps the *matawain*, who wear sandals themselves, are too busy monitoring mass morals to notice sexy footwear.

Twelve years ago, the Saudi American Bank, once solely owned by Citibank and now a joint venture between the two countries, became the first in the kingdom to have all-women branches. Appropriately, the decor, even in the rest rooms, is predominantly pink with black marble touches. "It is normal for women in Saudi Arabia to manage their own finances," said Mrs. Kifaya Hashem, the forty-two-year-old branch manager. Before such banks were opened, women had to ask male relatives to bank for them.

Like other Muslim women, Kifaya's salary is truly discretionary income. Although she earns more than her husband, he still pays all family expenses, as the Koran requires. "I'm building a seven-bedroom house with my savings," she told me, "which I will rent out when it is completed for at least Riyals fifty thousand [$14,000] a year. The land, eleven hundred square meters, was given to me by the government when I graduated." In another independent financial move, Kifaya said that while she tells her husband when she gets a salary increase, she never tells him how much. "He doesn't know how much I earn, and I don't inform him."

Despite its strict religious orthodoxy, Saudi Arabia chooses to ignore the clear Islamic injunction against usury. "Do we pay interest on our customers' accounts?" asks Kifaya. "Oh, very, very rarely. Only if the customer asks, which they usually don't, because paying or receiving interest is anti-Islamic. On such rare occasions, we pay a maximum of 2.5 percent."

Does the bank charge interest? "Oh, yes, of course. We are not an Islamic bank. If a woman takes a loan from us, we charge anywhere from seven to fifteen percent interest."

Kifaya stressed, "There is no real Islamic bank in all the world. We must deal with other non-Muslim banks, and they charge interest. And whether we call it interest, or bank charges, which sounds better, it is the same. One day, we hope we can be truly Islamic in our banking, but right now it is not possible. Also, we have a very few people who have studied Islamic economics. We wouldn't even know how to manage banking in accordance with the Koran."

When it comes to management meetings, however, Kifaya is barred from attending because it would be "un-Islamic" for her to mix with male managers. "Any business I have with other bank officials has to be done via the phone," said Kifaya. "And because I am not permitted to attend meetings, they send me full written reports. Sometimes, of course, I feel handicapped as a manager since I am not allowed to attend such official gatherings. But that is our system, and I'm not used to being with other men."

Just as governments and mullahs feel free to ignore Koranic dictates that directly benefit them, so, too, do the religious authorities force Saudi women to obey the letter of religious law even when they are aware that in reality what is happening is close to farce. When sisters Lamia and Nadia Baeshen were going to the United States to study for their doctorates at the University of Arizona, they were informed they must take a *mahram* with them for the duration of their stay abroad. Their father was unable to leave his business for several years, and their only brother was eleven years old. The authorities insisted that he would have to accompany them as their *mahram;* otherwise the two women could not go. "Not only was he only eleven, while we were adults, but the government also knew he is retarded and has a mental age of two. We had both graduated at the top of our classes before we went to the U.S. We felt competent and capable of being independent. We are, however, female. Our brother, being male, met the requirements of being a chaperon, no matter that he is mentally handicapped. In the end, our mother had to come with us to look after our brother, because he is unable to care for himself."

• • •

Despite the innumerable constraints and limitations on women in Saudi Arabia, I met many who, as in other Muslim countries, impressed me with their strength, intelligence, and determination to succeed, regardless of the considerable shackles on their lives. One such individual in Jeddah was Huda Awad, whose achievements would be impressive in any Western country; in Saudi Arabia she was as refreshing as a cool breeze in the desert.

Huda owns and runs a construction subcontracting company, which hires up to four hundred men, depending on the size of the project. And some of Huda's projects are sizable. Her company was responsible for the Ministry of Interior, Beladi and Redec office and shopping plazas, the Al Noor Hospital, plus four of the king's homes in Jeddah, Mecca, Taif, and Dhahran. In all, she has completed over one hundred major sites. When I called her, she suggested we meet for tea at the elegant Intercontinental Hotel on the Corniche. As she came toward me, I saw that her head was uncovered. She was the only Saudi woman I met in my entire trip who appeared in public without a *hijab*. Her nose was smudged and there was fine dust clinging to her hair. "Excuse me," she said, as she removed an equally dusty *abaya*, also the only time I saw a woman in the kingdom remove her Islamic coat in public. "I've just come from one of my building sites. Phew! It was hot, and as you see, very dusty. I normally go early in the morning so that I can return home to shower before going to the office."

Patting her hair, she remarked, "Ah yes, no *hijab*. I was wearing a hard hat and forgot to put it back on."

Under the sprinkling of dust, Huda was dressed for success. With her crisply elegant green-and-white linen suit, tasteful but expensive jewelry, black high-heel pumps, sophisticated wedge hairstyle, and very businesslike briefcase, she would have looked at home in any Western boardroom. Very much at ease in her skin, she is vivacious, with a ready chuckle, and appears supremely self-confident. "Yup," she said jokingly when I commented on the latter. "When things in business go bad, I always make sure I go and cry in the car, so no one can see me."

Huda began her career in advertising, but quit because she found it boring. "When I looked around for something else to do, I realized few Saudis were involved in subcontracting in the construction business. Saudis don't like to get their hands dirty; here everybody is a sheikh. But I don't mind dirtying my hands." Her family was totally opposed to her starting such a business. "They were afraid for me, convinced I would be raped or assaulted." Without financial support and unable to get licensing, Huda went into partnership with a French man. Two years later, she was able to register her own company and found herself installing concrete slabs in high-rises. Now she can talk knowledgeably about gypsum, marble flooring, and weight-bearing loads. "I was lucky — just as I went into business for myself, the building boom began here. We were so busy, I would go out and hire laborers off the street."

To assist her in the office, she hired a female secretary. "Suddenly the Ministry of Labor descended on us. They threatened to close me down and take away my registration because I had hired a woman in a company where other men worked. They also said it was forbidden for me to go into my office for the same reason. When I asked them how I was supposed to run my business, they told me to get an office at home. I requested they show me the written laws that stipulated this, but they couldn't. I still don't understand the system. Here they say, Don't do this, Don't do that. But they can never tell you why."

After the Ministry's visit, Huda complied with their stipulation and hired a male manager to attend meetings, negotiate, and take over business activities she was not permitted to handle. "It was a decision that cost me a million riyals. I later learned that he was cheating me constantly. The capital had disappeared from the company, work was done without contracts, my signature was forged on contracts I knew nothing about. As soon as I realized what was going on, I got rid of him.

"No one takes better care of you than yourself, I learned the hard way. When large amounts of money are at stake, a company owner has to be personally involved. In such situations, dependency is a liability. And if tradition doesn't make sense, I won't tolerate it. But I also didn't want to step on the Ministry's tail. I want to work."

The Ministry of Labor informed Huda that she was not allowed to spend the entire day at her office, but she could visit when there were major problems. "Well, as any contractor will tell you," she told me, "this industry is fraught with problems, all the time."

Huda had already come a long way from the young woman of twenty-six who was forbidden by her family to go shopping in the local *souk*. But although she is now in her early forties, she still has trouble convincing the authorities that she is not a small child. Not so long ago, Huda, who does a lot of business with European corporations, had arranged a two-week intensive trip to Paris to sign business contracts and purchase raw materials. "I had been working around the clock making appointments, setting up everything, and running the business here. I'm very serious about my work, and a bit of a perfectionist. I was exhausted when I left for the airport."

Following Saudi law, her brother accompanied her to the airport, and she was equipped as required with written approval from her father and the Ministry of Interior to travel abroad. "When we arrived, my brother took my documents to the official who checks that they are in order, and he told him I couldn't travel. My brother returned to me, and said, 'Forget your trip. You are not permitted to travel.' 'What do you mean?' I asked. 'Everything is booked, I have contracts to sign, I worked hard setting all of this up. And I have all the proper papers to travel.' The official refused to discuss the issue with Huda. She sent her brother back four times to protest, and four times he returned with a negative reply. Swissair, the airline with whom she was traveling, even intervened on her behalf to say that all of Huda's documents were in order. The official still refused to change his mind.

Finally, her flight took off. "When that happened I just completely lost my temper, something I rarely do. I realized that all the hard work arranging this trip was for nothing, that contracts might collapse. I couldn't help myself, I picked up my travel bag, which was very heavy because it was full of documents, and threw it at him. He ducked into his office, and closed the door. I chased him and began to pound on the window. I wanted to beat him, I was so mad. It was ridiculous really. I was pounding on tempered glass, a complete waste of time. Deep in the logical part of my mind I knew it wouldn't break. Normally, I'm a very calm, mature person, but then I was shouting at the man. I saw four policemen running over and I thought I would be in trouble, but they told the official not to be such an idiot, and to let me board the plane. Of course by then it was too late.

"The official's reasoning afterward when he explained to my brother, not to me, was that he wanted to protect me. He didn't want me to leave Saudi Arabia at two A.M. and arrive in Europe alone." Huda growled to illustrate the fury she felt at the time. "I told the fool that I had purposely taken that flight so I would arrive in Europe during the day. Now he was forcing me to take a daytime flight that would arrive in Paris after midnight, which was what I had been trying to avoid."

Huda talks about her fear of rape with the same intensity as many Muslim women. "I couldn't live alone, I would never feel safe," she said. Her apartment is in her family's compound. "It is the ideal arrangement: I have company when I want it, and can be alone when I need to work."

Huda said she learned fear in the early eighties when she lent a friend her car to go to the hospital, and then took a taxi to meet her there. "It was only about eight P.M. and the driver was a Saudi driver, so I didn't think twice about it. My mind was on my work. I hadn't noticed where we were going when suddenly I realized he had turned off the asphalt road, and was driving me to a deserted area. I was petrified. The moment he stopped the car, I threw myself out and began running for my life. Eventually, I came to a building and ran inside, sobbing hysterically. I called a friend to come and pick me up. I was too ashamed to phone my family. I was also too scared to wait inside the building with the four doormen, although I am sure they were perfectly respectable. They put a chair outside the door under a street lamp for me until my friend came. After that I refused to use taxis. I learned they are not safe.

"They tell you Saudi Arabia is the safest place to be, that the crime rate is so low. If it is so safe, why don't people ever walk, why are children always accompanied?"

Now when Huda takes her early morning keep-fit walk along the beach promenade, wearing her *abaya, hijab,* and sneakers, she makes her Egyptian driver accompany her. "I don't want to take a chance, even though I never make eye contact with anyone. At first my driver walked in front of me to be inconspicuous. But what shocked me, and also shocked him, is that all the time as we were walking, he was pestered by men trying to pick him up. It happened every day, and he is just an ordinary-looking man. This kind of male lust occurs here because of segregation. They can't get a woman because women are so protected, so they go after the men. My driver told me he realized for the first time how belittling and disrespectful such behavior is for women. Now to avoid his being sexually harassed, he drives in the car slowly alongside me as I take my morning exercise."

In her business dealings, either with the men she employs or with the men with whom she negotiates, Huda said, they treat her with consummate professionalism and respect. "My peers know I am knowledgeable, the company has a good reputation. My employees respond to my authority, and they know who pays their salaries. Of course, I cannot joke at work; it would be misinterpreted, so I censor my behavior."

The only time she has run into difficulties is when dealing with government ministries and departments. "With one ministry, I went on official business. I was totally covered, even my face, because I would be dealing with men I didn't know. I was trying to get some papers processed. And even though I was fully veiled, the man I dealt with made it very clear to me he would give me what I needed only if I gave him what he wanted, and he made it very obvious what that was. I forgot the paperwork and just walked out. I wanted to kill him, but instead, when I reached my car, I burst into tears. It hurt me that I couldn't follow up on a contract because of this kind of behavior. We really need to clean the minds of the men here, and teach them to behave responsibly."

On another occasion, Huda met the reverse situation. Because of her gender, Huda was treated as a pariah at the Saudi equivalent of the chamber of commerce when she went to have a contract dispute adjudicated. "The judge's first comment to me was, 'Why are you wearing a beige *abaya* instead of a black one?' I told him I was cold, and this one was warmer. Then he said he would prefer not to have me in the courtroom and would rather handle the proceedings with my male lawyer. My lawyer objected, as the arbitration process was available to people who own their own companies, and women in Saudi Arabia may do so. But the judge said he couldn't talk to a woman. I didn't insist. We dropped the case because I knew it would have gone against me under such circumstances.

"In Saudi Arabia in the last few years, we are seeing more and more of this sort of thing coming up. People are getting the wrong message about Islam. They are becoming the way the British Puritans used to be, and some Muslims are abusing and manipulating the religion. I don't think there has ever been a time when we more needed to teach men how to understand women — that we have feelings, and that those feelings matter."

· · ·

Jeddah is considered Saudi Arabia's most liberal city because, being the gateway to Mecca, it has long been exposed to foreigners. Most women there do not veil their faces, and they often frequent restaurants in groups of women or with their husbands. The Saudi capital, Riyadh, on the other hand, is the heart of the conservative religious establishment. Women are rarely seen in public except at the special women's bazaars, and whenever they leave the house, all have their faces covered.

I had just left Riyadh's Al Derah Women's Souk, with shop after shop selling nothing but black face masks, head coverings, and *abayas,* when my Pakistani driver, Ashraf, pointed out to me the site for public beheadings. With great delight, he turned to me and said, "Memsahib, I show you something special close to here: Chop-Chop Square."

At first, with his thick accent, and broken English, I didn't understand what he meant. Drawing his thumb across his throat, he illustrated. Not far from the women's souk is the city's main mosque, which has a large parking lot. "Here, Memsahib," he said in a tone that seemed almost jovial. "Here they chop-chop heads on Fridays. They move the cars from the carpark, and then after prayers, everybody from mosque watch. They cut off head with long knife, big man, mostly he can do with one cut. If head not fall after three cuts, this mean Allah save man. Look, I am standing in place where they do. If you look carefully, maybe you can see blood." Fortunately we couldn't, and I suggested we continue our drive. Ashraf looked disappointed with my response. "If Memsahib still here when they do next one, I bring you. Many foreigners come. You can watch."

Despite the archconservatism of the capital, the city was the site of a recent restaurant scandal that illustrates the length to which people will go to bypass restrictions, and the risks they take for pleasure. One of the city's leading restaurants in Sulaymaniyah had recently reopened after a lengthy closure. The thirty-two-year-old British chef de cuisine told me why. He prefaced our conversation with, "Please don't use my name. Even though my contract is up shortly and I am leaving the country, the Saudi government has a long reach. I don't want to find myself having difficulty getting a job somewhere else."

The restaurant, one of the more expensive in the country, where dinner can cost $300 per head, is popular with Westerners and highly placed Saudis, including many princes and princesses. Royalty frequently takes over the entire restaurant for the night for a party of twelve. "When any of the royals are here, their bodyguards sit outside with guns under their arms. On those occasions, we are rarely bothered by the *matawain*. Those chappies know that if they hassle the wrong people, they might just find themselves being taken for a little drive in the desert late one night.

"The restaurant has a mezzanine, which is really the family section, where there are screens to hide women. It's very intimate — low lights, just four booths for a total of sixteen people. In recent years, it became the place for a little activity between couples, usually Saudis with Westerners. With the laws in this country, the hotels and expatriate compounds are too well policed; you couldn't sneak a Saudi into your room. People involved in illicit relationships would book the entire mezzanine for dinner just before *al-Maghreb* prayers began. Until recently, when the laws were changed, if you were already eating dinner in a restaurant, you were not required to leave during prayers when the restaurant was closed. You were simply closed inside when the staff left. If you had the mezzanine, that meant you had thirty unchaperoned minutes, which guaranteed no interference from staff, other guests, or *matawain*.

"But people forget: Riyadh is basically a small town, and everyone talks. There is not much else to do. The Saudi owners heard what was going on and went nuts. They closed the place down for a while because they knew if the authorities learned about it, they would probably put everyone up against a wall and shoot them. The restaurant manager, a foreigner, was on the next plane home, and believe me, he was lucky."

Westerners violate the laws banning alcohol, too. Currently in Riyadh, a British couple run an authentic but illegal pub from their home, patronized by many expatriates, including diplomats. It's open seven nights a week, and most of the liquor on sale is made locally. Imported whiskey runs $190 a bottle, vodka $135, and gin $162 in Riyadh. The prices are high, but so are the risks of smuggling it in. A few years ago, a British woman was sentenced to eighty lashes for serving alcohol at a party. The British embassy managed to have the sentence changed to immediate expulsion instead.

Prostitution is another industry that thrives in Saudi Arabia despite the risks involved. In fact, it received a boost in 1962 when slavery was banned. Women who had been slaves and now had no other means of support had little choice but to turn to the world's oldest profession to survive.

I was surprised to learn that Riyadh has an orphanage for children born out of wedlock and/or to prostitutes. The Dar Al Hadana orphanage comes under the women's welfare division of the Ministry of Social Affairs. The orphanage, spread over several floors, is large enough to house four hundred orphans.

"When an unmarried woman becomes pregnant in Saudi Arabia, she is sent to a special center where she is known only by a number for two years," said the orphanage's director, thirty-year-old Samha Al-Gamdi. In Saudi Arabia, as in many Muslim countries, a woman being admitted to a hospital in labor must produce her wedding certificate. If she cannot do so, the police are informed. "Sending her to a center is for her own safety. We are a tribal culture, and the girl's brother or uncle may try to come after her to take revenge. They may kill her. Her child is sent to us.

"At the end of the two years, the woman is whipped for the crime of giving birth to an illegitimate child. Ninety lashes is usual, but in some cases it has been one hundred and fifty. Then, if she wants, she may keep her child, but few choose to do so because the stigma is too big in our country, and also her life would never be safe.

"We have a prostitute at the moment who has had five babies by five different fathers without being married. Each time, she has been whipped, but she doesn't learn. She even has been put into prison for two years on three separate occasions to try to straighten her out. It doesn't work. She is not educated and she takes drugs. We have tried to talk to her about using contraceptives at least. But she just tells us, 'When I need money, I go and find a man.'

"We tested her and her last baby for AIDS. Fortunately, the baby was negative, and so far, so is the mother. We have also given her a house and financial support. She wants to look after her children, but always she goes back to prostitution. If this woman were married, the authorities would have executed her by now."

Children in Dar Al Hadana are told their parents are dead — never the truth — again, because the stigma in Saudi Arabia is too great. "We tell them their parents died in a car accident or a fire; we make up stories to protect them. But by the time they become teenagers, they understand. They realize that all Saudi children except for them have a family name. They only have a first name, which we give them. When the youngsters are around nineteen, the orphanage arranges marriages for them. "It isn't easy to find them spouses because of their backgrounds, but we always manage eventually. We give the girls Riyals twenty thousand [$5,500] as a dowry.

"Usually, the husbands we are able to find are very religious men who marry such a girl because they want to do a good act for God."

CHAPTER 10

Iraq: A Nation of Fear

*The deeper the wound to the body,
the greater the growth of the spirit.*

SADDAM HUSSEIN, JULY 1992

AS I WENT OVER MY RESEARCH MATERIAL on Iraq the night before I left for Baghdad, my stomach lurched when I came across reports and colored photographs supplied to me by a human rights organization of Iraqi torture victims. As a journalist, I was not new to such gruesome data. But these particular photographs, many of them of women, some of whom were still teenagers, illustrated vividly and sickeningly the cacodemonic abyss into which the imagination plunges when searching for new ways to inflict pain.

In Iraq, fear is a common denominator; it can begin even before one crosses the border. "Please be very careful," a Western embassy official in neighboring Jordan told me. "If you get into trouble in Iraq, there is nothing we can do to help you. Your hotel room and phone will be bugged. Hotel staff are required to report on you, as are taxi drivers, as well as the Ministry of Information 'minders' assigned to you, as are many of the people you will interview. Do not take the kind of risks you might feel safe taking in other countries. Iraq has what is probably the largest security police force in the world, and they are very good at what they do. Everyone is spying on everyone else. As in Stalin's regime, even children are expected to spy on their parents."

Like most journalists, no matter the country or the occasion, I pretty much bank on my profession to convey a certain protection. Acts of God excepted, the worst I expected was to be expelled, as I had been on one occasion when the country I was in was under martial law.

But in Iraq, the press credentials of British reporter Farzad Bazoft had not protected him. The Iranian-born journalist, on assignment for the London *Observer,* was hanged in March 1990 after being accused of spying for Israel. Iraq ignored many pleas of clemency from world leaders, including the Pope and Margaret Thatcher. What was particularly disturbing about the Bazoft case was that he was arrested for doing something that many journalists, myself included, might have done. He was attempting to investigate the cause of a mysterious explosion at a defense-industry complex, reportedly a missile development base, near Baghdad, which was said to have killed more than seven hundred people. Bazoft was caught taking soil samples from the civilian side of the security perimeter of the complex. He had planned to have the samples analyzed in Britain in an effort to ascertain whether the explosion had been of nuclear or chemical origin. It cost him six months of solitary confinement, torture, and ultimately, his life. Even now, Iraq's Ministry of Information uses Bazoft's name whenever it is trying to cow foreign journalists it considers too independent or argumentative.

After Bazoft's execution, there were those who said his Iranian origins were the reason Iraq had no qualms about killing him. But Robert Spurling's American passport, and Peter Worth's British nationality did not protect them. Spurling, the technical director of a luxury hotel in Baghdad, was jailed and repeatedly tortured for nearly four months in 1983. Never charged with any crime, he was released only when Iraq wanted to improve its relations with the United States. Worth, a British civil engineer, was jailed, beaten, and tortured in 1981 after he accidentally caused a picture of Saddam Hussein to fall to the ground at the construction site where he was working.

These thoughts skittered through my mind, as did images of the photographs, during the fourteen-hour drive from Amman to Baghdad. (Scheduled airlines have not been permitted by the United Nations to fly into or out of Iraq since the Gulf War.) What kind of human being is it who can take an electric drill to a living person's eyes, ears, and knees, or can ax off the breasts, arms, and legs of a teenage girl? How do you immerse someone in a tank of nitric acid, or burn them alive slowly with an acetylene torch, and then go home at night to your spouse and kids? And yet ordinary Iraqis have fallen victim to these kinds of horrors, plus the more "normal" tortures. Western human rights organizations estimate two hundred thousand Kurds out of a population of three million, and "tens of thousands" of the other fifteen million Iraqis have been executed under the

Hussein regime, the vast majority of whom are tortured before being killed.

Unfortunately, the trip to Baghdad supplied little to distract me from my morbid musings. The Iraqi desert through which we drove is flat and desolate. The modern highway is good, but seemingly never ending. My ancient Jordanian cab, arranged for me by the Iraqi consul in Amman, broke down repeatedly. And much of our precious drinking water supply went to cool down the frequently overheated engine, which rendered the driver and me close to dehydration in the searing desert temperature. By the time we arrived in Baghdad, we and the vehicle looked as though we had participated in the Paris-to-Dakar car rally.

I checked into the Al-Rasheed Hotel, named after the ninth-century Abbasid monarch Haroon Al-Rasheed, who ruled over Baghdad at the acme of its culture, development, and glory, and more recently made famous by CNN, which filmed the Gulf War from its grounds and windows. Seven months after my visit, a stray U.S. cruise missile crashed into the hotel, devastating the reception hall and killing two employees.

The moment I stepped into my hotel room, my phone began to ring and it continued to do so late into the night and early again the next morning. Baghdad's driver mafia were informed I had arrived apparently seconds after I had done so. And they competed frantically for my business. One, a Kurd, who arrived before my breakfast the next day, had to literally be pushed out of my room in the middle of his lengthy sales pitch.

That the competition was intense was not surprising. Iraq no longer has tourists, and since the Kuwaiti invasion, even its official and business visitors have been limited. Taxi drivers can go days, sometimes weeks without working. Latching on to a foreign journalist gives them access to foreign currency, and the opportunity to score points with the Iraqi authorities for turning in detailed daily logs of where the reporter went and to whom he or she spoke. But the major motivator is money.

Since the United Nations imposed worldwide trade sanctions on Iraq, on August 6, 1990 — four days after the Kuwaiti invasion — inflation has been dramatic. Incomes have been so severely eroded that Iraqi children are dying of malnutrition by the thousands. Problems are exacerbated by desperate shortages of food, medicine, vaccines, and just about everything else needed for everyday living. As with most oil-producing Arab countries that went from extreme poverty to extreme wealth in a few short years, Iraq imported more than it produced, if one discounts petroleum-based industries. With the U.N. embargoes in place, the average Iraqi is struggling to survive. The blockade exempts food and medicine, but, with Iraq's $4 billion foreign currency funds frozen abroad and the country unable to sell its oil, Baghdad says it cannot afford to purchase either commodity.

During my visit to Iraq, the official rate of exchange was the pre–Gulf War rate of $1 equaling Iraqi Dinars 3.30. On the burgeoning black market during my two-week trip, however, the rate grew almost daily, going from $1 equaling Dinars 15 to a high of D. 24; two months later, it had hit D. 40. Before I plugged into the foreign-exchange black market, I was charged $83.25 for a glass of orange juice at the hotel.

The average Iraqi salary is Dinars 200 per month and has an ever-diminishing buying power. Rice, a staple, and sugar were now D. 400 for a fifty-kilogram bag, the equivalent of two months' salary. Milk, when it could be found, was D. 160 for two liters, or D. 400 for a small container of the powdered variety. Two automobile tires, which had been D. 200, were D. 4,000 or twenty months' income.

Just as prices increase daily, so, too, do the chances of receiving forged banknotes. The Iraqi market has been flooded with fake dinars; the problem is so severe that banks, businesses, and even the currency black-marketers are all equipped with ultraviolet scanners to detect the forgeries. American dollars are just as risky. I exchanged large dollar bills for smaller denominations at the central Raifadan Bank, and half the notes I received turned out to be fake, as I learned when I tried to pay my hotel bill with them. Iraqi authorities claim the forged currency flooding the country is part of an illicit attempt by the Gulf War allies to destabilize the country. For the ordinary person it is just one more daily nightmare with which to cope.

The tension in Iraq was palpable — the last allied bomb and missile had fallen in Baghdad seventeen months before I arrived but many homes still had windows taped against bomb blasts (even though in this high-tech war, glass was usually pulverized to powder instead of shattering). "People are afraid, afraid the U.S. will bomb us again," said Asia Al-Tuhairi, aged fifty-five, who lives directly opposite the Al Dora Oil Refinery on the River Tigris in the city. Her fear was real.

In January 1993 — almost two years to the day from when the Gulf War began — one hundred American, British, and French planes carried out a bombing strike in southern Iraq in retaliation for Iraq's repeat incursions into Kuwait. Days later, Baghdad was bombed again by U.S. planes, which destroyed an industrial complex that was allegedly manufacturing components for use in nuclear weapons production. It was during this attack that the Al-Rasheed Hotel was hit. And then in June of that same year, American missiles rained down on Baghdad's intelligence complex, and also killed civilians in the nearby residential neighborhood.

Asia and her neighbors had watched in horror during the Gulf War as Cruise missiles traveled just yards over their homes as they neared the target of the refinery. "Some of those so-called 'smart bombs' fell in our residential neighborhood, obliterating houses, not strategic targets. And when they did hit the refinery, the flames were so intense they traveled more than halfway across the river toward our homes and burned for weeks. It was terrifying."

Scenes like those will never be forgotten by the people of Baghdad, but in conversation with Iraqis during my visit, I heard the same statement over and over: "As bad as the bombing was, it is worse now with the embargoes," Saad Taher, a thirty-four-year-old interpreter with the Ministry of Information told me. "There's a collective depression in Iraq now. It has affected my marriage, it has affected every family. We knew the bombing would end, but the sanctions feel as though they will go on forever. There is no hope in life, just death."

Worse hit in the economic crunch are the tens of thousands of war widows, most of whom lost their husbands in the eight-year war with Iran that ended in 1988. These women struggle to support six or more children on government pensions of between D. 60 and D. 130 a month, which no longer buys even a container of milk. Frequent scenes in the flea markets of the city, known locally as the Ali-Baba bazaars, are women and children peddling a few vegetables or the family's clothes. One undersized eleven-year-old stood in front of ten pairs of his sisters' equally tiny used shoes and slippers in the scorching noonday heat. (U.N. thermometers registered nearly 140 degrees my first week in Baghdad. It was certainly the hottest weather I have ever experienced.) "No, I haven't sold any today, and I didn't sell any the day before. But maybe later. . . . Unless I do, my sisters and I won't eat."

A recent program on the government-controlled television warned that any child found on the street selling or begging instead of in school would be taken from his parents. "The child's place is in school," the program lectured. A man with his own stall near the boy asked angrily, "Doesn't the government realize that food is more important than knowledge in Iraq today? If a kid doesn't eat, how can he study? And the government isn't feeding him." The same point had obviously been overlooked by a Baghdad mullah whose solution to the food crisis included telling girls to fast every second day. It was only when one teenage student fainted in her class that the mullah rescinded his recommendation.

In these markets of desperation, one of the more pathetic commodities for sale are the skeletal puppies priced optimistically at D. 400 and offered as potential guard dogs. The city's crime rate has climbed rapidly during the economic crisis; kidnapping for ransom is becoming an industry. The skin-and-bone puppies, mostly German shepherds, a number of whom are so weak they can barely stand, are bred by breeders who can't afford to feed them but are desperate for something to sell.

The scene that saddened me most was a young woman sitting on the ground in a black *abaya* and *hijab* trying to sell for D. 30 a chicken she had raised, even though she and her six children had not eaten meat for two years. Fatima, aged thirty, had lost her husband in the Iran-Iraq War in 1986. Her war pension of D. 112 per month barely kept her family in bread. She had brought two chickens to the market that day but in the crowd and rush a passerby had accidentally trod on the head of one and killed it. Since the chicken had not been Islamically slaughtered, Muslims considered it *haram*, forbidden, and were refusing to buy it. I purchased the chicken and told her to feed it to her children, but I wasn't sure that, as hungry as she and her family were, they would violate the Muslim code.

As the auction houses and secondhand furniture stores along Baghdad's Nidhal Street attest, many families have been forced to sell virtually all their possessions. Furniture, air-conditioners, ovens, refrigerators, wedding gifts, heirloom oriental carpets, paintings, toys, and even the former Dean of Baghdad University's treasured five thousand–volume book collection were available.

Who are the purchasers at the auction houses? The "new class" say the Iraqis scathingly, "the black-marketers who grow rich off our tragedy." They are the sanction-busters, who smuggle in foreign-label alcohol, whiskey, gin, arak, and a vast variety of beers, plus any other commodity that will find a ready market among the country's moneyed elite, Baath party members, and others close to Saddam Hussein. Said one, "Most of our stuff comes to Iraq through Turkey, Syria, and Iran, and always has." It is this new class that crowds the gambling tables nightly at the city's casinos, to which Saddam Hussein's son Udai is also a frequent visitor.

Two months after my visit, the government accused more than forty Baghdad merchants with profiteering, and hanged them from lampposts around the city. Seen as a government attempt to stall panic as the value of the dinar plunged 50 percent overnight and food prices again soared, the move backfired. Food shortages became more acute as other merchants, fearing the same end, refused to bring in supplies.

Fear in Iraq, I learned, comes in many shapes, textures, and colors. And it permeates every level of society, starting with Saddam Hussein, who has his own food-taster, bed-tester, and his own chair that travels with him (the last two to guard against poisonous tacks or hypodermics that may be embedded in either). Before the Gulf War President Hussein was highly visible and even held *diwaniyas* for the public at which he arbitrated in family or tribal disputes. At that time, Saddam's telephone number was listed in the Baghdad directory.

These days Saddam Hussein, like Cuba's Castro, sleeps at a different location every night to reduce the likelihood of assassination — and the attempts on his life have been many. But while Iraq's president now keeps a low public profile, his presence is everywhere. Giant portraits, some several stories high, stare at Iraqis in Big Brother style from buildings, lampposts, and any available surface. Many are connected thematically to the building they adorn. In front of the reconstructed telecommunications building, Saddam is talking on the phone. Outside the Ministry of Justice, he is a judge. At the Mukhabarat, security police headquarters, his expression is particularly severe. At the Communicable Disease Control Center, where all visitors to Iraq are required to have AIDS tests within five days of their arrival or go to jail, Saddam is pictured wearing a protective metal helmet! And at the main crossroads close to the Al-Rasheed Hotel, there are six enormous portraits of Saddam, several of them smiling. It may only be coincidental, but one of the main streets off that junction has become a center for a burgeoning industry in the city — prostitution. The oldest profession is increasingly turned to by Iraqi women who no longer have any other means to feed their children.

• • •

Although her husband is part of Saddam Hussein's inner circle, Amal Sharqi's life has not been an easy one, and it shows. Her face is gaunt, deep lines run from nose to mouth, and there are dark shadows under her eyes. She moves slowly and seems tired. Part of her physical appearance is due to what she describes as her "delicate health." Amal, aged fifty-two, has a longtime heart condition for which she daily needs four different medications, and which today in Baghdad even the elite have trouble regularly obtaining. But a lot of her apparent fragility stems from three decades of anxiety. She worries about her husband, she worries about her son, her only child, and she worries about her country's future. She weeps easily, and one understands why.

Her husband of thirty years, Abdul Jabbar Muhsin, is Saddam Hussein's spokesman, and he travels with him constantly, frequently in the same vehicle. I was surprised to learn that Hussein needed a spokesman. The president appears on Iraqi television almost daily and speaks at length each time. During my visit, an education seminar with the country's leading educators was televised. The president spoke without interruption for almost the entire three hours the seminar lasted, and devoted an entire twenty minutes to a monologue on the necessity for clean toilets in schools. He summed up that subject by promising to give raises to the toilet cleaners rather than the educators.

Saddam Hussein and Amal's husband were members of the Baath party when it was an illegal underground guerrilla organization in Iraq. And because of this political involvement, both men were imprisoned — Hussein once, but Muhsin thirteen times. "My son hardly knew his father when he was young," said Amal. "When we first married, I worked for the Iraqi News Agency. So many people wanted to fire me because of my husband's political activities. Once he was freed, no one would hire him. It was a very difficult time. When you are linked to a politically active person, you have to be prepared for the worst. I have never tried to stop him; we are in a pioneering period of our history. I believe it is more important to achieve something than to have a long and idle life. All cultures go through such a period."

Amal recognizes that Abdul's proximity to Saddam Hussein means that any assassination attempt on the president could kill her husband. "We've discussed that possibility," she said quietly. "We've written about it to each other in many letters. When Abdul was chosen to be spokesman for the Iraqi leadership, I sent him a congratulating letter in which I said, 'You've always had a noble cause to live for, and now you have one to die for.' I wrote about the Iraqi flag that we place over a dead body. After the funeral I said I would fold the flag and keep it, and give it to Abdullah, our grandson, at the time of his marriage. It would be his inheritance, I told my husband. Because in 1982, following the initiative of Mrs. Saddam Hussein, women throughout the country gave up their gold and jewelry to help finance the war against Iran. I even gave my wedding ring. I told my husband the flag would be a wedding dress for Abdullah's wife."

Without warning, Amal's stoicism and rhetoric suddenly collapsed. With tears streaming down her cheeks, she looked at me and, raising her voice, said, "Do you realize I'm talking about the death of my husband?" And just as quickly, her voice dropped again and she sagged in the chair in which she was sitting. "There are many reports of attempts on the president's life. . . . My husband rides with him often. . . . But if Abdul is killed, he will be a hero. It is a promise I made to my son."

Because of the nature of her husband's work, Amal is often alone, and I was reminded of the World War II slogan "They also serve who sit and wait." She was alone throughout the Gulf War. "My son was a soldier and I remained in Baghdad for the sole reason that when there was a raid, I could go up on the roof and see if there was any smoke from the direction of his base." Her voice quavered, and her eyes again filled with tears. "It was bombed repeatedly. Every time Baghdad was bombed, I waited on the roof to see if my son still survived or not." She wiped away her tears and sighed, "It was a very lonely period, very uncertain. My husband was with Saddam Hussein. And you don't know if you yourself will be here the next hour or not. You don't know whether your child, your husband, your home, even Baghdad will survive. We were threatened with a nuclear strike."

Amal, an intelligent, cultivated woman and a thoughtful speaker, told me she had agreed to see me only because she was "angry, and wanted to express that anger." We met at her publishing house, a company she formed two years ago after ill-health forced her to give up the government position of director-general of the Department of Culture for Children in Iraq. Since that time, her company has been able to publish only four books, two of those Arabic translations of E. M. Forster and Graham Greene, because of the extreme shortage of paper in Iraq under the embargoes. Iraq has lost half its newspapers and magazines for the same reason, and of those that survive, circulations have been cut by 50 percent. At *Alef Ba* magazine for women, I watched journalists write their articles by hand on both sides of scrap paper.

As many Iraqis are inclined to do with a foreigner these days, Amal veered into an attack on the U.N. embargoes, the responsibility for which, like most of her fellow countrymen, she places at the door of the U.S. White House. Amal was the author of a massive Iraqi letter campaign called "I Protest." She organized adults and children to fire off thousands of missives in many languages to world leaders and international media criticizing the sanctions. "I realized what the sanctions would do to Iraq, and I felt fear. We sent letters to the White House, to Downing Street, to the Vatican. They didn't reply.

"I have watched CNN showing film of the starving in Somalia. I can show you children here in Baghdad who look the same. Somalia suffered a famine. Iraq is a wealthy country. Our problem has been forced on us by Westerners who view us as less important than you view your pets.

"In the thirties, the Kuwait government took the decision to amalgamate Kuwait with Iraq. The historical fact is Kuwait is part of Iraq." While I was in Iraq, the state-controlled television launched a thirty-part series to document that fact. "But you are not punishing us now because you care about Kuwait. The West could care less. You simply do not want so much oil in the hands of a nationalist leader. The embargo will never be lifted until you can have a lackey in Baghdad. You are cornering us and driving us mad so that we commit suicide. You talk about political freedom and human rights. . . . If Saddam Hussein is toppled, there will be blood up to our knees." Her voice shook with emotion again as she spoke. "There are millions of people in the Baath party. Every one of them will be a target for slaughter."

It is for this reason that people in Iraq, even the many who are opposed to the current regime, insist that Saddam Hussein will not be overthrown soon. A ranking government official explained, "I'll tell you why there hasn't been a coup against Saddam Hussein. No one dares. Anyone who tries will not only be executed himself, but his children, his children's children, his brothers, his cousins, and all their children and grandchildren will lose their lives also. It will be as if that man's family never existed. The West may feel that if they squeeze us enough with the sanctions, Saddam Hussein will be overthrown. It won't happen. People feel like me. I would rather be a live rabbit than a dead and dismembered lion." It is a message that Saddam Hussein conveyed to the Iraqi people early on in his regime when he told the Revolutionary Council, "We have the strength of character to behead those, no matter how many, who betray their nation and conspire against their people."

Amal insisted that the West does not understand Hussein's role in Iraq. "He's not a dictator, he's a partisan. He's part of a very strong nationalist movement in Iraq that started at the beginning of the century. He's the culmination of a long struggle. In my lifetime, I have lived through six coups, one revolution, the recent war, and now this slow starvation of our country. Isn't it enough? If Saddam falls, your Western mercenaries will cause a bloodbath. There will be a reign of terror for Iraq.

"The West does not understand that in a society like ours a leader is a country's destiny. It is not a matter of whether a Democrat or Republican is in office. When Sadat took over Egypt he turned it one hundred and eighty degrees from the direction in which Nasser had taken the country. In our part of the world, a country's future is determined by one man. Saddam is a leader of a modern awakening, a renaissance of culture, social life, and politics. [*Baath* means "renaissance."]

"The West talks of pluralism and democracy. But pluralism is not a valid issue for Iraq currently. I think there should be an opposition, but we need time to prepare for this. After the nationalization of oil in 1972, sudden wealth poured over Iraq. People had a chance for the first time to buy a pair of shoes, build a decent house, send their children to school, buy televisions and washing machines. These people are still in the early stages of modern development. They are not yet formed. You can't have pluralism with a developing society. The West doesn't understand tribal or patriarchal leadership. In our culture, we feel safe and secure with a man who is confident to lead. You have to understand that. Iraq will have one-man rule as long as God wills it.

"Unlike my husband, I'm not a Baathist. I'm a nationalist and an Iraqi and a progressive woman. I have struggled to be a modern woman in an Islamic society, and I will not surrender to a country like Saudi Arabia that wants to cover all women and confine them to the house. The Baathist party is an avant-garde party for social change."

I commented that the Iraqi version of Baathism was more commonly known as a brutal totalitarian regime. A nation proudly referred to a thousand years ago as "People of Opinion" now was permitted only one — that of their president. Saddam Hussein, after all, is a man who has systematically killed any threat to his authority or any dissenting voice, even those of his close friends. And Iraq's penal code states that anyone criticizing the president, his party, or the government will be executed.

"When people raise the issue of totalitarianism, I point out that without it we would never have been able to achieve the present status of women in Iraq," said Amal. "When the state owns the media, and when the goals of the state are to initiate emancipation of women, you put all the media into service to achieve this goal.

"I can remember when the rights of women were not as respected in Iraq as they are now. Without totalitarianism, women's emancipation would have been much more difficult, and it would not have happened so quickly. Look at Western suffragettes, how they suffered. I am not defending totalitarianism; I am asking people with other forms of government to try to be open-minded enough to include other visions and approaches.

"To bring about change, to enable women to be educated, to go to school, to be economically active takes time and effort. In the West, it took a century to change the status of women. You have to build an infrastructure for it, and Saddam Hussein did so and did so quickly."

The irony is that in a country where human rights are not recognized, Iraqi women, on paper at least, have more rights and freedoms than in any other Arab state. I visited the General Federation of Iraqi Women to interview its longtime president, Manal Younis Abdul Razzaq. As I waited for her to finish a lengthy phone call, the three government "minders" who each took verbatim notes of the interview, told me, "President Younis is a very busy person. She is Iraq's First Lady." They then explained that unlike in the West, the president's wife was not designated First Lady. "It is a position of achievement. Mrs. Hussein has family responsibilities, which preclude her much of the time from playing a role in public life. When a First Lady is needed to meet foreign guests or delegations, President Younis stands beside President Hussein."

The Federation of Iraqi Women, dedicated to improving the status of women, is the female arm of the Baath party, and it claims a membership of over one million, one in eighteen Iraqis. Its literature reflects the Socialist-Islamic tenor of the Baath party itself. All titles begin with "comrade," which led to the Iraqi president's form of address being an oxymoronic "Comrade President Saddam Hussein — May God Protect Him." Other aims of the Federation of

Women are to "combat Zionist and Imperialist activities and to fight against racial discrimination, race exploitation, and any segregation because of sex, language, religion, or social activity." If this seems at odds with life in Iraq today, it is no more so than Iraq's constitution, drawn up by the Baathists, which guarantees "freedom of speech and opinion, and freedom of the press."

Similarly, women aged eighteen and over may legally vote, a hollow right today for both sexes in Iraq, where the National Assembly is a parliament in name only. However, women are to be found in every profession, including the armed forces, where they undergo military training but fill noncombatant roles, including that of pilots. Women make up 70 percent of Iraq's pharmacists, 46 percent of its dentists and educators, and 40 percent of its physicians. Women are also engineers. The director-general of Telecommunications in Iraq is a woman. Engineer Azhair Abdul Wahab, aged forty-six and a mother of three, is the highest-ranking woman engineer in Iraq. She was charged with repairing all the damaged and destroyed telecommunications centers throughout the country, which were specifically targeted by allied bombing, and she was given twelve months by Saddam himself to do so. She managed to meet the tight deadline by having male and female students work around the clock as laborers. "Communications means everything during a war," she told me. "If you kill the means to communicate, you kill the country."

Iraq also has women working in the petroleum industry as specialists. And women are politicians: currently twenty-nine serve in the 250-member National Assembly, and the percentage at times has been higher. The first female cabinet minister of an Arab country was Iraqi. Iraq had its first female judge in 1948, the same year a woman was appointed ambassador. Today, 40 percent of all university students are women.

Working mothers in Iraq receive six months' paid maternity leave and benefits, plus a further six months' leave at half-salary, which is a substantially better arrangement than most women in the United States have. The Federation also operates heavily subsidized childcare facilities for working women, an unusual situation in Arab countries, where the extended family or foreign servants normally fill that role. And employment laws in Iraq state that a couple's home must be closer to the place of work of the wife than of the husband, a benefit many exhausted working-mother commuters in the West might envy. (How the Iraqis monitor such a ruling isn't specified.)

War widows receive government pensions, and until the current economic crisis, also homes and cars. A man who marries a woman whose husband was "martyred" during any war receives a bonus of Dinars 7,500 ($24,750 at the 1990 rate), whether she is his first wife or co-wife.

In Iraq, a modified *Shariah* law operates: both men and women may apply for divorce, which, after six months of required couple counseling, is at the discretion of the judge. The mother is normally granted custody of the children, and if she is not able to take them, custody goes to the mother's sister or her female relatives. The father is permitted to spend one day a week with his children. If a husband elects to divorce his wife Islamically, by announcing three times that he is doing so, he must leave his wife the house and the car, and pay family support for two years. "And if she has good reasons to divorce him," said Younis, "such as he beats her, is a drug addict, et cetera, then he is allowed to leave the house with only one suitcase containing his clothes."

Such rights and benefits are unusual in many Islamic countries. And they are the reason that Iraq is often called a model for women's progress in the Middle East, and in some areas even for the West. Saddam Hussein himself said in a public address not so long ago, "Unless the woman is liberated, there is no freedom in Iraq. When the Iraqi woman is well, the Iraqi people are well, and when her position is disturbed, the disturbance reaches all the Iraqi people."

But when one takes a closer look at the status of women in Iraq, all is not as rosy or progressive as it seems. In a 1987 speech meant to highlight the advances of modern Iraqi women, President Hussein pointed out that under the world's first legal code set down in Babylon nearly four thousand years ago by an early Iraqi, King Hammurabi, women were viewed as chattel. "The husband had the right to mortgage his wife to a creditor, until he was able to repay his debts, provided he did so within three years," said Saddam Hussein. "He also had the right to sell his wife if she was unfaithful to him." Four millennia after Hammurabi and three years after he made that speech, Hussein suddenly declared that men had permission to kill with impunity any female relative caught or suspected of "misbehaving," and a law was passed to that effect. A year later, in December 1991, in a televised broadcast, Hussein told the nation, "If you see a woman or her daughters flirting on the street, or if you suspect misconduct, you are a people's council. You are allowed to kick that family out of the neighborhood and confiscate their house."

Iraqis to whom I spoke considered both these rulings sops to the country's 60 percent Shi'a Muslims, most of whom are located in the south of the country. In the southern cities of Karbala and Najaf stand the two holiest shrines for Shi'as throughout the world. During the Shi'a uprisings after the Gulf War, the population of this region — Farsi speakers like their neighbors in Iran — displayed more photographs of Khomeini than of Saddam Hussein. Throughout the south, Shi'a mullahs have been following their counterparts in Iran and calling for a return to the strict Khomeini-style Islamic orthodoxy, including the banning of cosmetics, total veiling of women, and their confinement.

In times of growing insecurity for Hussein's regime, the Sunni Arab minority that makes up most of the Baathist government has looked for ways to pacify the hostile southern majority. For this reason, Saddam Hussein has become more "Islamic" since the Gulf War, particularly in his speeches, which frequently quote from the Koran. It is also why he has cracked down on Iraq's female population. Sacrificing women is an easy political gesture for him to make.

Iraq also has nearly one million Christians, and churches in cities such as Mosul in the north are common. The founder of the Baathist party, Michel Aflaq, was a Christian, as are most of Saddam Hussein's domestic and personal staff. He is said to trust them more than the competing Islamic factions in Iraq.

In the Shi'a south, women commonly wear *hijab* and *abaya,* while in the north they frequently wear only *hijab.* In the capital, many women dress in fashionable Western clothes. I was surprised to learn, however, that Islamic dress, as in the rest of the Middle East, is making a reappearance. A large number of the employees at the Federation of Iraqi Women were wearing *hijab.* "We are an Islamic society," said President Younis, who is married to a military pilot and is the mother of four. She herself was dressed in a black business suit, with her head uncovered. But the president said she never misses one of the five daily prayers, and she opened her desk drawer to show me her prayer rug. "We have nothing against the veil; it is voluntary. The Federation simply calls for conservative dress — long sleeves and long skirts. We encourage women to be discreet in their fashion. Islamic dress is on the increase here because it demonstrates women are against Western influences."

Earlier Amal Sharqi had explained the increase thus: "People seek spiritual serenity and security, which religion provides, in a time of crisis. People are weakened by strife, and they take refuge under a cape of religion. I understand it."

Added President Younis, "The *abaya* impedes the movement of women, the *hijab* is more practical. But what is most important is that women's minds are not veiled, and their progress is not impeded. Islam is a comprehensive social system. It defines the status of women in the society, and it provides equality for both sexes."

Despite such statements, contradictions abound in the Baath party concerning women. "When I was a young woman," a woman in her fifties told me, "I was able to study abroad and travel freely. Since the Baathists have been in power, women may no longer study abroad, and under the age of forty-five are required to travel with a *mahram* male chaperon." Khairallah Tulfah, Saddam's uncle, who was appointed mayor of Baghdad shortly after the Baathists came to power, is best known in the West for his government pamphlet entitled "Three Whom God Should Not Have Created: Persians, Jews, and Flies." Baghdad women, however, grew to fear his legion of employed vigilantes who pounced on them in public to paint their legs black if they were considered to be showing too much leg. "It was not as though we were wearing miniskirts," said the wife of a retired Iraqi diplomat. Fortunately for Baghdad's female population, Tulfah proved too corrupt even for Saddam Hussein, who was eventually forced to remove him from office.

Iraq's laws on rape are also extremely antifemale. "In cases of rape, the man is usually obliged to marry his victim if she is single," Dr. Sadoun Khalifa, a member of the National Assembly and director of Iraq's Commission on Health and Social Affairs, told me. "If the victim is married, the rapist must pay financial compensation to her husband. This may come to between Dinars fifteen thousand and twenty thousand, depending on her age. The younger the victim, the higher the compensation; the older the victim, the lower the sum."

Women in Iraq were urged to join the labor force in a two-prong Baathist government campaign. They were needed because of a labor shortage, particularly during the eight-year war with Iran. The government also intended to shift women's allegiance to the state and away from family or ethnic group. At this time also, women were told it was their patriotic duty to bear a minimum of five children to replace those fallen in the war. Financial incentives were offered to every woman who had six children or more. At the same time, birth-control devices were declared illegal. Abortion, as in most Islamic countries, is prohibited by law. Illegal abortions, however, have increased since the economic crisis. The procedure, done without any anesthetics, currently costs the equivalent of eight months' salary.

The order to procreate coincided with women being told it was their duty to fill the jobs vacated by men away fighting. It was at this time that the child-care program was born, as was a massive nation-wide campaign encouraging women to bottle-feed their babies. Even today, hospitals are plastered with posters from manufacturers of infant formula, such as Nestlé. The campaign against breast-feeding sadly has been too successful, and has contributed to the current steep rise in infant mortality. Women used to giving their babies powdered milk can now no longer afford to buy it. During my visit to Iraq, a small can of powdered milk cost more than a month's salary on the rare occasions when it was available. And much of the country still suffers from impure water caused by the Coalition Forces' bombing of water-purification and sewage-treatment plants. Time after time I spoke to mothers in hospitals where their children were being treated for malnutrition or severe dehydration from chronic gastrointestinal infections. These women told me they couldn't afford to give their babies powdered milk. They were giving them instead a heavily diluted mix of the milk with water, or simply unboiled water.

In the workplace, totalitarian-induced gender equality is also flawed. President Younis herself has said, "Women in Iraq are considered incompetent until it is proved differently. For men, it is the reverse." And telecommunications-engineer Azhair, who heads a staff of more than a thousand men, admitted it was hard proving herself as an engineer and a boss. "I had to work four times harder than the men." And while she handles an annual budget of D. 35 million, and has been regularly working sixteen-hour days in the massive reconstruction needed since the Gulf War, she still has to go home and cook. "No, no, my husband would never cook. Arab men don't do such things," she said sheepishly.

When I applied for an interview with Saddam Hussein's senior wife, Sajida, Younis told me, "No, no, only in a case of life or death can we approach her. . . . If I bang my head against a wall and it opens, it is okay. But if I bang my head and injure myself, then I don't do it." It was a curious comment, and it hinted at the fear that all officials show when asked questions, even the most innocent, about Saddam Hussein and his family.

No Iraqi official will discuss on the record Saddam Hussein's second wife. That is partly due to the unwritten Iraqi maxim "The less said, the longer you live," but also because the Baath party was embarrassed when he married again. The president ignored his own ruling that a man needed the prior approval of his first wife and court permission before taking a co-wife. But that of course did not faze Hussein, who rather cynically told the nation on television a year after he became president that "a law is a piece of paper on which we write one or two lines, and then sign it underneath: Saddam Hussein, President of the Republic of Iraq."

Having taken a second wife, he more recently rescinded the law requiring first wives to give permission for their husbands to remarry. The fallout over the president's second marriage to Samira Shahbandar cost the lives of several men. The first to die was Hussein's closest and most trusted aide for twenty years, his valet and food-taster, Kamal Hana Jajeo. He was bludgeoned to death by Saddam's oldest son, Udai, at a party given in honor of the wife of Egypt's president, Suzanne Mubarak, in October 1988. Jajeo was believed responsible for introducing Samira to Saddam Hussein.

President Hussein has long seen himself as a Lothario with women. On his tours through various offices, he hovers over the most attractive young female present. Singling her out to chat, he has often followed up a little later by sending her a gift, frequently jewelry. "It's embarrassing," recalled one woman. "We are an Islamic society, and it is not usual behavior here." It is said that some of those young women were ferried for a few hours to a house Saddam kept especially for the purpose of "entertaining" them in the affluent district of Al Mansour in Baghdad, close to the elite Hunting Club. The club is a hangout for Saddam's top-level Baathists, who drink Black Label scotch at the cost of a month's salary for the average Iraqi, and whose president told me with a leer, "We no longer hunt anything except ladies." It was Hussein's valet who was responsible for handling the logistics of his employer's dalliances.

In his younger years, Hussein was a handsome man. Tall and slim and looking not unlike his son Udai today, he took pride in his trim physique. It is recognized that both father and son have a taste for lithe blonds, which is why Saddam's first wife, Sajida, now fifty-six, has long dyed her brown hair strawberry blond. Not surprisingly, Saddam's second wife, Samira, a sophisticated and urbane woman, is also blond. The president always ensures his flings are limited to married women, which is usual in the Arab world. He is savvy enough to understand that if he starts preying on Iraq's unwed virgins, even the Revolutionary Guards would not be able to protect him forever from the revenge of an Arab family so dishonored.

As is also common in the Arab world, Saddam's first wife ignored his amorous peccadilloes; it is possible that she did not know about many. And as long as he eventually returned to the family, she was accepting. Allegedly, she felt the same way about Samira at the beginning of Saddam's interest in her. At that time, Samira, in her thirties, was married to Nuredin al-Safi, a regional manager for Iraqi Airlines based in Austria. The president was attracted to her not only because she is beautiful but also because she is from a prominent family in Baghdad.

Ashamed of his humble beginnings in a mud village in Tikrit, a few hours' drive northwest of Baghdad, Hussein has long sought to improve his family history. Earlier, with the assistance of a compliant genealogist, he claimed that his ancestors were Hashemites, the same tribe as the Prophet and also of King Hussein of Jordan, making him a direct descendant from Mohammed. And in the early eighties, he tried to marry his son Udai to one of Jordan's princesses. The Jordanian royal family was scandalized. Hussein's Hashemite claim made him a laughingstock among educated Arabs throughout the Middle East.

When the president met Samira, he tried once again to acquire what he could neither buy nor obtain with brute force — good breeding. The way he went about achieving that aim simply confirmed once again his lack of class. Samira's husband was "persuaded" to divorce her. He was then rewarded by being made the head of Iraqi Airlines, a meaningless position today as the airline was grounded after the Kuwaiti invasion and it hasn't flown since. The airline offices in downtown Baghdad are now locked and shuttered.

When Hussein's first wife, who is also his maternal cousin, learned that Saddam had secretly married Samira, she became distraught. Their children — two sons, Udai, twenty-nine, and Kusai, twenty-seven, and three daughters, Raghad, twenty-five, Rana, twenty-one, and Hala, aged seventeen and Saddam's favorite — and other family members became involved and the issue promptly developed into a nasty domestic feud.

The second marriage was a public slap in the face for Sajida, who, two years her husband's senior, was then fifty, and who was concerned about her fading attractiveness. She also recognized that any Muslim male who takes a younger second wife will probably favor the children of that union; the second wife is typically perceived as the traditional "wife of the heart." Sajida's arranged marriage to Saddam had been agreed upon when both were still toddlers. She knew that being married to her first cousin was a relationship intended to cement family relations; romance was never a factor.

Udai, the Husseins' eldest son, and the one closest to his father in temperament, took it the hardest. As proud and as arrogant as Saddam, he dreaded the loss in status and the concomitant trimmings that his father's second marriage could mean to him and his siblings. When the president began to appear in public with Samira, Sajida feared she had been completely usurped. Given his mother's visible distress (some Iraqis say she came close to a breakdown) and his own volatile emotions, it was only a matter of time before Udai acted. Unable to confront his father or his new bride, he took out his anger on a much more accessible target: Kamal Jajeo, whom he murdered.

Udai's action, brutal though it was, has many precedents in Islamic history. In the harems of royal courts, particularly during the Ottoman reign, favorite wives were frequently poisoned or their infant sons were murdered, because an earlier wife could not bear the humiliation of being replaced, or did not want to see her son's position in the line of ascension displaced.

Udai underestimated, however, his father's fondness of Jajeo, a man said to be one of his most intimate confidants. A stunned and outraged Saddam informed the nation via television that his son would stand trial for murder. An indication of the depth of his feelings came shortly after when he refused to eat food prepared in Sajida's home, a classic Arab insult, and a symbol of contempt.

Sajida's brother, General Adnan Khairallah, then Iraq's defense minister and reportedly one of Saddam's closest friends, intervened. He confronted the president on his continual public humiliation of Sajida; the general was one of the few men who dared criticize Hussein. But on this occasion, the president did not welcome his brother-in-law's comments; nor did he reportedly take kindly to Khairallah's criticism around the same time regarding Saddam's policy concerning the Kurds. The Halabja massacre of six thousand Kurds by chemical gas had been earlier that year.

Shortly after, it was announced that the valet's family had requested clemency for Udai, and he was briefly exiled to Switzerland instead. Much was made at the time of the fortuitous clemency appeal from the dead's man family. The assumption was that the appeal was made under duress, and this may well have been the case. Under Islamic law, however, such a move is not unusual. The *qisas* law of retaliation, which is based on the early Arab "eye for an eye" principle, permits a sum of money, literally blood money, to be paid to the next-of-kin in the case of a murder or fatal accident.

Two months after Udai's return to Iraq from Switzerland, General Khairallah was killed when his helicopter fell out of the sky. He was touring the north of the country at the time with President Hussein, and since the two were still not on speaking terms, they flew in separate helicopters. Reportedly, Saddam had ordered the assassination of his brother-in-law because of his interference regarding Sajida and/or the Kurds.

The death of her brother further weakened Sajida's position with Saddam. She must have found her husband's earlier comments on family life ironic indeed. Hussein had told Iraq's women, "The most important thing about marriage is that the man must not let the woman feel downtrodden simply because she is a woman, and he is a man. If she feels this, then family life is over."

Saddam married Sajida in 1960, when he was twenty-one, and she was twenty-three and was already working as a schoolteacher; she recently retired from her position as a school principal. Western media commonly claim that Sajida is better educated than her husband, and cite the fact that he was in his early twenties before he graduated from high school. In the Islamic world, where education is still not available to many, this is not uncommon even today. In Egypt, he attended Cairo University Law School, which had an excellent reputation in the Middle East then and now, but he did not graduate. He later enrolled at Baghdad University.

People who know Hussein well insist he is not the uneducated buffoon he is commonly made out to be in the West. Tyrants are idiosyncratic by nature, and Saddam Hussein is no different, which may help to explain some of his more unexpected behavior or apparent miscalculations. Those close to him claim he is an avid reader and that he reads in French and English as well as his native Arabic. He is also mocked for his parochialism due, it is said, to his lack of interest in traveling abroad. This reluctance is not uncommon in Arab leaders, and in fact his nemesis, the Emir of Kuwait, feels exactly the same. When most of the Kuwaiti family leave for cooler shores during the scorching Gulf summers, the Emir refuses to join them. Syria's Assad and Libya's Qaddafi also rarely leave the Middle East.

Like Pakistan's leader, Benazir Bhutto, Saddam has a great interest in parapsychology. He prefers to consult astrologers from India, where astrology is a respected profession, one Iraqi couple who are close to the president told me.

For all the criticisms of Hussein, he is also the man who modernized Iraq. It was President Hussein who built up Iraq's oil industry and began ploughing most of its annual $20 billion–plus profits back into the country. He launched massive literacy campaigns, upgraded hospitals and the educational system, and made both education and medical care free. Saddam has always been a major advocate of education, which may date from his own battle to attend school when he was eight, when his stepfather preferred he herd the family's sheep, and may also have been influenced by his wife's career. Hussein's oldest daughter, Raghad, who has an M.A. in English, has taught, and both her younger sisters are expected to do so when they graduate from college.

Prior to the Gulf War, Iraq produced more doctors, engineers, and scientists than any other country in the Middle East. The Saddam Central Children's Teaching Hospital in Baghdad was recognized as the finest and most advanced of its kind in the Arab world. Most Iraqis own their homes, having received interest-free loans from the government. Hussein also modernized the country's highway system, and introduced electricity and potable water to the majority of Iraq's rural areas.

Driving through Baghdad, a large modern city straddling the silt-laden Tigris, I was amazed at how little evidence of war damage there was. Only one of the many bridges across the river was still out of commission. And the Presidential Palace and Ministry of Defense, which were pretty much leveled, were still being reconstructed. In the country's capital, there was less visible apparent war damage than in Kuwait, so promptly had around-the-clock repair crews been put to work. In Baghdad, however, the war mood had not disappeared. There were antiaircraft guns on the roofs of most government buildings, and tanks were parked outside the television and radio center.

One building has not been included in the reconstruction program: the Amiriyah Shelter on the outskirts of the city, which was bombed by American planes because the Pentagon believed it was Saddam's military command bunker. Whether it was or was not, the first two below-ground floors were a civil defense shelter for the local community. The third floor and lowest level is off-limits to civilians. Amiriyah sheltered approximately seven hundred women and children on the night two two thousand–pound "smart bombs" pierced the ten feet of protective reinforced concrete with such pinpoint accuracy the second bomb went through the same four-foot hole made by the first.

In the fireball that engulfed the shelter, corpses were fused together in the intense heat. Because of the intense heat inside, it took three days for the last casualties to be brought to the surface, many of whom were so badly burned they could not be identified.

Today, the Amiriyah Shelter has become an informal memorial to those who died in it. When I visited it, the only illumination came from the shaft of sunlight shining through the bomb-perforated roof. No light entered from the doorway because the tunnel turned several times to protect the entranceway from the force of any external bomb blast. Inside, every surface of the shelter was charred black, intensifying the already caliginous atmosphere. Twisted girders and chunks of building debris made walking through the gloom a hazardous process. Families whose loved ones had perished here had written the names of the dead on the blackened walls with chalk. Here and there, large photographs of children were propped against the walls and were adorned with garlands of plastic flowers like small shrines. The sound of *azan* for midday prayers filtered down to us, and it was a welcome reminder that life goes on.

Outside, I blinked in the noonday sun, and the heat felt good after the chill of the shelter. Looking at the small suburban houses that surrounded the shelter on all four sides, I couldn't imagine how they could bear to see the building every time they glanced out of a window or stepped outside. Most of these homes had lost four to five people each in the shelter conflagration.

What happened at Amiriyah was obscene, but the shelter more than any other place in Iraq symbolizes that while President Hussein may have modernized Iraq, if his current policies continue, history may also recognize him as the man responsible for destroying what he created. We may never know whether the public shelter in Amiriyah also served a military purpose. However, Western intelligence sources have verified that since the Gulf War, strategic offices and centers have been moved into civilian buildings, such as schools and apartment buildings, in case Baghdad is bombed again. In today's high-tech hostilities, when military centers can be specifically targeted with great precision, this kind of duplicity only guarantees the death of more and more ordinary Iraqis.

One of the biggest fears in Iraq today, next to a new wave of bombing, is the dread of having a family member fall sick. Many medicines and items such as I.V.'s are no longer available or are in short supply, and diagnostic machines, such as X-ray or dialysis equipment, have been rendered useless because of lack of spare parts or X-ray film. During my visit, the Ministry of Health announced that dentists had begun extracting teeth without anesthetics because none was available. Even supplies of antibiotics are depleted.

The Saddam Central Children's Teaching Hospital in Baghdad, Iraq's showcase medical facility before the U.N. sanctions, now, like most public buildings, has elevators and air-conditioning that no longer work. Tiny patients swelter in what is one of the highest summer temperatures in the world, as doctors battle to treat them with ever-diminishing technology. Pediatric cancer patients, their skin yellowish and beaded with sweat, deteriorate daily because chemotherapy has long since run out.

Toddlers suffering from zinc deficiency caused by malnutrition scream in agony when they have to be moved or touched because their skin has peeled off due to the once-rare condition. The raw flesh over her entire body made eighteen-month-old Zainab Rashid, who weighed just twelve pounds, look like a third-degree burn victim. Iraqi doctors told me that zinc deficiency, which also causes the hair to fall out, is a condition they once saw only in medical literature, and is as painful as severe burns. The child's forty-year-old mother, A'isha, sitting by Zainab's side, was exhausted, and appeared ten years older than she was. A mother of nine, A'isha had already lost three sons in the Iran-Iraq War. Now she wondered whether Zainab would survive. Out of earshot, doctors told me they were not sure, and if the child does live, the condition can cause irreversible brain damage and sterility.

"Why, why do Americans do this?" A'isha asked me. "Is it because we are Muslims and they hate Muslims? Does your Christian God permit you to do this to babies?"

Entering any hospital in Iraq today, a Westerner is likely to be the target of the ordinary Iraqi's anger. Many of the mothers whose children are dying are simple people, and a number are illiterate. They do not understand international politics or sanctions; they only know their child is sick, in pain. Cut off from any access to the outside world, even the educated are limited to the state-controlled media that daily disseminate Saddam Hussein propaganda.

At the Al Qadissiya Hospital in Saddam City, an impoverished section of the capital, the pediatrics chief, Dr. Tamalher Al-Dhahir, told me children were dying from typhoid, cholera, hepatitis, and measles. Polio, diphtheria, and whooping cough are making a comeback. Before 1991, Iraq had a model vaccination program. Today, the vaccines and even the hypodermics are not available. "It is easy to forget that measles is a killer disease. It weakens the immune system and the child often dies from chronic gastroenteritis," said a UNICEF official in Baghdad. "Before the sanctions, Iraq had the best and most efficient health system in the Middle East, the best doctors, the best infrastructure."

By early 1992, the death rates over the previous year had nearly doubled, and the incidents of kwashiorkor and marasmus, more commonly associated with Somalia or Sudan, and other severe forms of malnutrition had quadrupled. According to a UNICEF report, prior to the sanctions, malnutrition had not been seen in Iraq for at least the last decade. Due to the crisis, maternal death rates also have more than tripled, rising from 37 per 1,000 before 1990 to 117 per 1,000 eighteen months later.

Nearly 50 percent of Iraq's population is under the age of fourteen. The United Nations' figures stated that 340,000 Iraqi children were expected to die in 1992, and one-third of the 3.5 million youngsters under five then suffering from moderate malnutrition could die if the situation in Iraq didn't change. International and Iraqi health authorities were predicting a major crisis if the sanctions continued. And as one doctor commented, "The first and last person who suffers under sanctions is always a child. These are not economic sanctions, but sanctions against life."

As I was leaving the hospital ward, a male doctor grabbed my arm and spun me around. "Why are you here?" he shouted angrily. "What is the purpose of your visit? Where is your mercy? This conflict is between our higher authority and yours. What is the sense in making these children suffer? Do you have children, do you? I do, I have two," he yelled. "I know how it feels to be a parent. Do you think these mothers talk to the government? Can they change anything? Why does America's president want to starve children, babies, to death?" Attracted by the noise, three nurses tried to calm him and lead him away. Dr. Al-Dhahir apologized, "He's tired, and he's seen so many children whom he no longer has the means to help."

Raskia Mansi, heavily pregnant, was asleep in the sweltering afternoon heat next to her six-year-old daughter, Zara, who had been hospitalized with late-stage malnutrition. Raskia awakened as we drew level with the bed. The wife of a factory worker, she was expecting her thirteenth child the following week. "I didn't want to get pregnant again," she said, "but I can't afford or find the birth-control pills I used to take." She also cannot afford to feed the children she already has. Twenty-five days before, her eighteen-month-old daughter, Marwa, had died in this same hospital from the same problems as Zara has. Her husband, a retired factory worker, receives a pension of D. 220 a month.

"To buy food, medicines, we have sold everything — my wedding jewelry, our furniture, our heater, our blankets, even our clothes. This is the only dress I have left," she said, pointing to the one she was wearing. What was a typical family meal? I asked her. "A soup made with water and rice. One of my children was so hungry, she ate a candle," she said, as her eyes filled with tears. Raskia is anemic herself, and doctors expect her new baby to have a low birth weight. Six-year-old Zara is expected to die, and doctors believe the new baby also will not survive.

• • •

At the beginning of 1992, the Iraqi government began distributing food rations. Each month, one person was entitled to eighteen pounds of flour, two pounds of sugar, three pounds of rice, eight ounces of edible oil, one and three-quarter ounces of tea, and four fourteen-ounce cans of powdered milk. Each family was to get four-and-a-half pounds of meat. By the time I arrived seven months later, the meat and the milk were rarely available, and the other rations were intermittent.

I visited one mosque responsible for distributing the rations in the city. There was a large crowd of women outside, but the mosque health center where the rations were stored had already closed its doors because supplies had run out. "We turn away thousands all the time," said Mullah Adnan Abdul Wahab. "It is very hard to do; I have seven children of my own. But we don't have any more to give. If we had enough, the entire eighteen million population would come. There is such a need."

Among the crowd of women, virtually all of whom were garbed in Islamic black, was one very underweight girl, thirteen-year-old Najan Hassan. "I have traveled for an hour, and waited for eight hours," she said. "My father is sick, he hasn't been able to work for seven years, and my mother is dead. I have three smaller brothers and three sisters. Mostly we live on tea and bread. A lot of days, we do not eat." She, too, had been turned away. Najan, however, finally received three pounds of rice, perhaps two days' food for her family.

She clutched it carefully to her body, as if its value was beyond measure, as she began the long and hot journey home.

Robert Yallow, program manager of CARE (Australia) had been based in Iraq for twelve months. His agency runs a supplementary feeding program for infants and children in southern Iraq in conjunction with the Iraqi Federation of Women. "We ran a television appeal in Australia for Iraq. Normally, our appeals receive tremendous support, but this time we had hardly any calls. The few letters that came said, 'We've always supported CARE in the past, but we will not feed Saddam's children.' My God, that is grotesque. I was too ashamed to tell my Iraqi staff what had happened. Kids starving to death have nothing to do with politics. You can't mix government politics with humanitarian needs."

In a speech addressing the current embargo hardships in Iraq, Saddam Hussein called on the nation's women to work harder. "Many Iraqi women, particularly in the cities, now work at only one-quarter of their capabilities," he charged, as he launched a campaign entitled "Work to Deprive the Blockade of Any Meaning." The president continued, "When the Iraqi women provide the largest portion of their needs through their work, the blockade will no longer be of value. We want women to be productive instead of paying attention to secondary matters as they currently are. If men provide the food, and women the clothes, the blockade will end."

The speech that was already remarkably out-of-touch became spectacularly so when Hussein accused Iraqi women of frittering away their families' money on gold or new dresses. "The Iraqi woman, whenever she finds that she has money, will go to the market to buy jewelry or a dress. Is that not true? We are experiencing circumstances that do not permit you to purchase a new dress for Dinars two thousand or more. The Iraqi women's role has become more and more enhanced and its influence on life is now bigger than the role of the man. It is not sufficient to say that we work so many hours; we are required to work the whole time. Even our dreams must be about work. Iraqi women should not only shop." It was an amazing harangue in a country where conditions for the ordinary person are already so severe and deteriorating daily.

I could only contrast Saddam Hussein's comments about women buying dresses priced at ten times the average Iraqi's monthly income with the look of joy and excitement on one woman's face because a friend had given her a birthday gift of a small can of tomato paste.

CHAPTER 11

Jordan: When Islam Is the Solution

Beating a woman does not hurt her dignity.
This is impossible, because woman is born
without dignity.

JORDANIAN FUNDAMENTALISTS, 1989

ENTERING JORDAN BY ROAD FROM IRAQ, one acquires an almost immediate sense of well-being. Part of that, of course, is attributable to the fact of having left the most repressive police state in the world. The natives are welcoming, even those whose walls are plastered with posters of Saddam Hussein. In the summer, the temperature drops 30 or 40 degrees on the Jordanian side of the border to a more livable high 90s. And there is a clarity of light over the tiny kingdom that intensifies as one nears the capital, Amman.

Jordan has long been considered one of the most Westernized of Arab states. And its British-educated monarch and his American-born, blond, and blue-eyed consort, Queen Noor, only serve to confirm that image. King Hussein attended Harrow and Sandhurst, Britain's West Point, where he acquired his flawless English; his wife, the former Lisa Halaby, is a graduate of Princeton University. Until the Gulf crisis, the country was a "must-see" for tourists to the Middle East, and Jordan's 3.8 million population increased 50 percent each year with foreign visitors. Herod the Great built his fortress here, where he imprisoned John the Baptist, and where Salome danced for the Judean king, who gifted her with the head of the unfortunate John. It is in Jordan that the exquisite Petra, the fortress city "half as old as time," was carved by the Nabatean Bedouins from rose-red sandstone. Lawrence of Arabia was also based here at Wadi Rum during the Great Arab Revolt, and eight centuries before so were the Crusaders, whose castles still stand.

Amman, once built on seven hills like Rome, now seems to extends to at least twenty-seven, and it is hard to find a street that isn't steeply inclined. At first glance, the capital has an air of affluence, its limestone and marble villas glistening white in the sun, and topped with their Eiffel Tower–shaped television antennas. Fashions in Amman range from the imported expensive chic to the conservative completely covered. A women's boutique that caters to the ladies-who-lunch set sells only Nolan Miller labels, the look-rich, be-rich fashion designer for the *Dynasty* television series. Sunset in Amman is heralded nightly by the clink of glasses as servants serve cocktails on the myriad patios overlooking the city. And because this is Jordan, conversation at any such gathering invariably turns to the issue of a Palestinian homeland — more than 60 percent of the kingdom's population is Palestinian. With their baby and wedding photographs, many Jordanian Palestinians also keep photographs of their confiscated properties in Israel's occupied territories and their homes in Jordan that were sacked in the 1970 Black September civil war. "Next time we must try not to be born in a land promised by God to other people," one Palestinian wryly told me.

Jordan's apparent wealth, however, is as much an illusion as a desert mirage, particularly since the Gulf War. Crossing the Iraq-Jordanian border, one exchanges Saddam's superbly maintained four-lane highway for the pitted and potholed meandering route that leads to Amman. Jordan, like its neighbor Israel, missed out on the oil deposits that are so plentiful in the rest of the region. Instead, the kingdom, a country about the size of South Carolina, and much of it barren desert, is the impoverished cousin of the Middle Eastern and Gulf states.

King Hussein grew up in a five-bedroom villa in Amman, where, as a boy, he saw his imported bicycle sold to help his parents make ends meet. Hussein's father received a state stipend of only pounds sterling 1,000 per year. But while Jordan struggled to stay afloat financially, King Hussein was acknowledged by his plutocratic Muslim neighbors as the head of the First Family of Islam; his Hashemite lineage dates back unbroken fourteen hundred years to the Prophet Mohammad.

Until the Gulf War, when the man once referred to as Jordan's "plucky little king" backed the "wrong side," the kingdom received much needed aid from the United States, Saudi Arabia, and Iraq.

Once he aligned himself with Iraq, which until the war had been Jordan's main trading partner and the supplier of most of his country's oil, the United States and Saudi Arabia froze funding to the kingdom. The enforcement of U.N. sanctions also made it virtually impossible for Jordan to import from and export to Iraq. And as other Arab states boycotted the kingdom, Jordan was isolated politically and economically.

Another major blow to the country's economy was Kuwait's simultaneous expulsion of three hundred thousand Palestinians, most of whom returned to Jordan. These migrant workers — one in twelve Jordanians — helped swell the country's unemployment level from 8 percent to 30 percent, and deprived Jordan of its substantial remittances revenue. Not surprisingly, the Gulf crisis also dented the kingdom's tourism industry. (In an effort to turn Jordan's economy around, King Hussein announced in mid-1993 that he now opposed Saddam Hussein's continued leadership of Iraq.)

As the economy seemed increasingly shakier, and all but the minority moneyed elite were affected, the fundamentalist slogan "Islam Is the Solution" was increasingly heard. Unlike the oil-rich Arab states, Jordan does not have a comprehensive welfare program, and time and again the Islamists have stepped into that breach. Four years ago, the Muslim Brotherhood started its *hijab* campaign in Jordan's refugee camps that house nearly one million Palestinians. Through the mosques, men were told that a monthly "charity" allowance was available for "good Islamic" families. All that was required to qualify was that every female in the family begin wearing *hijab*, and for each one who did, there would be a payment of Dinars 15, or $22.54, per month. Families with the typical six to seven women and girls could receive between $135 and $158 every month, a valuable sum in a country where the average monthly income is $300. The financial incentive program was so successful that it was extended to Jordan's educational institutions.

Like the Christian missionaries before them, Islamists invariably begin proselytizing through the charitable organizations that they first establish. And in Muslim states, the services that the government cannot or will not or is too corrupt to supply, the fundamentalists frequently offer. The Muslim Brotherhood, the largest and best-established Islamist organization in Jordan, began offering medical, educational, and social services in the early sixties. Today, they run one of the biggest hospitals in the country, the Islamic Hospital in

Amman, which treated half a million patients last year. They also run 25 medical clinics, 40 Islamic schools, and 150 religious-studies centers. These establishments are seen as the underpinnings for an Islamic state infrastructure.

Islamic orthodoxy received the king's imprimatur in Jordan in 1957, when the monarch, whose popularity in the country was at an all-time low, was fearful of the spread of Nasser's socialist pan-Arabism from Egypt. In the crackdown after a member of the Muslim Brotherhood tried to assassinate Nasser, many of the fundamentalists fled Egypt and found asylum in Jordan. King Hussein was following the ancient Muslim maxim "The enemy of my enemy is my friend" when he supported the Muslim Brotherhood in Jordan at the same time as he banned all political parties in the country. To keep up an appearance of evenhandedness, the Muslim Brotherhood was registered as a charity.

In 1989, at the time of the first national elections in a generation, the country was still under martial law and the ban on political parties still stood, which meant most candidates had to run as independents. Only the Muslim Brotherhood was able to present candidates for election because of its legal status as a charity and not a political party. Consequently, of the eighty seats in parliament, twenty went to the Muslim Brotherhood and an additional fourteen went to independent Islamists, giving the fundamentalists 40 percent of the parliamentary seats and making them the largest block in government.

Those same elections were the first in Jordan for which women were permitted to stand as candidates, and twelve women ran, although none succeeded. But for one of the candidates, Tujan Faisal, the campaign waged against her still continues, and robbed her of her career, her marriage, her comfortable lifestyle, and her security. Until she ran for office, Faisal, a mother of three, was Jordan's Barbara Walters.

• • •

"Kill the apostate! Kill the apostate!" The words still haunt her. The blood the fundamentalists were calling for was her own. That phrase was shouted for hours each day outside the courthouse, and the chanting followed her to her home and was also repeated over her phone. Even her husband's medical office and his patients were plagued by the same thing on their phones.

In accusing her of apostasy, the Islamists asked the court to declare

Faisal incompetent, dissolve her marriage, confiscate all her property, strip her of all legal rights, ban any of her works, and grant immunity to anyone who shed her blood.

Her crime? In response to a two-month campaign waged in the nation's media by fundamentalists that claimed women should not be permitted to run for political office because they are not mentally competent to do so, she wrote a newspaper article castigating the crusade. Daily in the nation's press, the Islamists claimed that "women are deficient and lacking in religious education and understanding, rash, and guided by their emotions."

Said Faisal, then Jordan's top female television commentator, who had her own show and was also a newspaper columnist, "The newspaper articles stated that women are minors all their lives, and need male guardians to run their affairs and keep them on the straight path. Another said, 'Women are so deficient they are only capable of cleaning, cooking, and serving members of the family. They possess a physical makeup suitable only for menial tasks. In return for these services, a woman's remuneration will be that she is fed, given shelter, and clothed.' A third read, 'It is permissible to beat a woman if she disobeys her husband's instructions. Beating does not hurt a woman's dignity. This is impossible, because woman is born without dignity.'"

Having ignored the smear campaign against all women for as long as she could, Faisal decided the fundamentalists had gone too far. "They were portraying women in a very cheap way," she told me. "It was ridiculous. They claimed women go crazy when they have their period, and they also said that the fact that women love their children is a sign of their weakness. I was angry that the Islamists considered the entire female population not qualified for political office."

Faisal struck back with an article entitled "They Insult Us . . . and We Elect Them!" In it she wrote that the critics of women's rights had misinterpreted the Koran. "They were claiming, 'A woman's deficiency lies in the fact that she becomes pregnant, gives birth, and menstruates.' This clearly means that they feel motherhood (revered by Islam) is the cause of her deficiency. Should we, therefore, deduce from this that the barren woman is more complete than one who is fertile? Or whether women who do not menstruate are more complete than those who do?"

Despite Faisal's own prominence, when her article was published in the *Al-Ra'y* Arabic newspaper on September 21, 1989, there was no response to it for twenty-three days. "No one saw any apostasy in what I had written until I registered my political candidacy on October fourteenth," said Faisal. The elections were to be held on November 8, and Jordanian political campaigns, like many of those in Europe, are brief. But once she declared her candidacy, things moved fast. That same day, she was declared apostate by two conservative clerics, one of whom was a *Mufti* (a religious leader and interpreter of Islamic law) in Jordan's army, who claimed the case was filed "in the name of the people and in defense of Islam."

The charges against Faisal were also quietly backed by some leading Jordanians as a means of keeping the country "intact, conservative, and not so liberal as Western societies." The case, the first of its kind against a woman in Jordan, was seen as a test of strength for fundamentalists in Jordan as they opposed secularizing trends in the country.

"The two mullahs went from one *Shariah* court to another for two days, to find a judge who was sympathetic to their case," recalled Faisal. "The court close to my home rejected it, the judge said it was nonsense. But they didn't give up, and eventually in south Amman they found a judge who shared their views and who registered the case. I was notified at noon on the seventeenth of October that the court hearing would be the next day at nine A.M. Legally, I was entitled to forty-eight hours' notice, but the judge ignored that.

"We decided it was best if my lawyer went alone. But at the court, the judge refused to permit him to represent me, and he was told I would be tried in absentia. My lawyer was not allowed to speak, he could only take notes, and no one would provide him with a copy of the hearing, to which I was entitled."

The courtroom was jammed with Islamists, and the area in front of the building was even more crammed. Those outside began to chant what became their battle cry: "Kill the apostate." During the lengthy hearing the judge permitted only evidence against Tujan Faisal to be heard. Throughout the presentation, the hearing was frequently interrupted by shouts of *Allahu Akbar*, "God is Great," from the fundamentalists inside the courtroom.

"That first hearing was intentionally used to give the Islamists a major platform," says Faisal. The continuance of the case was postponed for ten days. "The second time, the family decided my father, my brother, and my sister should go and that I should stay at home. It was no longer felt safe for me to attend my own court hearing. My family and friends feared for my life."

Sitting in the living room of her apartment in Amman, Faisal, forty-three, recalled how her life spun out of control in a matter of days. The walls of her third-floor walk-up apartment need repainting, but Faisal can no longer afford the expense. There is a large crack in the plaster of one wall that runs almost from floor to ceiling, but there is also no money to fix it. "And when furniture wears as it does with small children, I won't be able to replace that," says Faisal. Her two daughters and a son are aged four, ten, and twelve.

"Before this happened, we led a very comfortable life. My salary was very good, and my husband's medical practice was large and successful. I had worked in television since 1971, and had my own show from 1983."

Faisal had been targeted by Islamic conservatives before the election. The first occasion was in 1984, when she organized a seminar on child abuse with the Amman's Women's Club. The data they collected showed a high incidence of child abuse, many cases of which were sexual in nature. "The irony in Jordan is that no one except the child's father or male guardian can register a case of incest with the courts," said Faisal. After the seminar, Faisal was attacked in the mosques. Mullahs accused her of trying to "break down the solidarity and moral structure of the Islamic family." Recalled Faisal, "They said child abuse was a disease that existed only in the West. They claimed it did not exist in Jordan, and I should not have brought foreign ideas here."

Then four years later, she did a program on battered wives. Faisal asked why, given that Jordan's criminal law no longer included stoning or hand amputation for theft, it was still permissible to beat wives. "When a woman goes to the police to complain, she is told she must have disobeyed her husband. I was amazed by the flood of mail we received from women after the show. Even my close friends had been victims and I didn't know.

"But religious sheikhs accused me of attacking Islamic law and said I had tried to abolish it. They went to see the Chief Justice of the *Shariah* Court, who in turn approached the Director General of Television. They wanted to ban me from appearing on television. I was banned for a week, but then the minister of information became angry over what had happened to me, and restored my show."

Early in 1989 she had planned to do a program on polygamy. "It was not very common in Jordan before," said Faisal. "But today polygamy is spreading more and more because the fundamentalists are promoting it. No wife feels secure these days, and women were coming to me with their fears." Faisal approached the *Shariah* Court to ask if they could send a representative to present the Islamic point of view in the program. "All I wanted was for them to explain why Islam permitted polygamy. I told them that my show presented both sides and left viewers to make up their own minds."

The polygamy program never developed beyond the planning stage. "The director-general and minister of information were both threatened," said Faisal. "They were told by the fundamentalists that they must have political reasons for wanting to air such a program. It was claimed that such a show was intended to be an attack on Iraq [then Jordan's closest ally], because Saddam Hussein now had two wives, and the Iraqi government was also encouraging men to marry again as so many women had been widowed in the war. I was told the minister did not want to risk his political career. The program was stopped.

"At the time of the election, the fundamentalists raised the polygamy program issue again, and claimed I had called for women to marry four men. They said it was un-Islamic, and it was the reason I should be killed."

"Apostasy is the easiest accusation in Islam. I argued in my article that a political candidate should be judged on merit, on intellect. The fundamentalists said for that, too, I deserved to be killed because I worshiped the human mind instead of God. Then for good measure, they claimed I had also sinned because I wanted a degenerate society."

Finding herself attacked in such a manner was obviously very frightening, but Faisal was also deeply offended. A devout Muslim, she is very well versed in Islam. She knew that the charges against her were in reality simply slander, but she also was aware that a mostly illiterate mob could be whipped into a hysterical fervor by manipulative clerics using the mosques to their own ends. And if she had any doubt of that, she received proof after the first court hearing.

The chanting mob left the courthouse and massed outside Faisal's home. "We closed the metal shutters, afraid someone would throw a rock or even shoot through the window. Our phone began to ring day and night with obscene and threatening calls. But I was determined not to give in to these extremists. I was scheduled to address political supporters at the university, and I kept that appointment. When I showed up, there were huge crowds, and we had to park blocks away. Then we realized all the seats in the front of the hall had been taken by veiled women, all Islamists, who had intentionally arrived hours earlier. They tried to embarrass me by asking many religious questions but I know the Koran very well, so that is hard to do. Then when they realized that wasn't working, they began chanting, 'Kill the apostate.' Men in the audience started screaming and shouting Islamic slogans and someone pulled the mike from my hand. Then the lights were turned out and we heard breaking glass. My supporters grabbed me and dragged me out the back exit. By then they were afraid someone would physically harm me. The police were contacted and I accepted police protection.

"My husband didn't trust the police. He said they had been infiltrated by the fundamentalists. He was convinced I would be assassinated. He refused to sleep at night, and sat up armed with a large knife in case anyone broke in. We were nervous every time we heard a car slow down outside the house. My eldest daughter, Dina, began to have nightmares that bearded men and veiled women would kill me. I was particularly concerned that someone might try to harm the children. I told their schools that the children were not to be permitted to leave with anyone except our family. I couldn't eat or sleep, I started losing weight rapidly, my clothes were hanging off me. We felt besieged, there was nowhere we could escape these people."

The second court hearing was a replay of the first. The same chanting mobs, although the crowds were larger, the same call for Faisal's death, and the same refusal from the judge to permit anyone to talk on the defendant's behalf. This time also, the Jordanian media gave the hearing major coverage. As before, the judge listened for hours to evidence only from the Islamists, and then adjourned the case until two days after the election. "My sister returned from the second hearing shocked and scared. She said it was like the Middle Ages; it was a witch-hunt. What was equally scary was how well organized the hate campaign was.

"Then a day before the election, and after these public performances, the judge announced that he was turning down the case. He said it was not because I was not guilty but because his court did not have the jurisdiction to try a case of apostasy. But he would have known that from the beginning. The case was referred to the Appeals Court because if I were found guilty, they would be the court that would have to dissolve my marriage." (Jordan's legal system is a complex and often contradictory mix of Ottoman, British, and Islamic law.)

The Appeals Court heard the case in camera, and demonstrations were limited to outside the courthouse. "When the clerics' lawyer began with Islamic slogans again, he was told that no more evidence was allowed." The three Appeal Court judges found Faisal not guilty. The fundamentalists, however, refused to give up. Claiming the authorities had pressured the court — and certainly the king had been embarrassed by the case and had warned against "those who exploit religion for political designs" — the Islamists asked parliament for a retrial at another court. "The case was accepted, and again dismissed in early 1990," said Faisal.

"This campaign against me, however, has never ended. Ever since then, they attack me from every corner." Despite her journalist contacts and sources, Faisal has not been able to learn which Islamist organization was behind the campaign against her. "Throughout the entire hearings, they never declared themselves. They simply said they represented the people. To this day, I do not know who masterminded it or funded it." The Muslim Brotherhood publicly opposed the case against Faisal at the time. Jordanians I spoke to saw their stance as a tactical move. "They didn't want to lose female votes in the 1989 elections."

For Faisal, the issue of who organized the crusade against her has been superseded by the damage it has done. "I was found innocent," she said, "but many of the punishments asked for by the fundamentalists at the beginning of this case have been carried out by these extremists.

"I can no longer get a job in television. I was told, 'I can't put you on the screen, I have to appease these people.' No one will publish my articles for the same reason. I have a Master's degree in English, so I applied for teaching jobs at the university, at community colleges, at schools. No one will hire me. The director of one college admitted they had been warned by the fundamentalists not to hire me, but he said he would ignore it if the other board members agreed. They refused. They were scared.

"It was the same when I received invitations to speak in the private sector. They would receive bookings, and then they would have to cancel me. Each time I was told that they received threats that my lecture would be violently disrupted.

"The extremists used the same intimidation tactics against my husband. He was fired from the medical college because of the threats from the extremists. So many of his patients were threatened that he was forced to sell his clinic. And he was unable to find a government job. In the end, in order for my husband to practice medicine he had to leave Jordan.

"Today, my father supports me and my children. We live on one-tenth of what my income used to be. It is just enough to buy essentials, nothing more.

"The fundamentalists ruined my husband's career, they ruined mine. They have forced the two of us to separate. They have destroyed my life, which is what they intended to do from the beginning."

Despite her own problems, Faisal is particularly concerned about "infiltration" of Jordan's education system by the Islamists. "We have a very young population. Fundamentalism is spreading rapidly in Jordan, because the children are being taught it in school and college." Prominent Jordanians share her concern.

Initially, after the last election, the new government did not include any of the elected members of the Muslim Brotherhood, although three independent Islamists did serve in the cabinet. The MB had declined to participate after its demand for the sensitive education portfolio was rejected. A year later, the king reshuffled the cabinet to include five of its members. And bowing to pressure from the Islamists, Abdullah al-Akayra, a member of the MB, was appointed minister of education.

Akayra's impact was immediate. His first step was to segregate the sexes in the Ministry and to do the same in schools throughout the country. He ordered veils to be drawn on illustrations of women in all Jordanian school textbooks. But the issue that brought him the most publicity was his banning of fathers from attending their daughters' school events on the grounds that the girls sometimes wore shorts or exercise clothes on these occasions. In a lengthy essay entitled "Thank Heaven for Little Girls (in Shorts)," the country's leading male columnist, Rami Khouri, reflected the feelings of many Jordanians. He claimed the issue was one of "raw political power," and asked whether this was the beginning of establishing absolute Islamic rule. "Does the fact that the MB and other Islamists won 40 percent of the Lower House seats mean that ministers have the authority unilaterally to start applying regulations that reflect their thinking? . . . This is not a controversy about shorts and girls' legs. It is about power, public authority, national identity, and the future of the Arab world. . . ."

The public outcry was loud and long, and Akayra was replaced as minister after six months. However, the changes he made in the educational system in Jordan live on in the fundamentalists he appointed at nearly every level during his tenure. Haifa Melhes, the highest-ranking woman in the Education Ministry, has gone to her office daily since 1991 to sit at her desk with nothing to do. Before Akayra's appointment, she had been the director of cultural affairs. After Akayra informed her, "I oppose women holding leadership roles," he gave her position to a male colleague. More far-reaching, however, is the fact that Akayra's many Islamist appointees are still in charge of the country's educational curricula, textbooks, and administrative affairs. "If you organize the schools along fundamentalist lines, you are already directing society," said Melhes. "This is the educational system from which the leaders of tomorrow graduate."

Professor Aarwa al-Amiri, a psychology professor at the twenty-four-thousand–student University of Jordan in Amman, like many academics in the country, is now teaching defensively. "I've been trying to avoid a clash with the fundamentalists at the university," she told me. "They have a great influence on campus, which means anybody can be a scapegoat. I've had to change my attire, and I've lost the freedom of speech.

"When I first started teaching here in 1973, I could freely say in class what I thought. Now we have to be very careful that we do not say anything that is construed as anti-Islamic. Islam is my religion and I respect it. It is a great spiritual and cultural movement that has shaped the entire Arab world for the last fourteen hundred years. The fundamentalists, who are much stricter and literal, are making many changes.

"In psychology I teach about evolution, and in the seventies I would discuss Darwinism, and my personal opinions on it. Now today, I don't.

"Equally, I am very conscious every morning of what I wear. A couple of years ago, some Islamist students came to see me in my office and said, 'Doctor, we care for you, but we are afraid you will go to Hell because of the way you dress.' I have always been a conservative dresser — long skirts, long sleeves — but in the seventies on campus you saw sleeveless and backless dresses and short skirts and nobody made a fuss. In those days you never saw a veiled student. Veiling happened gradually. Now more than fifty percent of our women students are covered."

Amiri has watched the fundamentalists take over student and faculty elections. "Nonfundamentalist men in Jordan are very apathetic politically." The forty-six-year-old academic feels that part of that apathy is fear. In the student riots of 1978 and 1979 at Jordan University, during which six professors were fired, employment regulations underwent a draconian change. "The university may now dismiss any professor, whether tenured or not, and without giving a reason why," said Amiri. "You don't get a reason, you just get kicked out, and unemployment in this country is very high."

The fundamentalists at the university have now handicapped female students on acceptance grades: the levels at Jordan University are higher for women than they are for men. The ruling came into force without opposition. In the faculty of education, for example, female students must get a grade of seventy-seven or over, male students only seventy-three. "Girls are handicapped as soon as they start to get ahead," said Amiri.

The professor herself was targeted by Islamists at the university a couple of years ago over a seemingly minor issue of an empty coffee cup on her desk during Ramadan. In the month of fasting, no food or drink of any kind should be consumed between sunup and sundown. The Koranic ruling, however, is usually strictly enforced only in the more orthodox Islamic states, such as Saudi Arabia. And women are exempted from observing the fast during pregnancy or when they are menstruating, although they are meant to make up the time later.

"I had a meeting in my office early on the second day of Ramadan, and I offered my guests coffee. Later, when I went to class, I noticed an empty cup on my desk, but I didn't really think about it. Shortly after, I was summoned to the dean of *Shariah* for violating Islam. Apparently, an Islamist student in my class had reported me, even though the cup was empty and no one had seen me drink from it. And I pointed that out at the time. Two days later, the dean of education sent for me. He began screaming his head off. 'How dare you? You can be kicked out for this,' he shouted at me.

"I quietly asked him, 'I can be kicked out for an empty coffee cup?' The furor went on for days over such a silly thing. It was too ridiculous, and offensive to Islam. What really bothered me was that my students had reported me, when the Koran clearly states that if someone makes a mistake, they should be corrected by soft words. Sometimes I feel the fundamentalists are abusing Islam. The religion is not oppressive. There was no greater man than the Prophet Mohammad. To trivialize the religion he brought to the world is a great pity.

"If Muslim fundamentalism continues in the direction it is heading, they will govern here. They will come to power and the impact for women will be very negative."

A number of leading Jordanians, including the king himself, feel that if the Middle East peace negotiations break down, extremism could take over. "If the talks collapse, the result would be too devastating and disastrous for this entire region, maybe the world," said King Hussein in 1992. "Despair and extremism will be the order of the day." And while he made that statement a year before the 1993 PLO and Israeli accord, as Arabs and Jews both recognize, implementation of the agreement could be undermined by violent rejectionists on both sides.

Dr. As'ad Abdul Rahman, a highly respected Jordanian political scientist, agrees. "The Muslim Brotherhood, of which Hamas in the Occupied Territories is a part, is against the Middle East peace settlement. (Hamas and other Palestinian extremist groups have long insisted that they will settle only for the complete destruction of Israel.) If those talks break down, the Islamists could dominate. Fanaticism is a function of the other party's [Israel's] obstinacy. You put your destiny in the hands of God, because you cannot solve your problems. Ordinary people, when there is hope, do not join fanatical organizations. Extremism is the politics of despair."

There are those who would say that forty-seven-year-old Rahman, now also the director of the Shuman Foundation, which promotes science and culture in the Arab world, knows better than most that that is accurate. In the early eighties, when the PLO was still viewed by many as a terrorist group, Rahman was a close adviser to Yasser Arafat. He resigned the position because he couldn't "keep up" with the ever-peripatetic Arafat, who travels so much he appears to live in his specially equipped plane. "There was no time for a family life," he said with a smile. Today Rahman, the deputy chairman of the political committee of the Palestinian National Committee, advises the PLO leader only when specially contacted.

Rahman's affiliation with the PLO caused him to be banned from teaching at Jordan University from 1973 to 1989. During that time, he spent eleven of those years on the faculty of Kuwait University. It was there that he learned that many of the Islamic charitable organizations in the Gulf are Muslim Brotherhood, including the Society for Social Reform. "The Saudi government or Rabitat may fund them but the organizations' allegiances are MB," he said. "The international organization of the MB is semicentralized, not a real confederation. But while it is a loose relationship, it is a definite one.

There is a great deal of money lubricating its wheels, particularly in Jordan. And it spends its money very effectively politically. Compared to other organizations in this part of the world, there is very little corruption. Religious fervor makes people more committed and active; it is a well-known psychological factor."

Another psychological factor that the Islamists understand, says Rahman, is the importance of targeting women. "If you really want to control the family and the future, then target women. The woman is, if you will, the Ministry of Interior of the family. She is the one shaping the youth."

Rahman agreed with Professor Amiri that Jordanians are, on the whole, politically apathetic. "And any vacuums get filled by the MB," he said. Western anti-Arab biases also play into the hands of Islamic fundamentalists. "There are many sayings of the Prophet that give Arabs a special role in building up Islam. The Koran says there can be no dignity in the Islamic world without the dignity of the Arab."

A leading political journalist in Amman told me, "The MB is beginning to rule our lives. A Palestinian film on arranged marriages that was to be shown in Amman was disrupted with a smoke bomb. A real bomb was used when they blew up the movie theater at the Al Baqaa refugee camp because they claimed they were showing progressive films. A poetry recital by a famous Lebanese poet was halted for the same reason: his works were considered too progressive. Such acts indicate the growing strength of the MB and other Islamists. If incidents like these continue to go uncontrolled, they can eventually undermine the government. Jordan's secret police always kept a sharp eye out for communists, but since the fifties, they have turned a blind eye to the MB.

"The MB has penetrated numerous Jordanian institutions, and it is making a profound change in the structure of our society. Politically, the MB may appear compromising, but its power base is not; it is becoming more and more radical. It works against any Muslim who challenges its authority.

"I believe that it is inevitable that the Islamists will win in the Islamic states through coups, revolutions, and elections. I think we also will see more and more blacks in the U.S. resorting to Islam as a political force, not just a religion."

There are times in Jordan when it seems that more moderate Muslims are conducting a smear campaign against the Islamists. Interestingly, however, when one talks to members of the Muslim Brotherhood, their comments about their organization and its aims are very similar to those of their detractors. At the Jordan University Hospital where he is an internist, Dr. Kandil Shaker Shubair, a graduate of the University of Illinois and a prominent member of the MB told me, "Just as salt infiltrates the food it is cooked with, the MB is infiltrating every society. There is no major city in Europe or the U.S. where the MB does not have a presence. Communism fell because it was an unjust system; capitalism will suffer the same fate because people who have money are putting their foot on the neck of the poor. Look at the U.S. — it consumes forty percent of what the world produces. Islam is spreading like wildfire because of the injustices of other systems. It is the future religion of the entire world."

Sitting in his office, where the major artwork is a large calligraphic quote from the Koran, his prayer rug casually draped over a chair, Shubair, who is also a professor of medicine at Jordan University, explained, "Our members are highly educated doctors, lawyers, engineers, or students, and those who are working are earning good incomes. All give a percentage of their income to the movement."

Sixty-one-year-old Shubair, who sports a long beard in the tradition of Islamists, is the father of eight children, four of them daughters. On women's role in the Islamist movement, he says, "We believe that women are the most important members of society. It is a crime to hold them back. The Muslim Sisterhood, which has a separate party structure from the MB, is very active. My wife goes anywhere I go, she even drives. The Saudis are blockheads regarding women and driving. Which is better, to have a woman travel in a taxi with a male driver who is a stranger, or for her to drive her own car? To drive her own car, of course."

Like any follower of an orthodox religion, Shubair feels Islam should be interpreted literally. If one of his daughters were to commit adultery, he says she should be flogged if unmarried, and stoned to death if married. And, in the case of pregnancy caused by rape or incest, he says, "She should bring forth her child." What about the feelings of the mother? "My sympathies are with the fetus."

But Shubair feels also that the MB is frequently misrepresented. "The MB does not discriminate or engage in acts of violence. Never, never, never!" he said emphatically. "We do not assassinate or threaten. We condemn such actions. It is the radicals who do such things. We are not radical, we are involved in preaching and the spread of Islam. We condemn violence."

Shortly after I left Jordan, two members of parliament who are senior officials in the Muslim Brotherhood went on trial, accused of subversion and plotting to overthrow the king and the government. The state prosecutor asked for the death penalty, but the men received lengthy jail sentences. Days later, however, the king, who had earlier warned that "Jordan would stand up to the ambitious and the renegades," pardoned both politicians. The move was perceived by many as reflecting the king's ambivalence about the Jordanian Muslim Brotherhood.

. . . .

Zuleikha Abu Risha, who was married for nineteen years to a senior MB policy maker, and was herself a founding member of the MB's Islamic Women's Society, would disagree with Dr. Shubair's denial that the MB engages in violent acts. After her divorce in 1987, Risha began writing critical and probing articles on fundamentalism and the MB. Since then she has received hundreds of death threats and has been under police protection for several years. Finding Risha was not easy. For security reasons, friends are very reluctant to reveal her whereabouts. After numerous phone calls that invariably led to dead ends, I mentioned the difficulty I was having to one of the women I was interviewing. Fortuitously, she was a close friend of Risha's and was able to set up a meeting for me.

I finally caught up with Risha at the small hotel where she was staying temporarily. She was the antithesis of how I expected an Arab woman to look having spent most of her adult life completely veiled and living in the shadows of a senior officer of the MB. Her smart black linen dress had a fashionably short hem, very short sleeves, and a definite décolletage, all of which complimented her shapely figure. Her heavy earrings and ornate Bedouin necklaces jangled as she moved. And her vivid red lipstick heavily stained the elongated brown cigarillos that she chain-smoked.

Once divorced, Risha began writing articles about the "strategies" of the Islamist's movement, particularly as it pertains to women. "I thought it was time to open the files of the MB," she said. "When they speak out against women, separate men and women in offices, employ their authority to hold women back, I write about it. These are not things that Islam gives them the right to do." Almost immediately she began receiving death threats and abusive and obscene phone calls. "They called me a prostitute, sent me photographs of naked women and said they were of me. They said I would be killed, accused me of having polluted thoughts, claimed I was working against Islam. I received a lot of very ugly calls.

"At first, I was very upset, and my friends became very frightened for me. They told me I shouldn't write so much about fundamentalists." Risha realized, of course, that the threats were intended to silence her. The more the extremists wanted her to stop writing, the more she felt it was necessary that she continue.

The campaign against her stepped up when a leading Islamist newspaper joined the crusade. "Every week they publish one to three articles attacking me. A few are polite about it, but most are very insulting." In an Islamic culture where a woman's honor and reputation are supposed to be closely guarded, any hint of sex is usually censored. But public attacks on Risha are frequently prurient and puerile, and in an Islamic society, all the more shocking. "One article was devoted to my sex life with my husband and ended with, 'When she speaks about women she forgets she was waiting for her husband in bed while he was with his other wife.'

"The attacks became particularly bad two years ago," she said. "The shutters of my house were closed permanently so that no one could see when I was home. Then they started saying they would plant a bomb under my car. Every time I left the house I would check my car for bombs. Do you know what that is like to live with all the time? It is a horrible way to exist." At that stage, Risha, now forty-nine, asked for police protection and has been under it ever since.

While journalists may have trouble locating Risha, the Arabic Islamist newspaper that attacks her weekly does not. When she was in Europe recently for six months completing her Ph.D. in Arabic literature, she received every issue. "They sent them to me. I don't know how they found out where I was." Returning to Jordan from that trip, the hate mail and death-threat letters that had accumulated in her absence "weighed kilos," she said. "I keep every one; maybe I will do something with them one day."

The daughter of a prominent Sufi religious leader, Risha met her husband at Jordan University when she was a twenty-two-year-old student, and he was a faculty member in his thirties. "He was very charismatic, I was a total innocent, naive, with no experience of men. I was mesmerized by him, and when he asked me to be his wife, I agreed. My father was enraged. 'We come from a distinguished family, you could choose anyone,' he told me. He was very much against my choice because my husband was MB and also because he already had a wife and three children. But in the end, my father gave his permission."

Risha does not talk about her marriage easily, particularly the early years. "My husband had told me before we married that I could finish my studies, and promised to send me to Cairo to do my M.A., but once I became his wife, he changed his mind. 'Education spoils women. The only knowledge a woman needs is how to be a wife and a mother,' he said." Risha had also been teaching part-time at a teacher training center. "He made me stop that, too. I had to ask for permission to go out, and he invariably said no. He told me he would divorce me if I went out without his permission." Risha's husband also forbade her to wear colorful clothes, push up her sleeves, or show any hair.

According to Risha, the marriage was a violent one. "If I was slow in obeying, I was beaten black and blue. My nose was broken. When my family saw me, they told me to use the beatings to get a divorce. But I was afraid of divorce; it is shameful for a woman. And he always told my family, 'She's stubborn, she doesn't obey.' And in the end, I would think he was right." In the first seven years of marriage, Risha had several miscarriages, which she attributes to the tension she was under. "Then my husband divorced his first wife and kept the children. I raised them, and eventually had two of my own."

By the early 1970s, Risha's husband was already a senior official in the MB. More recently, he's had several offers of ministerial positions. "But he has always refused them. He says he has a mission to educate students according to his Islamic beliefs." Risha and her husband's life became dominated by the MB. Over the years, she came to know many of the movers and shakers of the international Islamist movement. "The MB in Jordan was funded by Iran and Saudi Arabia, both the government and Rabitat. Our life was one long round of meetings, and more meetings, most of them political, and many of them held at our house. It became very clear that the organization was seeking power, total power.

"The Islamists want to change our modern society to what they refer to as 'pure' Islam. They want the country to be ruled completely by Shariah law. And they want to return the woman to the harem, where she will have a very restricted role in life — sitting at home and taking care of the children and the husband. She is to have a limited education, and no role in political or economic life. She is simply to obey the man. They want to turn us back into slaves.

Even now, five years after our divorce, my former husband still tells me my place is at home with the children. He says it is my own fault that I am threatened, I should not be writing against Islam.

"I am not against Islam. It is part of my identity, but it is also time that educated women read the Koran for themselves and make their own interpretations of it, not live with the misinterpretations of Islam that go against their rights, which is happening so much now."

• • •

As the Islamist pendulum swings wildly back and forth in Jordanian society, some things remain the same. A Jordanian woman marrying for the first time, no matter what her age, must be a virgin. And if she isn't, it is a simple matter to become one again. Hymenorrhaphy, or hymen restoration, is a medical procedure offered in countries throughout the Islamic world. It takes just a few minutes, in Amman costs $300, and is done on an outpatient basis and without anesthesia. "It is quite common in Jordan," said Dr. Efteem Azar, one of the country's leading obstetrician/gynecologists. "It is a very simple procedure and quickly done. Anesthesia isn't necessary because if you work with a very fine needle it is less painful than an injection of painkiller would be. Hymenorrhaphy must be done three to seven days before the wedding, because the tissue is simply pulled together and the procedure doesn't last."

Another service gynecologists in Muslim countries are called on to supply is post–wedding night verification that the bride was a virgin before the event. "It is not uncommon for a gynecologist to find in his office a blushing young bride surrounded by a whole horde of male relatives demanding that she be examined," says Dr. Azar. She did not bleed during sexual intercourse on her wedding night, and the men all want to know why.

"You always have to favor the girl, because if you don't, she'll be killed by her family. Sometimes, if the girl has the opportunity, she'll beg you to cover for her. They are very frightened, they know they will be killed. So you tell the male relatives the bride had an elastic hymen, which many women do anyway, and in such cases she wouldn't bleed.

"Honor killings are still carried out in Jordan. A family will arrange for an underage brother or male relative to do it. Then when there is an investigation, nothing happens. The case is dropped."

• • •

It doesn't take a visitor much time in Jordan to recognize that the country is a lot less Western than it is frequently perceived to be. In fact, Jordan is a country in the middle of an identity crisis. The next national elections, due at the end of 1993, are being called the first fully free vote in the Arab world in more than thirty years. King Hussein insists the country is moving toward democracy and pluralism, but at the same time, the government has banned three of the nascent political parties. Press censorship was only eased in 1989, and now a new law is to be passed forbidding criticism of the royal family and the military. And the Hashemite Kingdom can't seem to make up its mind whether it is Islamically secular like Turkey, or becoming neoconservatively religious.

If visitors and natives alike are confused, how is American-born and -bred Queen Noor coping? After being vetted by the queen's closest Jordanian woman friend, I was invited to the palace to find out. The royal family's real estate holdings have improved substantially since the king lived in a conventional villa as a child. Today, they have homes in Saudi Arabia, Switzerland, and in England in London and Ascot. The latter is said to be worth more than $12 million and was loaned to Prince Andrew and Sarah, the Duchess of York, while they were waiting for their own home to be built. In Jordan, the First Family is domiciled in the Royal Palaces, a collection of smallish regal residences scattered around a compound, and clinging to a steep hillside overlooking bustling downtown Amman. Living with them in the royal compound is Crown Prince Hassan Bin Talal, the forty-six-year-old younger brother of King Hussein.

The two very high stone walls around the royal compound are topped with metal railings, then metal spikes, and then frequent gun emplacements filled with soldiers bristling with automatic hardware. The main entrance gate has more of the same and nasty-looking spikes across the road leading to it. The tight military security bore witness to the fact that while the king was celebrating his fortieth year on the throne that year, it was only because he seemed to have as many lives as the proverbial cat. In a region where monarchs rarely die of natural causes, King Hussein has survived coups, riots, wars, and at least nine assassination attempts.

Hussein was only fifteen when his grandfather, King Abdullah, then Jordan's monarch, was shot to death next to him as they were about to enter a mosque. As the teenager lunged at the assassin he, too, was shot at, but the bullet ricocheted off a medal on his chest. He was sent flying by its force but was only bruised. Hussein became king two years later when his father, a man plagued with depression serious enough to require hospitalization, abdicated. Almost immediately, the attempts to assassinate the boy king began when Arab nationalists poisoned his food and put acid in his nose drops.

Hussein has also survived family tragedy, losing his third wife, Queen Alia, in a helicopter crash. When Lisa Najeeb Halaby, an American of Syrian descent, became Hussein's fourth wife, she was twenty-six. Barely out of college, she was suddenly stepmother to eight children from his earlier marriages, the oldest of whom was only four years younger than she.

Obviously, Jordan's royal couple have been subject to more traumas than most families. And they were being battered again at the time we met. The week before our interview, Queen Noor's mother had been rushed in the royal jet from a Mediterranean vacation to Amman for heart surgery. And then just days after our meeting, Noor flew with the king to the Mayo Clinic in the United States, where he was diagnosed as having cancer, and his left kidney and ureter were removed.

The queen, not surprisingly, looked pale and tired, but, despite the tension she was under, she was gracious in her attentiveness and focused. She has the same elegant but reed-slim build of Princess Diana, and, like Diana, is taller than her husband. Official photographs of the royal couple usually have been posed so that she looks shorter than he. The residence in which we met was the suite of rooms in which Noor had stayed between her engagement and marriage to the king. A romantic, she had commandeered the complex. And I could understand why. The heavily carved rosewood doors and *mashrabiyya* screens were set off by Jordanian Bedouin carpets and antique oriental brass lamps and light fixtures. An Arabic incense soothed the senses, as did the cooling sound of fountains in the plant-filled atrium directly off the room.

Despite her Syrian heritage, when Lisa Halaby met King Hussein she seemed an unlikely choice as consort to an Arab monarch. This was, after all, a country where women are preferably neither seen nor heard, and where the slightest misstep or misstatement by the wife of a king could trigger a full-blown political or religious crisis. At the time also, she was not Muslim, nor did she speak Arabic. How did the Architecture and Urban Planning graduate, who also had been a Vietnam War demonstrator in her student days, adjust to monarchical rigors and demands in a culture where protocol, politesse, and tradition can be rigid and unbending?

She freely admits it was a challenge. "I had a great deal to learn, and there were no guidance, instructions, or any kind of recommendations given me at any point on how to do it." Noor, whose name means "light" in Arabic, became a Muslim shortly before her marriage, and then set about learning Arabic, in which she is now fluent. "At the time I married, in 1978, adjusting to my role was easier then than it might have been later on. Since that time, there has been an increasing conservatism in the region generally, and in our society.

"Politically, economically, this society has been under enormous pressure throughout its history, and perhaps never more than it is today. As you know, there is a great deal of pressure here on young people, in the school system, and on their parents in the mosques and elsewhere [from the Islamists]. There is an economic incentive for young women to wear *hijab*. Of course, during economic difficulty, Islamic dress for women is an equalizer: it removes competition regarding clothes and does not place an economic burden on the family.

"Also, during a time of economic difficulty, people look for spiritual comfort and even spiritual solutions. And that leads to a time of reassessment as we have right now in Jordan, as to whether parliamentarians are able to provide spiritual solutions to the mundane material problems of the day. Therefore, it isn't surprising that you find many people very susceptible and receptive to the very easy, encouraging, and comforting slogans such as "Islam Is the Solution." But if it doesn't provide answers then, and this is the benefit of a democratic system, we hope people will educate themselves about whether they can find fast solutions, or whether they just have to work it through.

"One of my stepdaughters experimented with the *hijab*. She wanted to see what kind of impact — how can I put it? — to see if it would have a positive impact on her image." The queen herself favors Western dress, and rarely covers her head. "She was about fourteen at the time. I didn't say anything to her, but I think some of her cousins made their views known to her. It didn't last very long, less than a year. She didn't discuss it with me or her father, and she didn't wear it in front of us, which is why I didn't say anything. Obviously, it wasn't something she wanted to discuss with her parents.

"At the time, the *hijab* was increasing in Jordan, and perhaps she thought she ought to wear it. None of her friends were wearing it at the time . . . but I don't believe that superficial signs of faith and political ideology are really the issue. As a mother, I want to raise my children to have faith and confidence in themselves and in their ability to play a constructive role in society."

Because of the rising conservatism in Jordan, Noor has started, like Professor Amiri, to self-censor. "Yes, one is more sensitive, particularly in my position, in the way one presents oneself. And you have to differentiate between people who are conservative and those who are fanatic, people who are conservative, yet responsibly constructive, and those who are intolerant and rejecting any other viewpoint. I try to keep a low profile in my work, and especially abroad. I try to take care that I am not overemphasized discussing political issues, or that people are not presented with an [inappropriate] image of me on television or a video. I have always tried to present myself as I really am, but also sensitively to the traditions and expectations of people.

"We are still very much a male-dominated society, and the establishment around my husband is very conservative and very male-dominated. I probably had to make more adjustments in this area than I did in my marriage, which I have always tried to approach as a partnership. My husband has been very supportive of my taking on roles that even women in the West don't assume for their husbands, especially in communicating to the West on political issues. And in very special circumstances, I sometimes speak on behalf of my husband, clarifying for the government or for my husband rather key critical policies at critical junctures. In normal circumstances, these efforts are my own with my staff, and not in consultation with his people."

The queen does admit, however, there are times when her position vis-à-vis her husband causes jealousy among those in the king's entourage. "I'm optimistic and idealistic by nature, and believe that with all that has to be done everyone must work to do it together. It comes as a bit of a shock every time you realize there is a great deal of resistance and competition . . . and people who show their feelings directly, which makes it much more difficult. But there are a few special individuals whose vision I share, and from whom I can learn and understand in what way I can contribute positively to this society.

"There are also days when I call up my closest woman friend and say, 'Let's talk.' She and I are more liberal than much of the establishment here. And there are occasions when we have both been very concerned about some of the problems and pressures on this society. Right now the issue is how to safeguard the democratic pluralistic spirit that has begun in recent years, and to find a way it can evolve more meaningfully, when there are both economic and political pressures from all sides."

Not surprisingly, Noor is heavily involved in women's issues in Jordan, and in 1985, the eponymous Noor Al Hussein Foundation was begun. "It was very evident here that we were not developing a potential for women to work, and yet for economic reasons it was becoming necessary for family incomes to be supplemented. Our incoming-generating programs are linked to health awareness and educational programs so that a woman can improve the quality of life for her family and also enhance her position, her standing within the family and the community.

"We were concerned about a regression for women in the aftermath of the Gulf crisis, because many families were pulling their girls out of school. It is still happening in enormous numbers. They can't afford to send all their children to school, so they send the boys. The girls are kept home to help around the house. And in many cases, even boys in the same family go to school on alternate days because the family can't afford more than one uniform.

"We also need to get Jordan's women involved in the political process. It's not going to happen very quickly, but it is an area we are working on." Would such a move not trigger a conflict with the Islamists, who do not want women in leadership positions? "I don't think their position is consistent with early Islam. And I don't think one should fight against words. The struggle is for women to prove themselves, to establish their credibility. And where that has happened, we've seen change. Women have become major forces, economically or otherwise, and conservative men begin to recognize and acknowledge it. It may not sound like a great achievement, but it is a beginning."

Another of Queen Noor's concerns is the refugees in her country, who nearly doubled in population during and after the Gulf War. "I had such a feeling of responsibility and grief for what was happening in Iraq." Responsibility? "Responsibility in that each of us as a human being cannot ignore what happens to other human beings elsewhere. I had such sadness . . . my husband worked so hard to avoid war, to avert the destruction of Iraq and the loss of so many lives. For both of us it was a source of anger and disappointment that there was such little response to those efforts. We both also had a great concern about what kind of world we are becoming: How can we become more humane, and constructive, rather than constantly destructive?"

Noor admits that she and her husband "had discussions, debates, and sometimes disagreements" about the way they were presenting their point of view during the Gulf War. "There were times when I counseled other than the way things went. Coming from America, I understood U.S. media and public opinion, and I felt strongly that our position was not presented clearly enough. I found out very quickly that in the States it was being so distorted and twisted, and we were not addressing that fact. We needed to really ensure that we were communicating clearly." Declining to give a specific, the queen would only say, "They were simple things that were made use of to reinforce a negative image of our position, an image that was not accurate.

"We had discussions, but I didn't succeed in every respect. And we were caught in such a bind between the feelings of people here over what was taking place and their outrage because of the statements being made in Washington and elsewhere, and His Majesty's larger view of the region. My husband so believed that a peaceful solution could be found through reasonable discussions with other world leaders, but that was not the case.

"Although my husband and I had discussions about different ways of approaching the crisis and dealing with the world's press, I felt very strongly that his position was right. At the end of each long day, he would come home to his best supporter, someone who really believed that this was the struggle of a lifetime. I felt we were locked in a battle of survival for what we believed in and for the future of our children."

Did she feel split loyalties between the country of her birth and her adopted land, a woman born and educated in America married to an Arab man at the epicenter of the crisis?

"He is very much an Arab man, and I am a woman who was raised in a Western culture and that has influenced both of us. But I still see us as a man and a woman, and our family, which is a naive way to look at it, I know. It was not a question of split loyalties, because many of my friends in America felt the way I did: very concerned about the military buildup and the absence of meaningful dialogue, and very concerned about many aspects of the crisis that did not reflect the best spirit of American society as I grew up knowing it. And here in the Arab world, the traumas of the crisis tended to narrow minds and intensify emotions in a very irrational and intolerant way. On both sides of the divide, I saw two societies that I care for very much and am very much a part of, not presenting themselves in the best possible way."

During the Gulf crisis, Noor and the king rarely saw their days end before 2:00 A.M. While he was involved with political negotiations, she was helping the evacuee efforts. "I tried hard to be there for him, to listen to his frustrations, and try to inject where possible a sense of humor. And also to let him know that we were not isolated. There were people all over the world writing to us and I would read him letters from people in the U.S., Europe, and elsewhere. Sometimes the best thing to do was just be there and not say anything at all. And there were moments too, when to decompress, veg out, my husband would pick up the children's computer games.

"At the time of the war, we had two children at school in America and two in England. It was a confusing and difficult period for them when their father was being criticized in the West. We tried to give them the larger picture, but it was a very rude and shocking lesson in life for them, but also part of the preparation. It is the kind of thing that has happened to their father ever since he has been king of this country. Jordan has been predicted to be on the verge of dissolution over and over again."

Being married to a man who has survived many assassination attempts, and living in a politically very unstable part of the world, how did she deal with the feeling that every time her husband went out, it might be the last time she would see him?

"I'm philosophical. I believe, as he does, that you have to make the most of every moment you have on this earth. I don't share my husband's fatalism that my number is up on a certain day. But there is so much to be done, and if we concentrate on the dangers and threats, we weaken our energy."

Queen Noor insists that she and her husband have not discussed contingency plans in case of a possible coup or other national emergency, as have many sheikhs in the volatile Middle East and Gulf. "We have never even discussed it. During the war, so many others taped their windows and provided a shelter in case chemical weapons were used. Our family didn't do that. We simply decided not to develop a fortress mentality. This is our country, and our destiny. God forbid anything violent and tragic should happen to any one of us, but this is our society. If anything goes wrong, we are not going to live in exile abroad."

I asked her whether she was concerned that as an American woman in a country where the Muslim Brotherhood is growing, she could be targeted. "Oh yes. Zuliekha Abu Risha has been targeted, all sorts of people have. Nobody has actually told me that I've been threatened with violence. But I've certainly been included as a target for slander. I'm not going to change the way I live. I move around freely and have the same relationships with people as I did before."

Queen Noor believes she was targeted when newspapers around the world in 1992 claimed King Hussein was taking another wife. The woman in question was Rana Najem, then an attractive twenty-five-year-old press secretary at the palace. The story first broke in *Al-Quds,* an Arabic newspaper in London, and quickly rippled through the Arab world. There were rumors that the king had bought Najem a large apartment in Amman, had asked her to leave her job and prepare herself to become his wife and take on the court duties that would correspond to her new position.

"It's not the first time; this has happened before. It has happened throughout the king's life," said Noor. "Any time he encourages someone, or shows any kind of interest, there is a jealous reaction. Men and women are targeted in an environment like ours when any special favors are shown to them by a head of state. Rumors abound of supposed details of our private lives. The reason this one took on such proportions is that it was fed to the international press by people working with the Kuwaitis. It became a politicized campaign against us. We know who did it.

"It became much bigger than the average rumor and began to affect the lives of our children. We received phone calls from the children abroad. You're raised to view the written word as almost sacred. But these are not the first rumors they've heard about either one of us. There was a slanderous campaign against my husband from the beginning of the Gulf crisis. And it was very upsetting for us."

Raising sons and daughters in an Islamic world, did she, I wondered, raise them differently than she might have in the United States? "I am a stricter parent than is the king. I wish I weren't, but someone has to be. His Majesty is much more permissive with them. I think raising children of a Hashemite head of state, who inherit spiritual obligations to be the finest examples of Hashemite Muslims, is a great challenge. It is a very confusing world here. But it's very confusing out there, too. We don't have a drug problem, or a major

AIDS epidemic, or fragmented families. We try to teach humility and human values so they can carry on the tradition of their father's special position in society."

Looking back, I asked her, if she could change anything in the last fourteen years, since her marriage, what would it be? She smiled, "I would have found a way to avert the Gulf War." It was my turn to smile. "Ah, yes, but you're only a queen, not God," I joshed her.

"You always wonder, what if I had . . . ? Should I have been more aggressive?" Noor said thoughtfully. "In life there are so many moments when you think, If only I hadn't been so diplomatic. . . . I just hope and pray that I will make good use of my experience in the times ahead.

"And, God willing, if a Middle East peace settlement is successful, it could be a major catalyst for women, and the most effective way of neutralizing extremist forces who are seeking to narrow the horizons of our societies."

CHAPTER 12

Israeli Occupied Territories: Next Year in Jerusalem

*Hamas considers the unveiled as collaborators of a kind.
It is our religious duty to execute collaborators.*

HAMAS GRAFFITI, GAZA

A S BORDER CROSSINGS GO, the Allenby Bridge between Jordan and Israel is unprepossessing. The rickety wood-slatted bridge with its institutional-green metal supports is barely the length of the aged bus ferrying travelers across. The River Jordan it spans is about seven feet wide and looks to be knee-deep. What is memorable about traveling from Jordan to Israel, however, is not the scenery, but how the crossing is conducted.

Segregation begins at the border — Arabs to the left, all other nationalities to the right. The journey from Amman to Jerusalem is only forty-two miles on good roads. But it can take seven hours or more, with most of that time spent sweltering in the heat through what may be the toughest security examinations in the world. For holders of Palestinian travel documents, that same trip may take as long as a week, or even two, depending on the time of the year. When I crossed, in late August, Jordanian newspapers were reporting that twenty thousand Palestinians were camping out for that length of time at the bridge waiting to enter Israel. Many of them were returning from the Hajj pilgrimage. The backup occurred as Israeli border authorities arbitrarily changed the number of Palestinians they would permit to enter on a given day. "It may be three thousand, fifteen hundred, or just eight hundred," I was told. "They are equally arbitrary about the times the border is open. It's supposed to be eight A.M. to two P.M., but they frequently close it at eleven A.M. or twelve P.M."

Inside the large warehouse-type sheds used for immigration and security, Americans of Arab origin are culled again from the lines containing mostly Western tourists. Once a Palestinian, always a Palestinian, no matter the passport he or she carries, has long been the philosophy of the day. Shunted to one side, they are curtly told to wait. "You have to understand, we must be very careful," a young female guard told me. "Israel has many security problems. If we make a mistake here, many people — Israelis, tourists — may be killed."

Outside the immigration shed, Star of David flags fly from rooftops. Arab communal taxis take passengers the short distance from the Allenby Bridge to Jerusalem via Jericho. Reportedly the oldest continuously inhabited town in the world, Jericho is impoverished and scruffy, as are most Arab towns in the Occupied Territories. A few miles on, one passes the pristine settlement of Ma'ale Adummim. One of the largest Jewish settlements in the West Bank, it was expensively built and is expensively maintained.

Ma'ale Adummim demonstrates clearly that the term "settlement" is a misnomer; this is not a small community but a complete new town. Such settlements cover entire hilltop ridges throughout the Occupied Territories and use most of these regions' resources. The River Jordan is little more than a trickle today because most of its water is now piped to Tel Aviv and Jewish settlements in the West Bank. When Arab wells in the region run dry, Israeli law forbids the sinking of new ones. The Arabs' Jewish neighbors in the new settlements enjoy the luxury of swimming pools, and regularly water their lawns. Today, only 4 percent of Arab-owned irrigated farms receive irrigation water.

Minutes later, Jerusalem comes into view. The high-rise buildings of the modern metropolis disappear into a distant heat haze. In the foreground is the crenellated wall of the Old City of Jerusalem. This ancient city, which can be traversed on foot in twenty minutes, is the center of three of the world's most important religions. Here is the Via Dolorosa (the Way of Sorrow), which leads from Gethsemane, where Christ was arrested, to Calvary, where he was crucified. A short walk away is the large Dome of the Rock mosque, whose golden cupola dominates Jerusalem's skyline. The blue-mosaic mosque is one of the more beautiful in the Islamic world, and it is built over the rock from which the Prophet Mohammad is said to have ascended to heaven; hence its name. The third-holiest shrine in the Muslim world/ after Mecca and Medina, the mosque stands on the platform where the Second Jewish Temple, which was destroyed by the Romans in A.D. 70, once stood. Immediately below it is the Wailing Wall, believed to be a retaining wall for the temple. The Temple Mount above, a quadrangle between the Dome of the Rock and the Al Aqsa Mosque, is the most sacred site for Jews.

The proximity of such sacred sites has been perilous for both the Muslim and Jewish religions. One of the more violent occasions was the Temple Mount massacre on October 8, 1990, when it was rumored that Messianic Jews planned to lay a cornerstone for the Third Jewish Temple. The fundamentalist Jewish sect, known as "The Faithful of the Temple Mount," has long spoken of its plans to do so, and maps sold throughout Jerusalem show a Jewish temple in place of the mosque. A Muslim crowd, armed with stones, gathered between the two mosques to halt such an act. Fearing attacks on Jews praying at the Wall below, Israeli border guards sprayed the Muslims with automatic gunfire, even shooting at ambulances and wounding medical personnel. When it was all over, 21 Palestinians were dead, and 145 were injured. The initial comment of the Israeli authorities was as follows: "Fortunately, no one [meaning no Israeli] was killed." The government later refused to accept a U.N. investigating commission into the incident.

"The tragic event at Temple Mount galvanized the Palestinian resistance movement, breathing new life into the Intifada and especially into its Islamic vanguard, the fundamentalist movement, Hamas," says Dr. Scott Appleby of the U.S. Fundamentalist Project. "The October eighth confrontation unleashed what Hamas has termed 'The War of Knives' — a new round of knifings and reprisals in the Occupied Territories and in Israel proper."

The Islamic Resistance Movement, known by its Arabic acronym, Hamas, was born at the same time as the Intifada, in December 1987. But its founder, religious sheikh Ahmed Yassin, with longtime connections to the Muslim Brotherhood, had formed its forerunner fourteen years before to strengthen Islamist values in Gaza. Ironically, that earlier movement was supported by Israel, who viewed it as welcome opposition to the PLO. Today, fundamentalist Hamas is a major organization in the Occupied Territories, and a challenger to PLO leadership.

When the Middle East peace talks began, Hamas increased its level of violence against Israelis in an effort to derail any chance of a settlement, to which they are violently opposed. As their attacks on Israelis escalated at the end of 1992, Jewish authorities arrested

1,400 Hamas members and deported 415 of them to Lebanon. The peace negotiations immediately floundered.

The strategies of both the PLO and Hamas have been hauntingly similar to those employed by Jewish factions during the struggle against the British for the creation of a State of Israel in 1948. Radical extremists in the Irgun, led by Menachem Begin, bombed and assassinated their way to an independent state, while the moderate Jewish Agency and its military branch, Haganah, took the path of political negotiation, according to Israeli historian Yehoshua Porat in an interview with the *Christian Science Monitor* newspaper. "The Haganah was more moderate in its use of force, while the Irgun was more extreme, and much readier to use violence," he explained. The PLO, like the Haganah, is prepared to accept a two-state solution. Hamas, on the other hand, demands the abolition of Israel, just as Irgun insisted on the whole of Israel. Even the mass deportations are similar. In an effort to break up Irgun leadership, the British deported four hundred Irgun members to East Africa without trials.

• • •

Palestinian women today live under a double burden: the Israeli Occupation and cultural patriarchy, which has increased with the growing Islamic fundamentalism. "As Arab women we have two battles, one against the Israeli Occupation, and the other against the fundamentalists," says Fawdah Labadi, whose two brothers have been deported for life, one of whom had married only a month earlier. His new bride was not permitted to go with him. Labadi is an unpaid spokeswoman for the Women's Studies Center, a research and resource organization in the West Bank. Commenting on the role of Palestinian women in a future state, she laughed wryly, "It's on our agenda that women should participate, but eighty-five percent of our men don't want women to rise. They want to be able to dominate them, and overcoming this attitude will not be easy."

A former schoolteacher, Labadi was fired from her position by the Israelis because they claimed that the Women Teachers' Union, of which she was a member, was a political movement. "All we were trying to do was improve our working conditions. Our salaries were half what the Israelis were getting. Instead, I ended up being forbidden to work or travel. I've been appealing to the High Court since 1988, but until now they have not scheduled a hearing or produced any proof against me. With my brothers deported, I became a major breadwinner for the family. Now that I am not able to work, it is very difficult financially for us to survive, and we are trying to grow our food. I have received a scholarship from England to do my Master's, but I have not been able to get permission from the Israelis to go.

"The hatred and the violence . . . there has been so much abuse on both sides. Jews and Muslims lived together before, and I would like to think they can again. The problem is, Will Jews and Muslims forgive each other for these years? I fear not. The fundamentalists on both sides, Muslim and Jew, are really the ones keeping the fighting going."

Palestinian women have long participated in their nationalist movement, and many removed their *hijabs* for the first time in demonstrations against the creation of Israel in 1948. Despite this, in the first year of the Intifada, Hamas zealots, many mere teenage boys, forced women in Gaza, where the extremists then had more control, to wear the Islamic head covering again. Having achieved that goal, Hamas then insisted that women wear the full-length Islamic coat or *abaya,* and more recently women have been bullied into wearing face veils and gloves. In Gaza today it is rare to find a woman who does not dress like her counterpart in Saudi Arabia. In East Jerusalem and the West Bank, an estimated 50 percent of women are now veiled, and that number is steadily growing even in towns like Ramallah, where not so long ago Arab women could and did wear shorts.

In June 1992, an international festival of women's films and books, the first of its kind and one that was expected to be an annual event, had to be closed down after its organizers received threats. "The extremists claimed the films were inappropriate," said Suha Hindiyeh-Mani, the head of the Palestinian Women's Studies Center, who organized it. "They said if Palestinian women want to learn about divorce, marriage, et cetera, they must not do it from foreigners. Ironically, the films had been shown in Gaza without any problems, although they did generate a lot of debate among members of the audience. But the school in Ramallah where we planned to show them in the West Bank received threats, so we were forced to close the festival."

Palestinian society was long considered secular, but this has been changing. "Palestinians are again embracing Islam. In another generation, Islam will govern here," said one Islamist. Certainly, pressure from Islamist organizations like Hamas is reshaping Palestinian society. And as always, they are doing so with substantial funding from the Gulf states. Charities and institutions run by such groups are proliferating, and they now operate the best schools, clinics, and hospitals for Palestinians.

The increasing budget of Hamas was particularly important at a time when the PLO was forced to cut back on funding to needy Palestinians. There were also indications that Arafat's power in the Occupied Territories was waning, and this was exacerbated by his recent fragile health. And as his position within the organization was perceived to be weakening, so, too, did the role of the PLO in the lives of Palestinians. A younger generation is finding the religious extremists' virulent anti-Israel rhetoric and militancy far more appealing than peace negotiations.

For many years, Palestinians were considered among the most educated of Muslim women. With the advent of the Intifada, women and girls were active participants in the uprising. According to a U.N. study on the status of Palestinian females in 1990, 10 percent of the fatalities and 23 percent of the injured in the first three years of the Intifada were women. Women are frequently arrested, and, like men, frequently tortured, often without being charged with any crime. The incarceration rate of Palestinians in the Occupied Territories has been the highest in the world — in the first two years of the Intifada, one in six of all Palestinian males between the ages of fourteen and fifty-five were jailed under Israeli emergency laws.

For Palestinians in the West Bank, Gaza, and East Jerusalem, having a prison record is a common denominator, like having brown eyes or black hair. It is almost impossible to find a family who has not had at least one member incarcerated in an Israeli prison or military detention center.

Being female has not been grounds for special treatment from the Israeli security forces. Intisar El-Qaq, a social work student from Silwan, East Jerusalem, was in the early stages of pregnancy with her first child when she was arrested at the age of nineteen. Despite her condition, she was kept in solitary confinement, her hands and feet were shackled, and she was denied exercise, a suitable diet, and sufficient medical supervision. Throughout her labor, her legs were cuffed to the hospital bed.

Khitam Moluch, a thirty-five-year-old mother of five from Beit Anan in the West Bank, was arrested for embroidery. Together with the relief agency World Vision, she had organized a Palestinian folklore bazaar to raise money to buy educational materials and food for a village kindergarten. Hours after the bazaar opened, police stormed it. Moluch was arrested, and bazaar items such as wall hangings, scarves, and so on, were confiscated. Why? The offending embroidery had been done with red, green, black, and white threads, the colors of the banned Palestinian flag. She, too, served time in jail.

And the same day that Terry Boullata had a liver biopsy, and was still bleeding from the operation and unable to walk unassisted, the twenty-three-year-old was arrested. In that condition, she was interrogated and then confined to what is known in Israeli detention as the "coffin." The container, made of concrete with a steel door, measures 6 feet by 2 feet by 2.6 feet. "It is like a tomb," said Terry, who was then a research assistant for the Palestinian Human Rights Information Center. "It is completely dark; there are three or four small airholes near the top that are too high to see out. The coffin is very hot and reeks of human excrement. Prisoners have to eat, sleep, and shit standing in the coffin."

Terry had originally been arrested two years previously, after representing the Palestinian Students' Union at a conference in Greece. On her return, she was accused of meeting Arab organizations in Greece and engaging in political activity. On subsequent arrests, she was accused of being a leader of the Intifada. "But they accuse nearly everyone they imprison of that," said Terry.

On that first occasion, she was placed in solitary confinement in an underground cell 9 feet long and 4 feet wide. "Every twenty-four hours is like twenty-four years," she recalled. "You are told only your tongue will save you, nobody knows where you are, and you will die alone unless you talk. In the summer, it is so hot and humid, and insects crawl on you. In the winter, your breath freezes. You lose track of the days; all you know is that the Shin Bet [General Security Services] come and take you time after time for interrogation. I was threatened with rape. I was also hooded and chained to a bar in the same position for hours." The hood, made of a feltlike material and usually dampened, tightens over the heads as it dries and makes the wearer feel as though he or she is being suffocated. Prisoners describe the hood as smelling of perspiration and vomit, which further nauseates the wearer.

"There is no shame in saying that the first time you are jailed, you are frightened to death. And every time they come to arrest you after that, you are very scared," said Terry. During her first prison experience, Terry began to experience joint pain, and then edema of her limbs. Eventually she collapsed and was finally hospitalized.

"My arms and legs blew up, they were enormous. My hands were double their normal size. As they cuffed me to the hospital bed, I screamed with pain. The cuffs were cutting into my flesh. One policeman realized I couldn't walk, so I couldn't escape, and he took the cuffs off. When his colleague returned, he chained me again." The prison doctor told Terry she needed more complicated tests than they could do, and since he could do nothing further for her, she was returned to her cell.

Almost immediately, the Shin Bet came to interrogate her again. "By this time, I was in such agony, I was sobbing. I told them, 'I can't do any more, just let me die in peace.'" Shortly after, she was released until her health improved, and was immediately hospitalized for two months.

Terry was eventually diagnosed as having developed chronic active hepatitis and Crohn's disease, a painful autoimmune condition in which the body attacks its own digestive system and can cause internal hemorrhaging. She also had developed arthritis, which frequently accompanies Crohn's disease in women. The stress she experienced from her prison conditions is believed to have helped trigger her autoimmune problem. Because of her poor health, she required regular blood monitoring tests and the liver biopsy that she had just undergone when she was arrested again.

"When they put me in the coffin, I thought it was all over. I couldn't breathe, I was gasping for air. I kept banging on the door. Eventually, one of the guards opened the door. 'Aren't you dead yet?' he asked me. He could see I was having trouble breathing." Terry collapsed and lost consciousness. The following day, she was again hospitalized.

Shortly after, through human rights activists, French President Mitterrand learned of her case. "Yitzhak Rabin was visiting France at the time, and his trip coincided with the first TV news footage showing Israeli soldiers deliberately breaking the arms of boys in the Intifada. He was not well received. Perhaps because of this and Mitterrand's personal intervention, Rabin gave orders from Paris for me to be released." Terry was flown to France and later Chicago for medical treatment. She was eventually given a fourteen-month sentence that was suspended for three years. As with most such court hearings, no proof against her was offered.

According to the Al-Haq Human Rights Organization, which is affiliated with the International Commission of Jurists in Geneva, under emergency laws in the Occupied Territories, administrative detention and deportation can be solely for unspecified "security reasons." "The Israeli military commander just has to have reason to believe a person is a threat. They do not have to disclose evidence. In fact, evidence is considered classified information. It is that simple," said Dr. Said Zeedani, director of Al-Haq. "The most you can do is get a lawyer and challenge the charge in the High Court, but even then, evidence against you is not disclosed."

Today, Terry, twenty-six, is married and the mother of a healthy daughter, but even her wedding was delayed for two weeks when her husband was arrested at a road block "on suspicion" as he was driving to the ceremony. "I was following in the vehicle behind his, dressed in my wedding clothes. They held him eight days. I was very nervous. When we finally got married, he was under town arrest. And then for what would have been our honeymoon, there was a twenty-two-hour daily curfew. We had been married eighty days when my husband was arrested again, and he was detained without charges for ten months. So far, he has been arrested ten times.

"Of course I feel bitter, although I try to retain a sense of humor — you have to try. But I would so like to have a normal, ordinary life — to make a lunch date with a friend and know they won't be arrested before we meet, to plan a picnic and not have it canceled because your community is placed under collective town arrest or because of a curfew. My husband said to me once, 'You know, Terry, all I really want is to walk with you and the baby freely in Jerusalem. Not have to apply for a permit to go there and probably have it refused.'

"I hope my daughter gets the chance to live in a dignified, respectful way," says Terry, who was born one year before the Occupation began. "I may not live to see the dream of freedom come true. I can only hope in her lifetime it does. But I do know that freedom is never freely given. You have to fight for it."

Women's groups are also frequently targeted, and members are detained on suspicion of political activities against the state of Israel. Zahira Kamel, the forty-seven-year-old head of the Palestinian Federation of Women's Action Committees and an adviser to the Palestine peace delegation, has been arrested and jailed three times, but never charged. From June 1980 until March 1987, she was also placed under town arrest, the longest such arrest for any Palestinian. Town arrest meant being confined to her small village near Ramallah in the West Bank for seven years, and from sunset to sunrise for that period being confined to her home. Additionally, she had to report to the police twice daily, and was subject to frequent unscheduled visits from the police to her home. What were the charges against her? "The order stated simply, 'for security reasons.' No further explanations, no proof, et cetera offered," she said.

Kamel's Women's Federation was originally established to help change the role of women in Palestinian society. It offers social and legal advice to its members, and because so many men are imprisoned, teaches women skills to help them support their families when the customary breadwinner is absent. Since the Intifada, Kamel has observed many changes in the lives of Palestinian women. "Illiteracy has increased due to so many schools being closed by the Israeli authorities for long periods of time, and families frequently choose to keep girl students home because of the violence. [In one year, high schools were permitted to be open for only twenty days, elementary schools for thirty-five. And Bir Zeit University only recently reopened after a four-and-a-half-year closure.] The marriage age has decreased in an effort to keep girls from participating in demonstrations. Marriages are now arranged for girls at sixteen rather than at the previously more common twenty. Polygamy has increased, encouraged by the Islamists. And there has been a dramatic increase in domestic violence."

A Palestinian study showed that in two or three of every ten marriages Arab women are now subject to domestic abuse: "Houses are small here, often only one room. When there are a lot of curfews, men are locked at home with their families, and tensions rise. During curfew, it is forbidden even to use one's backyard or balcony. Violators are shot, as was one woman in Nablus who was sitting on her balcony breast-feeding her baby. She was killed, the infant survived. When violence is used against a people, when they are treated inhumanly and humiliated, they themselves become more violent."

This also applies to the Israeli forces themselves. In a twenty-six-year occupation, both sides were exposed to ever-increasing hatred and brutality. In the Gaza refugee camps, throwing rocks at Israeli soldiers was a daily event, and a ritual the Israeli troops, often the same age as the Palestinian youths, came to dread. Increasingly, too, rocks were replaced by knifings, petrol bombs, and gunfire. Armed Palestinian groups such as the Red Eagles and Black Panthers, and known collectively as the "Red Intifada," triggered special undercover Israeli commando units whose job it was to combat them. "Stones and bullets and sudden death in the Gaza are so common that foreign newspapers have long stopped bothering to record them, except on days when the casualty counts are so high they cannot be ignored," reported the *New York Times* in early 1993.

Many Palestinian scholars feel that the brutalizing of Arab men by Israeli forces has contributed to the increasing popularity of Hamas, particularly the fundamentalists' campaign against women. "Part of what we are seeing now regarding women and Hamas is a psychological backlash," says Dr. Suha Sabbagh, the Palestinian executive director of the Institute for Arab Women's Studies in Washington, D.C. "The Palestinian male, a father, the authority figure in the house, has lost all his authority. At work in Israel, in the streets, Palestinian men have been continuously pushed around, humiliated, treated very badly by the security forces, and have been unable to resist. Much of this belittling has taken place in front of their children and their womenfolk. The Israelis have used public humiliation as a systematic policy of cutting down the image of Palestinian men as the hero figure in the family. For Arab men, that is the same as losing their masculinity.

"At the same time, there have been tremendous gender shifts in relations between Palestinian men and women. Arab women risking their lives by participating in the Intifada were less likely to bow to former Muslim traditions." As forty-three-year-old Rehab Essawi, a woman professor on the West Bank, whose entire adult life has been dominated by her loved ones being in prison, told me, "I had a country and its name was changed. We have political parties, but they are banned, so we cannot say if or to which one we belong. I cannot stand in front of you and say who I am. Women started organizing in small groups for sewing and knitting, then they became politicized and participated in the Intifada. Women were also the ones who answered the knocks at the door in the middle of the night, to protect their men from arrest. After all this, women had to be given their rights.

"Do you think one of my brothers can say to me today, 'Get out of bed and prepare food for me'? Before they did force me, slap me, and say, 'This is the right of men.'"

"Honor, too, began to shift from the value placed on a woman's virginity to how much she had done to liberate her land," said Dr. Sabbagh. Women who were sexually assaulted during interrogation and torture sessions in prison were less frequently ostracized by their communities afterward. The Israeli army, however, may be the only one in the world routinely to sexually expose themselves and begin to masturbate as a means to disperse Arab women demonstrators or groups of women.

"Men were also away from home a lot, either in prison or in the Gulf trying to earn a living, and children began taking orders from their mothers," explains Dr. Sabbagh. "When men returned home, they felt left out, and that they were no longer respected by their wives or children.

"Another factor was that the Intifada raised hope. It brought about greater recognition of the Palestinian plight by the world outside. Palestinians believed the uprising would be a solution to a lifetime of oppression. When there appeared to be no change, something had to give. Instead, men began returning to religion as a solution. Hamas told them that it was correct for them to bring their women home. Men were told to remove their women from the political arena, bring them back into the home, and once that happened, the old order of women obeying men would be reestablished."

Dr. Sabbagh feels that women, too, are partially responsible for their recent regression under the fundamentalists. "Women's involvement in the Intifada initially was very spontaneous. As the uprising became more organized, the Unified Palestinian Leadership did not provide the kind of programs necessary to keep the women's activities going. It was a secondary issue to them. In the focus on national liberation, the needs of women were ignored. Consequently, many women felt they were no longer a part of the uprising and returned home."

The Unified National Leadership of the Uprising (UNLU) was also very slow in speaking out against the fundamentalist violent campaign to force women to veil, even though youths attacked girls at a Gaza school for not being covered, and women in both Gaza and the West Bank have had nitric acid, stones, and rotten eggs thrown at them for failing to do so. Graffiti, too, began appearing, ordering women to veil or accusing them of being collaborators if they did not do so.

It was two years before UNLU finally stated that "nobody has the right to accost women and girls in the street on the basis of dress or the absence of *hijab*," and by then it was too late. "Once you put on the veil, you accept everything it symbolizes, your life changes completely, and it is very hard to take it off again," one woman told me. "There are times when I think I would rather stay as we are [without peace] than have an Arab and not a Jew come to arrest me at midnight," said another Palestinian woman, who, not surprisingly, did not want her name attached to that statement.

Terry Boullata fears that Palestinian women may be treated the same way as women in Algeria's fight for independence. "They struggled with the men, suffered the same way as men, and then, when it was over, women lost all their hard-won freedoms and were pushed back into the home. Whenever the moderate Palestinian factions become weak, Hamas becomes stronger. I've been told to cover, but I don't intend to. I'm a liberal woman. And I didn't go through what I've been through to be forced into an existence of emptiness, which Hamas seems to feel women should lead."

As in all Muslim countries, there are strong women like Terry and Professor Essawi who resist pressure from religious extremists, and in most cases they are able to do so because the men in their lives share their opinions. It is much more difficult for Muslim women to make a stand for independence if their brothers, husbands, fathers, or other male relatives do not support such a move. Time and again, women give in to male pressure — even an uncle's or cousin's opinion may carry sway on such issues — because a woman is told that she, and hence the family, will be less respected, or that she may be physically harmed unless she complies.

Even in America, an Islamic extremist stabbed his sixteen-year-old daughter to death because she wanted to live a Western existence like her classmates. Palestinian-born Tina Isa, a St. Louis, Missouri, honor student died in 1989, four years after her family moved to the United States from a village near Jerusalem. Her father was outraged that she wanted to date a local boy and had taken a part-time job at a fast-food restaurant. When she returned home after her first day at work, her father claimed she had shamed the family's honor and for that she should die.

Two years after Zein Isa was convicted for his daughter's murder, he was indicted for being a member of the Abu Nidal terrorist organization, a breakaway group of the early PLO, and for plotting to kill American Jews and blow up the Israeli Embassy in Washington, D.C.

In Terry Boullata's case, she married a man who is not conservative, and who shares her progressive views. Rehab Essawi is an articulate, outspoken, and take-charge woman, who is well known in Palestinian circles, but she also receives a certain amount of reflected respect because of the man to whom she was engaged, who is now dead.

Rehab is an education professor at Bethlehem and Hebron universities. An attractive, energetic woman with a quick laugh, she is, in her forties, still unmarried, which is unusual in her society. At nineteen, she was engaged to Omar Kassem; the two had grown up together in a small village on the outskirts of East Jerusalem. It was an engagement that would last twenty-one years, the length of time Omar served in an Israeli prison. The sentence ended only with his death. It was, of course, also a sentence of a kind for Rehab.

When the Israeli occupying forces took over the West Bank and Gaza in 1967, Omar Kassem was a twenty-seven-year-old English-language teacher. A member of the Arab Nationalist Movement, he became a senior official in the early PLO. Months after the occupation, Kassem was part of a group of Palestinians who illegally went to Jordan in an effort to strengthen the Resistance against the Israelis. As the group were attempting to infiltrate their way back into Israel, they were detected. During the ensuing border skirmish, Kassem was arrested. He received three life sentences, and was the highest-ranking PLO official to be jailed. "It was an extremely harsh sentence," says Rehab. "Today, he would probably receive only about six years. But none of us believed that the Occupation would last as long as it has. We thought it would be over much sooner, and our lives would return to normal. We lived in hope. Omar and I were so sure that we would be married one day."

Instead, the next two decades were marked for Rehab by her twice-monthly visits to her fiancé. Those precious thirty minutes each time gave them both strength. "We talked to each other through wire mesh, and put our hands up to press fingers through the wire. For years, that was the only intimacy we had.

"Political prisoners are separated from their visitors by the wire. For criminal prisoners, the wire windows were lifted so they could kiss or touch their visitors. One time, the prison guards forgot to close the window, and Omar and I were able to hug each other. The first time my fiancé hugged a woman was when he hugged me that day. It was such an emotional moment, he began to tremble.

"Throughout all those years, I lived for his letters. He wrote beautiful letters to me, and expressed such love in them. Prisoners are limited in the amount of mail they can send, and to get around this, some of mine from Omar came to me with the names of other prisoners signed at the bottom. Whenever I became lonely, I would take out his letters and read them, and as I did I could see him and hear his voice. I still do this when the loneliness for him gets bad."

The only visits to Omar that Rehab missed were when she herself was jailed three times in the seventies. "I was accused of getting in touch with an illegal organization. I had gone to visit my brother in Iraq." Rehab is very matter-of-fact about her own prison experiences. "During my interrogation, I was beaten, spat at, told I would be raped. They placed me in a cell where I could hear men screaming with pain, although I believe it was a psychological-torture tape they played. The worse time was when they made me stand facing a wall with one leg lifted. If you move even slightly, they kick or beat you.

"One way or another, my life has revolved around prisons since 1967. But that is true of every Palestinian family. After Omar was imprisoned, my brother was jailed for ten years. And since then, two of my brothers-in-law have been, one for fifteen years, and the other for three-and-a-half." (Rehab's mother died of a heart attack triggered by tear gas that was being fired at demonstrators but that also filled the small room in which she was sitting. In confined spaces, tear gas is particularly dangerous.)

In the summer of 1989, Omar contracted hepatitis, a common problem in Israeli prisons. "He became so yellow, his lungs failed. By then, he had lost so much weight, he had wasted away. But they still chained him to the bed. He couldn't stand, let alone walk, or escape. He had painful bedsores because being chained meant being kept in the same position.

"The second and last time I was able to hug him in all the years I knew him was just a few hours before he died. As I held him in my arms, he closed his eyes, then opened one, and a single tear rolled down his face. By that afternoon, he was dead."

Omar Kassem received a hero's funeral, the largest Palestinian funeral in Jerusalem. "The PLO held a commemoration ceremony for him. They talked about his being a teacher, a Palestinian, who had won the respect of everyone who knew him. But they didn't talk about him as a human being, the man I knew and loved." Now, all that Rehab has left of Omar are a twenty-one-year collection of yellowing letters, a few photographs, and the memory of two brief hugs.

A year to the month that Omar died, Rehab's sister gave birth to her first child, a daughter, Lara. Since Rehab's brother-in-law was jailed four months after his marriage, Rehab has been a surrogate parent to the little girl. "He's been in jail two years so far, and he still hasn't been tried. When will this child see her father?" Lara, a high-spirited toddler, launched herself into her aunt's lap from the opposite side of the room, and Rehab cuddled her and said softly, "You know, Lara fills my life. She's the child Omar and I were never able to have."

•   •   •

Driving between Jerusalem and Gaza, I noticed how green the Israeli countryside was, much more so than it had been twenty-two years ago, when I had last come this way. Now there was acre after acre of well-tended cultivated land where little had grown before. The journey confirms how small this country is; as many Israelis are quick to point out, if the West Bank is given up, from Tel Aviv to the Jordanian border is a scant fifteen miles. The distance from Jerusalem to Gaza is approximately sixty miles; in all other respects, the two places could not be more remote from each other. Jerusalem is a cosmopolitan city overflowing with tourists year-round, who congregate in the evening around Zion Square, Israel's Montmartre, with its winding streets, sidewalk cafés and bars, and musicians and street performers. Gaza is a fly-blown strip of sand measuring twenty-eight by five miles; its refugee camps have some of the highest population densities in the world.

Better known as Misery-by-the-Sea to its Arab residents, Gaza was four years into a nighttime curfew at the time of my visit. Violators of the curfew could be arrested, shot, or killed, at the discretion of the soldiers manning the frequent checkpoints. Gaza's nightlife those days was limited to Israeli patrols in armored vehicles and jeeps covered in protective screens to guard against the local ammunition of choice — rocks. And in Gaza there is little shortage of rocks, much of it building rubble from homes that have been dynamited.

Large-scale demolition of houses was an extrajudicial punishment in the Occupied Territories that was introduced by Rabin in 1985, when he was minister of defense, as part of Israel's "Iron Fist" policy. Typically, a family was informed that their home would be blown up and were given thirty to sixty minutes' notice to remove their belongings, and sometimes less. There were no charges, no trials, and no appeal. The explosions were occasionally so powerful that neighboring homes were also damaged.

Unemployment in Gaza was running at 60 percent even among university graduates when I was there, and the majority of its eight hundred thousand inhabitants live well below the poverty level. Six months later, in March 1993, both Gaza and the West Bank were completely sealed off "indefinitely" because of escalating violence against Jews. Fifteen Israelis had been stabbed to death or shot in the month prior to the order. During that same period, twenty-six Palestinians died in street clashes with Israeli troops. The closure of the Occupied Territories meant that the 110,000 Palestinians, 30 percent of the Arab workforce in both the West Bank and Gaza, who cross over daily into Israel for below-minimum wages, were unable to work. Indigenous employment in the Occupied Territories for Palestinians is limited because for years Arab businesses that might compete with Israeli monopolies have been banned.

Driving through Gaza was a challenge: many side roads were completely blocked by high barricades of oil barrels constructed by the security forces to minimize crowd mobility; donkey carts and the occasional camel were more frequent than cars, and children ran alongside barefoot. The refugee camps are breeze-block hovels with corrugated metal roofs and windows with shutters but no glass. Flimsy home additions, some two stories high, are constructed from any available scrap materials. Most roads are unpaved, and large piles of rotting garbage mark many intersections. Basic services — water, electricity, and garbage disposal — are erratic.

My first stop was at the Palestinian Women's Union, founded in the early sixties by Yussa Barbari, a cultivated and formidable seventy-year-old and the former principal of the only girls' school in Gaza. The Union's original objectives were "to raise the social, cultural, health, and economic standards of women, and to help women achieve equality with men in public life." Today, concerns of gender equality have given way to issues of simple survival. The union supplies often the only support the women crowding the building and its yard receive. All have had husbands killed during the occupation, or forcibly deported, or they are serving long prison sentences. Virtually all the waiting women were also completely veiled, with floor-length coats, gloves, and face coverings. To spend time at the center is to listen to a litany of adversity.

"The world thinks that Islam is full of fanatic Muslims," says Yussa Barbari. "I will tell you frankly, the veil is their last hope, the hope that religion will save them. They know that nothing else will. They realize that U.N. resolutions are only implemented against Arabs and Muslim states: Libya, Iraq, and the Palestinians. When you lose everything, there is only religion left to turn to."

And certainly, the women waiting to receive their allowances of 100 Israeli Shekels ($44) per month, mostly from European sponsors, have lost much. Iman Sardiah is twenty-four years old and the mother of three. Her husband, accused of killing a collaborator, "a spy for Israel," is serving a life sentence. "They took him in the night," she told me. "The next time I saw him, he was blind in one eye from the torture. They demolished our house and they did it one year before my husband even had a trial. I was eight months pregnant at the time. They didn't even give us time to take anything out. There were three families living in the house. We just had a few rooms, but they dynamited the whole building. We lost everything, and the other families were punished, too. The Red Crescent gave us a tent to live in."

"The Gaza Strip has been a laboratory to test all rules violating human rights conventions," says Barbari. "We are living in a jungle and jungle law prevails. The U.S., with its support of Israel, has demolished our Arab State. We have lost seventy-five percent of our land to Jews, we've lost our properties, our young men. The world doesn't know this. And it is *we* who are called terrorists. Russian immigrants and Ethiopians have had the right to come here; what history do they have with this region? And we who belong here have had no rights, none at all." Palestinians and Jews alike were surprised when Israel accepted three hundred Bosnian Muslims in March 1993. Both sides saw the gesture as little more than a public relations step to remove the focus from the 415 deported Palestinians.

Shallabiyah Schewda, aged forty-seven, the mother of eleven, told of her fifteen-year-old daughter's being badly beaten on her way home from school as she passed a clash between Palestinian youths and soldiers. The girl became hysterical and couldn't stop crying, and the child's father sent their son out to get tranquilizers for her. It was after curfew, the boy was arrested, and soldiers went to his home. Schewda's sixty-year-old husband was clubbed with guns in the subsequent assault, and he collapsed vomiting blood. He died a few hours later in the hospital. "Several days later, three Israeli officers came and apologized to me. They said it shouldn't have happened. My husband was killed because none of the soldiers who beat him that night could speak Arabic and we couldn't explain my daughter needed medicine."

Each woman waiting to see Barbari brought with her a history of horror. Near the house where the Union is located, graffiti six feet high reads "Hamas Is the Base of Israel." There is also the ubiquitous "Islam Is the Solution." "Thank Allah for Hamas," said one of the women. "The roads are sealed by the Jews, Hamas opens them. Just like Hamas will free our country. They are doing something for Palestine. Everyone else has forgotten us."

In Beach Camp later, which was built in 1952 and is home to forty-eight thousand Palestinians, many of whom were born there, a group of women invited me into one of the houses. The original two small rooms, each about nine feet square, once opened onto a tiny courtyard and outside kitchen area. Today, a corrugated metal roof over that area has given the family a living room, but sections of the roof are still open to the elements, flies, and the powerful stench of trash rotting outside on the street. A brightly colored woven plastic rug partially covered the floor of the living room; other floors were bare cement. The only furniture were a few thin mattresses and pillows made from flour sacks and then embroidered. Lines slung across the room served in lieu of closets and also to dry towels.

Once again, the women defined themselves by their own or their families' prison records. Where an Arab woman might previously have been introduced as the mother of Khalil or Khalid, instead I was told, "This is Widad Dahman. She was in jail. Three of her four boys are in jail; they were all tortured, of course." Widad interrupted, "Ah, yes, Khalil, who is twenty-two, has been arrested eight times," and then, as if talking of her son's football scores, she said with total recall, "The first time they took him it was for three months, then for four months, the next time was six, then they took him for five months, then six months, after that fifteen months, and then for two months. Now they have him again. The last time they shot him in the leg and head. He's never been charged or been to court.

"They haven't taken my fourteen-year-old boy yet, but they will. He's been beaten by soldiers already. Sometimes I think they should put us all in jail. It would save them and us a lot of time."

Widad, now forty, was born in Beach Camp, where her father died when troops shot randomly into crowds. "Peace talks? Don't talk to me of peace talks. The Palestinian flag should fly on all the land from the River Jordan to the sea. It should all be Palestine. Anything less I reject."

It was Habiba Alyian's introduction, however, that disturbed me most. "My daughter is *shaheed,* martyred, and I am glad she gave her life for the just cause of Palestine."

Wafa, the youngest of Habiba's twelve children, was seventeen when she was shot. "It was her last day at school, and the last day of her final exam. As she left the school, there were some boys throwing stones at soldiers. The girls joined in. Then more soldiers came and the boys began to run away, but the girls couldn't run as fast. Wafa was shot in the head with a real bullet, not a rubber one."

The teenager underwent five hours of brain surgery, and three more operations in the next eighteen days. "She couldn't see anything, she couldn't speak, she couldn't move, they were feeding her by tube." Eventually, Wafa was flown to a special brain-injury unit in Cairo, Egypt. After eighteen months, and regaining some vision and ability to speak, the young woman died from a massive kidney infection caused by the shunt draining fluids from her brain injury. "Wafa was very successful in school. She was a flower in our lives," said her mother. Habiba paused in her story to show me a dog-eared photograph of Wafa in a wheelchair taken shortly before she died.

"I have always ordered all my children to throw stones at the soldiers," said Habiba, now fifty-five. "Why? Because of the Intifada. Four of Wafa's brothers were in jail for the same thing when she was shot. Thanks be to God, Wafa loved her land enough to die for it. Thanks be to God, my daughter is martyred for Palestine." For Habiba Alyian, the martyrdom of a child in what she considers a Holy War is an honor. Since she herself was a child, she has been aware of the Koranic verse "Those who are slain in the cause of Allah are not counted among the dead. They are living in the presence of their Lord and are well provided for."

Later, at the home of one of the two leaders of Hamas in Gaza, physician Mamoud Zarhar echoed similar sentiments on Islamic martyrdom. "Islam is the only system in the world that can cope with deaths of its people to further its cause, and that is a strength. Americans do not *want* to die for their faith or their country." He was talking of Hamas's goals. "We cannot establish a separate state without its being Islamic. We attempted in the past and we failed. We tried Moscow, we tried being secular, and the end result was the shameful defeat of the Arabs in 1967. Then we came back to the West with Camp David. But we are not Western. Palestine can be restored only by Muslim power; it is the only way to restore the dignity of Arabs."

Dr. Zarhar, a surgeon, is on the faculty of Gaza's fundamentalist-run Islamic University. Until 1982, he was a physician at the Government Hospital, and chairman of the Arab Medical Association, but he was dismissed by the Israelis because of his political activities. After three years of running a private clinic, he was invited to teach at the university. He looked tired as he greeted me at his sparsely furnished home, and he limped from an old knee injury as he crossed his large reception room every time the phone rang, which it did constantly during our conversation.

"So many meetings, so many phone calls. We have asked the Israelis to let us go to Jordan to meet with the PLO on the peace talks. But they have refused our request. Windows are opened for some, but not for us." As he sat down again, I noticed the large prayer callouses on his forehead and the tops of both feet, formed by decades of daily kneeling to touch his head to the ground in worship.

"Hamas is a misunderstood organization. It is not an organization of religious sheikhs, but an organization of intellectuals. It is part of the Muslim Brotherhood, which can be found everywhere in the world. Even American Muslims are members. People are afraid of Hamas but that is because of the propaganda of Palestinian spies working for the Israelis. We don't want to push Israel into the sea, although the Jews say we do. Look at history: when Jews were expelled from Spain, we opened North Africa to them. We recognize Jews, they don't recognize us, and that is the problem.

"The peace process will produce a big zero. Israel will never give up all the land it took in 1967. And Palestinians are very weak. How can we alone withstand all the pressures? Other Arab countries in the region represent Western interests. But the U.S. is fully ignorant of the behavior of the Arab leaders they support, and the U.N. is totally neutralized. But we are not a separate entity in the Muslim world; we are linked to the current Islamist wave. If Israel will not give up our land, it must be taken by force with the assistance of other Arab countries. Our problem is the leadership of other Muslim countries. Those who have never helped us must be eliminated. Every secular leader, except Sudan, will be overthrown by the Islamists. This will be quicker than trying to negotiate a Palestinian state with Israel. By the end of this century, the Muslim Brotherhood will have launched a big wave against such authorities."

As our conversation wound down, Dr. Zarhar asked whether I was married. When I told him no, he wanted to know why not. "You were created for children, your uterus was created to produce children. Your breasts were created to lactate and feed children. You have a brain, yes. But you are also a woman, and to have children is your purpose." I did not respond, having learned early on in my travels that such dialogue tends to be circular.

"In my sermons in the mosques on Fridays, I am teaching about your Western phenomena. You are legally permitted one marriage, but your world allows many adulterous relationships at the same time. This is against humanity. For family unity, we Muslims have multiple wives. We do not need adulterous lovers, we have no problems with AIDS. I am preaching that it is good for family unity to have multiple wives if it is necessary for the husband."

At the time when I met him, the physician had one wife, and six children. Three months after our meeting, Dr. Zarhar was one of the 415 Hamas members who were deported to an exposed, windblown strip of no-man's-land between Lebanon and Israel. The Lebanese refused them entry, and Israelis fired at them if they moved too close to the Israeli border. It was their expulsion that caused the peace negotiations to falter. As Dr. Zarhar's group dominated international headlines for weeks, I wondered how his wife and young children were faring as they became just another Gaza statistic, children without fathers, a wife without a husband. What price for them family unity?

• • •

Returning to Jerusalem, I faced the inevitable mammoth traffic jams that build up some miles from the city and that can take an hour or two to clear. In an effort to avoid the worst of the traffic, the taxi driver cut through back streets. Suddenly we were in the middle of one of several newly developed Jewish Orthodox suburbs. Women were dressed in long skirts and long sleeves, and they covered their hair with snoods rather than wigs. The men in their long black coats, black hats, and *peyot* sidelocks looked little different from their forebears in Polish and Russian villages nearly 250 years ago. Since contraception is forbidden for Orthodox Jews, it was not unusual to see couples with eight or more children. In the Mea Shearim Orthodox district of Jerusalem, signs are widely posted in English and Hebrew cautioning women who enter the area that they must be dressed modestly.

Jewish Orthodoxy has grown substantially in Israel in the last fifteen years, and, as with similar religious movements around the world, it has spawned its own militant fundamentalist groups. Since Orthodox Jews are the only Israelis excused from military service on the grounds that war needs "both physical and spiritual strength," and they supply the latter, the acts of terrorism of these factions is ironic. Included among the Jewish militant organizations are the pro-Zionist Gush Emunim, which began the settler movement in the

Occupied Territories; the anti-Zionist Neturei Karta, which has been involved in stoning moving cars and buses that violate the Sabbath; and the Kach, members of Rabbi Meir Kahane's party, who, along with Gush, have demanded the forced evacuation of Palestinians in the Occupied Territories, areas they call by their ancient names of Samaria and Judea.

In the early eighties, Gush Emunim stepped up a campaign designed to increase the tension between Israelis and Palestinians. "These terrorist acts included the 1980 planting of bombs in the cars of two Arab mayors, the 1983 killings of three Palestinian students in an Islamic institute in Hebron, and, most significantly, a 1984 plot to blow up the Dome of the Rock mosque in Jerusalem," said Dr. Scott Appleby. Gush Emunim radicals working with high-ranking Israeli army officers planned "to plant twenty-eight precision bombs to destroy the Muslims' third-most sacred shrine without damaging the surrounding area. Had it been successful, the bombing would have undoubtedly led to a profound crisis and an Arab-Israeli confrontation of unpredictable magnitude." Fortunately, the plot was uncovered shortly before it could be carried out. The Jewish fundamentalist underground also began killing individual Palestinians (the preferred modus operandi is drive-by assassination) in an effort to force them to leave the Occupied Territories.

Gush's most successful campaign, however, has been that of building Jewish settlements on Palestinian land. The settlement program began in the seventies and gained impetus in the eighties with the support of right-wing Housing Minister Ariel Sharon and government funding even though it contravenes the 1949 Geneva Convention. The campaign was designed to isolate and surround Palestinian population centers and make it difficult after such extensive Jewish development for those regions to revert back to Palestinian control. When the Labor party took office in the summer of 1992, Prime Minister Rabin promised to suspend the construction of new settlements, but not those in Jerusalem or the eleven thousand units already begun. The suspension was made under pressure from the United States, which threatened to withhold $10 billion in loans. Western diplomats, however, say that it is not a construction freeze, just a partial slowdown.

Today, three-quarters of the settlers, who include many American Orthodox Jews, are not Gush members, according to Appleby, yet, Gush Emunim continues to administer much of the settlements' infrastructure. One of the leaders of the Gush settler movement is

Daniela Weiss, a mother of five, who is proud of her fanaticism, and believes that "Samaria" and "Judea" can only be Jewish land. Sounding very much like her Hamas counterpart, she says, "I am very far from tolerant. Extremism in the defense of God's commandments is no vice."

• • •

It is the first thing one sees on entering and the last image one leaves with. The painting dominates the small room. It depicts a teenage boy on his back in a garden, his glassy-eyed stare indicating he is dead more surely than the blood seeping into his shirt from a chest wound. "It happened two days before Yusef's eighteenth birthday," said the boy's mother, coming into the room behind me. "His father had given him a watch for his birthday, the first watch he'd ever had. It was a golden color, not real gold — we couldn't afford that — but my son was as proud of it as if it had been."

Yusef, in his final year at high school, had been working part-time for a neighbor as a plumber on a building site in Bethlehem. Returning home at the end of the day, he took the public bus to his village, Silwan, which sits immediately below the southern wall of the Old City of Jerusalem. On the bus with him were a group of teenage boys, Jewish settlers. "We learned later that they claimed the sun reflecting off his watch was shining in their eyes. When Yusef got off the bus, they did, too. As he took a shortcut through a public garden, they attacked him. Yusef was stabbed through the heart and left to die." His body was discovered thirty minutes later, at four P.M., by a journalist taking the same shortcut.

"When Yusef did not return on time, I began to worry. He never stayed out. Where is there for Arabs to go in the Occupied Territories?" asked his mother, Widad Yabani. "I had been thinking that afternoon about making him a yellow cake for his birthday; it was his favorite. But mother's intuition told me something was wrong. I asked the police and the local hospitals if there had been a bomb on a bus or any accidents. They said no. At seven P.M., I was so worried, I took a taxi to his job site. I called him but no one answered. On the way back, a message came over the taxi radio that the police wanted me. They said my boy was in Jaffa Hospital. They had taken him there to do an autopsy."

The Jewish youths who killed Widad's son were arrested. "We found out later they spent two months in jail. If it had been Arab boys killing a Jew, they would have been in prison for life." B'Tselem, an Israeli-run organization that monitors human rights in the Occupied Territories, has long documented the unequal treatment of Jews and Arabs. "Whenever an Arab is tried for murdering a Jew, in all instances the convicted parties receive life sentences and their homes are demolished," states one of their reports. "In the reverse situation, when Arabs are killed, the files are often closed without any charges being brought. And when Jews are convicted, their sentences may be just months long."

The next time Widad had any dealings with Jewish settlers was in August 1991, when many families in her village, including her own, received letters informing them their homes now belonged to Israel, and they had twenty days to vacate the properties. The letters arrived one month after they were dated, ten days after the deadline. Silwan, the village in which Widad lives, was part of Jordan until 1967. To the militant Jewish settlers, however, the Palestinian village, five minutes' walk from the Wailing Wall, is on the site of the City of David, and for this reason they want to force Arabs out.

"They came at midnight on October fourteenth, two months after we received the letters. They broke windows of houses and jumped inside and threw out furniture and clothing. There was a lot of shouting, and we saw men with beards, skullcaps, and Uzi machine guns. We thought it was the police looking for Intifada activists. Then we realized they were Israeli settlers.

"The police came and there were long conversations in Hebrew, which we could not understand. Our landlady, Fatima Karim, who lived above us, refused to come out, and the police said they would shoot her if she didn't. She was finally carried out forcibly. Then the police sealed the house behind her. This meant that since that night no one has been permitted to enter her home. The family's entire possessions have been locked inside. The fridge had meat in it and vegetables, and everything had to be left.

"The settlers said Fatima didn't own the house even though it was left to her by her grandfather, and her family had lived in it for generations. She had all the papers; she even had proof that we pay her rent. The authorities told her that because her father lives in Amman, the house now belongs to the government." (Widad's family continues to live in its part of the house and continues to pay rent to Fatima.) Israel has long contended that any properties in the Occupied Territories with absentee owners can be claimed by the government.

Over the next few weeks, armed midnight raids by Jewish settlers continued. In one of the forays, Jewish settlers forcibly took over the house next to Widad's. "My neighbor was hurt in a fight and had to be taken to the hospital. Now my new neighbors are a young Jewish Orthodox couple. He is about twenty, she is about eighteen. We never speak, yet we live so close that we share an adjoining wall. We can hear them as they move."

The small house next door is identical to Widad's except that it has an Israeli flag flying from the water tank on the roof, and the building is surrounded by high barbed-wire fences. Outside the house around the clock are posted two Israeli guards armed with Uzi machine guns, pistols, and knives, and linked by walkie-talkies to the Israeli security forces patrolling the area in armored jeeps. The plainclothes guards claimed they were private security, not military.

"Settlers killed my son. I don't want to live with them, and we can't afford to move," says Widad. "And I don't understand why they want to live with us if they have to live behind barbed wire to do so. Their security has made a prison for them."

During the weeks of settler raids on Silwan, Widad was surprised and touched when Jewish students from the Peace Now organization showed up in the village to aid the Palestinians. The Israeli organization has long advocated giving up land in exchange for peace between Arabs and Jews. "We were afraid to sleep at night in case the settlers came back. We didn't know these students, but they slept on our floor to protect us. We were very grateful.

"In 1967, when the Jews first came here, it was not so bad. We worked with Jews, we had Jewish friends, then things gradually began to get worse, until in the end each side became afraid of the other."

• • •

"When there is violence against Arabs by Jews, we should make their people suffer equally." Mariam Shakskier seemed just another harried mother when I met her in her apartment at the top of five very steep flights of stairs in Nablus in the West Bank. Her six-year-old son, Ysar, and several of his friends were squabbling loudly over a TV computer game. Her four-year-old daughter, Sumood, who has Down's syndrome, was feeling irritable and demanding attention. Mariam herself, slightly built and whose face showed the premature lines of a heavy smoker, was trying to make her voice heard above the din. She repeated her comment, "When there is violence against

Arabs by Jews, we should face it and make their people suffer equally. That is what I was thinking at the time when I did it. Nothing more."

Mariam was describing the day she placed a bomb in the crowded cafeteria of the Hebrew University. The explosion sent terror through the lunchtime crowd, and shock waves through the Israeli public. The final casualty count was twenty-eight people wounded, but no fatalities.

As we sat in her neat living room, with its black-and-white sofa set, framed family photographs, and a vase of artificial flowers on the coffee table, our conventional surroundings made the conversation seem all the more surreal. As Mariam served bologna sandwiches and coffee, only the occasional twitching of a nerve in her cheek suggested that we were talking about anything other than last night's television program.

"Palestinians were being forced out of the West Bank. My people, our children, were suffering. I wanted to help them. Women should share in the revolution. I was searching for a way to help end the occupation. I kept thinking, What can I do?" It wasn't long before Mariam made contact with a group that gave her the answer to her question.

"It was a pipe bomb, homemade, and my job was to take it into the university and place it on a chair in the cafeteria just before lunchtime. The university was targeted because there were a lot of Israeli soldiers there. We thought a bomb explosion there would make people think about why it had happened, and then they would understand our cause. It wasn't my choice to put the bomb in the cafeteria. I was told to put it there. I did, and half an hour later, it detonated.

"I knew it had worked when I heard the news on the radio of the explosion. I was pleased since I had succeeded in doing something for Palestine. I had no guilt or regret. I just continued with my normal life."

Mariam, who was eighteen at the time, says she does not remember whether she was scared or not as she carried the bomb into the university. "No, I did not think about the people who were hurt or their families. No, I have never seen injuries caused by that kind of bomb. All I thought of was how my people had suffered. Later, when the Israelis tortured me, I wished I had exploded the whole university, not just the cafeteria."

Seven days after the bombing, Israeli soldiers surrounded the house where Mariam lived with her parents, four sisters, and five brothers. "They began to ask each of my sisters her name. When they came to me, they just said, 'You, come with us.' They took me to the Russian Compound." The Compound, a large stone building near Jerusalem's Old City, was, in the last century, a resting place for pilgrims. Today, the forbidding building is known for its torture, not its hospitality.

"The Russian Compound is a slaughterhouse," said Mariam. "They asked me where I was on the day of the bombing. I told them I was in school. They called me a liar. There were three men. One of them hit me in the stomach and twisted my arms as if he was going to pull them from my body. Then the three of them began to beat me, all the time they kept calling me a liar. They said they would hang me and cut me into pieces. When I didn't speak, they said, 'You will see what will happen to you.'

"At three A.M., they came for me again. They told me to take off my clothes and I refused. They forcibly stripped me. Then they tied my legs to a chair, and a man began to hit me on the head, hands, and legs with a club. It hurt so much, such pain. They stopped and then told me I was going to be raped, and they would watch." Mariam passed out, she doesn't know whether from fear or her injuries. "There was water beside me when I came to, and they brought a paper for me to write my confession." Mariam, still naked, continued to resist until they brought into the room a man whom she knew. "His head injuries were very bad, and they had screwed two of his fingers together; they were mangled. They beat his injured hand with the club in front of me. He screamed. And they kept asking him crazy questions, like, 'What color is a car?' He would scream, 'Yellow,' and they would say, 'No, red,' and smash the club on his fingers again. They wanted him to confess that he was involved in the university bombing with me. But he didn't know about it.

"Finally, they said they wouldn't waste any more time on either of us. They would take us as we were, naked, and hang both of us. It was at this point that I confessed to planting the bomb, but I said I worked alone. They weren't satisfied, and the beatings and the torture continued for forty-five continuous days. Then one day they brought me a Hebrew newspaper with a picture of my father. They said they had sealed our house, closed his restaurant, and taken away everything our family owned. 'Now your family is dirt poor,' they told me. I couldn't speak, my face was too swollen from the beatings." Mariam also learned that one of her sisters, Najwah, was arrested as

Mariam's accomplice and sentenced to three-and-a-half years' imprisonment. "My sister had no idea about the bombing, I never discussed it with anyone." Mariam received two life sentences.

While in prison she learned English and Hebrew, and matriculated from high school. On a number of occasions, the informal prison classes were stopped. The woman teaching foreign languages was accused of political agitation because she had the prison students recite in English "I am a Palestinian." "In those days, we couldn't even admit out loud that our country was Palestine." During her incarceration, Mariam learned that her brother, Samir, had been killed in the fighting.

After serving ten years in jail, Mariam was freed in a prisoner exchange. An Israeli pilot was exchanged for seventy-five Arab prisoners, including ten women, one of whom was Mariam. "Nobody knew we were being released, and I didn't know where my family was now living. I returned to our old neighborhood and someone contacted my father. My mother didn't recognize me. I had been one hundred and thirty pounds when they arrested me. I was eighty-three pounds when I was released.

"But after my release, I felt as though I was in a bigger prison. All the restrictions on Arabs had taken place while I was locked up. For example, I haven't left Nablus since I was eighteen." Today, Mariam is forty-two.

"By the time I was released, the PLO was changing from its armed militancy to discussing the possibility of a Jewish and an Arab state side by side. It was the first stage of realism inside the PLO." The PLO's new moderation matched Mariam's. "Ten years in jail changes you completely," she said. "I don't regret what I did. But today perhaps I would choose a different way to resist. No matter the problem, I now believe that bombing is a bad idea. Before we used to say all Palestine should be for the Palestinians; we didn't want to share our home with someone else. Eventually, you learn to compromise.

"I will always remember, however, the faces of the Palestinian women and children being driven from their homes. The fear in their eyes. That was what obliged me to do what I did. Palestinians felt defenseless. I never gave a thought to the Israelis, except how to get rid of them. Your enemy had a state, and you did not. Certainly, the Israelis were not thinking of my pain when they tortured me.

"But I remember Arafat's speech to the U.N., when he said, 'I have a rifle and an olive branch. Don't let the olive branch fall from my hand. I want peace.'"

Recently, Mariam has put the Hebrew she learned in jail to good use. "I have been participating in dialogue meetings between Jewish and Arab women. We live so close to one another, but neither side really knows the other. It is necessary to sit and talk together, to understand what the other side wants and fears. We try to explain that we have rights, too, that we must also have a state. That what statehood means to them, it also means to us.

"We tell them we are just struggling to free ourselves. We don't want to suffer more, to lose more children. I want to know I can send my son out to play near the house, something he has never been able to do because I fear he will be shot. In prison once, we had a remembrance party for all the women whose sons had died during the Palestinian Resistance. The list of dead boys was so long. So much pain, so many tears. . . .

"But one thing I have noticed in these meetings is that Israelis, despite being strong, always see themselves as victims because of the Nazis. We know the Jews suffered in the Holocaust, but we didn't participate in their suffering. Today, the Palestinians are the victims, and the Israelis need to recognize that. Even now the Jewish women ask us, 'Do you really want peace?' We tell them we don't want to use violence only to receive more violence from Israel. The occupation affects the occupied and the occupier. It is a disease affecting civilians and soldiers. For this reason, both sides must have peace."

• • •

"Enough of blood and tears. Enough!" The rhetoric was emotional, the media hyberbolic, as the Declaration of Principles between Israel and the PLO was signed in September 1993. Long in coming, the much-trumpeted agreement caught both Jews and Palestinians off guard. But despite the dancing in the streets on both sides of the Green Line, less optimistic voices — some would say more realistic ones — were much less sanguine. "It is too early to declare that we are facing one of the great moments of history," cautioned Chaim Herzog, former president of Israel. "These developments could lead to peace, economic prosperity, and even confederation. They could lead to tragedy."

Palestinian-American Edward Said, a Middle East expert at Columbia University, echoed the feelings of many Palestinians when he admitted to being "very disturbed" by the agreement. "It's very flawed. It leaves too many things unclear, too many things to [be decided in the] future. It is still a dominant and a subordinate relationship. It's disastrous in many ways."

Ordinary Palestinians were left wondering if what they had been offered was a hollow victory. The sectors ceded to Palestinian authority under the agreement, such as health and education, are little different from what they already possessed before the Intifada began six years before, except for control of taxation. Rehab Essawi pointed out, "Thirteen years ago the Israelis offered to return to us considerably more land than we will get now. At that time also they said they would withdraw Jewish settlers from the Occupied Territories. Now Palestinians are to be given partial rule of less than seventeen percent of our land, the settlers are to stay, and still more settlements are being built. It is also common knowledge that the Israelis would have paid money to get rid of Gaza. They've wanted to get it off their hands for a very long time."

Other Palestinians are concerned that they may have exchanged one form of oppression, the Israelis', for another, Yasser Arafat's. "The Chairman talks democracy but has always run the PLO as a dictatorship. An Arab prison will be just as miserable as a Jewish one, Arafat's iron fist just as painful as Rabin's," said one Gaza resident. Similarly, there is fear that much of the foreign aid pledged for Gaza and Jericho will not reach its destined beneficiaries. Fiscal accountability will be new for the PLO; in the past, Arafat has maintained tight and secret control of the organization's coffers.

Meanwhile the blood and tears continue, wives are still becoming widows, children orphans. Shortly after the signing of the historic document, one of Arafat's lieutenants in Gaza was assassinated, and that incident was followed by suicide bombings in Gaza and the West Bank, and violent clashes between Palestinians and Israelis, all of which illustrated just how fragile such an accord is. Three weeks after Rabin and Arafat's symbolic handshake on the White House lawn, the PLO leader was firing off to the Jewish prime minister an angry letter denouncing the Israeli military's rocket assault on homes in Gaza City. The killing of two Hamas commanders and the arrest of other members of the organization were violations of the spirit of the peace agreement, Arafat insisted. As if nothing had changed, Rabin responded that such armed attacks would continue if necessary.

And while Israel continues to insist that Jews and Arabs have a common enemy in the form of Islamic fundamentalism, the two sides still remain far apart on key issues such as the sovereignty of Jerusalem, water rights, and border control. Ultimately, however, the survival of the peace agreement is likely to depend on the Palestinian economy. Twenty-six years of enforced poverty and despair has bred extremism. The choice is simple, say experts: Singapore or Somalia — stability with the former model, chaos and violence with the latter.

CHAPTER 13

Egypt: The Mother of the World

A Woman's Heaven Is Under the Feet of Her Husband

ISLAMIC PROVERB

I
T IS THE CONTRASTS and the contradictions that one remembers: Egypt, the ancient center of Islam and learning, the "Mother of the World," also has long been known as the "Land of Licentiousness" to which Gulf Arabs flock for the wine, women, song, and gambling that are banned at home. Egyptian belly dancers, frequently a synonym for prostitution, make the annual Hajj pilgrimage to Mecca to expiate their transgressions of the past year so they can return to Cairo's sleazy nightclubs and begin sinning again. In Egypt also, men feel pious for giving up whiskey, which is banned under Islam and yet readily available throughout the country, for the Ramadan month of fasting.

It is a country where employment is guaranteed "as a right" under the constitution, yet more than one-fifth of the workforce, 50 percent in some places, are unemployed and the numbers continue to climb. Media censorship is "forbidden" under that same constitution, yet the state tightly censors all newspapers, TV, and radio, and the authors of books considered to "threaten national security," which can include feminist literature, are jailed or banned from publishing.

It is in Egypt that the Grand Sheikh of Al Azhar, the ultimate authority on all things Islamic for 85 percent of the world's Muslims, is a state-paid employee; as such, the Ministry of Information prescreens his sermons and, it is also said, his *fatwas,* and he needs its authorization before granting an interview. But while the Grand Sheikh is the symbol of religiosity and morality, his staff pad their salaries by illicitly selling access to him for $100 a visit, thus continuing the *baksheesh* tradition that permeates all Egyptian bureaucracy and may well predate the eleven hundred–year-old Al Azhar.

Egypt was the first Arab country to begin education of women in the 1880s, but today, 110 years later, 63 percent of all women are still illiterate. The first feminist movements in the Muslim world were founded in Egypt in the twenties and yet the "Law of Obedience" enacted in 1979 requires a wife to submit totally to the authority of her husband, and the "Law of Return" enables police to forcibly return her to him even if she has fled from her husband's physical abuse. Twenty years ago Egypt prohibited female circumcision, but 80 percent of rural girls, and an estimated 40 percent of urban ones are still forced to submit to this practice, which mutilates their genitalia. In Egypt 25 to 30 percent of all household breadwinners are female, yet the fundamentalists campaign for women to stop working.

Egypt's split personality is especially visible in Cairo: the Corniche El Nil is lined with five-star hotels overlooking the historic river, where beggar children sleep on the sidewalks and the penetrating pungency of donkey, horse, and camel urine is almost overpowering as it evaporates in the hot sun. The city's schools are so overcrowded they operate three shifts daily often with one hundred students per class, and yet the government routinely slashes education and health budgets in favor of the Ministry of Interior, which controls the secret police and internal security. In Cairo the five-year-old state-of-the-art Opera House plays host to world-class performers for the silk-and-diamonds set, yet the city's housing shortage is so acute that one million people now live in the tombs of the capital's necropolis.

Life in the City of the Dead, however, is considerably more comfortable than it is for many Cairenes. The stone mausoleums, some of which predate the thirteenth century, are cool and dry. Most now have electricity and indoor plumbing and many have small enclosed gardens. The wide boulevards that run between them are blessedly free of the fume-belching, horn-honking traffic jams that contribute to the chaos and cacophony of most of the city. And in fact, the necropolis is frequented by picnickers on holidays and weekends.

It is the dwellers of Cairo slums such as Bulaq who exist in conditions that would have appalled Dickens; the homes were tenements in the last century. Today, the narrow, dark, and rickety buildings appear to hold one another up like wasted gutter drunks, and only a deranged optimist would step onto the treacherously decaying balconies. Most buildings appear to be in danger of imminent collapse, and they do so with deadly regularity, burying their occupants. During my visit to Egypt, newspapers featured these headlines a few days apart: "18 Crushed to Death in 7-Story Building Collapse" and "Housing Dangerously Unstable, 30 Narrowly Escape Death as Building Crumbles."

But it is the capital's garbage collectors, the *zebaleen*, who live in squalor so soul-crushing that to call Cairo "Calcutta with pyramids" is to slander Calcutta. The two communities of *zebaleen*, one Coptic Christian and the other Muslim, make their homes in the festering dumps of Cairo's garbage. Trash stacked fifteen feet high towers over the hovels of the *zebaleen*, and the narrow routes into the warrenlike communities lie over decades of foot-flattened waste. The noisome assault is overwhelming; a miasma of putrescence seems to invade every pore, and far from closing down, the nose in olfactory-flashbacks recalls the stench for days. To be at the bottom of the detritus chain in a Third World city is to be poor indeed. In the Christian section, one mother and her small children, all barefoot, sorted mounds of used disposable hypodermics for recycling, seemingly impervious to the constant prickings and scratchings from the needles, and ignorant of the risk of infection. "AIDS is dangerous?" snorted the woman. "So is going hungry."

In the Muslim garbage collector's community in Ain El Sira there are other dangers. The air is turbid with smoke and ash from the numerous garbage fires set by the contractors dumping construction debris on the top of a 150-foot cliff of refuse immediately above the *zebaleen* shacks. In the six weeks prior to my visit, four homes had been buried under landslides started by the trucks' dumping, which continues around the clock. The last had occurred at night. "We woke up to shouts from the truckers for us to get out, and seconds later the roof caved in," said Ibrihim Abdul Razak. "We all got out except my seven-year-old son, Tahir. The debris smashed on his leg." Tahir was hospitalized, the family's home destroyed. The other *zebaleen* wait for it to be their turn.

"Nobody cares if we live or die," said forty-five-year-old Samira Hassan. "We have lived here for thirty-five years. The city promised us electricity and water. We paid for the electricity to be installed five years ago. They took our money — we still have the receipt — but they never came back." Samira has never left the community, never visited a park or seen the countryside. "We don't have time, we don't have money. I tried to grow a flower once, but nothing green grows here."

Samira is a mother of nine. "I had six more children but they died when they were very young. It is common here. We have many problems — scorpions, mosquitoes, rats, and *ersa* [weasels], always *ersa*. They are our main problem. They bite our babies, feed off them, in the night. Children get sick, fevers, and then they die. In the winter, the roofs leak, it is very cold at night, more children die."

A quarter of the Egyptian population now live in Cairo, a city of fifteen million people, swollen daily by three million commuters. The remainder of the fifty-eight million population of Egypt, which increases by one million every ten months, is crowded onto 3.5 percent of the country's territory. Egypt covers 385,000 square miles but most of it is desert or marsh and little more than the narrow Nile valley and the Delta is settled. Cairo's infrastructure long ago stopped keeping pace. Collapsing buildings, exploding sewers, overtaxed transportation systems, water shortages, and air pollution that rivals Mexico City's are all greeted by Egyptian officialdom with little more than "*Malesh, malesh* [Never mind]. Tomorrow, *Inshallah*, things will improve."

It is in conditions such as these that the religious extremist movement was born and has prospered. It was the Islamists who supplied emergency services — tents, food, and water — to Cairenes made homeless in the October 1992 earthquake, which devastated parts of the city, killed more than five hundred, and injured ten thousand. When the earthquake victims rioted over a lack of any government response to the disaster, Mubarak pleaded for their patience, but offered little more. And in a classic government blunder, when the Islamist organizations began distributing cash and relief supplies to homeless families, the government, embarrassed by the criticism, arrested forty of the two hundred doctors distributing the aid. The authorities claimed that under emergency laws only official channels could distribute emergency aid. Once again, the Egyptian government's failure to act helped the cause of the Islamists.

Today, the Islamic militants are waging an increasingly violent battle to hasten the collapse of Mubarak's secular government, which it accurately accuses of being inefficient and corrupt. Egyptian bureaucrats routinely demand bribes to carry out the simplest task, even to process forms. Bomb attacks throughout the country, tourist buses sprayed with machine-gun fire, and assassinations of and death threats against well-known Egyptians have all become regular events.

"Every government gets the opposition it deserves," says Fahmy Howeidy, a fifty-five-year-old columnist for *Al Ahram*, Cairo's largest daily newspaper, whose offices border on the Bulaq slums. "The Islamic movement in Egypt was moderate when it began in 1928," insists Howeidy, a moderate Islamist himself. "The Nasser government started violence against the Muslim Brotherhood. The movement was banned, fifty thousand members were jailed and severely tortured, and others were executed. They were not freed until Sadat came into office in 1970." Other chroniclers of history would disagree with the columnist's assessment of the violence against the Muslim Brotherhood.

Hassan al Banna, a schoolteacher and the fiery founder of modern Islamic fundamentalism, preached overthrowing the secular government "by any means including militancy," in his quest to return Egypt to "true Islam." Throughout the 1940s, MB terrorist squads targeted prominent Egyptians. In 1949, Banna himself was targeted by the security forces of the last monarch of Egypt, King Farouk, who reportedly had him assassinated. Five years later, the MB attempted to kill President Nasser, and it was this event that triggered what in essence was a pogrom against the Islamist movement in Egypt. In the face of Nasser's mass arrests and executions, many MB members sought refuge in neighboring Arab countries, exporting the movement with them.

One of Nasser's victims in his massive anti-Islamist crackdown was Zeinab al-Ghazzali, the founder and Supreme Guide of the Muslim Sisterhood, the women's arm of the Muslim Brotherhood. She was sentenced to death by hanging for attempting to overthrow the government; her husband suffered a stroke when he heard the sentence, and died shortly after. At the time of Ghazzali's arrest, the MS claimed one million registered members in Egypt, and while those figures may have been inflated, rioting broke out when it was announced she would be executed. Shortly after, her sentence was reduced to twenty-five years, much of it to be served in solitary confinement. King Faisal of Saudi Arabia intervened on her behalf but Nasser lied to him and told the monarch she had already been freed. In fact, she was in a Cairo jail, where Nasser's secret police were trying to ensure she would never again lead a movement against the state.

The torture of Ghazzali was particularly brutal and something she can scarcely bear to talk about even today, although she remembers every detail with great clarity. "I was tortured for months at a time," she says at her home in a comfortable suburb of Heliopolis in Cairo. "In one cell they placed me in I was up to my shoulders in water for twelve hours a day. For the remainder of each day I was kept in another cell, which measured six feet by three feet, with rats for company. They hung me up for hours by my hands, beat me constantly, threatened me with sexual assault." From the change in the tone of her voice, it is apparent, however, that the most frightening incident was when she was locked up with snarling dogs that, she was told, had not been fed for several days. "I prayed. It is what I always did when I was being tortured, and as I continued to pray, the dogs didn't touch me," said Ghazzali. After Nasser's death, Saudi Arabia's king petitioned Sadat for a full pardon for her, which this time was granted and she was released.

Sitting in her study with its floor-to-ceiling shelves of leather-bound books, Zeinab al-Ghazzali, now aged seventy-five, has lost none of her early fire and passion. "I didn't believe in Sadat, and I don't believe in Mubarak. I want a government of the Koran and the Sunna [hadiths], and I won't retire until then or until God sends for me." Even at her advanced age, she continues to head the MS, and today she claims that 50 percent of Egypt's women follow her, a gross exaggeration, although the movement does have tremendous support. "I never had children; the Muslim Sisters and the Muslim Brothers are all my offspring," she said. Ghazzali still gives weekly lectures at her home, and is currently writing three books on Islam, one on the Koran, another explaining the names of God, and a third on the *hadiths*. She is aided in her work by female acolytes, all of whom dress as she does in Islamic garb, but in white. "White was a favorite color of the Prophet," she explained.

After decades of preaching and proselytizing, Ghazzali is not easily interviewed; her style instead is to lecture, displaying as she does, teeth broken in prison. One asks her a question, and one receives the answer to another, and that will lead to a tangent that she will enthusiastically pursue. The quality of her Arabic mesmerizes her listeners in the same way the Arabic of the Koran has inspired Muslims for fourteen hundred years, and, like the Koran, the poetry of her language does not translate into the more mundane everyday English. "Ah, the beauty of her Arabic," say both our interpreters a number of times, neither of whom wanted to interrupt her when she was in full voice. Her pet African parrot, "Bengo," however, was not as considerate. His piercing squawks of *"Saalam Aleikum"* and *"Allahu Akbar,"* and "Islam Is the Solution," in fluent Arabic frequently drowned his owner's voice.

One of eleven children, Ghazzali was born in Mit Yaish, a village eighty kilometers from Cairo. Her father, an Al Azhar scholar, had two wives. While she was still an infant, her father had a vision that she would play an important role in religious life, and to that end, he determined that she be fully educated. Ghazzali was thirteen when he died and her elder brother refused to let her continue her education. "He said I was already too argumentative. Instead, I devoted myself to my father's religious books and by the time I was fifteen, I had read three hundred and fifty." But at seventeen she made an unexpected detour and joined the Women's Union, founded by Huda Shaarawi, an early Egyptian feminist, who began a campaign in 1919 for women to unveil. Three years after joining, Ghazzali resigned and founded the Muslim Sisterhood. (Today, she is also one of the leaders of the Muslim Brotherhood.)

"I had become convinced that Islam was the real answer — that when Muslims come back to the right path, as Allah desires, then Islam will rule the world. This is not something that should scare the West; it should comfort them. Islam is the justice of Allah on earth." And then, as if explaining to a simpleminded child, she smiled broadly, served me cake and tea and said, "You have to understand, Allah's message that was sent through Judaism ended when Jesus came. And Allah's message through Jesus and Christianity ended when Mohammed came. Adam, Noah, Abraham, Moses, Jesus were all Muslims, but they were messengers only. The final and future religion, the religion of God, is Islam. Judaism and Christianity are now obsolete.

"The world has only to look and see that Islam brings happiness. It is the fastest-growing religion in the world because it is the most suitable to the life of human beings. It suits the mind, the emotions; it doesn't fight the emotions as other religions do. The mind comes to Islam first and then the heart follows. The only reason there is a conflict between the West and Islam is because of the Crusaders, because they were beaten by the Muslims. That is why people in the West are so fanatic about our religion. If you read the history of Saladin, you will know the humanity of Islam and his good soul. The way he treated the Christians when he captured them — he looked after the officers personally. The image of Islam for the West was ruined by the Crusades, and further damage was done by your biased history books and your education.

"The current rebellion here among the young revivalists of Islam is because they are angry with our ruler and the government, and with the support the regime receives from the West. A lot of the

Islamist groups are not dealing with the problem as they should. The threats, the killings, the robberies by groups like Al-Jihad. . . . The Muslim Brotherhood, on the other hand, deals with the ruler as a mother would a small son who has made a mistake, in a reasonable manner.

"It is not right that Islam should be blamed for the uprising. It is caused by the cruelty of the ruler and his regime. It is also true that Western and Muslim agents in the Islamic world, and even here in Egypt, are trying to separate the different Islamist factions. It is the work of hidden and/or foreign hands, just as France's Mitterrand said he would not permit the Islamists to rule Algeria. But we do not want our countries ruled by leaders who are ruled in turn by the West.

"Unfortunately, Christians do not follow the Bible as it was originally written, and it is the same with the Jews. If both faiths followed their holy books, there would be no fighting between us. Islamic beliefs do not change, our prayers, *Shariah*, our behavior are unchanging. But you people have changed your Bible and you had no right to do it." Her voice rises as she becomes excited, her face mobile with passion.

"The role of women has deteriorated because of so-called modernization in the West. Your fashions, short skirts, dancing, women having boyfriends and not husbands, having babies and not being married — this is unlawful. It is also against all women. The Prophet said that women are sisters to men, women fought in wars with men, women work like men. Islam does not prohibit women from working, but the rules . . ." — she thumped her desk with her fist until the objects on it bounced — "the rules. These *must* be followed. The door to the room must *never* be closed, a man and a woman must never be alone together. In this way the thoughts of sex are prevented from forming. . . ."

Ghazzali segued back to an earlier point she had forgotten to make on Islamist assassinations of supporters of secularization. "Under Islam, if a person has rejected his religion, then, yes, he must be killed. But he is entitled to a trial. If found guilty, he should be imprisoned, so that he can reflect on what he has done. And if he then comes back to God, he must not be killed.

"The Koran says that religion must not be forced, even with apostates. But if you have not accepted Islam on the Day of Judgment, you will not be accepted, you will be the loser for all time. Islam has fulfilled mankind's needs from its first day until today, and will do so until the last."

She smiled broadly again, and sat back in her chair and suddenly relaxed, the intensity fading from her features. Clearly, the session had ended.

· · ·

Although Sadat emptied the jails of fundamentalists in 1970 in an effort, like Jordan's King Hussein, to counter Nasser's socialism, the Islamists were ultimately responsible for the president's death. They could not forgive him for the Camp David Treaty with Israel. It was an army lieutenant who tossed a hand grenade at the president's feet as he stood at the reviewing stand during a 1981 military parade. The young officer was a fanatical member of Sheikh Omar's Al-Jihad, a violent splinter of the Muslim Brotherhood.

"The Muslim Brotherhood is still banned here. They should have the right to exist," says journalist Howeidy. "When these organizations are legal, they are moderate. But when you see how oppressive the police are in this country . . . just look at what is happening. Some months ago in a town of about fifty thousand people in upper Egypt there were about thirty troublemakers. But the authorities burned mosques with innocent people inside, destroyed houses, arrested so many. The government now recognizes the Islamists could be an alternative regime and they feel threatened.

"Now their position is not to accept even moderate Islamists, and the more oppressive the government becomes, the more people flock to join the movements. This is what happens when the authorities are too heavy-handed." Certainly, Egypt's record on human rights is dismal. "Systematic torture and long-term detention without charge are two of the most egregious abuses, but not the only ones," says the U.S.-based Middle East Watch. "Despite Egypt's projection of a democratic face to the international community, the list of violations is lengthy and well documented." More recently, other human rights groups have accused Mubarak's regime of taking children as young as eight years old as "hostages." The children are jailed and tortured in an effort to make family members who are wanted by the police give themselves up.

In December 1992, government troops sealed off Imbaba, a sprawling Cairo slum, for several days and sent more than fourteen thousand heavily armed troops equipped with a hundred armored vehicles storming through the area. Imbaba, a district of a million, has long been a fundamentalist stronghold. Few women living there now venture out in public without being swathed from head to toe in black. On the first day of the operation, seven hundred people were arrested, at least four people were killed, and twenty-eight stockpiles of arms and explosive devices were discovered, as were tapes of militant clerics, including Sheikh Omar. It was the biggest crackdown on dissidents since Sadat's assassination. The Islamic militants, who want to replace the current government with a Muslim theocracy, warned they would step up their attacks against foreign tourists.

The threatened backlash came a few weeks later. On the same day as the bombing of the World Trade Center in New York City, militants linked to Sheikh Omar's organization detonated a bomb in a crowded café that is popular with tourists in the heart of Cairo. It killed three people and seriously wounded twenty, including two Americans. Since then, other bombs have been exploded in crowded areas of Cairo, including outside the Egyptian Museum, which houses the Tutankhamen exhibition along with many other ancient Egyptian treasures. Explosive devices have also been placed in the pyramids and pharaonic temples at Giza, on the outskirts of the capital. The zealots, including Sheikh Omar, claim the ancient monuments are nothing more than pagan idolatry and should be destroyed. Daily, the cycle of violence continues.

Nawal El-Saadawi is a prominent Egyptian who is in the unfortunately unique position of being viewed both as an enemy of the state of Egypt and an enemy of the Islamists. One of the Arab world's leading feminists, the silver-haired, sixty-three-year-old physician and writer is outspoken to the point of occasional stridency, in a style reminiscent of the early women's rights movement in the West. Both the Egyptian government and the Islamists have long sought to silence her, the former by banning her articles and books for twenty-five years (she has authored thirty and only one has been published in Egypt); they also closed her women's organization, her feminist magazine, and on one occasion Sadat jailed her. She was released only after Sadat's death. The extremists were even more aggressive: they placed her on their death list in August 1992. Since then, Saadawi has had twenty-four-hour guards supplied by the government, which wants her muzzled but apparently not dead. Both sides, however, have failed to silence her.

Saadawi first drew attention to herself when she was the country's director-general of health education and she started speaking out on prostitution and other forms of sexual exploitation in the Arab world. She also tackled subjects never openly discussed before, such as female circumcision, incest, and sexual diseases. Many of her books, some fiction and some scholarly, deal with the same subjects. "My troubles started the day I held a pen in my hand," says Saadawi.

Sitting in her study decorated with postcards from feminist colleagues all over the world, Saadawi launches her first salvo. "Women are suffering from state-created fundamentalism, both here in Egypt and in the United States.

"Sadat encouraged the fundamentalist movement in an effort to neutralize the power of Nasser's groups. He encouraged the confinement of women, the veiling of women, because the fundamentalists wanted it. When I was in medical school in the fifties, there was not a single veiled woman at Cairo University. By the time my daughter was a student twenty years later, thirty percent of women in universities and schools were veiled." Today, the figure is closer to eighty percent. Saadawi is equally critical of Sadat's wife, Jihan, who was viewed in the West as a progressive feminist. "She did nothing for women," she said curtly, referring to the 1979 Jihan law. "It meant that a man who wanted to marry again had to inform his wife and she could choose to stay married to him or get a divorce." In 1985, the law was overturned. "Today, an Egyptian woman has to go to court and prove the second marriage is damaging to her, and this is very difficult to do. Once she is divorced, she also loses her home; the husband can take the children and the apartment.

"The American government has also encouraged fundamentalists to oppress American women. The Christian fundamentalists want biblical law to rule in the U.S., and your presidents have supported them in this. Similar movements exist in many other countries, and they are responsible for the relapse of women and the global backlash against them." (Indeed, the Christian fundamentalist movement in the United States does frequently sound like its Islamic equivalent. Rousas Rushdoony, known as the "father of Christian reconstructionism," considers democracy "heresy," and wants all Americans, even non-Christians, to be ruled by biblical law. He also campaigns for "the death penalty, preferably by stoning, for adulterers, homosexuals, abortionists, heretics, blasphemers, and disobedient children." One of the leaders of the Coalition for Revival — the umbrella organization for Christian fundamentalism — Rushdoony, along with other COR members, believes that women should be under the control of men in their families, whom they must obey at all times.)

"Fundamentalism is why women in the Islamic world are now veiled again," says Saadawi. "It is why I'm censored, still, after all these years. I cannot speak on television, I cannot be published by newspapers or magazines, and my books are banned. The government is against me and is censoring my voice. The fundamentalists want me dead."

Saadawi first learned of the death threat against her when she was awakened at 2:00 A.M. by security police the day after writer Farag Fouda was assassinated in June 1992. "I thought they had come to take me to prison, as before," she recalled. "Why else would the police ring my doorbell in the middle of the night? But they told me Fouda had just been killed and that I was being given around-the-clock guards. The Islamic terrorist organizations had placed on their death list writers who had taken a stand against the establishment of a theocratic state.

But while the government took steps to guard her life, Saadawi accuses Mubarak's regime of stepping up the "systematic campaign" against her in recent years. It began when the feminist magazine she founded, *Noon,* which was run by her daughter Mona, supported Saudi Arabia's women during their driving demonstration. Saadawi, who has long insisted that Islam need not be misogynistic, then wrote an article criticizing Saudi Arabia's Sheikh Bin Baz. "He had written an entire book on why women should be completely covered. He said that Islam allows women to show only half of one eye. This, of course, is simply not true. I responded to Sheikh Bin Baz's book with a very critical article stating that one can be a good Muslim woman with a naked face. The Saudis were furious.

"I was attacked in newspapers in Saudi Arabia, and also in the newspapers here that have Saudi affiliations. A lot of journalists here are paid by Saudi Arabia. One Egyptian newspaper called me corrupt and against Islam, and said I wanted to teach women to be immoral. But morality has nothing to do with hiding the face.

"Saudi Arabia is a country that preaches many things, but when you look at their daily behavior, examine their lives, you find a lot of decadence. But as long as they are covered, that's okay. It is the superficiality of religion. Saudis call Egyptian women loose, and then they come here for prostitutes, for nightclubs. In Saudi Arabia, the more you find segregation of sexes, the less you find morality."

Shortly after Saadawi's article on Bin Baz, the Egyptian Ministry of Social Affairs closed her international organization, Arab Women's Solidarity Association, which focused on women's social and economic advancement. Issuing a decree to dissolve AWSA in 1991, they claimed that the association spread ideology offensive to Islam, and that its activities did not comply with the general interests of the country. They also stated that AWSA was, in fact, damaging relations between Egypt and some foreign (but unspecified) Arab states. At the same time, the government transferred all AWSA's finances to an Islamist women's group.

Until recently, the Egyptian government was schizophrenic in its approach to fundamentalists. While opposing their movement, it frequently tried to appear more Islamic than the Islamists. Considerable TV and radio time was and still is devoted to religious programming. And many religious leaders who have been deemed moderate and therefore controllable, were appointed to official positions.

Like many Muslim women, Saadawi believes that men interpret the Koran to benefit their own interests. Unlike many Muslim women, when she tackles such subjects, Saadawi's eyes sparkle, she grins almost impishly, and it is clear that she receives an adrenalin charge from doing battle. "The fundamentalists always focus so much of their energy on women because they want to divert people from the serious problems of the day, such as poverty.

"But they don't speak about the double standard. They have one for women and one for men; they are very strict with women, and very lax, lenient with men. They encourage corruption and promiscuity among the men, and then they say they are good Muslims. Polygamy, encouraging men to have four wives, is promiscuity. This damages the family, but they allow that. This kind of double-standard morality is corruption."

It is comments like those that outrage the religious militants. Was she afraid of being accused of apostasy? "Oh, this happens to me all the time," said Saadawi, dismissively. "My God, this is happening every day here. Daily, they say we are not Muslims, we are atheists, we are against Islam." Such labels do not bother Saadawi. Her concerns as a physician and a writer are to improve the lives of women by "changing the system."

"You cannot separate health from policy. I come from a village and I have practiced medicine in villages, so I know the conditions. The men and women who came to me are sick because they are poor, because they don't eat well, or their housing conditions are terrible. The women have had illegal abortions because they have too many children. Girls came to me hemorrhaging from circumcision. I couldn't tackle all these problems just as a physician. I have to know why these problems exist, why they are hungry, why they circumcise girls. You cannot separate health from politics, from poverty, or economics. They are all important to women's health problems.

"Why should a girl be a virgin, required to bleed, on her wedding night? Thirty percent of girls are born either without a hymen or with an elastic one that does not bleed on their wedding night. Men are not supposed to be virgins. Why is it required of women?"

A major campaign of Saadawi's organization before the government closed it was to halt female circumcision. "The majority of rural Egyptian women are still circumcised. Here they remove only the clitoris; they do not do the much more extensive procedure, but even so, there are many problems. Infection, bleeding, damage to the urinary tract, sepsis, even death. Later, it may cause pain during coitus, and psychological damage. In the villages it is performed on girls just before puberty, by untrained village midwives using any kind of knife or razor, without painkillers, and in unsanitary conditions. In the middle and upper classes, it may be carried out by a doctor. The reasons given for clitoridectomies in Egypt are 'cleanliness,' and 'so that girls will not run after men.'" In many societies, it is also believed that if the baby's head touches the clitoris during delivery, the infant will die.

Female circumcision is frequently described as an "age-old Muslim ritual," when in fact it predates Islam and is even believed to be pre-Judaic. There is no mention of it in the Koran, and only a brief mention in the authentic *hadiths*, which states: "A woman used to perform circumcision in Medina. The Prophet said to her: 'Do not cut severely, as that is better for a woman and more desirable for a husband.' But because of this still debated *hadith*, some scholars of the Shafi school of Islam, found mostly in East Africa, consider female circumcision obligatory. The Hanafi and most other schools maintain it is merely recommended, not essential. In the nineteenth century, women in the United States and Europe were sometimes circumcised because it was believed to relieve epilepsy, hysteria, and insanity.

Today, an estimated one hundred million women have undergone the sexual mutilation. It is performed in many African countries, including Sudan, Somalia, Ethiopia, Kenya, and Chad. It is also a tradition among Muslims in Malaysia and Indonesia, and in a number of countries in the Middle East, including Egypt, the UAE, and parts of rural Saudi Arabia. Coptic Christians in Egypt and animist tribes in Africa as well as Muslims, undergo the ritual.

More than 90 percent of Sudanese women undergo the most severe form of circumcision, known as "pharaonic," or infibulation, at the age of seven or eight, which removes all of the clitoris, the labia minora, and the labia majora. The sides are then sutured together, often with thorns, and only a small matchstick-diameter opening is left for urine and menstrual flow. The girl's legs are tied together and liquids are heavily rationed until the incision is healed. During this primitive yet major surgery, it is not uncommon for girls, who are held down by female relatives, to die from shock or hemorrhaging. The vagina, urethra, bladder, and rectal area may also be damaged, and massive keloid scarring can obstruct walking for life.

After marriage, women who have been infibulated must be forcibly penetrated. "This may take up to forty days, and when men are impatient, a knife is used," recounted Sudanese women at a conference that I attended several years ago in Cairo on the "Development of Women in the Islamic World." They also told of special honeymoon centers built outside communities so that the "screams of the brides will not be heard." At this time also, the risks of infection and hemorrhaging are high.

During childbirth, the scar tissue must be cut and the opening enlarged, otherwise mother and child may die. In the mid-eighties, American *Nursing* magazine began advising medical practitioners in the United States how to treat such patients, since the influx of women from countries where circumcision is standard meant that U.S. health-care providers were now seeing them in hospitals here. And if such cases are not handled correctly, major complications can ensue. The tradition of female circumcision in many countries is so strong that circumcised women even in the United States usually request reinfibulation after each delivery.

• • •

Halla Sarhan also considers herself a feminist, but her style and her world could not be more different from Nawal El-Saadawi's. The editor of an Egyptian woman's magazine, she sent her chauffeur-driven white Mercedes complete with mobile phone to pick me up, and I was shown into her white and pink office during an editorial meeting. Her nearly all male staff danced attendance and addressed her by the honorific "Doctura" while Sarhan, rapidly approving or rejecting layouts, constantly plucked grapes from a large bowl. She was impeccably made up, her lipstick and nails matching a bright-red silk blouse, her hair tied back in a black velvet bow. A mass of diamonds sparkled from both hands.

"We deal with a lot of material like in your *Cosmopolitan* magazine, even sex," said Sarhan, who, after seven years in the United States studying at George Washington University, and then working at Voice of America in Washington, D.C., is familiar with the American magazine. Despite her publication's subject matter, Sarhan manages to sell her magazine both in Egypt and in the Gulf states. "In Arab society there is terrible government censorship, and also from the religious community in Saudi Arabia, where we sell. If they don't like an article or an advertisement, they will tear it out, ink it out, or, in some cases, confiscate the entire issue.

"The Ministry of Information here has told me not to put a pretty woman on the cover because the mosques are saying it makes men excited and is, therefore, against Islam. My magazine, like all others, depends on pretty women to sell.

"We are going backward in this part of the world as far as women are concerned. But I have found a good formula to be able to publish what other people would not dare to print. In a recent wedding issue, for example, we had a section on what happens on the wedding night. Nobody talks about it here. The brides must be virgins, and the men are either virgins or their only previous experience has been with prostitutes or house servants. There is a tremendous misunderstanding of sex in our culture. Our youths are really ignorant on this subject; they can't talk about such problems and it causes such difficulties in relationships. Friendship doesn't exist between a husband and a wife here. And the man is still often told to be violent with his wife the first night, "to slaughter the cat," so that she becomes scared of her husband and obeys him. Instead, the experience is very traumatic, painful, and frightening for many women." Arabic folklore includes a tale in which a bridegroom brutally kills a white kitten in front of his wife before he deflowers his bride. The quivering bride is told that if she ever disobeys her husband, her fate will be the same as the cat's.

"If I simply write about sexual problems, the pages will never pass the censor," explained Sarhan. "If, however, I wrap the whole section in verses from the Koran, which is what I did, the articles are taken seriously by the authorities. Because of this, we were able to run a piece entitled "What Do I Do on My Wedding Night, Mama?" We were also able to have a gynecologist explain how the hymen is lost. Another feature in that issue was about how sixty percent of Arab women refuse to have intercourse on their wedding night because of their fears; with this we ran a Koranic verse that tells the man to go to his wife with kisses and soft words. In an article on frigidity, which is a common occurrence in the Arab world because of the problems between couples, we explained that the Koran instructs men to give their wives the right of sexual pleasure."

Listening to Sarhan describe the sexual dysfunction among many men and women in the Arab world, which was also confirmed by a number of women I interviewed as I traveled, one thing became clear: Arab classics such as *The Perfumed Garden* and *A Thousand and One Nights* notwithstanding, the reputation in the West of Arab men being a race of superlative lovers may well have more to do with Rudolph Valentino's trend-setting Hollywood version of a sheikh and of the size of royal harems than it does with reality. In Israel's Occupied Territories, for example, a West Bank biology professor, Mohammad Haj Ali, was so concerned about the level of sexual ignorance among married Palestinians that he wrote and published a sex education manual for Arab adults in 1992. The book, according to the author, included biological and health sections, plus discussions of the psychological, social, and moral aspects of sexuality.

"Women are really crushed and maltreated in this society," said Sarhan. "Men realize that the religion gives them a license; even my six-year-old son knows that because he is male he is automatically powerful. The man is the one who can desert or divorce the wife at whim; the man is the one who can do as he pleases, not the woman. It is men who can take secret wives without informing their first wife. It is so common here to be at a funeral when a woman and a child walk in whom nobody knows, and she turns out to be the dead man's secret second wife. Even with my husband I fear polygamy; it puts all women in jeopardy. Generations of mothers have taught their daughters to give their husband everything he wants, never confront him, even if they know he is fooling around.

"The women I talk to or who write to us tell me that married men care only about their needs. The wife must never express her needs. Arab men want their wives — the mother of their children — to be very passive, very conservative. Then, if she doesn't satisfy his needs, he goes to a prostitute. And in or out of bed, the Arab male must always be in control. Here, if a man beats his wife in the street, people will tell him to stop, until he says she is his wife. Then they say okay, and stop interfering.

"Violence against women is being reinforced by the Islamist movement. I have attended sessions where they claim to teach the women the Koran, but many of the things they teach they invent. I was shocked to hear women being told, 'Hang a whip in a very visible spot in the house so you, the wife, and others can see it,' so they will obey their husbands at all times. What is worse, women are now beginning to believe this rubbish, and are starting to enjoy being slaves. Oriental women are brought up to be very obedient. They are taught that strength and violence equals masculinity. Soft and tender is considered weak, stupid. Women here want dictators, not a man who is decent, gentle and polite."

Sarhan first married at seventeen, "to escape my father's domination, to feel free," she said. "But I had just exchanged one form of control for another. My husband wouldn't even let me attend college." Sarhan's second marriage was equally controlling, and this time she was also a battered wife. "To escape him and avoid being forced by police to return under the "Law of Return," I went to the U.S. and refused to come back." Eventually, her husband divorced her. She met her third and current husband, Eman, a Pavarotti look-alike who is also her publisher, in the United States. "We knew each other for three years before marrying and had a chance to really get to know each other. We were in a society where we could do that, and nobody would kill us for it. In Egypt, a couple must be engaged before they can talk. Our way was much healthier, and very romantic. But when we returned to Egypt, the dynamics in our relationship changed. Men feel more powerful in this society. Overseas, we were equal partners. Here, it is a pyramid and the husband must always be at the top, or else society will condemn him. I was boss all day at the magazine. How was I supposed to switch hats at home? It was difficult for me, and we had a lot of differences. But I care about him . . . if it makes him happy . . . In the Muslim world, men prefer to marry a girl who has never been exposed to life or touched by human hands, so they can form her. It's like Pygmalion: you shape the woman you want sexually, physically, how she talks, how she dresses. She's clay in her husband's hands."

Sarhan does not consider herself a feminist "like Gloria Steinem," but she is worried about the changes in Muslim society. "Things are getting worse for women, much worse. I find it frightening." This was particularly brought home to her after a recent and well-publicized case of a rape on a Cairo bus that triggered a campaign for Sarhan's magazine.

The young woman, known only by her first name, Shahinaz, boarded a bus during Ramadan with her mother and sister in Ataba, a working-class area of the capital. Buses in Cairo give new meaning to the phrase "jam-packed," and, unlike in some other Muslim countries, they do not have a separate section for women. Separated in the crush from her mother and sister, twenty-three-year-old Shahinaz, a secretary in a law office, found herself at the rear of the bus wedged between two men. Despite her screams, which went ignored by commuters, one man held her while the other deflowered her with his hand. Only after the young woman became hysterical, and a police officer at the next bus stop realized there was blood on the victim's skirt, did the police give chase. Both men were captured, but have not yet been tried.

Working women in Cairo have long complained of being sexually assaulted on the buses by men who take the opportunity of rare proximity with the opposite sex to knead, rub, and fondle female commuters. Sarhan and others attribute the problem to the late marriage age. "Most men can't have sex until they get married, and they can't get married until the couple have a place to live, and since there is such a housing shortage here, it's become a big crisis. The average man is in his mid-thirties before he can afford to marry. So frequently his sexual frustration is channeled into manhandling women on buses. And since being manhandled is so shameful in our culture, decent women suffer in silence rather than be accused of having encouraged the man."

That is exactly what happened to Shahinaz after the first wave of national outrage that a young Egyptian woman could be sexually assaulted on a public bus. "The fundamentalists began saying it was the girl's fault: she was wearing a skirt, even though it was a long one, and not *hijab*. The media also began to blame her, and even women started saying it was the girl's fault because she was working and not staying at home. Nobody was attacking the animal who had taken her virginity. I was so stunned by the response to such a public attack, I ran a symposium on rape. We invited women, police, lawyers, psychologists, the men in my office. All the men sat there and insisted it was the woman's fault if she is raped. It was very depressing. Then I ran a series of articles and we received faxes from women as far away as Saudi Arabia telling us it wasn't just Egyptian society, but the attitude of Middle Eastern men and society in general."

For Shahinaz, the daughter of a mullah, the trauma continues and her marriageability has diminished. She sleeps badly, cries frequently, and refuses to leave her home. "The minister of interior said that what happened to me was not unusual. I swear to God that if this is a common thing, I will take my sisters and kill them and kill myself so that what happened to me does not happen to them."

Islamists often attribute unbridled male lust to Egyptian movie actresses and belly dancers. Egypt, after India, is the second-largest producer of films for the Third World. Luridly colored billboards dot Cairo depicting scantily clad actresses, promising more than the censored film itself delivers. Despite this, cinemas have been attacked and video stores burned by the militants, who consider both a corrupting influence. One of their more successful campaigns has been offering large financial inducements to well-known actresses and belly dancers to give up their professions and embrace the veil as a good example to ordinary Egyptian women.

Taxi driver Said Abdel Wahab "knows that Cairo is sin city," and is determined to protect his wife and daughter from any exposure to what he considers the capital's libertine lifestyle. In his profession, he frequently ferries tourists to nightclubs, bars, and casinos. He is particularly shocked when he sees Muslim visitors to Egypt, especially women, frequenting such places.

Thirty-six-year-old Said considers himself a "moderate conservative," and, like many Cairo taxi drivers, he carries a Koran in his cab, which he studies between fares. I met him on the first day of my trip, and finding him helpful and honest, I hired him for the remainder of my visit. Toward the end of my stay, he invited me to his home to meet his wife and family. Said and his family live in Shurba Al Khima, one of the more densely populated areas of Cairo. His building was cheaply constructed, like so many in Cairo. A narrow steep staircase, dramatically contorted by subsidence, led to the cold-water apartment consisting of four minute rooms, the largest no bigger than eight feet square. Only the two front rooms had windows, which overlooked a narrow lane. Said lived here with his wife, Wafa, aged twenty-four, his four-year-old daughter, Safar, thirty-month-old son, Ahmad, and his very elderly father and blind mother.

It was in this dimly lighted, claustrophobic apartment where one had to step over furniture to move around, that Said had virtually incarcerated his wife "to protect her." In a village, Wafa would have lived with an extended family and would at the very least have had a compound to wander through and the company of other women. Instead, she was not permitted to visit other women in her building, or to go out even to buy bread, or even to attend weddings, a social highlight in the lives of most women living in *purdah.*

Both Said and Wafa are college educated. He holds a degree in commerce. She was studying for a commercial diploma when they married six years ago, but Said refused to let her continue. "It is better she sit home and teach the children. There are many problems in the street, and I would never let her work with men. No, no, no," said Said. "I want to control her and my daughter wherever they go. She cannot meet other people. She has no permission to go anywhere without me, and, as a taxi driver, I work from seven A.M. until midnight, so she must stay home. I buy the food. I do not permit her to visit the women in the building, not even for an hour. Women sitting together talking make problems — it has always been so — so I have never permitted it and she must be one hundred percent obedient to me.

"Of course, I visit my male friends, we sit and talk, but men are different from ladies; they don't make problems, men are wise. The mind of a lady is not like the mind of a man. She is not equal to a man. Why? Because man is man, and woman is woman. It is better my wife sit every day in the house with the children."

I asked Said how he spent his free time, particularly in the winter, when there was less demand for taxis. "In the summer I sleep, and after the tourist season in the winter, I go for picnics, for drives, to the beach. No, I never take my wife. It is not necessary. I go with my friends, all men, many times. Why should I take her? I go to such places with men. It is the same when I go to weddings. I go alone. I don't take my wife, because it is too crowded." Similarly, Said does not permit Wafa to attend a mosque even at Ramadan. "She can pray at home. It is better."

Said is not intentionally being harsh; he considers himself a kind man and is perceived by people that way. He is sharply critical, for example, of men who beat their wives. "There is a difference between a woman and an animal," he says, and he does not agree with polygamy. As far as he is concerned, he merely takes his role as guardian of his wife and children very seriously.

"It is very difficult for me. I get very lonely," says Wafa. "Before, when I lived with my parents, my mother's friends visited. They were as close as relatives. When I married Said, we knew each other for only two weeks; there was no time to discuss how he wanted our life to be. I married him because people said he was calm and good. When he refused to let me attend weddings, my father spoke to him and tried to make him less strict, but Said said, 'This is my character, I cannot change.'"

When I asked the couple if they could alter anything in their lives what it would be, Said responded immediately, "A new car. That is my dream." In front of her husband, Wafa said, "I would change Said, so that I could at least go to weddings." When Said stepped out to fetch sodas for his guests, Wafa gave a tight little smile and added, "He is a good man, but if I had known his character before, I would not have married him. I guess this was my fate."

• • •

Kariman Hamza is one of the better-known female faces throughout the Middle East and certainly in Egypt, and, like her country, she is full of contrasts and seeming contradictions. A leading Islamist, the petite, slightly plump, very stylish woman is given to wearing *hijabs* made from chiffon, ornate lace, or even gold lamé, draped over a pillbox hat to give them more flair. "You can be elegant and religiously conservative," says Hamza, who is the general manager for religious programming on Egypt's state-run television, and has a biweekly interview show of her own on Islamic issues.

The fifty-year-old grandmother and mother of nine claims she was the first Egyptian woman in public office to wear the veil, in 1970. Since then she has waged a battle with the government over wearing it on her show. "The minister has tried to stop me from wearing *hijab* eleven times, always insisting I not be so conservative. My response continues to be that a higher power, Allah, has ordered me and all the women of the world to wear it, and I obey him."

The government did, however, close down Hamza's televised fashion show, which ran briefly and showcased Islamic styles for women in rich fabrics and colors that were usually decorated with beads, flowers, lush embroidery, or even fur trim. These dramatic outfits are the kind of clothes she wears, and they are a long way from the black shrouds male Islamists insist women must wear. When her fashion show was closed, Hamza, undaunted, turned the format into a successful Islamist women's fashion magazine instead.

Her television show is syndicated in eleven countries in the Middle

East, Gulf, and North Africa. On assignment, she has dined at Buckingham Palace with Queen Elizabeth, and interviewed the empress of Iran, the king of Morocco, and other international luminaries. Recent program topics include Islamic banking, life after death, male-female relations, and whether Islam should undergo a reformation. On the subject of the latter, talking in the sound bites perfected after twenty-three years on television, she says, "When we go back to God, we go beyond modernization. Islam is far ahead of modernization; technology is running behind. The only reason that Egypt is undeveloped is that as a country we moved away from our religion."

Hamza is the only woman in Egypt with a religious TV program. "The government has always refused to approve others, and many have tried." She admits that the station frequently receives letters saying that a woman's face should not appear on the screen, or that she has interviewed somebody the viewer considers inappropriate. "When that happens I contact the person or Islamic group and try to explain why Islam does not bar a woman from appearing in public. Many of these Islamists I pity because they do not know their religion very well." The American University in Cairo has become so concerned about the Islamists' distortions of Islam that they have started holding seminars for students to clarify the true teachings of the religion.

It is because of this lack of knowledge, Hamza insists, that many of the fundamentalist groups refuse to let women work. "True Islam does not impede women's progress, does not forbid her being a leader, nor prohibit her from working. The Prophet permitted his wife Zeinab to work after their marriage. She made excellent leather saddles, and Mohammad was very pleased with her work." Hamza can sound almost as progressive as Gloria Steinem one minute, and as antifeminist as Phyllis Schlafly the next.

"However, it is true that women are more fragile and more sensitive than men. They need men to lean on. Physically, a woman is weaker than a man in everything, for example, her heartbeat, her muscles, her hemoglobin. She *needs* to be a mother and a wife; her reason for being is marriage. Islam prefers a woman not work, which is why the man is more powerful, but Islam also does not prohibit her from working if it is necessary, if her husband is sick, dead, or if she is divorced." And just as Phyllis Schlafly herself traveled the United States while she lectured women to stay at home with their children, Hamza, recently widowed, explained her more than two decades in television. "I love my job, and I wanted to tell the world about Islam. I began to work when my children were in school."

Due to Hamza's position, she is well acquainted with the religious sheikhs of Al Azhar. And she is concerned about the *fatwas* issued by the theological institution because of government control of the Islamic scholars attached to the mosque. "Al Azhar sends religious scholars all over the world to teach Islam, which is good. But the Grand Sheikh of Al Azhar, the pinnacle of Islam in the world, is appointed by the government, not through election, which is a big mistake because this means his decisions will be made to please Egypt's ruler. If Al Azhar could have elections to select the Grand Sheikh (in the same way new popes are elected), then Muslims would be more confident of the *fatwas* issued."

Like Hamza and other prominent Muslims, I also questioned whether the man to whom 85 percent of all Muslims looked to for rulings on all aspects of their lives, should be an Egyptian government–appointed bureaucrat. This means that whenever the governments of other Islamic countries consult him on policy, the response that he gives is monitored by the authorities and reflects Egyptian policy. Despite this, heads of states still turn to Al Azhar as the ultimate arbiter in many of their government decisions, and invariably accept such decrees as being absolute. "Al Azhar has been oppressed since 1954 (when the Islamists were first forced underground) and because of this, Islam has lost its independence," said columnist Fahmy Howeidy. "As long as we do not have democracy, Al Azhar is not allowed too far from the regime's line on Islam."

• • •

Meeting His Excellency, the Grand Sheikh Gad Al Haq of Al Azhar, took time. Not only was a personal introduction required, but so, too, was approval from the Ministry of Information, which requested written questions in advance, and which also needed a recommendation from the American Embassy. The quest also required tremendous diligence to ensure that the many necessary documents were shunted from one official location to another. The Ministry of Information, like all Egyptian ministries, is heavily overstaffed, dating from the days when all university graduates were guaranteed a job in one of them. But despite this, official studies show that civil servants in Egypt work little more than thirty minutes a day.

Al Azhar was built in the tenth century, and was originally Shi'a and the religious center for the Fatimids, who forcibly converted

Egypt to Shi'a Islam during their two centuries of rule. It was Saladin, then a general from the same village as Saddam Hussein in what is now modern Iraq, who restored Egypt to Sunni Islam in 1171.

The Grand Sheikh of Al Azhar's office is as modest as the man himself. The grimy building, marked only by hovering beggars, sits at the edge of one of Cairo's busiest traffic junctions. The dust, fumes, heat, and the constant clamor of traffic are the same inside the building as out on the street. A soiled and tattered narrow red carpet leading directly to Sheikh Al Haq's suite indicates his rank and office. Other floors are bare.

The grandfatherly figure sitting behind a large desk, with his hands clasped gently over the beginnings of a paunch, smiled warmly in greeting. His simple gray galabia was little different from that of thousands of Egyptian office workers, a red fez with a white scarf wrapped around the brim topped the outfit, and his black spectacles and trim white beard bestowed a scholarly air. Only his three telephones, a modern and efficiently working air-conditioner, and his paper-shredder suggest that this is no ordinary cleric; I was never able to discover what a man of God needed with the latter.

The Grand Sheikh opened our meeting with a brief prayer, "Praise be to Allah, and peace and prayers be upon his Prophet," and his initial comments sounded similar to those of the Muslim Sisterhood's Zeinab al-Ghazzali. Like her, he attributed Islam's current global resurgence to its being the natural religion of mankind. "It is similar to the nature of man, his thoughts and his behavior. And because the laws of the religion and the *Shariah* are not rigid, and are flexible enough for man to embrace without fanaticism, it is logical that the religion should be spread."

Blaming any antipathy between the West and the Muslim world on the leaders of some Western countries, he said, "They want again to colonize Muslim countries in the Middle East to gain access to their resources. Islam is known for its tolerance and peace. Muslims are not aggressors or aggressive people. But you must learn about our religion from qualified scholars, not from the new Islamist movements. Such movements and groups are against the authorities. They began using violence against the people, and the authorities had to respond to their acts with violence."

There are those who would say that Al Azhar has been instrumental in that violence since the highest Islamic authority has condemned a number of writers who have been subsequently placed on death lists and even killed by militant Islamists. "It is the responsibility of the writers whether they put themselves in a dangerous position with their writing," responded the Grand Sheikh. "They are asked to write only what is good and in accord with the faith of the people. Material that is not should be kept from society. If there is a small child playing with matches, and they are not taken from him, he can burn himself and others. Therefore, Al Azhar objects to any publications, films, plays, and art that will harm society or go against the principles of Islam, and reports them to the courts so they can be stopped. And it is the courts who must decide if someone has committed apostasy. The ordinary man has no right to kill such a person."

While such comments on censorship may seem paternalistic and outdated to non-Muslims, the Grand Sheikh rejects any suggestion that after fourteen hundred years a religious reformation might be needed to adapt Islam to the modern world. "The basic pillars and principles of Islam were revealed by Allah. Therefore, Islam is valid for all times and all places. Reformation is unnecessary and unacceptable."

But there have been some changes made in the Koran, I pointed out; slavery and concubinage, for example, have both now been Islamically proscribed. If Islam could be reformed in these instances, why could other changes more in keeping with modern life not be made? "In the case of slavery and concubinage, these changes could be made because both existed prior to Islam."

On women's issues, Sheikh Al Haq's initial comments sounded not unlike those of the Prophet Mohammad's: "Men and women are equal under Islam in education and every other part of life. If there are some rules specifically for women in Islam, it is for the benefit of society. Regarding the covering of a woman's face and hands, for example, this is a tradition of her culture, not an Islamic requirement." But he quickly proved himself to be a cultural traditionalist. "Women cannot be judges," he insisted, "because from very early on, religious scholars and imams of Islam recognized that women are too sensitive to face dealing with bad crimes, criminal laws, executions, and such things."

Similarly, the seventy-five-year-old sheikh's sentiments on women as political leaders appeared more rooted in the conservativism of his generation than they did in Islam. "A woman can have any leadership position except head of state. She cannot be president. Why? Because once again, if we look at her feminine emotions, her sensitivity, we can see that she will not be able to face those great things that confront the people and the government." I asked him, What about Pakistan's Benazir Bhutto, for example? "There will always be mistakes," said the Grand Sheikh, laughing. "This was the fault of democracy. When she visited me, if she had asked me whether it was right for her to be head of state, I would have told her it was not."

Islam's foremost cleric disagrees with fundamentalists, however, on whether women should be able to work outside the home. "Islam does say that the financial support for a wife should be the responsibility of the husband. But in unfortunate circumstances and times of poor economy such as now, it is permissible for women to help support their families by working. All that Islam asks is that women who work behave correctly with men, keep themselves above suspicion, and not try to seduce men." Once again, it appeared as if the onus for propriety between the sexes was placed on women. I was confused, I told the sheikh. The Koran clearly states that both men and women must be modest in their dress and in their behavior with the opposite sex. Islamists force women to adhere to these requirements, but not men. Why was this? I asked. In a response that sidestepped the issue, he said, "Men who harass women know nothing about the teachings of Islam. If they did, they would know that Islam says men are prohibited to touch, look at, or bother women."

I mentioned to the Grand Sheikh that a number of prominent Muslims were concerned that the highest authority for 85 percent of the world's Muslims was an Egyptian government bureaucrat. Did he find himself involved in a conflict of interest between the requirements of Islam and those of the state? "There may be some differences, but the Grand Sheikh of Al Azhar always gives the opinion of Islam to the government, and the Egyptian constitution compels the government not to go against the *Shariah* of Islam."

My final question was whether, in the foreseeable future, he thought that Egypt might become a theocratic Islamic state, ruled by *Shariah* law as the Islamists demand? "*Inshallah*, God willing, Egypt will complete the instructions of Allah in the future." It was another diplomatic response. To say otherwise, the Grand Sheikh of Al Azhar would have appeared to be calling for an end to the current government, to which he himself also belongs.

• • •

"How did you get my home phone number? Who gave it to you? Who are you?" Egypt's High Court Chief Justice Sa'id al-Ashmawy is understandably cautious when approached by people he doesn't know. For the last twelve years, apart from his hours in court, he has been forced to be a virtual recluse, living behind the tightly closed wooden shutters of his apartment. In the lobby of his building, armed guards scrutinize all visitors and accompany them in the elevator and to his door. It's been years since Ashmawy enjoyed going out to dinner, or took his once regular evening stroll, and the pallor of his skin reflects the fact that he is mostly homebound.

The fifty-five-year-old justice, who completed his postdoctoral studies at Harvard, is a man with very strong views, and they have dramatically curtailed his security and freedom and deprived him of a wife and children. Al Azhar and other leading mullahs consider Ashmawy's opinions heresy, and the Islamists have been trying to kill him since 1980. The only reason they have failed so far is that the security surrounding him rivals that of some heads of state. His heinous crime? He declared that *Shariah* law is mostly manmade, not divine, and therefore is able to be replaced by a new and modern jurisprudence that could incorporate human rights. As far as his opposition is concerned, the justice who describes himself as a liberal Muslim is the worst kind of dissident because he supports his argument with Koranic facts.

"The legal rulings in the Koran are limited and relatively few indeed if we compare them to the total number of verses. There are some sixty-two hundred verses in the Koran, but only two hundred, most of which have been abrogated, deal with legal matters. The remaining eighty legal verses mostly concern personal status and inheritance law. The Koran is mostly a code of ethics, not a code of law.

"Despite this, the militant Islamists believe that Islamic law was revealed by God, without differentiating between religious law and the jurisprudence that was added later. Much of what is now considered *Shariah* was added in the centuries after the Prophet's death by self-serving rulers who wanted to bestow sacredness on themselves under cover of religion. This was mere dictatorship, and did not reflect the spirit of Islam. Justice, prosperity, and opportunity were the possessions only of the caliph and his ministers, to be distributed as they wished. Such benefits were not the rights of the people. No opposition was allowed. When it arose, it was called heresy and damned as atheism.

"There are only four legal penalties mentioned in the Koran: amputation of the hand for theft; lashing for adultery; lashing for falsely accusing a woman of adultery; and imprisonment or death for highway robbery. The Koran also has a number of prerequisites that must be met before the enforcement of such penalties. For example, amputation is not to be applied if a thief is poor and in need. And the death penalty for apostasy is not mentioned in the Koran; in fact, the Koran stresses the religious freedom of everyone. It also includes some legal rulings that are temporary, which is how slavery and concubinage were abolished. And since there is this precedent, the *Shariah* could be updated, and amputation for theft, for example, could be abolished as well.

"Similarly, the term *Jihad* in the Koran means principally self-control and self-refinement. *Jihad,* as in fighting a war, is meant only as an act of self-defense; the Koran forbids its being purely an act of aggression. The doctrine of the militants not only poses a threat to peace and humanity, it undermines Islam itself, falsifying its great teachings, terminating its vital spirit and its humaneness."

When Ashmawy authored his first book twelve years ago stating that *Shariah* was manmade and not sacred, there was an instant furor in the religious community. Several subsequent books by the justice have caused further outrage, although moderate Muslims and secularists use them as a basis for their opposition to the Islamists. "The Al-Jihad extremist group began a revolution against me. I was attacked by many, in newspapers, by the Grand Sheikh, and Al Azhar had demonstrations against me. The first death threat came after the minister of religious affairs spoke out against me in mosque prayers. Then a leading religious sheikh said I was an apostate, and deserved the death penalty. Another mosque in Cairo openly asked people to murder me. At that point, I complained to President Sadat, and that particular mullah was fired. Since then the government has given me around-the-clock guards.

"I was preparing to marry at the time, but I realized it would be unfair to a wife and children. They would be terrified by such threats, and my concern for their safety would weaken my resolve. I've had to modify my life dramatically since these death threats were made. I don't go out any more, and I'm very cautious in accepting people to the house. But I feel passionate about this issue. God protects me. Although after Farag Fouda's death, I'm more nervous. I hope to die an old man of natural causes. . . . But I will never yield. I prefer to lose my life rather than my work. I am trying to further the understanding of Islam.

"Militants are doing nothing for mankind, and any opposition is met with threats of death. Their arguments are ill-conceived and without substantiation. For example, if you follow the Islamist reasoning on why women should veil, then both men and women should be covered. It is this simple. To this movement, a woman is always under the custody of a man whether he is her father, brother, husband, or even a son. They claim she has no right to leave the house without permission from her custodian, or to work if she is married. To the Islamists, a woman has no right to wear what she wants, she must be covered, or be declared a heretic.

"Theirs is not a rational movement, just a political movement with slogans. They are encouraged by Saudi Arabia and Iran, and have infiltrated all aspects of Egyptian life, through television, newspapers, everything."

Ashmawy claims the totalitarian rule of most Islamic countries has pushed Muslims into religiously militant organizations. "Most countries where Muslims are in the majority are in fact ruled by military or semimilitary governments. And it is characteristic of such governments that they aim to create permanent external threats to draw the attention of people away from the internal problems of such regimes. For the Islamic world, Western colonization and the state of Israel are permanent external threats. Consequently, in the absence of any real democracy, people lacking moderate channels for the expression of emotions aroused by such distrust are driven to extremism.

"The existence of totalitarian regimes throughout the Islamic world has enabled rulers to make use of public funds and foreign subsidies for their own profit, which has resulted in a wave of corruption. Freedom, education, and accountability are the correct remedies for such a situation. Lacking such things, many people maintain that the establishment of a theocratic government will cure all societal ills. Such a government, they believe, will create a new utopian society and will provide them with identity, security, and hope in a world in which they feel themselves to be strangers.

"True Islamic government, however, if one follows the tradition of the Prophet, is the government of the people; a government that they freely elect and in which they share; a government that they may change peaceably, without bloodshed and without being denounced as heretics. But Al Azhar sheikhs are government civil servants. Should Muslims be looking to Al Azhar for the final word on Islam? I don't see any sophisticated scholar there; they have degenerated a lot. Now some are educated and some are not, and the religious scholarship is poor. For these reasons, I am surprised other countries look to Al Azhar for the final word on Islam.

"I am afraid of the future for Egypt: the Islamists could destroy the country through sectarian strife. Their movement is out of control, and it could also devastate, do tremendous damage to, many other Islamic countries. The Islamists will soon be causing a lot of problems for the West, as well. In fact, it has already started there."

CHAPTER 14

Epilogue

*And if two parties of believers fall to fighting,
then make peace between them.
And if one party of them doth wrong to the other,
fight ye that which doth wrong till it return unto
the ordinance of Allah;
Then make peace between them justly, and act equitably.*

KORAN 49:9

"FUNDAMENTALISM IS NO FAD, but the preference of a generation." This opinion, expressed by Martin Kramer of the Washington Institute for Near East Policy, is shared by many Middle East analysts and also Islamic leaders themselves. "Only Islam remains in this part of the world. There is nothing else left to inspire the young, to mobilize them, and give them a sense of history," says Hassan al-Turabi, the militant leader of fundamentalist Sudan. "It is a force that is going to come anyway because it is a force of history. The West will simply have to learn to live with this new and growing power bloc."

And as Turabi recognizes, the Islamist movement continues to proliferate. As it does, its oppressive politics are increasingly governing the lives of Muslims, particularly women. Advancements made by Muslim women in recent years are being overturned either by the fundamentalist movements or by the ruling regimes themselves, which are fearful of the Islamist threat to their power. In a world where education for females was generally accepted only a generation or two ago, women are again being infantilized. In the name of religion, they are being banned from traveling, working, studying, divorcing, voting, holding positions of power, in effect, from making their own decisions about major or minor aspects of their lives. And because the same Islamic scriptures that legitimized their rights are distorted and used against them, women refusing to bow to such dictates put their lives at risk if they are labeled un-Islamic by the zealots.

"Such restrictions on women are necessary," insist Islamists. "They are to protect women's honor, and they are also a symbol of our enormous respect for women." In reality, the Islamic neoconservative political organizations demean women in myriad ways that have no basis in the religion.

And while female honor continues to be the fulcrum around which Islamic society pivots, the level of women's confinement remains the barometer of change in the Muslim world. The changes taking place in women's lives reflect and foreshadow the course that Islamic nations will follow as we move into the next century.

Already many countries, in addition to the ten written about here, are being affected. In Sudan, the National Islamic Front, a militant branch of the Muslim Brotherhood, led by the urbane and Western-educated Turabi, has turned the country into a violent theocratic state. Forcible conversions of the three million Christians in the southern provinces have been so brutal that the Pope has denounced them. And Sudan, with the assistance of Iran, is also helping to spread Islamic extremism to moderate Arab countries and a number of Africa states.

Even in mainland China, Islamic fundamentalism is on the rise, "particularly among the Hui around Xian," according to American anthropologist and Islamic demographer Richard Weeks.

Malaysia, like Sudan, has plans to implement *Shariah* law, which will also have jurisdiction over the 10 percent of the population who are non-Muslim. In Indonesia, the country with the world's-largest Muslim population, photographs of Khomeini now decorate school walls.

In the former Soviet Central Asian states of Azerbaijan, Uzbekistan, Kyrgyzstan, and Tajikistan, where Muslims already number more than sixty million and their population is expected to reach one hundred million in the next fifteen years, the hegemonic jostling by Iran, Pakistan, and Saudi Arabia is well under way. The former Soviet republics, now being dubbed collectively "Islamistan," are resource- and technology-rich. "The fortunes of fundamentalist Islam as a worldwide political movement that is capable of directing material, as well as spiritual, development, may rise or fall with its success in rallying Muslims in the Central Soviet states," says fundamentalist specialist Dr. Scott Appleby.

And just as Islamic extremism was imported into Afghanistan,

Afghans have now begun to export their newly acquired ideology and military expertise to other Islamic states. In Tajikistan, where thousands have died since 1992 in clashes between socialist and Islamic forces, Afghanistan has supplied Central Asians with arms and military training. They have done the same for Muslim Kashmiri insurgents fighting Indian troops. Thousands of Saudi-supported Arab extremist mercenaries, veterans of the Afghan-Soviet war, have joined forces with Algerian fundamentalists. In Bosnia, Afghans and Arabs have participated in military action and training of the former Yugoslavian Muslims; Iran has helped supply the arms.

The Islamist uprising that most concerns Western and Middle Eastern analysts alike, however, is Egypt's. It is feared that if the current regime falls to fundamentalism, many other countries in the region may well follow suit. "The key case is Egypt, and other Muslim countries are keeping a close eye on how the regime handles things," says Appleby. "If Egypt falls, if the secular regime is overthrown or run out of office, then there will be a sea change in the Middle East and North Africa. Western policies, U.S. policies in the region, are linked to the fate of Egypt. And Egypt, of course, is a major player in the Middle East peace process. If Egypt can't hold it together, the dominoes will just fall geopolitically." Of equal concern as Egypt appears increasingly less stable, is the October 1993 report by CIA director R. James Woolsey to a U.S. Senate committee, in which he admitted that Egypt possesses biological weapons. Should such arms fall into the hands of fanatics, Tel Aviv and Jerusalem would be far more vulnerable than they were to Saddam Hussein's SCUDs.

"Egypt is always the leader of them all, the 'mother of them all,'" adds political analyst Alon Ben-Meir. "If Egypt's desperate economic situation is not turned around, the fundamentalists are going to take over. Egypt is desperately in need, but it doesn't need two or three billion U.S. dollars in aid a year, more than half of which is stolen. It needs major, major investment, development of its infrastructure."

Since the Camp David accord was signed in 1978, Egypt has received $30 billion from the United States, the second-highest recipient of American aid. Only Israel has received more. However, the United States and Egypt both acknowledge that much of that aid is siphoned off and/or wasted. One of the major offenders of corruption, according to Egyptian critics, is the Mubarak family. They accuse the president and his two sons, Ala and Gamal, of skimming money from the Egyptian treasury and American aid to amass a personal fortune estimated at nearly $2 billion.

And while Egypt is officially a multiparty state, Mubarak is increasingly perceived by many as unofficially appointing himself "president for life." This view was strengthened in 1993 when, as the only candidate for the presidency, Mubarak was "renominated" to a third six-year term despite his party's apparent inability to deal with the many problems assailing the country. The Egyptian government's only response to the unrest has been a campaign of armed crackdowns and stepped-up execution of dissenters.

"The failure of democracy to take root in the Middle East has enabled Arab leaders to slaughter their people while convincing the survivors that their real enemy was Israel and the West," wrote a *New York Times* columnist last year. "Since World War II, the Arab world has failed to produce a single government that shares power with its people, a single government that holds itself accountable to its people, a single government based on genuine parliamentary process, religious freedom and democratic restraints."

It is increasingly likely, however, that Egypt, along with other autocratic Islamic governments, may soon be forced to recognize that the only alternative to rebellion spawned by repression is genuine reform. The ordinary Muslim citizen is currently confronted with an impossible choice, says Washington scholar Hisham Sharabi. "On the one hand, are the fundamentalists; on the other, the dictatorial, authoritarian tyranny of the state, of the one party, of the army. Muslim society is being torn between the two." The lack of real choices in the Muslim world only inflames an already incendiary situation.

At the same time, and due to the Western world's increasing dependence on their oil, Islamic nations have assumed an increasingly important role in the post–Cold War world. And three years after the Gulf War, the threat to our interests in the region is still very much alive. "We haven't seen the end of Gulf crises," insists Dr. Appleby. "The Gulf situation — Iraq and Kuwait [and Saudi Arabia] — is not settled, nor is the situation with Iran. For anyone to assume otherwise is foolish. The whole area remains very unstable."

Certainly, as far as the United States is concerned, it would now seem time to reassess our foreign policy in that region, particularly regarding arms control and oil. "The facts are clear and jarring," says Thomas A. Cardamone, Jr., a Washington, D.C., arms-trade analyst. "The U.S. increasingly imports more oil from Saudi Arabia, more now than it did before the Gulf War. This growing reliance on Saudi crude, even after fifty thousand Americans risked their lives to protect the supply, limits the number of options the U.S. has if that source is threatened again. The need for Arab oil encourages weapon sales to the region, which are fueling a destabilizing arms race.

"After the Gulf War, the Bush administration ignored the causal link between America's reliance on Saudi oil and the need to send troops to the Middle East. No effort was made to modify U.S. policy. Instead of finding less volatile oil sources to reduce the risk to such a large portion of the U.S. supply, the administration flooded the Middle East with weapons. This was done in the belief that if the Gulf states were threatened again, the weapons could prevent the oil states from being overrun before American troops save the day — again."

In a speech given after the Gulf War, President Bush called for regulating arms sales to the region, saying it would be "tragic" if a new weapons buildup occurred in the Middle East. Just months later, the United States announced weapons sales to the region worth $35 billion. Those sales continue unabated. In 1993 the United States, the world's-largest arms merchant, supplied 57 percent of the global arms market according to congressional figures. Since the Gulf War, nearly three-quarters of that amount has gone to the Middle East and Gulf.

The lesson of Afghanistan apparently has also not been learned by Washington. After a massive U.S. supply of arms to the Afghan Resistance throughout the eighties, Washington has admitted that since the country fell to anti-American Islamic extremism, millions of dollars of arms, including antiaircraft Stinger missiles, are turning up on the international black market. The "disposal problem" of such arms is only now being considered by the CIA, which is reportedly trying to buy back the missiles to keep them out of terrorist and/ or Islamic fundamentalist hands. And the arms the U.S. supplied the Afghans with were neither state of the art, nor in anywhere near the quantity of those going to the Middle East and Gulf.

"If the U.S. were to reduce its imports of Gulf oil, risk to the supply would be diminished and less military hardware would be needed," says Cardamone. "Without such a policy, the likelihood of a new Gulf war involving the U.S. remains."

The total American reserves of oil number 24.7 billion barrels, less than one tenth of Saudi Arabia's; and our Alaskan oil reserves are declining. Areas that have shown promise, such as the Arctic National Wildlife Refuge and the continental shelves of California and Florida, are barred from drilling for environmental reasons. And since U.S. oil is found at much deeper levels than Arab oil, and because our labor costs are much higher than theirs, it is considerably more expensive to produce American oil than to purchase oil from the Gulf states.

Alternative fuels are a long way down the road, says the federal Department of Energy. "GM, Ford, and Chrysler are competing with Germany and Japan to produce an effective electrical car or a hybrid — those with electrical- *and* petroleum-run engines," says a spokesman. "However, the battery is still the major sticking point."

If Saudi Arabia, the nation with the world's largest oil reserves, can run industrial plants on solar energy, why has the United States not aggressively pursued alternative fuels? Professor Ben-Meir claims it is because of an informal agreement made with Saudi Arabia shortly after the 1973 oil embargo that the Saudis would maintain reasonable oil prices if the United States did not invest too much in or subsidize too heavily any corporations wanting to develop technologies to produce non-oil-based energy. I was unable to corroborate such an agreement, but the issue was raised during congressional hearings in the eighties to determine whether Arab investment in the United States posed a threat to the U.S. economy. At that time, it was suggested that their mammoth investments might be used to press the United States to slow its efforts to become less dependent on oil imports.

Arab oil reserves account for 70 percent of the world's total, and the vast majority of that, 88 percent, is in the hands of four Arab states: Saudi Arabia, with 260 billion barrels; Iraq, with 100 billion barrels; UAE, with 98 billion barrels; and Kuwait, with 97 billion barrels. Three major oil-producing states — Libya, Iran, and Iraq — are already vehemently anti-American. The other three — Saudi Arabia, Kuwait, and the UAE — are all ruled by autocratic regimes, and have growing fundamentalist opposition movements. All three countries also have large Shi'a populations — Kuwait and the UAE are 30 percent Shi'a, and Saudi Arabia is an estimated 15 to 20 percent Shi'a — that have been subject before to external agitation from Iran.

"The U.S. is trading with disaster. It is dangerous, so dangerous, to allow ourselves to be so reliant on oil from the most volatile and unstable region on earth," says Ben-Meir.

It is Salman Rushdie who said, "The U.S. has become all too painfully familiar with the nature of the holy — rather, unholy — terrorists of Islam." Rushdie described the Islamist uprising as "a great struggle for the soul of the Muslim world." He went on to say, "And as the fundamentalists grow in power and ruthlessness, the courageous men and women who are willing to engage them in a battle of ideas and moral values are rapidly becoming as important for us to know about, to understand and support as the dissident voices in the former Soviet Union used to be."

Rushdie's opinions are not welcome, of course, in much of the Islamic world since Iran's *fatwa* sentencing him to death. But one of the more prominent and respected Islamic thinkers in the Middle East, Egyptian scholar Kamal Abdul Magd, speaks for many Muslims when he says, "When religion becomes coercion, it becomes more pernicious than terrorism. It becomes subversion seeking not only to intimidate but to subvert society's moral and physical underpinnings." And the oppression and fear engendered by the religious extremists is invariably felt first by women. The Islamists apparently have forgotten, or choose to ignore, the Prophet Mohammad's teaching: "There is no compulsion in Islam."

Index

abortion, 69, 248–249, 334
Acquired Immune Deficiency Syndrome
(AIDS), 140; in anti-Western propaganda, 99; male sexual habits and, 132,
162; press censorship and, 132, 208;
prostitution and, 62, 63, 115
adoption, 6, 39, 67
adultery, 69, 310; honor killings for, 32,
114, 219, 279; Koran and, 41, 348–
349; punishments for, 51, 114, 218,
219, 275, 348
Africa, 125, 334, 353
A'isha bint Abi Bakr, 36–38, 40–43
alcohol, 68, 87, 121, 135, 231, 321
amputation, 111, 218, 348, 349
apostasy, 120; accusations of, 212, 263–
264, 267–268; Koran and, 349; punishment for, 10, 12, 212, 328, 346
Arab oil embargo, 18, 20, 26
Arafat, Yasser, 273; and Middle East
peace talks, 294, 317–318, 319; and Persian Gulf War, 16, 156, 176
arms sales, 19, 124, 356
al-Assad, Hafez, 253
Ataturk, Kemal, 34
automobiles: driving with niqab veils, 161,
187; oil consumption, 20; Saudi
women's driving controversy, 211–213,
214–215, 218, 275
Al Azhar: Gad Al Haq, Grand Sheikh of,
7, 321–322, 344, 345–347, 349;
mosque (Cairo), 172, 344–345, 350–351

Bank of Credit and Commerce International (BCCI), 21–22, 23, 61
banks, 223–224
bin Baz, Sheikh Abdulaziz, 211, 212, 215,
216, 332
Bedouin, 175–178, 212
Begin, Menachem W., 292
Bhutto, Benazir, 66, 216, 253; forced
from office, 59–60, 61; and Islamic
dress, 31, 86; Islamist condemnations
of, 57, 63–64, 347; as prime minister of
Pakistan, 57–58, 59, 60
Bible, 29, 183–184, 189, 328

birthrates, 19, 24, 34, 92, 113
breast-feeding, 189, 249
bribery, 324
bride-price. See dowries
burqa veil, 56, 81. See also veiling

censorship: in Egypt, 321, 332, 336, 345–
346; in Jordan, 280; in Kuwait, 165–
166; in Pakistan, 61; in Saudi Arabia,
208; in UAE, 132, 147
chador, 5, 55, 94, 98. See also veiling
chaperon (mahram) requirement, 190, 209,
220, 224
child abuse, 6, 266
childbirth, 43, 92, 248, 335
child care, 32, 88, 245, 249
childrearing practices, 133
children: abandoned, 67; beggars, 68; cultural importance of, 152; custody
rights, 71, 114, 150, 246; degradation
of girls, 35, 43–45; disease and illness,
256–257, 324; Iranian revolution and,
106, 118; Islamic fundamentalism and,
270; malnutrition and starvation, 177,
235, 237–238, 249, 259; marriage of,
92, 113–114; martyrdom of, 308; murder of, 30, 35, 67; orphans, 231–232;
prostitution slavery, 62; spying on parents, 233; torture of, 329
Christian fundamentalism, 331–332
concubinage, 34, 346, 349
confinement. See purdah
contraception, 68–69, 89, 113, 248, 310
corruption, 18, 170, 350, 354
crime, 9, 72, 111, 228, 238

dancing girls, 61, 62–63
death penalty: for adultery, 51, 114, 218,
219, 275, 348; Afghanistan, 9; for apostasy, 10, 12, 212, 328, 349; Iran, 110–
111, 114, 115, 116, 121, 125; Iraq,
234–235, 239, 244; Koran and, 349;
Pakistan, 51; for prostitution, 116;
Saudi Arabia, 212, 218–219, 229–230
Death of a Princess (film), 219–220